# Literacy in Society

# APPLIED LINGUISTICS AND LANGUAGE STUDY

*General Editor*
Professor Christopher N. Candlin, Macquarie University

For a complete list of books in this series see pages vii–viii

# Literacy in Society

Ruqaiya Hasan
and
Geoff Williams

LONGMAN
LONDON AND NEW YORK

Addison Wesley Longman Limited
Edinburgh Gate
Harlow, Essex CM20 2JE, England
*and Associated Companies through the world.*

*Published in the United States of America
by Addison Wesley Longman, New York*

First Published 1996

ISBN 0 582 21792X PPR

**British Library Cataloguing-in-Publication Data**

A catalogue record for this book is
available from the British Library

**Library of Congress Cataloging-in-Publication Data**

Literacy in society / edited by Ruqaiya Hasan and Geoffrey Williams.
    p.  cm. – (Applied linguistics and language study)
  Includes bibliographical references and index.
  ISBN 0 582-21792-X
    1. Written communication – Study and teaching. 2. Literacy.
3. Sociolinguistics. 4. Semiotics – Social aspects. 5. Language and education.
6. English language – Study and teaching.  I. Hasan, Ruqaiya.
II. Williams, Geoffrey.  III. Series.
P211.L727  1996
302.2′244–dc20                      96-12698
                                      CIP

Set by 8H in 10/12pt Baskerville
Produced through Longman Malaysia, ETS

# Contents

# APPLIED LINGUISTICS AND LANGUAGE STUDY

GENERAL EDITOR

PROFESSOR CHRISTOPHER N. CANDLIN

*Macquarie University, Sydney*

**Error Analysis**
Perspectives on second
language acquisition
JACK RICHARDS

**Stylistics and the Teaching of
Literature**
HENRY WIDDOWSON

**Constrastive Analysis**
CARL JAMES

**Language and Communication**
JACK R. RICHARDS *and*
RICHARD W. SCHMIDT (EDS)

**Learning to Write: First
Language/Second Language**
AVIVA FREEDMAN, IAN PRINGLE
*and* JANICE YALDEN (EDS)

**Strategies in Interlanguage
Communication**
CLAUS FAERCH *and* GABRIELE KASPER
(EDS)

**Reading in a Foreign Language**
J. CHARLES ALDERSON *and*
A.H. URQUHART (EDS)

**An Introduction to Discourse
Analysis**
New Edition
MALCOLM COULTHARD

**Language Awareness in the
Classroom**
CARL JAMES *and* PETER GARRETT

**Bilingualism in Education**
Aspects of theory, research and
practice
JIM CUMMINS *and* MERRILL SWAIN

**Second Language Grammar:
Learning and Teaching**
WILLIAM E. RUTHERFORD

**The Classroom and the
Language Learner**
Ethnography and second-language
classroom research
LEO VAN LIER

**Vocabulary and Language Teaching**
RONALD CARTER *and* MICHAEL
McCARTHY (EDS)

**Observation in the Language
Classroom**
DICK ALLWRIGHT

**Listening to Spoken English**
Second Edition
GILLIAN BROWN

**Listening in Language Learning**
MICHAEL ROST

**An Introduction to Second
Language Acquisition Research**
DIANE LARSEN-FREEMAN *and*
MICHAEL H. LONG

**Language and Discrimination**
A study of communication in
multi-ethnic workplaces
CELIA ROBERTS, TOM JUPP *and*
EVELYN DAVIES

**Translation and Translating:
Theory and Practice**
ROGER T. BELL

**Process and Experience in the
Language Classroom**
MICHAEL LEGUTKE *and*
HOWARD THOMAS

**Rediscovering Interlanguage**
LARRY SELINKER

**Language as Discourse: Perspectives
for Language Teaching**
MICHAEL MCCARTHY *and*
RONALD CARTER

# Acknowledgements

The Publishers are grateful to the following for permission to reproduce copyright material:

Addison Wesley Longman Australia Pty Limited for our Figure 2.4 'Describing features in a place' from M. Stacey and J. Lucas (1987) *Investigating Geography: Environment,* and our Figures 2.6 'Describing processes in a place: salination' and 2.7 'Post-geography: exploring issues, both from M. Stacey and J. Lucas (1988) *Investigating Geography: Contemporary Issues;* Jacaranda Wiley Ltd for our Figure 2.2 'Pre-geography realised by cartoons' from L. Scott (1982) *People and Places: Our World in Change, Vol I* and our Figure 2.5 'Map of Melbourne's central business district' from R. Pask and L. Bryant (1982) *People in Australia: A Social Geography;* and Thomas Nelson Australia for our Figures 2.1 'Pre-geography realised photographically' and 2.3 'Transition to stage 2', from pages 1 and 5 of *Learning to Look through a Geographer's Eyes, Book 1* by Gallagher, Oliver and Wilson (1987).

# Introduction

GEOFF WILLIAMS AND RUQAIYA HASAN

To even a casual observer it is apparent that any 'literacy event' in social life (Heath 1983) is necessarily one which implicates readers, writers and texts understood as language in use in social contexts. This simple observation suggests that analysis of social functions of literacy, and perhaps even more of the ontogenesis of literacy, is a highly complex task since all three components in the literacy event create a potential for significant variation. Texts are by definition socially situated acts of semiosis, and therefore necessarily variable as a function of their relation to the social context of use, which both defines and is defined by them. Equally, readers/writers are socially situated subjects who, on the one hand, have – at least in theory – the freedom of the entire rich resources of their language, including the discursive practices it puts at their disposal, but who, on the other hand, must select from only a range of these resources which come to represent their 'ways of meaning'; it is only an aspect of this practical condition of social life that the ways of saying and meaning of differently socially positioned readers/writers are non-equivalent.

It follows that for any pedagogic discourse concerned with questions of social equity, careful analyses of the variable relations between texts and writers/readers are an essential prerequisite. This highlights the problem of developing sensitive descriptive resources which would enable such a deep analysis of textual variability, and which would simultaneously enable scholars of pedagogy to relate their findings about features of pedagogic discourse both to social conditions of human existence and to the semiotic practices of subjects who have variable access to the institutional processes of education.

The chapters presented in this volume move within this vast landscape, being concerned with *literacy in society*, without necessarily touching on every aspect delineated above. All were first heard on some occasion organised by scholars and students of language who use the systemic functional framework (SFL) as their point of departure: the majority of the papers were in fact presented at the 19th International Systemic Functional Congress, held at Macquarie University in July 1992. It is not our intention to provide the customary synopses of each chapter by way of leading the readers to the offerings of this volume: it is our readers' prerogative to approach them as they will. What we would like to do in this introduction is to discuss briefly some issues in literacy seen from the perspective we have outlined in the previous paragraph. That perspective itself is one associated closely with the SFL framework. From its very early stages, SFL has viewed language as a social semiotic (Halliday 1978), with the consequence that variability in language, variability in social positioning, and their relations to education have always attracted the SF linguists' attention. The commitment to this perspective was already apparent, for example, in the early SFL literacy education research projects directed by M.A.K. Halliday at University College London which began as a Nuffield Project in the mid 1960s and continued up to 1970 as the *Schools Council Project on Linguistics and English Teaching* (Halliday 1978; Keith 1990). The interest in educational linguistics has continued in the work of many linguists, notably J.R. Martin and associates (Sydney University), Margaret Berry, Ronald Carter and associates (Nottingham), Lemke (CUNY), and many others. This interest ranges from studies of lexicogrammar in discursive processes as they impinge on pedagogy through to what has become popularly known as the genre-based literacy program, guided by Martin.

Turning first to the writing/reading subject, the deeply social nature of literacy processes is perhaps nowhere as evident as in ontogenesis, what Hasan, in this volume, has referred to as the natural line of literacy development. If learning language is *Learning How to Mean* (cf. Halliday 1975), then the semiotic processes of verbal exchange which very small children engage in are at once a resource for learning language, learning about language and learning through language about the world in which the children and their meaning group live. The last of these perspectives has been the focus of Hasan's research in semantic variation – how the social conditions of existence dialectically relate to the speaking subjects' ways of meaning, creating a variability in points of view which finds its expression in every sphere of semiotic activity (Bernstein 1990; Bourdieu 1984). What Vygotsky referred to as semiotic mediation is not limited to simply specialised contexts of learning: the semiotic mediation by means of language functioning as an abstract tool suffuses much of human experience. And to the extent that this semiotic mediation is dialectically engaged with the social conditions of human existence, to that extent the natural development of mental functions must take variable forms. This has obvious implications for literacy pedagogy in schooling environments, which typically operate with a single standard, which is itself typically semantically congruent with the views of a specific segment of industrialised capitalist societies. We believe that the role of language as an abstract tool in the intellectualisation of concepts (cf. Vygotsky) is highly relevant to issues of literacy development. Painter's research (see this volume for a partial account) is a beginning in this area, which needs to be supplemented with large-scale studies of how the development of language and the development of mental functions are shaped by varying social conditions.

It is in the context of this natural line of semiotic development that one must view the ontogenesis of literacy in the specific sense of engagement with print. It is clear that what children come to take as literate activity is to a large extent a function of recurring features of linguistic semiosis in interaction with caregivers. From those first interactions mediated by an object text children begin to form their literate practices which are, therefore, not surprisingly responsive to the social positioning of caregivers (Cook-Gumperz 1986; Heath 1983; Ninio and Bruner 1978; Wells 1985). But since such positions are differentially related to school literacy practices, not all children entering schooling can clearly establish the same relation to schooled literacy (Williams 1995). The problem of variable ontogenesis is an important signifier for a more general situation in literacy education. Though pedagogic handbooks often acknowledge variation in the ontogenesis of literacy, particularly following Heath's ethnographic description (1983) of oral and literate 'traditions' in three 'communities' in the south-east of the USA, in fact the majority elide any systematic consideration of variation in caregivers' literacy practices and its consequences for children from a sociologically informed perspective. The result is that a majority of accounts of the difficulties which children experience in pedagogic literacy are framed in terms of individual cognitive or perceptual deficit. We identify the tension between the quotidian, natural line of literacy development and the exotic, pedagogic one as a major area needing an informed sociolinguistic approach which can identify the parameters of semantic variation (cf. Hasan this volume).

A remarkable feature of pedagogic discourse is the fact that so little attention is given to the nature of object texts (Meek 1988) and their consequences for literacy development. The majority of analyses of reading take no account of the effects of text features on reading. Instead, they investigate readers as socially un-located, generalised subjects who are more or less efficient processors of language, but bereft of any point of view. (For a contrast to this approach see Cranny-Francis in this volume, who focuses on the reading of a text at the secondary school stage.) Reading is thus made to resemble a unitary process across types of discourse, irrespective of the interpretative activity required by texts in specific types of social context (Eco 1994). Literacy pedagogy would, in our view, benefit from developing theoretically coherent methods of the analysis of meaning relations in texts typical of the various stages of schooling. Certainly, some specific questions of relations between features of texts and the formation of literate consciousness have been extensively discussed in the last decade, with broad critiques of the representation of class, race and gender in children's early reading materials. Interest in the effects of stereotypical representation on pupils' consciousness and students' variable readings of texts designed to challenge cultural stereotypes has been noticeable (Davies 1989; Gilbert 1992). However, these discussions typically do not exploit the powerful analysis of ideology construal through the systematic workings of identifiable lexicogrammatical patterns; the analysis is typically presented in commonsensical terms which makes it somewhat difficult to build further research on it.

While still on the topic of texts, an obvious fact is that school texts have always deployed multiple semiotic modalities. The implication is that the description of texts cannot be entirely linguistic. In the early stages of literacy development illustrated texts are typically most prominent. In later schooling and in a wide range of adult literacy learning, texts deploying multiple semiotic modalities are equally crucial, as for example the interaction between language, maps, illustrations, diagrams and images. Until quite recently the questions posed by the presence of multiple semiotic modalities have been ignored (cf. Doonan 1993; Meek 1988). A recent encouraging contribution in this area has been the work reported by Kress and van Leeuwen (1990) and on displayed art by O'Toole (1994). Their analyses of systematic meaning relations within and between visual and verbal elements of text drawing on Halliday's multifunctional perspective open new possibilities for pedagogic discourse. (See for example van Leeuwen and Humphrey in this volume who explore some of these issues in geography texts.) One hopes for a framework that might permit a coherent analysis of meaning relations between the linguistic texture and structure of a text such as Sendak's *Where the Wild Things Are* and the texture and structure of its pictorial text in such a way as to reveal the seamless transition in reading from one modality to the other.

In the educational linguistic work associated with the SF linguists, the best-known work concerning literacy texts is in a framework introduced by Martin, which is generally known as the genre-based writing movement (Christie 1990; Martin 1985; for one account of its history see Rothery in this volume). This movement has attempted to provide explicit linguistic descriptions of the main 'stages' in educationally valued texts. The aim behind this enterprise was to develop a literacy pedagogy which might help learners in gaining access to educational discourses of the type which they might otherwise not become familiar with in the natural course of their life. A common criticism of this work has construed its analyses of text stages as prescriptive. We are not convinced that the analysis of text stages, *per se*, is any more prescriptive than the analysis and identification of the elements of the structure of the clause. It is perhaps the fate of any analyst who aspires to draw features of implicit textual practice to consciousness to be either accused of prescribing simply because one is drawing attention to typical inclinations to behaviour – an attack on our ability to behave as 'unique individuals'! – or it is one's fate to be castigated for being insufficiently sensitive to highly delicate aspects of textual practice in specific contexts. The first is often a misreading of the aims of the research, the second is usually founded on differences in views about the nature of semiosis (Bakhtin 1986).

Because genre-based pedagogy has used existing educational discourses as models for teaching the structure of such text types, criticism of this approach has focused on possible harmful effects in reproducing existing social practices, and for failing to equip students to critique such practices (see Luke in this volume). The issues in this debate are fairly complicated (for a discussion of some of the issues, see Hasan in this volume), but this sort of criticism is in fact an argument against the explication or presentation of any existing social institution and in this sense it is self-defeating. This is not to suggest that we consider the genre-based writing movement perfect (no self-respecting academic would ever concede this of any one except themselves!). Thus, in the context of a sympathetic evaluation of the genre-based writing movement, Carter, in his contribution to this volume, draws attention to some of the problems, as does Hasan from a different point of view. From the perspective of literacy development, we would like to see the genre-based literacy pedagogy developing more explicit accounts of (i) the relation between lexicogrammar and the identification of textual 'stages'; and (ii) a clearer demonstration of what is meant by connotative semiotic, especially how the structure of the text and the social occasion of the text relate to each other. For a critique along these lines and a somewhat different conception of the relation between social context and text structure, see Hasan (1995). Genre-based educational linguists have responded to criticisms objectively and positively. It has led to a dialogue with critical literacy, and deeper and better analyses, thus providing richer materials from these scholars. An example of this might be seen in the work reported by Macken and also by Veel and Coffin in this volume.

In our view no literacy education program is worthy of that name if it ignores the richest and most effective resource which resides in the lexicogrammar. We should hasten to add that we are not talking here of traditional grammar, the pedagogy of which has been altogether too disappointing and wasteful. In suggesting that grammar is the richest and most effective resource, we have in mind a functional grammar, whose uses in literacy education are far removed from those which are envisaged by certain educators who promote traditional grammar in the hope of recovering an Arcadian literacy – or to maintain certain standards and thus to gain implicit social control. It is encouraging to note that more recently the teaching of grammar has begun to receive support as part of students' development of knowledge about language. Nonetheless there are educators who defend the exclusion of grammar – specifically functional grammar. They advance arguments of the following kind for their position:

- grammar teaching is an unproductive use of curriculum time, which is better used in 'actual' reading and writing;
- grammatical knowledge is boring for learners;
- grammatical knowledge is generally inaccessible to learners;
- grammar teaching is necessarily a prescription of the forms of a standard language.

Each of these is in fact an empirical claim about relations between an unspecified pedagogy and an unspecified grammatical description. In so far as the arguments are advanced against teaching functional grammar, each makes untested assumptions about relations between this grammar and pedagogy. However, as Candlin (1995: v) has remarked, 'Grammar is one [subject] on which pretty well everyone has strong views, even if they haven't had very much direct or thoughtful contact themselves with any of its various meanings. Grammar simply is a topic which excites an enormous amount of active and sharp debate.' This form of the 'popularity' of grammar often prevents cool and objective assessment. There is for example no *a priori* reason why learning about the grammar of one's language under conditions which illuminate how language is used in social life is boring, any more than *a priori* it should be assumed that teaching functional relations between elements of an ecological system is boring. No doubt both can be made very boring, as the teaching of traditional grammar has been! (See Hasan's comments on recognition literacy in this volume.) Whether we treat knowledge of grammatical concepts as inaccessible to learners depends on assumptions about the nature of human developmental capacities, including assumptions about how scientific concepts are internalised (cf. Vygotsky). We note with interest Carter's view (1990) that an SF grammar such as, for example, Halliday's (1994) or Matthiessen's (1995) makes obsolete the results of previous research in (a) the teaching of grammar; and (b) its role in literacy development. A functional grammar is one which offers descriptions of language form in relation to semantics, and descriptions of semantic categories in relation to the contexts of social living. The introduction of such a grammar appears to us to raise interesting new questions about the connections between learning language – i.e. pursuing literacy development – and learning about language. The final argument we noted above from the opponents of grammar is particularly significant given the enormous political pressure on (and within) educational bureaucracies to exclude  minority uses of language from institutional schooling. No doubt the teaching of traditional grammar did effectively support these exclusions and indeed the rhetoric of many advocates of a return to teaching traditional grammar indicates just how effectively those lessons were learned! However, the exclusion of a *functional* grammar on these grounds simply reveals ignorance of the nature and scope of that framework. And through this lack of understanding it deprives learners of the very metalinguistic tools through which it would be possible for them to give a sustained defence of minority linguistic usage in education. Without some theoretically coherent means of describing how and why language varies in relation both to groups of users and to uses in social context (Halliday and Hasan 1985) learners are sadly prevented from understanding the politics of language standardisation.

Among those educators who do support the role of grammar in literacy pedagogy there are important differences of views on uses of technical metalanguage. A widely held position is that 'explicit' teaching of grammar should follow 'implicit' development of metalinguistic knowledge. At a commonsensical level this view has some credibility, suggesting that it would be difficult to understand the concepts of noun and verb without some understanding of the division of the experiential world into entities and processes. But note the disturbing view underlying this position about the relation between linguistic semiosis and abstract thought. Language is reduced in this view to the role of nomenclature rather than being seen as a semiotic tool for the mediation of abstract concepts. We suggest, following Vygotsky's views, that metalanguage is precisely the resource which enables learners to develop the means of reflecting on language. Also following such thinkers as Vygotsky, Luria, and Whorf, we might expect that qualities of thought about language, in fact what a learner comes to understand about *how to act* on language reflectively, are substantially dependent on qualities of the metalanguage, and on how the learner has come to encounter that metalanguage. Since the metalanguage is not a transparent labelling system for concepts implicitly developed through commonsense means, it is precisely the theoretical qualities of the grammatical descriptions which are of primary importance. In summary, one might expect rather different outcomes for learners who have been given opportunities to learn about linguistic meanings through a functional grammar in constructive discursive contexts in comparison with outcomes deriving from the traditional teaching of traditional grammar.

Teaching about language, especially the lexicogrammar, remains one of the most controversial aspects of literacy education. There seems little sense in continuing to make *a priori* assertions about its learnability, its usefulness, its inherent interest, the relative merits of functional and other kinds of grammar, and the like. What is needed is action in the form of actual research in order to advance current understanding. Summing up our discussion of the place of grammar in literacy education, we suggest that serious attention to the following foci is definitely needed:

- linguistically well-informed accounts of the ontogenesis of grammatical knowledge, especially accounts which move beyond short-term, general assessments of development, and which consider the evolution of metalinguistic concepts over periods of years, preferably in children in different social positioning;
- complementing these, detailed accounts of learning contexts in which grammatical knowledge is developed, including accounts of how learners begin to understand the multiple purpose of grammatical descriptions;
- comparative studies in order to establish which grammatical features might best act iconically to introduce learners to the possibilities of functional grammatical description, especially in the development of critical language awareness (Fairclough 1995);
- explorations of means through which teachers might learn to use functional grammar as a professional resource, not only in teaching students about language as part of a literacy curriculum but also for a wide range of other educational purposes, including the assessment of children's language development.

That we emphasise the need for the understanding and for the learning of grammar in the language education contexts should not be a matter of surprise. Literacy education will remain incomplete until pupils have a conscious understanding of how patterns of language are systematically used in the construal of our social universe, and this means not just being able to write 'correct' sentences, or to reel off definitions of noun and verb or to parse correctly. Above all this, it means, as the ultimate goal, the ability to realise how invidious systems of relations are developed, how they are maintained, and what part our discourses play, and where they derive their power from for playing those parts. An understanding of the role of grammar is a necessary step in engaging with problems of exploitation. This is indeed a far cry from any notion of grammar or language teaching that traditional literacy pedagogies have ever worked with.

# References

Bakhtin, M. 1986. *Speech genres and other late essays.* Translated by V.W. McGee, edited by C. Emerson and M. Holquist. Austin: University of Texas Press.

Bernstein, Basil. 1990. *The structuring of pedagogic discourse. Vol. IV: Class, codes and control.* London: Routledge.

Bourdieu, Pierre. 1984. *Distinction: a social critique of the judgement of taste.* Translated by R. Nice. London: Routledge & Kegan Paul.

Candlin, C.N. 1995. Introduction. *Using functional grammar: an explorer's guide* by David Butt, Rhondda Fahey, Sue Spinks and Colin Yallop. Sydney: NCELTR, Macquarie University.

Carter, R. 1990. The new grammar teaching. In *Knowledge about language and the curriculum,* edited by R. Carter. Sevenoaks: Hodder & Stoughton.

Christie, F. 1990. The changing face of literacy. In *Literacy for a changing world.* Melbourne:ACER.

Cook-Gumperz, J. 1986. *The social construction of literacy.* Cambridge: Cambridge University Press.

Davies, B. 1989. *Frogs and snails and feminist tales: preschool children and gender.* North Sydney: Allen and Unwin.

Doonan, J. 1993. *Looking at pictures in picture books.* Stroud: The Thimble Press.

Eco, Umberto. 1994. *Six walks in the fictional woods.* Cambridge, MA: Harvard University Press.

Fairclough, N. 1995. *Critical discourse analysis.* London: Longman.

Gilbert, P. 1992. The story so far: Gender, literacy and social regulation. *Gender and education,* 4(3).

Halliday, M.A.K. 1975. *Learning how to mean: explorations in the development of language.* London: Arnold.

Halliday, M.A.K. 1978. *Language as social semiotics.* London: Arnold.

Halliday, M.A.K. 1994. *Introduction to functional grammar,* 2nd edn. London: Arnold.

Halliday, M.A.K. and Ruqaiya Hasan. 1985. *Language, context and text: aspects of language in a social-semiotic perspective.* Geelong, Vic.: Deakin University Press.

Halliday, M.A.K., Angus McIntosh and Peter Strevens. 1964. *The linguistic sciences and language teaching.* London: Longmans.

Hasan, Ruqaiya. 1995. The conception of context in text. In *Discourse in society: a systemic functional perspective,* edited by Peter H. Fries and Michael Gregory. Norwood, NJ: Ablex.

Heath, S.B. 1983. *Ways with words: language, life and work in communities and classrooms.* Cambridge: Cambridge University Press.

Keith, G. 1990. Language study at Key Stage 3. In *Knowledge about language and the curriculum,* edited by R. Carter. Sevenoaks: Hodder & Stoughton.

Kress, G. and Theo van Leeuwen. 1990. *Reading images.* Geelong, Vic.: Deakin University Press.

Martin, J.R. 1985. *Factual writing: exploring and challenging social reality.* Geelong, Vic.: Deakin University Press.

Matthiessen, Christian. 1995. *Lexicogrammatical cartography.* Tokyo: International Language Sciences Publishers.

Meek, M. 1988. *How texts teach what readers learn.* Stroud: The Thimble Press.

Ninio, A.Z. and Jerome S. Bruner. 1978. The achievements and antecedents of labelling. *Journal of Child Language,* **5**.

O'Toole, Michael. 1994. *The language of displayed art.* London: Leicester University Press.

Wells, Gordon C. 1985. *Language, learning and education.* Windsor: NFER-Nelson.

Williams, Geoff. 1995. Joint book-reading and literacy pedagogy: A socio-semantic examination. Unpublished doctoral dissertation, School of English, Linguistics and Media, Macquarie University Sydney.

# 1

# Politics and knowledge about language: the LINC project

RONALD CARTER

Every time the question of the language surfaces, in one way or another, it means that a series of other problems are coming to the fore: the formation and enlargement of the governing class, the need to establish more intimate and secure relationships between the governing groups and the national-popular mass, in other words to reorganise the cultural hegemony.

(Antonio Gramsci, quoted in Crowley, 1985)

## 1  Introduction

The relationship between politics and knowledge about language is both comprehensive and complex. In this chapter only three main perspectives are offered: a brief overview of a national language education initiative in England and Wales with a particular focus on keywords in discourses about language, English and education; the place of genre theory in relation to such an initiative; some research and development questions for teaching school students about language.

## 1.1  Examining language

Here is part of a GCE examination paper set for 15–16-year-old pupils in Britain in the early 1960s. Questions of this kind about grammar constituted between 20–30 per cent of the total examination paper.

> Leaving childhood behind, I soon lost this desire to possess a goldfish. It is difficult to persuade oneself that a goldfish is happy and as soon as we have begun to doubt that some poor creature enjoys living with us we can take no pleasure in its company.

Using a new line for each, select *one* example from the above passage of *each* of the following:

   (i)   an infinitive used as the direct object of a verb;
  (ii)  an infinitive used in apposition to a pronoun;
 (iii)  a gerund;
 (iv)  a present participle;
  (v)  a past participle;
 (vi)  an adjective used predicatively (i.e. as a complement);
(vii)  a possessive adjective;
(viii)  a demonstrative adjective;
 (ix)  a reflexive pronoun;
  (x)  an adverb of time;
 (xi)  an adverb of degree;
(xii)  a preposition;
(xiii)  a subordinating conjunction.

Reference is made to such an examination exercise at the very beginning of this chapter because the views of language and of language teaching enshrined within it go right to the very centre of current debates in Britain about language teaching in the context of the new National Curriculum for English in England and Wales. The debate is characterised by different political positions and, in particular, by strenuous efforts by the British government to persuade teachers to a return to the 1950s and to the kinds of practices of language teaching illustrated by this examination paper.

What are the practices which are illustrated by this example? Why do government ministers wish to see them reinstated? What do teachers think of them? What is the view taken by linguists of such practices? Answers to such questions may begin to explain why the materials for teachers produced by the Language in the National Curriculum (henceforth, LINC) project were not only refused publication by the British government, but also became the centre of contesting views about language and education.

## 1.2   *Views of language and language teaching*

The different views of language and language teaching in respect of this representative examination paper held by government, English teachers and by linguists may be broadly summarised under three headings: (i) Government views; (ii) teachers' views; and (iii) linguists' views.

## (i)  Government views

1. The examination paper illustrates a manifest concern with measurable knowledge. A body of linguistic facts can be taught, learned by pupils and then tested. Answers are either right or wrong, the *body* of knowledge taught is definite and measurable, and teachers can even be assessed by how well they teach it.
2. The learning which ensues is disciplined and takes place within a clear framework. It contrasts vividly with what is felt to be the vague and undirected concern with creativity and personal expression which characterises work in many English lessons at the present time.[1]
3. Such practices will help to guarantee correct grammar and standard English. They will remove sloppiness in expression and eradicate a climate in which errors are viewed only in relation to a process of language development and thus not always immediately corrected.

The views of the government have received strong support in a number of public statements by HRH The Prince of Wales. In a speech reported in the British newspapers only seven days after the publication of the English Working Party Report ('The Cox Report', DES, 1989) Prince Charles was quoted in various papers as making the following statements (which represent a synthesis of what was reported):

> We've got to produce people who can write *proper English.* It's a fundamental problem. All the people I have in my office, they can't speak English properly, they can't write English properly. All the letters sent from my office I have to correct myself, and that is because English is taught so bloody badly. If we want people who write good English and write plays for the future, it cannot be done with the present system, and all the nonsense academics come up with. It is a fundamental problem. We must educate for character. That's the trouble with schools. They don't educate for character. This matters a great deal. The whole way schools are operating is not right. I do not believe English is being taught properly. You cannot educate people properly unless you do it on a basic framework and drilling system.

A prominent conservative politician, a politician who was chairman of the Conservative Party during the years 1984–7, adopts a not dissimilar position, equating illiteracy with crime in a series of 'logical' non-sequiturs which, it could be argued, it is a major responsibility for all concerned with English language education to deconstruct:

> ... We've allowed so many standards to slip. ... Teachers weren't bothering to teach kids to spell and to punctuate properly. ... If you allow standards to slip to the stage where good English is no better than bad English, where people turn up filthy ... at school ... all those things tend to cause people to have no standards at all, and once you lose standards then there's no imperative to stay out of crime.[2]

We will return to the use of certain keywords in such statements. We will return to them because they frequently recur in such statements. The articulation of concepts framed by words such as *correct, proper, standard(s)* and the equation of standards of language use with standards of hygiene and cleanliness should, however, be noted at this stage. We should also note how discussions of language by those with such persuasions are regularly framed in terms of social behaviour. Even the word *drills* connotes a view of the individual language user conforming to externally imposed norms almost as if s/he were marching in step on the parade ground.

### (ii)  Teachers' views

Until recently, teachers' views have been regularly dominated by what are described as 'Romantic' conceptions of English as a subject (see Christie, 1985/89).

Romanticism in English teaching involves a classroom emphasis on language use which is person-centred, which stresses the capacity of the individual for originality and creativity, and a concern that strict rules and conventions may be inhibiting to pupils, and in the process, restrict their capacities for using the language. There is a particular stress on the primacy of speech, even in writing where individuals are encouraged by the teacher to find their own personal voice.[3] In the context of such ideologies it will be clear that many English teachers reject the view of grammar and of language study illustrated in the above examination paper. It runs very obviously counter to Romantic influences on the subject. During the course of the LINC project, shifts in teachers' perception of formal language study were recorded, but strong resistance remains, on the above grounds, to the decontextualised study of language, to teaching practices and pedagogies which are necessarily transmissive and narrowly knowledge-based, and which allow little or no scope for an emergence of the pupil's own 'voice'.

### (iii)    The views of linguists

Linguists have taken a prominent role in the shaping of the National Curriculum for English in England and Wales.[4] Most linguists take the following main views of grammar-based teaching and testing of linguistic knowledge:

1. They point out how examination papers from the 1960s are preoccupied with the written rather than the spoken language.
2. They point out that the analysis is invariably decontextualised since the definitions required of pupils are *formalistic*. That is, there is no attention required to language use, to the functions of language or to the kinds of meanings produced by the particular forms which are isolated.[5] Examinations such as those above are exercises in the naming of parts.
3. They point out that such examinations are concerned with sentences rather than texts. In fact, the text here is genuinely incidental. The focus is on a bottom-up analysis of the smallest units of language with little or no interest in eliciting from pupils how such units might combine to form larger functional meanings and effects.

Accordingly, those linguists who advised the government did not recommend a return to the 1950s and to a teaching of grammatical forms by means of decontextualised drills. But they did not reject a formal study of language. Instead, they strongly advocated programmes of study for pupils in Knowledge About Language (KAL). It was felt that such a concentration was overdue, and had been neglected for too long, probably because of dominant Romantic philosophies of English teaching which resisted most forms of explicit analysis. However, to be successful, it was argued, and indeed eventually accepted in parliamentary statutes, that KAL needed to be based on a wider range of analysis than grammar, and needed to be clearly rooted in theories of language variation, both spoken and written. These views (of government-appointed committees) were grudgingly accepted by the government. The government were quick to recognise that knowledge about language, based on a variety of texts, includes discussion of language in context, and that discussion of context is often necessarily social. Such an orientation served only to reinforce for the government the desirability of decontextualised drills and exercises.

## 2    LINC: an in-service teacher education project

LINC stands for Language in the National Curriculum. LINC is a project designed to make the theories and descriptions of language in the new National Curriculum accessible to teachers, and to assist them with the language components of the National Curriculum for English in England and Wales. In this context it has to be remembered that, for many teachers in Britain, formal language study has not formed part of either their pre-service or in-service education. Indeed, in some teacher-training institutions there is a history of active resistance to the introduction of more linguistics-based courses in English, and for this reason English teachers and teacher-trainers did not give the publication of National Curriculum reports an unreserved welcome.[6]

Details of the remit and organisation of the LINC project are given in Appendix One. In basic outline the main project team was asked to produce study units for teachers which were to be used in in-service courses, in school-based follow-up and dissemination, and in self-study sessions. The resulting training package is therefore activity-based and open-ended. It contains many linguistically based tasks with accompanying commentaries so that teachers can work on the material in a range of contexts.

### 2.1    *The LINC ban*

The LINC project assumed an especial political prominence when the government decided, in the summer of 1991, that it did not wish to publish the materials produced by the LINC project. Neither was it able to allow commercial publication in spite of interest on the part of several international publishers in publishing the complete training package.[7] Although the project was allowed to continue and although the LINC training package could be made available in photocopied form for use on in-service training courses, such decisions amounted to an effective ban on widespread publication and dissemination of LINC materials.

Predictably, the government ban has served only to increase interest and, in particular, demand for the training package and other LINC publications. Both in the United Kingdom and overseas over 20,000 *samizdat* versions are being used in school and training college INSET sessions, LINC/BBC TV and radio programmes (DES approved) have been widely praised and LINC publications from Hodder and Stoughton have achieved sales five times higher than planned. Highest levels of interest overseas are in Australia, New Zealand, Canada, USA, Hong Kong and Singapore, where LINC materials are being integrated into teacher-training programmes. Particular interest has come from schools inspectors in France and Germany, who, increasingly concerned about the narrow formalism of their own language teaching, admire the balance achieved in National Curriculum English between attention both to the forms of the language and its use.

Debates surrounding the LINC ban centre on certain key words. They are the same key words which recur repeatedly at times of social and cultural change when questions of language and the nature of English as a subject are always central. There is nothing unusual about this. A recent collection entitled *Proper English?* (Crowley, 1991) contains documents ranging from Jonathan Swift's *A Proposal for Correcting, Improving and Ascertaining the English Tongue* (1712) – a key essay for understanding social and cultural pressures in the aftermath of the English revolution – to the *Newbolt Report* (1921) – published after the First World War explicitly with the aim of promoting English as a subject of national unity and cultural harmony – to the politically influential *English, Our English* (1987) by John Marenbon, which attacks much current theory and practice in the field of literacy. Over nearly 300 years the debates cover remarkably similar ground: the place of a standard language in relation to non-standard forms; the place of absolute rules of correctness in grammar and pronunciation; the perception of a degeneracy in standards of language use.

It is no semantic accident that words such as *standard*, *correct*, and *proper* are key words. Debates about the state and status of the English language are rarely debates about language alone. The terms of the debate are also terms for defining social behaviour.

The term *English* is synonymous with Englishness, that is, with an understanding of who the proper English are. A view of one English with a single set of rules accords with a monolingual, monocultural version of society intent on preserving an existing order in which everyone knows their place. A view which recognises Englishes as well as English and which stresses variable rules accords with a multilingual, culturally diverse version of society. Both positions include politically extreme versions. These range from a view that standard English is correct English and must be uniformly enforced in all contexts of use (with dialects extirpated) and that children not drilled in the rules of standard grammar are both deviant and disempowered (strong right-wing position) to a view that Standard English is a badge of upper-class power, and that to require children to learn it is a form of social enslavement (strong left-wing position I) to a view that Standard English must be taught to working-class children so that they can wrest linguistic power from those more privileged than themselves (strong left-wing position II). It is striking how these political positions converge in certain respects and how the pedagogical positions are often identical.

## 2.2   LINC and the middle ground

The overwhelming majority of teachers in the United Kingdom occupy a middle-ground position between these two extremes. They recognise and support the balanced view of language and learning provided by the Kingman and Cox Committees, in all National Curriculum documents and now in LINC courses and materials. They concede that attention to grammar and to the forms of language has been neglected and now willingly incorporate more formal knowledge about language into schemes of work which continue to stress the importance of the audiences, purposes and social contexts of language use. They are saddened that this determination to take a balanced and informed view of language learning should be constructed by some sections of the press and by some politicians as a form of left-wing extremism. They are disturbed that while research advances in medicine and other scientific domains are accepted, evidence from research into language and language development is lightly dismissed.

The LINC training materials adopt a balanced and moderate position on many of the above issues. For example, far from being opposed to grammar, in the LINC materials grammar occupies a central position. Indeed, there is more detailed description of the grammar of English there than in any mother-tongue English curriculum materials anywhere in the world, though, in keeping with all National Curriculum recommendations, there is no advocacy of a return to the decontextualised drills and exercises of the 1950s. Instead there is systematic exploration of grammatical differences between speech and writing, between standard and non-standard forms of the language, and between different varieties of English. In spite of being described in certain national newspapers as a dialect project, 97 per cent of the examples in LINC materials are of pupils speaking, reading and writing in Standard English. They also demonstrate that one of the most effective ways of learning Standard English is for pupils to compare and analyse differences between their own dialects and the dialect of Standard English, discussing explicitly how and when different forms are appropriate. Over sixty pages are devoted to helping pupils with correct spelling and to helping their teachers understand the complexities of the English spelling system. Throughout the materials an emphasis on texts encourages teachers to focus not just on content but on the relationship between *what* is said and *how* it is said. The success of LINC's approach to the language curriculum has generated innumerable further local publications which are eagerly sought and used.

Grammar is not neglected. Here is an example of LINC's approach to grammar taken from some local training materials:

> It had been so different three years ago, the night she'd met Stefan de Vaux. There'd been a party. Bella always threw a party when she'd sold a picture because poverty, she'd explained, was a great inspiration. She'd been wearing a brilliant blue caftan, her fair hair twisted on the top of her head, the severity of it accenting her high cheekbones, the little jade Buddha gleaming on its silver chain round her neck.
>
> Claire, pale from England and the illness that had allowed her to come to Tangier to recuperate, had been passed from guest to guest – "Ah, you're Bella's cousin" – like a plate of canapés, she thought ruefully, attractive but unexciting. Until Stefan de Vaux had taken her out onto the balcony and kissed her.
>
> "Well?" he'd said softly, in his lightly accented voice, letting her go at last, and she had just stood there, staring at him, at his lean, outrageously handsome face, his laughing mouth, amber brown eyes. "Angry? Pleased? Shocked?" And she'd blushed furiously, feeling all three.

There are many interesting grammatical features of this text which pupils can explore and investigate. For example, the use of incomplete sentences, e.g. *Until Stefan de Vaux had taken her out onto the balcony and kissed her.* The self-standing subordinate clause (with no accompanying main clause) is a not uncommon stylistic feature of popular fiction, functioning to create a sense of anticipation and, as it were, inviting the reader to close the sentence in their own imaginations. Another common feature is patterns of transitivity which regularly associate female characters with intransitive actions, e.g. *she blushed; she sighed; she moaned* and male characters with transitive actions, e.g. *he kissed her.* The equation between language use and the construction of different 'positions' for men and women (there are no examples of *she kissed him*) is something which readers need to be able to see through and resist. Of course, such assumptions simply reinforce existing ideologies within the culture, and it is the purpose of such fiction to do no more than reproduce such ideologies. It is one key feature of the LINC approach to grammar that pupils should, where possible, explore grammar in complete texts, in relation to social and cultural contexts and with reference both to forms and functions. For further discussion of this position in relation both to the development of reading and writing skills see Carter and Nash (1990) and Carter (1990b) which is an introduction to a collection of supporting articles for the LINC Training Package. It should be recognised, however, that detailed analysis of every grammatical component of the text is not an element of the LINC materials. In fact, one strategic decision taken in the early stages of the project was crucial and formative. In the time available, with curricular change encircling teachers all the time and, furthermore, in the context of uncertainties and anxieties about linguistics in relation to the English curriculum, the main project team decided that it was preferable to take a small but discernible step forward rather than to take a large step and lose balance completely. It was therefore decided that the materials had to work with the grain, had to accommodate existing assumptions, and had to build on those assumptions instead of attempting radically to change them. It was important to go with the not inconsiderable – though generally unformalised – knowledge about language which teachers already possessed and with what interested them about language.

Thus the focus on grammar may be felt by some linguists to be insufficiently formalised. In the context of in-service material for teachers of English as a mother-tongue it is, however, considerable and is primarily concerned with how grammar works to construct meanings in the kinds of text with which many English teachers are familiar.

## 2.3   Keywords

What was effectively a ban on the publication of LINC training materials probably had to be expected. The emphasis on language variation and on language in context led to a too frequent reference to social theory and an emphasis on socio-linguistic perspectives. For governments of a particular political persuasion the word *social* is directly equatable with the word *socialist*. The training package itself was designed, it was said, in too activity-based and open a manner. The government eventually made it clear that it had preferred all along training materials which emphasised right and wrong uses of English, reinforcing such an emphasis with drills and exercises for teachers and pupils to follow, and with a printed appendix containing the correct answers to the exercises. The emphasis should be on factual knowledge which is measurable and determinable, and which can be transmitted from a position of authority rather than be discovered through activity-centred processes. As we noted above, a key word here is the word *drill*. It derives in an important sense from the parade ground. It encodes an armed-services view of the individual learner. Marching in uniform and standardised linguistic steps with others ensures a language without differences and distinctions within a clear framework of order and authority.

Finally, it was said that certain key words do not appear in a sufficiently unambiguous way. Words such as *correct, standard* and *proper* are always relativised to specific contexts and practices of teaching.

In respect of such key words, linguists and teachers do, in fact, need to find a way of talking about language which better controls and engages with the existing public discourses, especially those of most sections of the press and media. In this connection, English teachers have to apply their knowledge about language to a major problem of communication. The very vocabulary currently available to talk about language variation – the essence of National Curriculum English in England and Wales – offers only apparently negative or oppositional terms which play neatly into the hands of those with the most simplistic notions of language and education. Thus, to talk about non-standard English can be seen as a departure from standards; to talk about the dangers of absolute rules of correctness is seen as an endorsement of incorrect English or as a failure to correct pupils' work; to suggest that proper English is relative to contexts of use is itself improper. Space does not allow further exposure of these antinomies (others are traditional vs. trendy; national vs. unpatriotic; basic vs. progressive; simple vs. complex) but it is easy to trace how the generally moderate and balanced English teacher is constructed as an offender against order, decency and common sense.

## 3    LINC and genre theory

There are many different emphases and inflections in the LINC Training Package. There is also a focus both on continuities with existing good practice and on important recent developments in the field of language education. One of the most significant of recent developments is in the field of genre theory and in the teaching, in particular, of genres of writing. It is a controversial area of teaching and learning and LINC in-service training courses and materials engage in places directly with key aspects of genre theory, as developed in the USA, within the context of European text linguistics and, in particular, of work in Australia within the context of systemic functional linguistics.[8] Detailed analysis of this work must await a separate paper, but listed here are what are felt to be some main points of conclusion from LINC's work with genre theory.

### 3.1    Reactions to genre-based teaching

(1)    LINC teams have been convinced by the strength and depth of arguments for making the language structure of texts more visible on the grounds that genuine intervention by the teacher and consequent development in pupils' language use are not possible unless the relevant patterns of language are identified. Australian genre theorists have expressed reservations about Romantic conceptions of English teaching which make language learning an invisible process, and which explicitly oppose attention to

language on the grounds that it inhibits sensitivity to language and the personal shaping of experience through language. Such arguments are directly engaged within LINC materials.

(2)    LINC teams have accepted that a primary concern with personal shaping of experience has resulted in classrooms in which there is an over-concentration on narrative to the exclusion of other genres.

(3)    In a related way LINC has adopted a more inclusive view of authorship, especially in the writing classroom. Pam Gilbert (1990:70) wrote that: 'Authorship is but one of the newest of a long line of discursive devices which serve to entrench personalist, individualist, speech-oriented theories of writing in schools.' Although such a position obscures important developmental connections between speech and writing, it establishes a basis for more impersonal writing modes, and thus a wider range of generic types of writing.

(4)    LINC's introduction of a more genre-based approach to writing has provoked some hostility on the part of British teachers. A major concern is that such writing practices are inherently conservative and are designed to produce unreflective operatives who will be able to do no more than sustain a market economy for a conservative society. The concern of genre theorists for a wider range of writing types which are in turn closer to the requirements of the world of work is interpreted as a narrow vocationalism. What has helped to change this perception is the notion of *critical literacy*, initiated in particular by Gunter Kress and incorporated in specific materials such as the *Language: A Resource for Meaning Project* developed by Frances Christie, Joan Rothery, Mary Macken and others.[9] Here, a functional literacy is augmented by a critical literacy designed to enable learners not only to comprehend and produce society's discourses, but also to criticise and re-direct them, if necessary. Inevitably, such practices link closely with the above arguments for making linguistic structure more visible. They clearly serve to differentiate such work from those ideologically conservative approaches to writing which would simply leave society's discourses intact, in so far as they were penetrated at all. As Michael Halliday has put it: 'To be literate is not only to participate in the discourse of an information society; it is also to resist it … it is rather perverse to think you can engage in discursive contest without engaging in the language of the discourse.'[10] Such work underlines the fact that genre-based teaching is both

revolutionary and reactionary. Teachers in Britain are more prepared to embrace genre theory if it includes more elements of
critical linguistic awareness.

(5)   British teachers have become increasingly impressed by
the precise analytical work which has enabled central, prototypical
features of particular genres to be identified. It is the same explicitness of analysis which has helped both pupils and teachers to
develop a critical linguistic literacy.

(6)   LINC teams have valued the overt, explicit and retrievable
arguments advanced in particular by Martin (1985/89) but also by
others as well. Taking such strong, clear argumentative lines
enables others to argue with or argue against in a systematic way.[11]

## 3.2   Problems and issues

Work on the LINC project has also enabled teachers to identify
what seem to them to be some problems with current work in
genre theory, and which may suggest directions for future
research and development. These observations are listed here
because of the extent of interest in this particular field of language education. Such is the extent of interest in Britain in
genre-based work that some solutions to some of these problems
are already being explored in a number of action-research projects in UK schools and teacher-training colleges. The main points
of concern are stated below.

(1)   Existing descriptions of genre within a systemic functional
tradition may have tended to neglect work in other traditions of
description. For obvious reasons there has been a concentration
on the realisations of schematic and generic structure in the
lexico-grammar of texts. There is now a large body of work within
the traditions of text-linguistics and written discourse analysis on
lexical patterning, cohesion, coherence and textual macrostruc-
ture. Even work within a Hallidayan tradition on cohesion and
thematic patterning has not been as extensively applied as it
might have been.

(2)   LINC teams keep coming across texts which do not conform to any single generic structure. They are the result of mixed
genres. Examples of mixed genres are arguments which make use
of narrative structures, narratives which have reporting or exposition structures embedded within them, and reports which are
simultaneously impersonal and personal in form, that is, they are

reports which also contain personal accounts of events and specific, person-based recommendations. LINC teams would thus want to emphasise that genres are not autonomous systems, and that accounts of genre and genre teaching may be limited in their considerable potential if they become too simplistic or narrowly monologic.

Terry Threadgold (1989) put it as follows:

> Texts are not necessarily formed or produced on the basis of single generic patterns. They may also be multi-generic. These are not random differences. They are historically, socially and functionally constrained: and we will need to be able to teach the differences between and the motivations for multi-generic and single generic texts.

However, our acceptance of this does not mean that we dismiss genre theory, as John Dixon (1987), Michael Rosen (1988), Dixon and Stratta (1992), among others, have tended to do, for the fact that we mix genres must mean that generic structures exist to be mixed in the first place.

(3)   Work within the framework of Australian and British genre theory on the genre of narrative tends to be a little too simplistic overall. It fails adequately to recognise that Labov's model for narrative description is a spoken model based on spoken data.[12] Because spoken narratives unfold sequentially in time, they do not normally have the characteristic embeddings, shifts in point of view, and complexities of narratorial presentation which characterise most written narratives. Within the general area of continua between spoken and written genres it is important, however, that literacy is not wholly construed as written texts.

(4)   Early examples within Australian work of teachers modelling genres to a whole class were perceived by LINC to be possibly over-rigid and deterministic. A common view is that there has been a tendency among some genre theorists to swing the pendulum too far in the opposite direction from Romantic conceptions of learning and teaching. Research in domains of both first and second language teaching shows that we do learn effectively by making things our own, and by being personally involved in the processes of constructing a text. It has also been demonstrated that process-based approaches to writing, with an emphasis on ownership of the text, lead to increased motivation to use language. In a parallel way, there may be among theorists in a systemic functional tradition a tendency to over-emphasise factual,

impersonal genres at the expense of the personal. Accordingly, British teachers and linguists have been particularly impressed by recent work on modelling in relation to joint and individual construction which operates successfully to show writing to be both *process* and *product*-based, and that work on genre can be integrated with more holistic approaches to language learning and development. (See again the relevance of the Australian materials cited in note 9.)

(5)    The identification of genres for description and teaching tends to be internal to the school. There is little attempt to identify the genres of writing commonly required in the workplace. Research directed by Margaret Berry on 'The Language of Business and Industry', which pays detailed attention to genre theory, has much to offer us all. It demonstrates, for example, that a report genre in junior school is markedly different from a report genre in industrial or business work settings, as demonstrated by Stainton (1990). It also underlines that text-intrinsic accounts of genre need to take fuller cognizance of the audience, purpose and context in which particular genres operate.

(6)    Encouragement to pupils to reflect on language has tended to be restricted to the patterns of language in the particular genre in focus. Instead, a general classroom climate needs to be established in which talking and writing about language leads to the need to analyse language. This can be stimulated and promoted in all kinds of ways. In the context of the National Curriculum in Britain there is an emphasis in LINC's work on *language awareness* – that is, general sensitivity to different styles and purposes of language use. These include differences between spoken and written language, explorations of the language of literature, the language of jokes, advertising, pop-fiction, and political rhetorics, and investigations of the continua between different accents and dialects, including Standard English. Such explorations, such encouragement to greater language awareness, are a necessary habit-forming prelude to looking more closely and analytically at the linguistic patterns which make up different genres. A climate of reflection is created which leads to fuller and more systematic analyses. Analysis is not always best fostered by practising analysis and reflection of language solely within the context of individual genres. (For an outline of attainment targets for knowledge about language in the National Curriculum for England and Wales, see Appendix Two.)

Several of these observations are hardly new, and many of them have been advanced by genre theorists themselves. However, the issues mentioned above have grown out of specific contexts of applied linguistic work in relation to the National Curriculum for English in England and Wales. Teachers in Britain interested in writing development are beginning positively to embrace work on genre theory and on genre within a functionalist perspective in particular. These observations should be viewed in a correspondingly positive light. Further detail about the whole LINC programme and the influence of Hallidayan theories of language on it is evidenced in the introductions to the *Training Package* itself and the accompanying Reader.[13]

## 4   Knowledge about language in the classroom

Once again, detailed exploration of this area must await a separate paper. It should also be recognised that the primary purpose of the LINC project was to develop *teachers'* knowledge about language more systematically. The project has, however, stimulated numerous central questions about the relationship between teachers' knowledge and pupils' knowledge, and stimulated, again in the context of National Curriculum requirements, high levels of interest in the teaching of knowledge about language to pupils aged between five and sixteen years. A recent LINC-based publication (Bain, Fitzgerald and Taylor, 1992) presents over thirty classroom case studies in pupils' knowledge about language collected during the course of the project (see also, Carter, 1995).

In the development of pupils' knowledge about language (henceforth KAL) work on the LINC project suggests the following main points which would all benefit from further classroom evidence.

1.  The kinds of language activity at primary and secondary level which most effectively reveal and extend pupils' work across the whole curriculum. What kinds of *experiences* most effectively prompt pupils' reflection on language and language use?
2.  The nature of progression in KAL. For example, should teaching about smaller units of language (e.g. vocabulary) precede teaching about larger units (structure of texts)? Should the

sequence be reversed? Can smaller and larger structures of language be taught simultaneously?

3. The precise relationship between implicit and explicit knowledge about language. Is the natural order always implicit before explicit or can explicit teaching deepen intuitions and unconscious awareness?

4. The connections between KAL and pupils' developing language use. What areas of knowledge about language most effectively stimulate language use? What kinds of interventions by teachers most effectively support such development? At what point is whole-class teaching about language effective and when is it least effective?

5. What kinds of KAL best support and underpin different genres of writing? What kinds of metalanguage are most appropriate for pupils at different ages?

6. What differences are there between teachers' knowledge and pupils' knowledge about language? What aspects of teachers' knowledge are best withheld, or can all kinds of linguistic and metalinguistic knowledge contribute to pupils' language development?

7. What kinds of evidence can be obtained concerning the relationship between metalinguistic knowledge and cognitive development?

8. Should KAL or language awareness be a separate curriculum component, or should it continue, as it is presently formulated with National Curriculum frameworks, to be embedded within the main 'profile components' of reading, writing, speaking and listening?

9. What kinds of assessment are most appropriate for pupils' knowledge about language?

10. What kinds of knowledge about language most appropriately support the development of critical literacies? What knowledge of specific linguistic forms should be developed? Is there a preferred order to this knowledge development?

## 5    Conclusions: the lessons of LINC

A project of the scale and complexity of LINC cannot escape criticism. It is important that the lessons of both success and failure are recorded. For example, for all their successes with teachers,

LINC materials need to be further adapted in three main ways. First, materials on reading should be developed to exemplify in greater detail what a mixed-methods approach to reading entails. More examples and case studies would illustrate how readers use a range of different cues and clues, syntactic and semantic, phonic and visual, in the process of learning to read. More action research would illustrate when to mix methods and when to concentrate on a single teaching procedure. Future LINC materials (or their derivatives) must also enable teachers better to analyse the linguistic differences between real books and books from graded reading schemes. Secondly, supplements to existing units are needed on differences between spoken and written English, particularly in relation to the teaching of punctuation which depends crucially on the relationship between grammatical structure and the rhythms and contours of speech. More examples are also needed of how Standard English varies across spoken and written modes while still remaining Standard English. Thirdly, more examples are needed to show how literary texts can stimulate enhanced knowledge about language, especially the history of the language, and how greater linguistic knowledge underpins literary appreciation. LINC materials show continuities with 'A' level English language.[14] Although this is one of the most rapidly expanding 'A' levels, it is vital that a balance is struck between literary and linguistic emphases.

## 5.1 Negative conclusions

Even if the general developments outlined above take place, they will take place against a cultural background in which both positive and negative factors are at work. The main negative factors are, first, that some teachers will continue to persist with the worst excesses of Romanticism in their view of language learning and teaching. They will continue to make linguistic processes invisible and regard language only in so far as it provides a window on to content, the expression of the individual self, the world of ideas. They will continue to refuse to see forms of language as a powerful resource for creating significant domains of meaning. Secondly, governments may want to intervene more directly in the shaping of the English curriculum. If so, and whatever their political persuasion, governments may not want to endorse classroom language study which explores relationships between language and society, and which subjects those relationships to interrogation and to question. They are likely to continue to be especially disturbed by classroom KAL work which encourages children to investigate such relationships independently and for themselves. They may exert their powers to impose a language study which is 'neutralised' by being more decontextualised, formalist rather than functionalist in orientation, and which, above all, can be easily assessed and measured. The currently very overt demands by the British government for greater attention to phonics in the teaching of reading is but a signal of an increasing emphasis on the basics in so far as what is 'basic' often involves a decontextualised language focus.

## 5.2   Positive conclusions

It is a positive factor that governments are drawing attention to language, recognising it as both medium and message, mounting arguments in relation to the 'proper' study of English, attacking the positions adopted by those with a professional interest in language.

Although the battles will continue to be between those who have the power but not the knowledge, and those who have the knowledge but not the power, the very fact that governments are increasingly forced to mount explicit arguments about language is healthy both for processes of public debate and for the cause which espouses the centrality of language to the school curriculum. Increasing attention to language on the part of teachers, coupled with high degrees of enthusiasm and conviction, will lead to pupils being progressively interested in language. Increasing knowledge about language among pupils will produce within a generation a society which is likely to be less prejudiced and ignorant and more informed and articulate about matters to do with language.

Finally, a more positive view of applied linguistics emerges from projects such as the LINC project. It is a view in which teacher and linguist work more collaboratively towards an increasingly common agenda. As a result, teachers become more aware of the problems of linguistic description and, in turn, linguists begin to address problems identified by teachers, rather than only those problems identified by linguists themselves – a process likely to result only in a narrowly linguistic rather than a genuinely applied linguistic agenda. Increasingly, all concerned with language have come to appreciate how notoriously fascinating, complex and ultimately *dangerous* language and language study are. In a project inspired by the work of Michael Halliday, the final word can only be left with him (Halliday, 1982):

> ... there is a real sense in which linguistics is threatening; it's uncomfortable, and it's subversive. It's uncomfortable because it strips us of the fortifications that protect and surround some of our deepest prejudices. As long as we keep linguistics at bay we can go on believing what we want to believe about language, both our own and everybody else's ...

> ... More than any other human phenomenon, language reflects and reveals the inequalities that are enshrined in the social process. When we study language systematically ... we see into the power structure that lies behind our everyday social relationships, the hierarchical statuses that are accorded to different groups within society ... .

# Appendix one

LINC stands for Language in the National Curriculum. It is a project funded by the Department of Education and Science under an ESG (Education Support Grant). The main aim of the project is to produce materials and to conduct activities to support implementation of English in the National Curriculum in England and Wales in the light of the views of language outlined in the Kingman and Cox Reports on English language teaching and English 5–16 respectively (DES, 1988, 1989). The LINC project was designed to operate from April 1989 until March 1992.

The LINC professional development materials (University of Nottingham, Department of English Studies, 1992), were prepared in the first two years of the project (April 1989–April 1991) and were used as a basis for training of key project personnel. For the duration of the LINC programme the materials were included in local education authority (LEA) in-service courses and teachers were supported in considering the development needs of their own schools with regard to language in the National Curriculum. The primary aim of the materials was to form a basis for the immediate training requirements of the project; however, a further aim was to produce materials which are of use to providers of both in-service and initial teacher training over a much long period of time.

The LINC materials are characterised by the following main features:

- There are ten main units in the package; each unit is designed for approximately 1–1½ days of course time or its equivalent. The units are supported by BBC TV and Radio programmes.
- Each unit is organised around a sequence of activities to support users 'doing' things with language.
- Each unit is designed to be maximally flexible and can be supplemented or extended according to need. The loose-leaf ring binder format means that units can be easily detached and/or combined with other material.
- Units are grouped under main headings of development in children's talk, reading and writing, together with a block devoted to language and society.
- Each unit has at its centre complete texts, usually drawn from recognisable classroom contexts; the activities promote analysis of language but scrutiny of decontextualised language is normally eschewed.
- The training package draws on the many available examples of good practice in language teaching and recognises that teachers already know a lot, particularly implicitly, about language.

The foci of the project are presented diagrammatically in the Figure 1.1.

Copies of the training materials are published in a printed desktop version and are available from LINC project, Department of English Studies, University of Nottingham, Nottingham NG7 2RD, England.

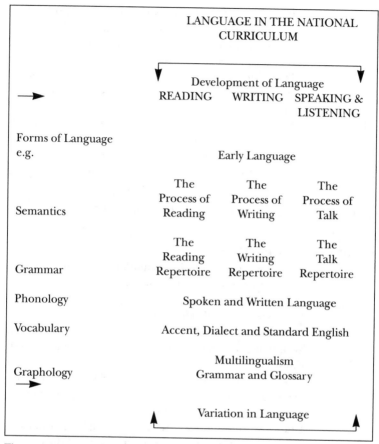

**Figure 1.1**

## Appendix two

### Statements of attainment in knowledge about language

6.22 In the SPEAKING AND LISTENING PROFILE COMPONENT pupils should be able to:

| LEVEL | DESCRIPTION |
|---|---|
| 5 | Talk about variations in vocabulary between different regional or social groups, *e.g. dialect vocabulary, specialist terms.* |
| 6 | Talk about some grammatical differences between spoken Standard English and a non-standard variety. |

7        Talk about appropriateness in the use of spoken language, according to purpose, topic and audience, *e.g. differences between language appropriate to a job interview and to a discussion with peers.*

8        Talk about the contribution that facial expressions, gestures and tone of voice can make to a speaker's meaning, *e.g. in ironic and sarcastic uses of language.*

9        Talk about ways in which language varies between different types of spoken communication, *e.g. joke, anecdote, conversation, commentary, lecture.*

10       Talk about some of the factors that influence people's attitudes to the way other people speak.

6.23    In the WRITING PROFILE COMPONENT pupils should be able to:

**LEVEL**    **DESCRIPTION**

5        Talk about variations in vocabulary according to purpose, topic and audience and according to whether language is spoken or written, *e.g. slang, formal vocabulary, technical vocabulary.*

6        Demonstrate some knowledge of straightforward grammatical differences between spoken and written English.

7        Comment on examples of appropriate and inappropriate use of language in written texts, with respect to purpose, topic and audience.

8        Demonstrate some knowledge of organisational differences between spoken and written English.

9        Demonstrate some knowledge of ways in which language varies between different types of written text, *e.g. personal letter, formal letter, printed instructions, newspaper report, playscript.*

10       Demonstrate some knowledge of criteria by which different types of written language can be judged, *e.g. clarity, coherence, accuracy, appropriateness, effectiveness, vigour, etc.*

6.23 In the READING PROFILE COMPONENT pupils should be able to:

| LEVEL | DESCRIPTION |
|---|---|
| 5 | Recognise and talk about the use of word play, *e.g. puns, unconventional spellings, etc.* and some of the effects of the writer's choice of words in imaginative uses of English. |
| 6 | Talk about examples (from their own experience or from their reading) of changes in word use and meaning over time, and about some of the reasons for these changes, *e.g. technological developments, euphemism, contact with other languages, fashion.* |
| 7 | Talk about some of the effects of sound patterning, *e.g. rhyme, alliteration* and figures of speech, *e.g. similes, metaphors, personification,* in imaginative uses of English. |
| 8 | Identify in their reading, and talk and write about some of the changes in the grammar of English over time, *e.g. in pronouns (from thou and thee to you),* in *verb forms, in negatives, etc.* |
| 9 | Demonstrate some understanding of the use of special lexical and grammatical effects in literary language, *e.g. the repetition of words or structures, dialect forms, archaisms, grammatical deviance, etc.* |
| 10 | Demonstrate some understanding of attitudes in society towards language change and of ideas about appropriateness and correctness in language use. |

(From Department of Education and Science, *Report on the English Working Party 5–16* (The Cox Report). HMSO, London, 1989)

# Notes

1 A much-quoted statement is this connection by John Rae, a head-teacher, appeared in *The Observer* newspaper in 1982. It is frequently cited in support of right-wing political views:

> The overthrow of grammar coincided with the acceptance of the equivalent of creative writing in social behaviour. As nice points of grammar were mockingly dismissed as pedantic and irrelevant, so

was punctiliousness in such matters as honesty, responsibility, property, gratitude, apology and so on.

2   Transcribed from a contribution by Norman Tebbitt MP to a BBC Radio 4 programme in 1985.

3   The most detailed expositions of these positions are found in Gilbert (1989; 1990).

4   Professor Gillian Brown and Professor Henry Widdowson were members of the Kingman Committee (DES, 1988); Professor Michael Stubbs and Professor Katharine Perera were members of the Cox Committee (DES, 1989). A relevant formative document is Perera (1987).

5   For a fuller analysis see Carter (1990a).

6   A representative collection of papers articulating a set of clear positions against anticipated curricular changes is Jones and West (eds) (1988).

7   Detailed accounts of the political context of the LINC project are contained in an edition of *The English Magazine* (April, 1992) devoted to LINC. An edition of *The Times Educational Supplement* (26.6.91) contains an explanation by Minister of State, Tim Eggar, of the non-publication of LINC materials. A valuable background paper is Bourne and Cameron (1989).

8   Recent debates on the value of genre theory appeared in teachers' journals such as *English in Australia* (1988) and *English in Education* (1992).

9   See, in particular, the publications from Harcourt, Brace Jovanovich in the series for schools *Language: A Resource for Meaning* (Harcourt, Brace Jovanovich, Marrickville, NSW, 1990–91). The authors of these materials are Frances Christie, Pam Gray, Brian Gray, Mary Macken, Jim Martin, Joan Rothery. Consultants to the project are Beverly Derewianka and Jennifer Hammond.

10  See Halliday, this volume.

11  See in particular Martin (1985/89) and Kress (1985/89).

12  We believe that Labov's model copes only with a specific class of spoken narrative; it cannot be easily applied to the true dialogic narrative (Polanyi 1985). [With reference to a variety of written narrative, Hasan (1984). Editors.]

13  See Carter (1990b) and Appendix One to this chapter.

14  'A' levels are school-leaving examinations for the 16–19 age group in Great Britain.

# References

Bain, R., Fitzgerald, B. and Taylor, M. (eds) *Looking into Language: Classroom Approaches to Knowledge About Language* (Hodder and Stoughton, Sevenoaks, 1992).

Bourne, J. and Cameron, D. 'No Common Ground: Kingman, Grammar and the Nation', *Language and Education*, 3, 1989, pp. 147–60.

Carter, R.A. 'The New Grammar Teaching', in Carter, R.A. (ed.) *Knowledge About Language and the Curriculum: The LINC Reader* (Hodder and Stoughton, Sevenoaks, 1990a), pp. 104–21.

Carter, R.A. (ed.) *Knowledge About Language and the Curriculum: The LINC Reader* (Hodder and Stoughton, Sevenoaks, 1990b).

Carter, R.A. *Keywords in Language and Literacy* (Routledge, London, 1995).

Carter, R.A. and Nash, W. *Seeing Through Language: A Guide to Styles of English Writing* (Blackwell, Oxford, 1990).

Christie, F. *Language Education* (Deakin University Press, Geelong, Vic., 1985/Oxford University Press, Oxford, 1989).

Crowley, T. (ed.) *Proper English?: Readings in Language, History and Cultural Identity* (Routledge, London, 1991).

Department of Education and Science *Report of the Committee of Inquiry into the Teaching of English Language* (The Kingman Report) (HMSO, London, 1988).

Department of Education and Science *Report of the English Working Party 5–16* (The Cox Report) (HMSO, London, 1989).

Dixon, J. 'The Question of Genres', in Reid, I. (ed.) *The Place of Genre in Learning: Current Debates* (Deakin University Press, Geelong, Vic., 1987), pp. 9–21.

Dixon, J. and Stratta, L. 'The National Curriculum in English: Does Genre Theory Have Anything to Offer?', *English in Education*, 26(2), 1993, pp. 16–27.

Gilbert, P. *Writing, Schooling and Disadvantage: From Voice to Text in the Classroom* (Routledge, London, 1989).

Gilbert, P. 'Authorizing Disadvantage: Authorship and Creativity in the Language Classroom', in Christie, F. (ed.) *Literacy for a Changing World* (ACER, Hawthorn, Vic., 1990), pp. 54–78.

Gramsci, A. 'Selections from Cultural Writings', quoted in Crowley, T. (ed.) *The Politics of Discourse: The Standard Language Question in British Cultural Debates* (Macmillan, Basingstoke, 1985).

Halliday, M.A.K. 'Linguistics in Teacher Education', in Carter, R.A. (ed.) *Linguistics and the Teacher* (RKP, London, 1982), pp. 10–15.

Hasan, Ruqaiya 'The Nursery Tale as a Genre', *Nottingham Linguistic Circular*, 13, 1984.

Jones, M. and West, A. *Learning Me Your Language* (Mary Glasgow Publications, London, 1988).

Kress, G. *Linguistic Processes in Sociocultural Practice* (Deakin University Press, Geelong, Vic., 1985/Oxford University Press, Oxford, 1989).

Marenbon, J. *English, Our English: The New Orthodoxy Examined* (Centre for Policy Studies, London, 1987).

Martin, J. *Factual Writing: Exploring and Challenging Social Reality* (Deakin University Press, Geelong, Vic., 1985/Oxford University Press, Oxford, 1989).

Martin, J. 'Intervening in the Process of Writing Development', *ALAA Occasional Papers*, 9, 1986, pp. 11–43.

Perera, K. *Understanding Language* (NAAE/NATE Publications, Sheffield, 1987).

Polanyi, L. 'Conversational Storytelling', in van Dijk, T.A. (ed.) *Handbook of Discourse Analysis*, Vol. 3 (Academic Press, New York, 1985).

Rosen, M. 'Will Genre Theory Change the World?', *English in Australia*, 86, 1988, pp. 4–12.

Stainton, C. 'Genre: A Review', *The Language of Business and Industry Project* m/s, Department of English Studies, University of Nottingham, 1990.

Threadgold, T. 'Talking About Genre: Ideologies and Incompatible Discourses', *Cultural Studies*, 3(1), 1989, pp. 101–27.

# 2

# On learning to look through a geographer's eyes*

THEO VAN LEEUWEN AND SALLY HUMPHREY

## 1  School geography as a register of the visual semiotic

In a social semiotic theory of language (Halliday 1978), the concept of register is central: language is seen, not as a unified whole, but as a set of registers, and these registers, rather than differing primarily in their phonology and syntax, as do dialects, differ in the kinds of meanings they realise, and in the ways in which they realise them, so constituting the discursive heterogeneity which, today, characterises languages like English. Definitions of literacy should take account of this, and define literacy in terms of plurality, as literacies, and in terms of register, as proficiencies in speaking and (where registers are also written) reading and/or writing specific registers. The question is not so much 'Can you speak, read and write English?', but 'What can you speak, read and write in English?'.

As literacy has become the focus of political debates on education, another question has become important: which literacies should be fostered at which levels of education? In the context of the 'genre debate' in Australia,[1] Martin and others have argued strongly that literacy should be seen as proficiency in registers which are highly valued in the dominant culture and enable those literate in them to formulate their interests in such a way that they will count with those in power and stand at least a chance of contributing to social change. As a result the literacies required for mastering school subjects such as geography and science have become one of the key issues in the literacy debate in Australia. The learning of geography, for instance, is mediated through language (more specifically through the textbook, cf Martin, Wignell,

29

Eggins & Rothery 1988: 168), and is therefore in the first place a matter of mastering the specialised register of geography, of becoming geographically literate. Only in this way can the specific and socially powerful discourse of geography be mastered.

School textbooks, however, no longer only use language, and have, in the past few decades, become increasingly visual, and the 'language of images', too, should be seen, not as a unified whole, but as a set of registers. There is, for instance, a great deal of 'technicality', not only in the language of school geography (Martin et al. 1988: 150–5) but also in the images of school geography, through abstract maps, charts and diagrams. And the apprentice geographer must learn to read images in a specialised way, 'to look through a geographer's eyes', and to read, and in many cases also produce, specialised kinds of visuals. As the beginnings of a systemic functional description of images are now available (Kress & van Leeuwen 1990, 1991; van Leeuwen 1992; O'Toole 1994), it has become possible to describe registers of the 'language of images', and hence to outline what is involved in geographical visual literacy. This is all the more important because visual literacies may embody their own discourses, and these discourses need not be identical to those realised in language, even within one field, such as school geography.

This chapter, then, a first attempt at describing a visual register in the context of the discourse of literacy, is a study of geographical visual literacy, based on a comprehensive set of Australian junior high school geography textbooks now in print. It is based on research conducted by (cf Metropolitan East DSP 1992), who has worked on (linguistic) geographical literacy. It follows a 'developmental' approach, in order to show how geography textbooks construe the learning of geographical visual literacy as passing through five stages: (1) pre-geography; (2) observing features in a place; (3) describing features in a place; (4) describing processes in a place; and (5) post-geography: exploring issues. These stages are similar, but not identical to those postulated in (cf Metropolitan East DSP 1992), who posits four stages: (1) observing features in a place; (2) describing features of a system in a place; (3) explaining interactions in a system; and (4) exploring systems at risk. The differences, we believe, are due not so much to a difference in interpretation, as to a difference in the roles played by language and the visual semiotic in the development of geographical literacy.

# 2   Pre-geography

The first page of the first volume of a relatively recent Australian series of geography textbooks (Gallagher, Oliver & Wilson 1987), called *Learning to Look Through a Geographer's Eyes*, contains three snapshots – snapshots of people doing things in places of potential geographic interest (Figure 2.1). Although addressed envelopes, foregrounded through partially overlapping the photos, already hint at the centrality of place in geography, the pictures are not yet geographical visuals. They are everyday rather than specialised visuals, snapshots rather than scientific illustrations. The people in these pictures are doing touristic, rather than geographers' kinds of things, and the places shown serve as backgrounds to these activities, rather than as the primary subject matter. The phrasing of the captions displays the same priorities. In 'Fishing at Loch Torridon', for instance, the touristic activity rather than the place is thematic, which contrasts with later stages in which circumstances of place frequently become marked themes (Metropolitan East DSP 1992).

The processes in pictures of this kind are for the most part 'presentational' (Kress & van Leeuwen 1990: 82–6): the pictures show actions, transactions and reactions involving human Actors and realised by the vectors formed by the Actors' limbs or eyelines. The settings are circumstantial, and often lowered in modality, softer in focus, or otherwise made less distinct than the foreground. Interpersonally, the pictures, like snapshots, may either be of the 'offer' or of the 'demand' type – the picture bottom right in Figure 2.1 is of the latter kind, and, like all pre-geographical 'demand' pictures shows the 'others' who live in places of geographical interest demanding our recognition, as realised by the look at the viewer. 'Social distance' tends to be close to medium. The vertical angle is eye level, positioning the viewer at a level of equality with what is depicted, and the horizontal angle is usually frontal, realising symbolic 'involvement' with what is depicted (cf Kress & van Leeuwen 1990: 32–43). Modality is low in comparison to the landscape photographs used in stage 1 and 2: the landscape is still to be read as a whole, and not yet to be scrutinised for its individual features.

Other pictures in the same category take the form of cartoons, as in Figure 2.2, the first page of a chapter on deserts in Scott (1982). Here, too, everyday 'touristic' activities are shown. The

**Figure 2.1** Pre-geography realised photographically (from Gallagher et al. 1987)

reader is addressed as someone who is not yet a geographer, someone who still looks through a tourist's eyes, or, a frequent variant, through the filter of an imagination fed by stories of intrepid adventurers, explorers and superheroes. But the cartoon modality lowers the validity of touristic experience by comparison to the geographical knowledge embodied in sharply focused landscape photographs. And the tourist, or the young geographer, is often depicted as comical, which further devalues pre-geographic experience. Progressive educationalists have long maintained that education should be built on the knowledge and experience children have already acquired when they enter education (Martin et al. 1988: 143–5; Hasan 1991). And at first sight this is what occurs in geography texts: the pictures show everyday experiences, or take their cue from the kind of adventure stories with which young geographers would already be familiar. But, albeit to differing degrees, they also devalue this experience, for instance by showing it in a comic way. Just as newspapers, in which factuality is the cornerstone for credibility, represent 'opinion' in the form of cartoons and 'fact' in the form of photographs, so geography texts, in which geographical knowledge has the highest credibility, use lowered modality to represent pre-geographical experience as less valid than geographical knowledge.

The landscape at the bottom of the page shown in Figure 2.2 no longer contains people and shows the landscape in sharp detail. But its angle is still that of someone who participates in what is going on in this place: the picture could have been taken from inside a four-wheel drive travelling down the road. It is a transitional picture, already closer to the geographical visual, but not yet quite there, already abstracting from human activity and pre-geographical experience, but not yet using the detached, objective high angle of the typical geographical landscape. The next page, however, shows someone climbing a mountain, and the mountain is not, by the looks of it, in the desert, so that one cannot help feeling that the picture symbolises the ascent to the high angle of objective knowledge. It is also the last picture in the chapter to depict people.

At the end of the chapter which opens with Figure 2.1, and in connection with the first exercise apprentice geographers are required to do, as the first step on the road towards becoming geographers, we find another set of transitional pictures (Figure 2.3). In one of them we see an Aboriginal girl looking up at the viewers as though asking them to acknowledge her presence. But the caption no longer acknowledges her or her activity. It merely says 'Shrubs at Port Hedland'. This, then, is the first lesson in looking through a geographer's eyes: ignore the human element, ignore what you would pay attention to first in an everyday

**Starting out on the desert safari**

**What climate will we experience?**

The police offered Tony and Helen some advice before the safari started out in search of Ayers Rock.

*"Remember, you are exploring a* **desert** *and the harsh climate makes it difficult to survive if you're not prepared. During the summer day, it will be very hot, maybe over 40°C, so take clothes to protect yourself from the sun. You should take some warm clothes too, because the nights can be cold — temperatures below 10°C are common.*

*"The desert is also* **dry***; even though you'll drive over many creeks or* **wadis***, each will be dry. The desert receives less than 250 millimetres of rain a year. Always carry plenty of water with you.*

*"You will notice that the wadis have sandy beds — don't camp in these. If there is a sudden storm, the wadi will flood quickly and wash you away."*

Just from these comments about the climate of the desert, you can learn a lot. Under the heading "Desert Climate" in your book, list the things the policeman said about desert temperature and rainfall.

I think we're ready to start. I'd better tell the police where we're going in case we get lost.

Figure 2.4   Ayers Rock

**Figure 2.2**   Pre-geography realised by cartoons (from Scott 1982)

context, and focus on place, on what would normally be background, turning that background mentally into a foreground. It is a lesson in reduction, in abstraction. And the same picture teaches the young geographer another lesson. The Aboriginal girl and the landscape are seen, not from eye level, from the angle of someone who is participating in what is going on in the place shown, but from a high angle. The picture takes the viewer one step towards that extreme high angle of the map, which is the angle of objective knowledge, the angle of knowledge-is-power, the God's eye view, or, to use a more contemporary image, the view from the satellite.

Transitional images, then, commute just a few of the features of the pre-geographical image. They increase the modality of the setting, and/or introduce the high angle, and/or remove the human element from the picture. In this way they consolidate the first stage in 'learning to look through a geographer's eyes': learn to observe features (usually features of place) which you might otherwise take for granted and see in a holistic way; learn to scrutinise analytically what you might previously have seen as mere 'setting' or 'background'; crane up slowly to those symbolic heights from which objective, detached knowledge operates.

## 3   Observing features in a place

The transitional image leads gradually into the next stage, which features landscapes, presented in high modality photographs, sharp, detailed colour shots, taken from a high and usually oblique angle and drily photographed without a trace of the iconography of touristic or artistic landscapes aimed at evoking a 'mood' or 'atmosphere'. Such pictures are no longer 'presentational' but 'analytical' (Kress & van Leeuwen 1990: 73–7), to be read as part–whole structures ('this landscape has feature a, b, c, etc.'). And the captions reinforce this: '*Note the hummocks of sandhill canegrass on the dunes and the drab greens of the shrubs and bushes of the swale.*'

When, in books or chapters on 'social geography', pictures of this kind do include human participants and activities ('workers in a factory', 'shoppers in a store', etc.), they show the people as though they were trees in a landscape: from a detached (oblique) horizontal angle, a high vertical angle, and far social distance. This reduces the vectoriality of the activities shown to a minimum and makes it difficult to see what the people shown are actually doing. Some books show analytical pictures of people from 'other cultures' (Amazonian Indians, Eskimos) which are to be scrutinised for the features of dress and body ornament which the people depicted display, and for the objects they carry, rather than that they establish a symbolic relation between the people depicted

**Exercise 6**

*Make a list of the four vegetation types shown in Figures 1.5(a)–(d). Alongside each, write the climatic zone where you would place it.*

**Figure 1.5(a)** Desert shrubland near Port Hedland, Australia

**Figure 1.5(b)** Dwarf birch trees near Kiruna in North Sweden, on the border of the Tundra

**Figure 1.5(c)** Savanna grassland in Zimbabwe

**Figure 1.5(d)** Light tropical forest in Tabasco, Mexico

**Figure 2.3**   Transition to stage 2 (from Gallagher et al. 1987)

and the viewer. Observation is now to become dispassionate, analytical. Pictures are now to be read as scientific documents, 'data'.[2]

# 4   Describing features in a place

It is significant that the maps are placed on the left and the landscape photos on the right. As argued in Kress and van Leeuwen (1990: 102–9), left and right have specific informational values. If a picture or layout has horizontal polarisation, with some (kinds of) element clearly positioned left of centre and others right of centre, then the elements on the left are presented as 'given' and the elements on the right as 'new'. For something to be given means that it is presented as something the viewer already knows, as a familiar and agreed upon departure point of the message. For something to be presented as new means that it is presented as something not yet known, not yet already agreed upon by the viewer, hence as something to which the viewer must pay special attention. The new is therefore problematic, the information at issue, while the given is presented as commonsense and self-evident. In the two pages shown in Figure 2.4, then, location is presented as the given of geography, as its uncontroversial point of departure, while description – analysis of the located elements – is presented as the new, as that which must be learnt by the apprentice geographer. A comparable structure is found, at this stage, in the verbal text, which now takes the form of descriptive and taxonomic reports, with a good deal of technicality in the terminology, and circumstances of time and place as marked themes (Metropolitan East DSP 1992).

Why are the maps given? Are not maps the kind of picture which young geographers must learn to read? Should not maps, therefore, be positioned on the right? Or is the map here just a not-too-closely-to-be-investigated token of geography-ness, like a scientific diagram in, say, a cosmetics advertisement? The question becomes even more interesting when we look at the two maps in more detail. The most complex and information-rich map is placed on the left, as the given in the syntagm formed by the two maps. The map on the right is much simpler. Rather than a 'resource' map, to be used to find specific information (in the way we use a street directory), it is a 'statement' map which, in one glance, reveals all it has to tell: 'the desert is in the heart of

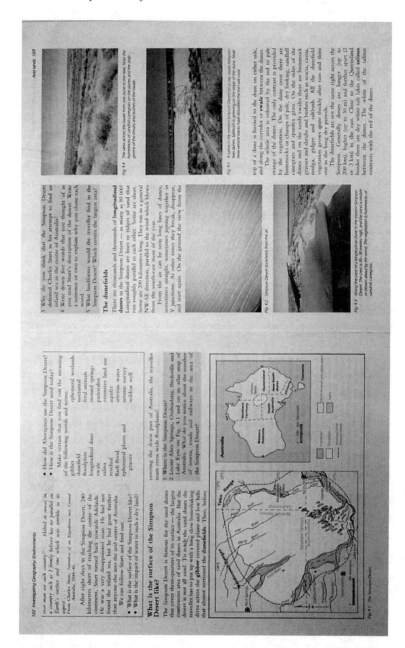

**Figure 2.4**   Describing features in a place (from Stacey & Lucas 1987)

Australia'. Most given, and therefore least open to scrutiny, is the 'given of geography': geography is about place, about locating. The next, more specific given relates to the topic of the chapter, and is the central role of the 'outback' and the desert in the imagination of Australians. With these two givens as a departure point, learning about the desert begins.

The conjunction between locating and describing is not always realised by the horizontal aspect of the layout. In other cases the map is on the top and the description on the bottom of the page. The map is then positioned as the 'ideal', presented as the idealised or generalised essence of the message, and the description is positioned as the 'real', which provides more 'down to earth' information – more specific information (e.g. details), more real information (e.g. evidence), or more practical information (e.g. directions for action, practical consequences) – (Kress & van Leeuwen 1990: 98–101): again location is given the ideologically privileged position. Or it may be realised by overlapping. In an illustration in Cox and Bartlett (1983), for instance, small colour photographs of landscapes are superimposed on a two-page black and white aerial photograph, and each landscape is connected to its location by means of a thin line, so that location is, as it were, the 'base', the canvas on which the descriptions are painted. An illustration in Stacey and Lucas (1985) uses yet another compositional device, the opposition between centre and margin. Verbal descriptions of the stages of the process of baking bread are arranged, in circular fashion, around a floorplan of the bakery, and each stage is connected to its location by means of a thin line which runs from the relevant part of the text to the location in which the activities described take place: location is here central, and description marginal. How useful is it to know exactly where in the bakery the various stages of baking bread take place? Maybe not very, but in order to turn the baking of bread into geography, it must not only be located, location must also become the central issue.

The conjunction of locating and describing works well in the case of sand dunes, or, to put it more generally, in the case of phenomena which are (a) bound to specific locations, and (b) describable in terms of physical features. But, as the bakery example has perhaps already indicated, modern geography does not restrict itself to phenomena of this kind. Pask and Bryant (1982), for instance, open a section on the central business district of Melbourne with a page containing a high angle, oblique long shot of the Melbourne CBD and a map locating Melbourne as the heart of a network of roads. How much can be learnt from scrutinising a high-angle photograph of the Melbourne CBD as though it were a landscape with distinct physical features? Not much: in the modern city all buildings look alike – hospitals, universities, business offices, government departments may all be housed in the same kinds of functional tower block.

Looking at a map of the same place, on the next page (Figure 2.5), we are confronted with a highly complex picture which, at first sight, reminds one of a painting by Mondriaan or Van Doesburg rather than a map (Kress & van Leeuwen, 1991, in fact see these kinds of painting as abstract maps). How much sense does it make to present maps of this kind when specific activities (the subject matter of this map) are less and less bound to specific locations? In the postmodern world everything is increasingly everywhere, and this does not sit well with the geographical discourse: geography is like a linguistics which can speak only of local dialects, only of varieties of language that can be located spatially, and not of the many varieties of language that come with social class, gender, age, occupation and so on.

## 5    Describing processes in a place

So far we have discussed visuals which either describe places or describe other things as though they were places, pictures which *spatialise* these other things – spatialisation is to the language of images what nominalisation is to verbal language, and the more technical and abstract visual language becomes, the more it is likely to spatialise what might also be coded in terms of presentational processes. Geography texts also feature visuals which describe processes, chains of events, for instance the process of desertification, or the processes that bring about cyclones, and visuals of this kind form the next stage in acquiring geographical visual literacy, in 'learning to look through a geographer's eyes'.

They differ from pictures which locate and describe places in several ways. First of all they are more abstract, because they are about things that require more than simple observation to be understood: underlying causes, generalised essences. Hence they use (often highly schematic) drawings rather than photographs:

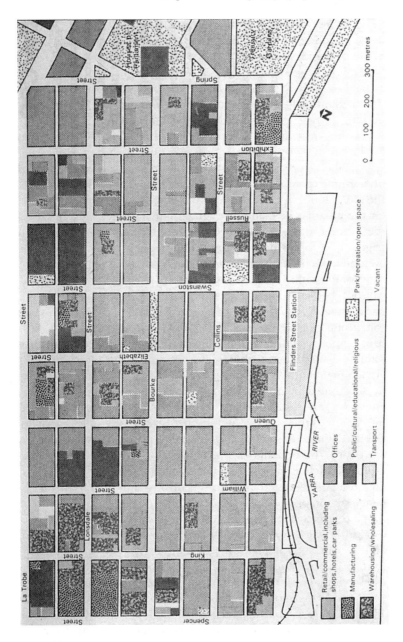

**Figure 2.5** Map of Melbourne's central business district (from Pask & Bryant 1982)

we move away here from naturalistic modality to scientific modality, to a mode of representation in which it is not the observation of surface appearances, but the postulation of more abstract or generalised processes – a deeper truth – that defines what counts as true or real (Kress & van Leeuwen 1990: 49–61). Despite this, the element of location remains, for without it the visuals would no longer be geography, would not become science.

Locating may, again, take different forms. The diagrams may, for instance, be superimposed on a 'setting', as when arrows and verbal labels ('precipitation', 'evaporation', etc) are superimposed on a simple drawing of a landscape, including only the essentials – the sun, clouds, a tree, the soil – to show the hydrological cycle. Or the link may be made through conjunction, with, for instance, the location of cyclones shown first on a map placed on the left page, or on top of the page, and the diagram which explains the cyclone next, on the right page or the bottom of the page.

Secondly, unlike maps and landscapes, diagrams are not analytical but presentational (Kress & van Leeuwen 1991: 37–51), paraphrasable as 'this pictorial participant (e.g. 'water') does something (e.g. 'evaporate')', or 'this pictorial participant (e.g. 'tree') *does something to* that pictorial participant (e.g. 'absorbs water')'. The processes themselves are realised by vectors, usually arrows or oblique lines, and the pictorial participants (they may be substituted by nominal groups) play the roles, not of 'whole' and 'part', as in analytical images, but of Actor, Goal or Converted in relation to the process. Action processes involve only one pictorial participant, the Actor, and Actor and process may be fused, as when an arrow on a map represents both a cyclone and the direction in which it moves (or rather, its movement in a certain direction). Transaction processes involve two pictorial participants, an Actor and a Goal. The Actor is the participant from which the vector emanates (or which is fused with the vector), the Goal is the participant at which the vector is pointed. In a picture of the hydrological cycle, for instance, an arrow may emanate from a cloud and point at a mountain, so that a 'literal transcoding' would be: 'the cloud (Actor) does something to ('rains on') the mountain (Goal)'. In Conversion processes, finally, the pictorial participants are both Actor and Goal, at the receiving end of a vector as well as forming the departure point for another vector. This is typically the case in food-chain diagrams, where every pictorial participant is at once 'eater' and 'eaten', contributing to the decomposition of some and the 'composition' of other participants.

These examples indicate that diagrams have many 'nouns' (diagrammatically depicted clouds, trees, mountains, etc) but few 'verbs' (arrows). In this they resemble expository writing, where most of the meaning is similarly contained in nominal groups, while verbs remain restricted to a small group of relationals like 'is', 'has', 'leads to', 'generates', 'develops', etc. And just as expository writing turns processes into things (e.g. 'raining' into 'precipitation'), so diagramming turns processes that take place over time into spatial configurations, 'systems'. And because the meaning of the vectors is so abstract and general, the same signifier (arrow) can signify fundamentally different processes *as if they were the same.* One model of interpretation is imposed on the idea of 'movement', of 'transport' from one place to another, and the idea of 'transformation', of 'change' from one thing into another. And because the signifier, the arrow, can and does represent both, the two meanings become conflated: Movement – transport – *is* transformation; mobility *is* the cause of and condition for change, growth, evolution. A food-chain diagram may be about the cyclical transformation of organic matter, but the arrows inevitably introduce a sense of movement: we cannot, it seems, imagine or visualise *the same place* changing. Conversion must be represented as movement, and movement as Conversion.

The cyclical process of nature, the food chain in which everything is 'eaten' by something else which, in turn, provides food for yet something else, or the hydrological cycle, in which water evaporates and then turns into water again, is a process of continuous conversion, which has no beginning and no end, and therefore no Actor and no Goal, unless it be the sun, depicted in many geographical diagrams as the 'prime mover' or original Actor of the process, the motor of the whole machine. Is it an adequate model for every kind of process geography texts may want to explain?

Figure 2.6 describes the process of salination. Three pictures, each representing several processes. But how are they connected? There is no vector to 'say': this state of affairs 'converts naturally' into that state of affairs, or this state of affairs brings about that state of affairs. Or, as is common in production-line diagrams and flowcharts: this state of affairs follows that state of affairs (although we do infer temporal sequence, despite the fact that the vertical time line is unstated). Three stages, three frames from an imaginary animation film which would show the transformation of the landscape as simply 'happening'. A process with a beginning and an end, and not a cycle, but who or what causes it? Not the first 'frame', the rainforest in its pristine state. In reality the process is caused by human agency, but this is not represented, either in the diagram or in the accompanying text, which only uses nominalisations like 'clearing', allowing agency to be obscured (the text even speaks of the 'poor farmers' who are the 'victims of erosion').

The process, caused by human agency, is represented as a natural process, and the link between the first and the second 'frame' is verbally glossed as temporal ('before clearing', 'after clearing'). Once the process is set in motion, however, it becomes a 'natural process', and the captions use an explanatory link to connect 'frame' 2 and 'frame' 3 ('affected by'), rather than a temporal one. Thus the processes which are embedded in each 'frame' are described as conversions or agentive processes. But the logic of the sequence of 'frames', of the way in which each stage leads to the next, is not represented visually.

It is at this level that the staging of visual and verbal literacy begins to diverge. This stage has been called 'explaining interactions in a system' (cf Metropolitan East DSP 1992) and shows how the movement from the preceding stage to this stage is that from describing and taxonomising to causal explanation. Visually, however, geography does not provide consequential or factorial explanations. It has only two models: agency and conversion, and while these are useful in relation to some processes, they are inadequate in relation to others.

# 6    Post-geography: exploring issues

When the process of 'learning to look through a geographer's eyes' has been completed, the human element at last returns into the visuals, in connection with contentious issues such as uranium mining, the conservation of rainforests and so on. But the texts do not argue for a particular stance towards these issues. Like the mass media, they introduce a variety of spokespeople to present different views, and the visuals serve to assign different degrees of credibility to these spokespeople. This can be done in a number of ways. Different spokespeople can be associated with different

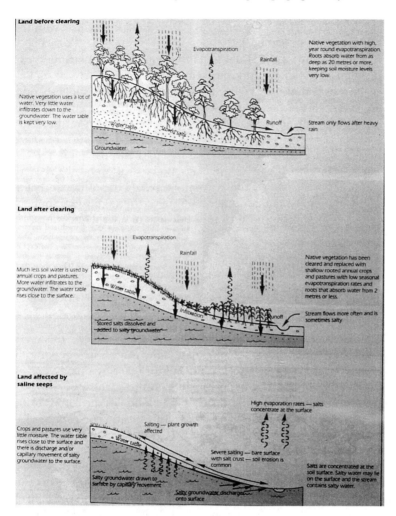

**Figure 2.6**   Describing processes in a place: salination (from Stacey & Lucas 1988)

kinds of speech acts – their views can, for example, be represented as images in thought balloons, hence as subjective and comparatively low in modality, or they can be represented as speech, in dialogue balloons. Their views can also be featured on banners and sandwich boards, in photos of demonstrations and sit-ins, which marks them clearly as minority opinion. Stereotyped drawings can affect their credibility, as is the case, for instance, with the spokespeople in Figure 2.7.

Selections from the visual systems of interpersonal meaning can position the viewer differently in relation to different spokespeople, as is shown in Figure 2.7 where some of the spokespeople are closer to the viewer than others, or shown frontally and looking directly at the viewer where others are shown from the side, looking away from the viewer. And the relative amount of space occupied by each spokesperson, as well as their position in the layout of this visual, gives their utterances different degrees of prominence. In short, the texts present a juxtaposition of viewpoints rather than an argument, but nevertheless favours some of these viewpoints over others, in subtle and often oblique ways.

## 7   Conclusion

The discourse of school geography, as it emerges from this study of visual geographical literacy, includes the following key elements:

1. In geography everything must be located – without this, geography would no longer be geography. And visual geography has developed a rich array of means for realising this.
2. The description of physical features is the cornerstone of geographical knowledge, and hence phenomena which cannot be described in terms of physical features must be spatialised if they are to be turned into subjects suitable for geographical discourse.
3. Visually, geography has only two ways of explaining processes: agency and conversion. Although certain kinds of processes involving humans (most notably processes of manufacture) may be turned into geography by locating them, a sharp line is drawn between 'natural' and 'human' processes, and this precludes relating human agency to ecological issues, other than in the form of non-geographical postscripts in which different viewpoints about ecological issues are juxtaposed in an ostensibly impartial manner which would appear to be a modified version of the way in which contentious issues are presented in the mass media.

From this I would conclude that 'critical literacy' should perhaps not, as Martin et al. (1988) maintain, concentrate only on describ-

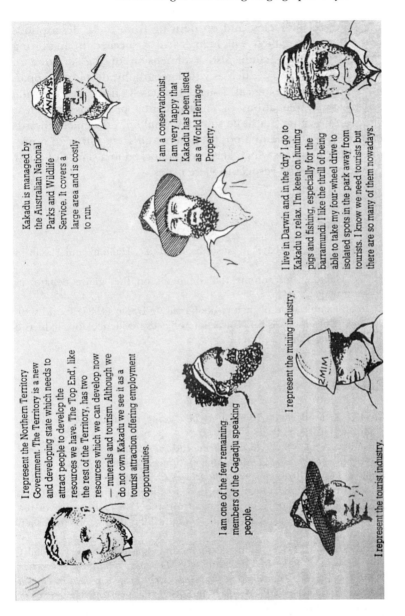

I represent the Northern Territory Government. The Territory is a new and developing state which needs to attract people to develop the resources we have. The 'Top End', like the rest of the Territory, has two resources which we can develop now — minerals and tourism. Although we do not own Kakadu we see it as a tourist attraction offering employment opportunities.

Kakadu is managed by the Australian National Parks and Wildlife Service. It covers a large area and is costly to run.

I am a conservationist. I am very happy that Kakadu has been listed as a World Heritage Property.

I live in Darwin and in the 'dry' I go to Kakadu to relax. I'm keen on hunting pigs and fishing, especially for the barramundi. I like the thrill of being able to take my four-wheel drive to isolated spots in the park away from tourists. I know we need tourists but there are so many of them nowadays.

I am one of the few remaining members of the Gagadju speaking people.

I represent the mining industry.

I represent the tourist industry.

**Figure 2.7**   Post-geography: exploring issues (from Stacey & Lucas 1988)

ing powerful literacies, and on deriving from these descriptions the pedagogies which will help learners succeed in mastering them. It should include also a dimension of the 'critique of literacies': if a literacy such as visual geography, despite its apparent focus on ecological issues, ultimately does not provide satisfactory explanations of environmental problems and clear views on how they might be solved, it would not do much towards empowering people in a positive sense, and seem rather to reproduce the discourses which keep people locked in a stance of guilty powerlessness with respect to these issues.

## Notes

\* On the 'genre-debate' in Australia, see Luke, Halliday and Hasan in this volume.
1 See Halliday this volume for comments on the 'genre debate' in Australia.
2 In an examination of picture-book reading Hasan (1987) found similar foci of emphasis on abstraction, objective evidence and deductive inference. (Editors' note.)

## References

Cox, B. & L. Bartlett. 1983. *Ideas in Geography I: Geography in Action.* Sydney: Jacaranda Press.

Gallagher, N., J. Oliver & I. Wilson. 1987. *Learning To Look Through A Geographer's Eyes. Book 1.* Melbourne: Thomas Nelson.

Halliday, M.A.K. 1978. *Language as social semiotic.* London: Edward Arnold.

Hasan, Ruqaiya 1987. 'Reading picture reading: invisible instruction at home and in school'. Proceedings from the 13th Conference of the Australian Reading Association, Sydney, July 1987. (no publisher, editor; n.d.)

Hasan, Ruqaiya 1991. 'Questions as a mode of learning in everyday talk', in Thao Le & Mike McCausland (eds), *Language Education: Interaction and Development. Proceedings of the International Conference held in Ho Chi Minh City, Vietnam, 30 March–1 April 1991.* Launceston: University of Tasmania at Launceston.

Kress, G. & T. van Leeuwen 1990. *Reading Images.* Geelong: Deakin University Press.

Kress, G. & T. van Leeuwen 1991. 'A Grammar of Diagrams, Maps and Charts'. Unpublished manuscript.

Leeuwen, T. van 1992. 'The schoolbook as a multimodal text', *Internationale Schulbuchforschung* 14(1): 35–58.

Martin, J.R., P. Wignell, S. Eggins & J. Rothery 1988. 'Secret English: discourse technology in a junior secondary school', in L. Gerot, J. Oldenburg and T. van Leeuwen (eds), *Language and Socialisation: Home and School. Proceedings from the Working Conference on Language in Education.* Sydney: Macquarie University.

Metropolitan East DSP 1992. 'A model for language development in Geography 7–10', (draft paper). Sydney: Disadvantaged Schools Programme.

O'Toole, L.M. 1994. *The Language of Displayed Art.* London: Leicester University Press.

Pask, R.& L. Bryant 1982. *People in Australia: A Social Geography.* Sydney: Jacaranda Press.

Reid, I. (ed.). 1987. *The Place of Genre in Learning: Current Debates.* Geelong: Deakin University Press.

Scott, L. 1982. *People and Places: Our World in Change,* Vol. 1. Sydney: Jacaranda Press.

Stacey, M. & J. Lucas 1985. *Investigating Geography: Communities.* Melbourne: Longman Cheshire.

Stacey, M. and J. Lucas 1987. *Investigating Geography: Environments.* Melbourne: Longman Cheshire.

Stacey, M. & J. Lucas 1988. *Investigating Geography: Contemporary Issues.* Melbourne: Longman Cheshire.

# 3

# The development of language as a resource for thinking: a linguistic view of learning

## CLARE PAINTER

## 1  Introduction

In this chapter I would like to outline the way that a theory of language development, as an aspect of a more general theory of language as social semiotic, contributes to a theory of learning. And I will do this in the context of describing some key aspects of language development and use in early childhood. The general issue I will be addressing concerns the relationship between developments in language and developments in thinking, and the particular focus will be on the way the linguistic achievements of the preschool years prepare a child cognitively for school learning.

## 2  Background: learning language and learning through language

As a background to thinking about the relation between language and learning, we can start by considering where language first comes into the picture for the learner. Research into neonatal behaviour has suggested that, as well as an innate predisposition to attend to other persons, human beings are in fact born with an innate motivation to come to know the world around them (Trevarthen 1980). Research into the ontogenesis of language, both by systemicists (Halliday 1975, 1979; Oldenburg 1987; Painter 1984, 1989, 1991) and by psychologists (Bates et al. 1979; Trevarthen & Hubley 1978) has shown how the first symbol system – what Halliday (1975) calls the 'protolanguage' – develops as a means of facilitating this learning about the world. It does so by allowing the infant to use other persons to mediate engagement with the environment. This is achieved when the infant develops symbols which construct meanings such as 'you give me that', 'you do that again', 'look at this with me', and so on.

However, although the protolanguage is developed in part as a resource for learning, it is eventually abandoned because of its limitations in this role. The protolanguage has no lexicogrammatical stratum and one limitation this imposes is that it cannot serve to categorise the phenomena of existence. For example, a protolinguistic child may have a symbol which embodies the meaning 'I want my dog', it could even have another different symbol for 'hallo dog' and yet another for 'look there's a dog', but none of these protolinguistic symbols would allow for the ideational meaning 'dog' to be constructed as a separable, identifiable meaning element constant across these different contexts. (Nor, indeed, does the protolanguage allow for the interpersonal meanings of 'I want' or 'hallo' or 'look' to be constructed as separable meanings which could then be freely combined with different ideational meanings like 'dog' or 'cat'.)

The protolanguage is therefore abandoned because the formal properties of the symbol system constrain the kinds of meanings that can be construed – not only the kind of dialogic interaction that can take place, but also the kind of ideational reflection that is possible. And an important point about the relation between language and thinking is that it is their own impetus to learn, together with their experience of making meaning with others, which encourages children to adopt a language system with the formal properties of the mother tongue. In other words, language proper is developed precisely because it is an optimal resource for learning.

This account, first presented in detail in Halliday's *Learning how to mean* (1975), thus attempts to explain language development in terms of the child's cognitive, as well as other, needs. An equally important point, though, is the fact that as soon as linguistic symbols become the medium of learning, then learning has to be understood as an inherently interactive, interpersonal process. This being the case, if learning occurs through the medium of others, through talk, then it follows that the world or the environment being revealed to the child for knowing is a semiotically constructed one. This is not to deny the material, but to argue that material reality can only be known – can only be an object of learning – by being construed as systems of meaning.

So the object of learning – what is learned – has to be understood as semiotic in nature. In *Learning how to mean*, Halliday took the 'what' of learning in its broadest sense as the social system. He argued that every conversational interaction between child and other reveals to the child not only information about the semiotic that is language but also information about the semiotic environment in which the text is occurring. From instances of language in use, or 'texts', children gain experience in the functions and structures of the language, which enables them to construe the underlying network of choices that constitutes language as a system. But, in addition, every text realises information about its semiotic context, a context Halliday describes in terms of 'field', 'tenor' and 'mode' components, glossing these as 'The ongoing social activity, the roles and statuses and the interactional channels' (Halliday 1975: 143). Because of its metafunctional organisation – its organisation into components which realise field, tenor and mode – the language allows the social context to be manifested in the text. This means that in construing the text, the learner simultaneously construes the social-semiotic context. On any occasion of language in use, then, a language learner is making sense of the particular text and the particular context, and from countless instances of text in context, the linguistic and social systems are construed (Halliday 1975).

Different components of the social context are realised by different components of the linguistic system. In this chapter I will be concerned only with the social-contextual system of field, and the 'ideational' component of the language system which construes it. As a gross characterisation of the area realised by ideational language choices, Martin (1992: 548) has suggested a provisional classification of fields into different domains as shown in Figure 3.1.

The basis for the kind of classification proposed is that the 'domestic' field is learned by doing, mediated by spoken language, and the 'exploration' fields of institutionalised knowledge are learned through instruction, mediated largely by written language. For my purposes here, the broad distinction Martin draws on between 'commonsense', everyday knowledge and 'uncommonsense' fields (based on consciously designed theories) will

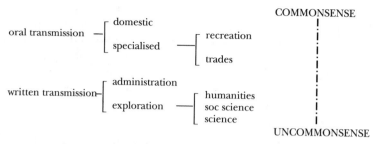

**Figure 3.1**   Martin's (1992) provisional classification of fields

be relevant. (See also Berger & Luckmann 1966; Bernstein 1975: 99.)

Now, if what has to be construed by the learner are systems of meaning, then it is axiomatic that our most important learning resource is language, our meaning-making and meaning-construing system *par excellence*. Using this resource for learning is to create or participate in the creation of text, where meaning becomes observable in its realisation as lexico-grammatical structures. This means that the strategies or processes of learning – classifying, comparing, generalising, making cause-effect links, hypothesising, inferring and so on – all are most usefully seen as strategies for meaning (realised in lexico-grammar), as ways of mobilising the linguistic resource into text, rather than ways of doing some essentially non-linguistic, non-visible mental process.

Moreover, if learning is manifested in the creation of text, then a study of a learner's texts will reveal instantiations of both their linguistic system and of their deployment of the system as a means of understanding. A study over time should therefore reveal something of the development of the linguistic system as a means of understanding.

With this in mind, I have undertaken a longitudinal case study of one learner's texts between the ages of two years and six months (2;6) and five years (5;0). Stephen, the child in question, is my son, the second child in the family, 4.5 years younger than his brother, Hal. Using audio-tape recordings and notebook and pencil jottings without his knowledge, I undertook a naturalistic diary study over this period. For practical reasons recordings were not undertaken at the childcare centre which Stephen attended and thus the data focus on parent-child talk rather than peer talk or conversations with other adults. I would like to use data from this study to illustrate the relation between new linguistic developments and new possibilities for thinking, and also to describe the way developments in the preschool period are crucial in enabling a child to embark on the move from commonsense, everyday, domestic knowledge to the uncommonsense or educational knowledge of school learning.

## 3    A case study of language and thinking : construing the things of experience

To return to the developmental story, then, I have already suggested that one of the first things a child gains as a thinker by moving into the mother tongue is a resource for naming. A common noun, such as *cat*, an adjective like *big*, or a verb like *open* names a class of things, qualities or actions respectively. Thus the initial move into the mother tongue provides, through naming, a crucial resource for learning. It is one which enables the myriad distinct, individual instances of phenomenal experience to be generalised (under the guidance of others) as *categories* of experience. This is one aspect of building up everyday 'knowledge of the world', that is, of building a semiotic construction of experience.

Once a child embarks upon the mother tongue, names are necessarily used on all occasions of speech. However, I wish to focus initially on those utterances which overtly classify or identify something by name. First let us look at Examples 1a–c, typical naming utterances produced by Stephen in the second half of the third year (between 2;6 and 2;8).

**Example 1    Naming**

| | | |
|---|---|---|
| 1a. | 2;6 | (S enters childcare centre and addresses staff member, A)<br>S:  I've got a paper<br>A:  Oh let's have a look. What's on the paper<br>(opening folded sheet) Do you know?<br>S:  Um, that's words (pointing) that's words |
| 1b. | 2;7 | (S pointing at the traffic from the car)<br>S:  A taxi, another taxi ... a tru- no, a van |
| 1c. | 2;8 | (S examining pattern on rug)<br>S:  That's a square. What's that?<br>M:  That's a circle |

In the early period of learning English as a mother tongue these are typical utterances where things are being classified by naming. They are typical in that the child can enquire about or tell how to categorise some observed phenomenon, by bringing it into intersubjective focus, either through pointing and/or through exophoric reference, and then using a relational process (see Halliday 1994: 112*ff*) to construe the category to which the observed instance belongs. The typical relational verb here is *be* and the clause can be analysed as having two 'participant' roles brought into a relationship by *be*, as shown below:

**Analysis 1**    Early relational process for naming with exophoric reference

| that | 's | a circle |
|------|-----|----------|
| Participant 1 <br><br> exophoric reference to observed phenomenon | Process <br><br> = | Participant 2 <br><br> category |

Having engaged in this kind of naming activity for some time, the process of doing so itself eventually gets named, using the metalinguistic verb *call*, as in example 1d:

> 1d.    2;10    (S fingering missing toggle on raincoat)
>         S:    I need a coat- a coat- what's it called?

By means of these relational processes, then, an instance is put into a general category. We can regard these utterances as occasions of practising signification, in that they all serve to construe the relation between a lexical symbol and the material phenomenon for which it stands. But, as Hasan (1985) has argued in her discussion of Saussure, working out the signification of a lexical item cannot proceed without simultaneously learning the value relations into which it enters. For example, to learn the accepted denotation of the word *van* depends on construing its oppositional relations to co-hyponyms such as *utility, truck, station wagon, car,* and this can hardly be done without simultaneously construing a semantic space which might be realised by a word like *vehicle* or *traffic.* So through the naming utterances where Stephen was practising signification he was also necessarily construing the things of his experience into taxonomies.

A superordinate category, such as 'vehicle', whether lexically realised or not, will be based on some shared similarity between the co-hyponyms. In the literature on initial category formation, similarity of functions (Anglin 1983; Nelson 1974; Rescorla 1980), perceptual properties (Anglin 1977; Clark 1973, 1975; Rosch 1978) and component parts (Tversky 1990) of objects have all been shown to be important, while Halliday (1975: 141) points out that the salience of any such factor for the child is not simply inherent in the thing, but derives from the social contexts in which it is encountered.

If we look at conversations from Stephen where things are described and compared, we find that he did, indeed, attend to various attributes of objects which might serve to discriminate them as members of a category. However, the status of those attributes was always left ambiguous. This can be illustrated from three text fragments focusing on observable parts and properties, Examples 2a–c:

**Example 2**    Possible criteria for categorising

| | | | |
|---|---|---|---|
| 2a. | 2;7 | M: | What did you see at the zoo? |
| | | S: | Elephants; they got big trunks |
| 2b. | 2;8 | M: | What cars have you got there? |
| | | S: | There's a fire engine one with a ladder on |
| 2c. | 2;9 | (S in bed with M & F reaches to M's earring) | |
| | | S: | I haven't got earrings |
| | | M: | No, you haven't got earrings |
| | | S: | And Hal hasn't got earrings |
| | | M: | No, Hal hasn't got earrings |
| | | S: | And (reaching to F's face) Daddy hasn't got earrings Daddy's got bristles |
| | | M: | Mm, he has, hasn't he? |
| | | S: | I haven't got bristles |

These examples are entirely typical of the period in that it remains inexplicit in every case as to whether any attributes described are seen as incidental to the individual in question or as important in determining the category.

The next developmental step in the use of language to construe categories builds upon experience with the kinds of texts described so far. The need to make sense of experience is the challenge which has led the child to classify its various aspects through naming and describing utterances. But having, in this way, created a meaning potential to construct a taxonomically organised knowledge of the things of his everyday experience, that lexical and grammatical potential is then available for use to do something more.

This can be seen if the earlier classifying utterances are compared with Example 3 from a year later:

**Example 3**   Classifying categories

3.   3;8   (S is examining animal jigsaw puzzle pieces)
   S:   There isn't a fox; and there isn't- is a platypus an animal?
   M:   Yes
   S:   And is a seal is an animal?
   M:   Yes (shepherding S to bathroom)
   S:   And is er- er- er- er-
   M:   You do your teeth while you're thinking

The difference in this text is that both participants in the classifying clauses are realised by nominal groups which name categories, as shown below:

**Analysis 2**   Relational process: both participant roles construing categories

| is | a platypus | an animal |
|---|---|---|
| Process = | Participant 1 (category) | Participant 2 (category) |

The first participant role here is not an exophoric reference item picking out some observable thing, but constructs a class lexically. Two levels of taxonomic hierarchy are thus brought into a hyponymy relation by this Relational Process clause. There are numerous recorded examples of such utterances from Stephen, but none was recorded before age 3;5. (The later appearance of such clauses is also attested by other case studies, such as Macnamara (1982) and Painter (1984).)

The importance of this development is that it constitutes a move on Stephen's part from using language to make sense of non-linguistic phenomena to using language to make sense of the value relations of the meaning system itself. Thus, by this time Stephen was not simply building the system of language (and knowledge) but was exploring it. In this sense he was not simply learning language and learning through language, but was simultaneously learning about language (see Halliday 1981).

My suggestion, then, is that the deployment of relational clause grammar has led inevitably to a new orientation towards making sense of the linguistic potential. But this, in turn, requires a further extension of the meaning resources. For example, in the fourth year, even when attention was still focused on categorising specific observable things, the impetus to explore the system required something new. This was the development of the internal causal conjunctive relation to make explicit the positive criteria upon which an entity was being assigned to a particular lexical class. This can be exemplified by the following texts, from the second half of the fourth year, between 3;7 and 3;11. The relevant utterances are underlined:

**Example 4**    The use of 'internal' causal links

| | | |
|---|---|---|
| 4a. | 3;7 | (M says something about her 'best boys') |
| | | H: We have to be your best boys cause we're your only boys |
| | | S: And Daddy |
| | | H: He's not a boy, he's a man |
| | | S: He is a boy, <u>cause he's got a penis</u> |
| | | H: He's a male, we're all males |
| | | S: He's a man and a boy too |
| 4b. | 3;9 | (M refers to airship overhead as 'spaceship balloon') |
| | | S: Not a spaceship – an *air*ship – <br> <u>cause a spaceship has bits like this to stand it up</u> |
| 4c. | 3;11 | (S is pointing at page numbers) |
| | | S: That's fifteen <u>because it's got a five</u>; <br> that's fourteen <u>because it's got a four</u> |

In these examples *because* has the 'internal' conjunctive meaning of *I know [it's an airship] because ...*; *I can tell [he's a boy] because ...* (Halliday & Hasan 1976). And while the 'external' use of *because* (*Do this because ...*; *I want this because ...*, etc) had already appeared, this internal conjunctive option was a fresh move. The importance of the internal conjunctive link is that it serves to explain the speaker's reasoning for asserting or inferring something – in this case for placing something in a category.

Another result of the new orientation towards making sense of the linguistic potential is the use of language to define language. Having begun to orient towards exploring the meaning system, the metalinguistic verb *mean* was taken up by Stephen as an additional resource for signalling relations between terms within his linguistic potential. This was obviously an important learning tool in itself, but experience in using *mean* to define words was also important in that it provided one of the earliest contexts for rank-shift (embedding).[1]

If we look at examples of Stephen's relational processes using *mean* we find that creating a synonymy relation by linking single words was often beyond him and that there was thus a need to embed whole clauses or clause-complexes into the second participant role, as in Examples 5a–b where embedded clauses are enclosed in square brackets.

**Example 5**   Embedding in the context of defining

| |
|---|
| 5a.  3;10   (S approaches M holding up a complicated duplo structure)<br>          S:  ... Balance means [[you hold it on your fingers and it doesn't go on the floor]]<br><br>5b.  3;7   M: You're naughty boys to throw them up there<br>          S:  Hal did it, by accident<br>          M: Well, Hal's naughty then<br>          S:  No, by accident; that's not naughty,<br>              that's mean (pause) [[you say sorry]] |

The defining Relational Processes can be analysed as shown in Analysis 3, following Halliday (1994: 115).

Thus the attempt to use language to explicate itself has created

**Analysis 3**    Defining relational process with embedded clause as participant

| Balance | means | [[you hold it on your fingers and it doesn't go on the floor]] |
|---------|-------|----------------------------------------------------------------|
| That | 's mean | [[you say sorry]] |
| Token | Relational Process | Value |

a context where the speaker has needed to manipulate the language in ways rarely needed before. Although the meanings constructed by the embedded clauses themselves are perfectly 'concrete' and familiar, the construction of a clause rather than a nominal group to realise a participant role is something new, and exemplifies an aspect of what Halliday (1994) has characterised as 'ideational grammatical metaphor'. The metaphor lies in the fact that a thesis referring to a state of affairs is treated as an object. In other words the grammar is being manipulated creatively to construe something simultaneously as an event and as a participant.

Indeed, the realisations of the Token roles in such examples similarly exhibit a limited kind of grammatical metaphor. In Example 5a above, in order to reflect on the meaning of a verb (*balance*) in this overt way, an action has been construed as a participant within the relational clause. In Example 5b, the Token role is realised by a reference item (*that*). However, it is different from the use of reference in the two-year-old examples, not only in being endophoric, but in being anaphoric to the whole of *doing it by accident*, which is then to be reinterpreted in the following clause as a participant. So once again a small new move is made, in this case a move into 'extended' reference (Halliday & Hasan 1976: 66), which will pave the way for the possibility of an entire text or for a 'fact' clause to be construed by the reference item – an even further abstraction from the exophoric origins of the use of the system of reference.

The linguistic developments described so far are summarised in Table 3.1.

**Table 3.1** Summary of selected developments in the system and use of Stephen's language: age 2–4 years

| Aspects of language use: 2–3 yrs | New developments in the language system and use: 3–4 yrs |
| --- | --- |
| Classifying/naming clauses (using *be, call*) with exophoric reference item realising one participant role (e.g. *that's a van; what's that called?*) | Classifying clauses with lexical realisations in both participant roles (e.g. *a bus isn't a truck*) |
| Describing clauses (using *be, have got*) (e.g. *Daddy's got bristles*) | 'Internal' causal option to link describing clause to classifying clause (e.g. *he is a boy because he's got a penis*) |
| No defining clauses | Defining clauses using *be* and *mean* |
| | Token Participant in defining clause realised by non-nominal elements (e.g. *balance means ...*) |
| | Extended reference in defining clause (e.g. *... that means ...*) |
| | Embedded clauses constructed into Value role in defining clause (e.g. *that means [[you say sorry]]*) |

Thus there have been developments in the meaning potential, such as the new option for causal conjunction or the new metalinguistic process *mean* and there have been new linguistic contexts for realising existing potential such as the various new realisations of the Participant roles in the Relational clauses. But the point I wish to foreground here is that the changes in the meaning potential itself are not just a matter of expanding the language but also, or rather, *by definition*, they constitute an expansion of the learning potential. The changes in the use of the meaning potential which create new forms of text also enable new ways of thinking and learning.

There is then a spiralling relationship between linguistic and cognitive development as schematised in Figure 3.2.

An exemplification of the way language development enables developments in thinking is provided in Figure 3.3, based on the texts discussed so far.

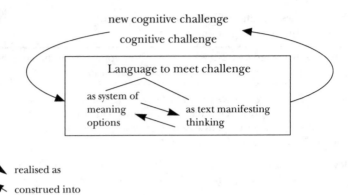

*Key*

➤ realised as

➤ construed into

**Figure 3.2**    The relationship between intellectual and linguistic development

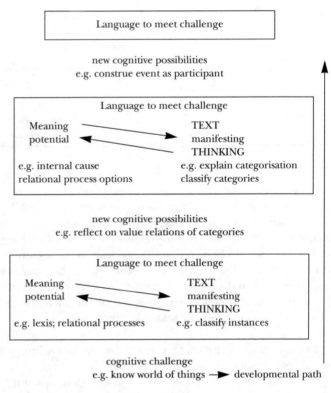

**Figure 3.3**    Exemplification of the relationship between intellectual and linguistic development

## 4   New possibilities for learning

The most important interrelated new possibilities for learning which arise from these developments are the following:

1. Building knowledge of the world can take place through overt exploration of meaning, rather than only by accumulating understandings through long-term observation and practice of language in use.
2. Abstract meanings become a possibility for the first time.

These new possibilities can be clarified and illustrated by the following conversations in which Stephen participated. Example 6 comes from the later period we have been describing, when Stephen was 3;8.

**Example 6**   Overt discussion of meaning

---

6.   3;8   (M asks S if he knows the word *dog*, which is in the book
             they are looking at)
      S:   No
      M:   It's an animal
      S:   Rabbit?
      M:   No, it's 'dog'
      S:   Dog's not an animal!
      M:   Yes it is. [some further talk omitted]
             What is it then?
      S:   It's, it's just a dog
      M:   Yes, but dogs are animals
      S:   No, they aren't
      M:   Well, what's an animal then?
      S:   Um (?a) giraffes an animal
      M:   Oh, I see, you think animal is only for zoo animals
      S:   Yeh
      M:   Dogs are animals too, they're tame animals. And cats,
             cats are animals too. Did you know that?
      H:   (chipping in) And people, we're animals
      S:   We're *not*

---

From this text it appears that in the twenty months or so that Stephen had been using his vocabulary for animals, and observing others use the word *animal* in specific contexts of use, he had constructed a taxonomy in which *animal* was in opposition to *pet*, or at any rate had a narrower signification than the adult term. Yet, because he was now able to talk about the relation of the categories to one another, this not only became apparent for the first time, but he could be directly and immediately tutored in the adult version of the meaning relationships (*dogs are animals too, they are tame animals*, etc) without reference to any observable instances of the phenomena being classified.

The ability to handle this kind of talk is crucial for school learning since many of the categories of educational knowledge cannot be inferred from observation because they depend on criteria which cannot be observed directly. In relation to Martin's classification of fields, domestic categories can be construed through acting on and observing things in context, whereas this is not the case with fields that explore, those of uncommonsense knowledge. The ability to construct new categories by relating them to known ones, even when no observable example is available is thus necessary. This can perhaps be further illustrated by the following brief text, Example 7:

**Example 7**   Learning technical classifications

7.   3;10   (S fails to find a picture of a seal in his fish book)
          H:   Seals aren't fish, that's why. They're mammals
          S:   Are seals mammals?
          H:   Yes, cause they don't lay eggs; they have babies

Whether something lays eggs or not is, I suppose, open to observation in principle, but in practice this is hardly the case for all individuals. While perceptual criteria, together with experience of the name in specific observational contexts, may allow the learner to discriminate a seal as a particular kind of water creature, they certainly won't inform the child about the category to which it is assigned within the field of biology. (Indeed, it is only his experience with books and with schooled children that have made the biological category relevant to Stephen.) But having had experience in justifying his own classifications using internal *because* clauses, Stephen was, by age four, in a position to take up a linguistically presented criterion of this kind. And, indeed, my argument is that he will have to do so once he moves into learning other than commonsense fields. This is the point of Vygotsky's distinction between what he calls 'spontaneous concepts' which arise from everyday activities and the 'scientific concepts' of school learning, the development of which he says 'begins in the domain of conscious awareness' (Vygotsky 1987: 216, cited in Lee 1987).

By the fifth year, there is fairly clear evidence that Stephen can manage this kind of learning from instruction.

**Example 8**   Learning from definitions

> 8.   4;4   (M & S are discussing whether whales kill people)
>          M:   There may be one kind of whale that can, but most
>                whales are nice creatures
>          S:   They're not creatures Mum, they're whales
>          M:   Yes; creature is anything that's alive
>          S:   Are *we* creatures?
>          M:   Yeh
>          S:   No, we're not! (laughing)

While Example 8 does not involve learning a new category, it does illustrate the way Stephen can revise a taxonomy from participating in a single text. Thus he can not only track the definition that is offered, but he can immediately draw from it a 'logical' inference and realise that this does not match with his current taxonomy.

The new mode of learning, then, is to learn from text where the language is distanced from the immediate context of situation, to learn by making an inference from a definition rather than from observation of language in the context of situated use. This is crucial for school learning, not only because of the time it saves and because the criteria for technical classifications may not be accessible to personal experience, but because the categories themselves may be inaccessible to observation.

This can be seen from Example 9, a conversation which took place just before Stephen's fourth birthday:

**Example 9**    Learning abstract categories

9.   3;11   (S overhears F mention *fifty*)
           S:   Is fifty a number?
           F:   Yeah
           S:   How does it go?
           F:   It comes after 49
           S:   A hundred comes after 49
           F:   A hundred comes after 99

Here we see Stephen being able to talk not just about things but about something more abstract and thus not accessible to being understood by rehearsing signification. As a material object, a particular graphic symbol can be identified as *fifty* in just the same way as an example of a cat can be named as *a cat*. (Indeed, Stephen was doing this in the previous year, as in Example 5c.) However, as a number, fifty is only an object of the symbolic world – it is a meaning not a thing. The linguistic development of the non-phoric relational clause structure has, however, allowed it to be classified as a symbol, rather than just identified as *fifty* – has allowed it to be understood in terms of value relations. And it is interesting that in further attempting to understand the symbol Stephen reconstrued the material processes *go* and *come* metaphorically as relations and, adopting F's model, discussed the sequence of enumeration by construing it in terms of relative locations.

Again, the importance of being able to manage this degree of abstraction is crucial to school learning. The business of early schooling is to learn the new symbol systems of written language and of mathematics. And whatever pedagogy is adopted, being able to talk about what they are doing at all will require children to use some degree of abstraction and metaphor in the language. Abstraction is needed because symbols as symbols are non-concrete meanings, and metaphor because those symbols also have a material aspect, as graphic shapes, which children must also come to grips with. (Some of the complexity of meeting the new medium of language is perhaps suggested by Stephen's enquiry at age 5: *Mum, how come everything starts with a letter?*.)

Although it will take much more than a single text to give Stephen an understanding of the meanings he is trying to explore here, I would argue that what has allowed him to address some-what abstract ideas is the path of linguistic experience he has travelled. That path has taken him from using 'context free' relational clauses to construing non-thing meanings as participants and eventually coopting material meanings to additional relational uses in overt attempts to classify and define. Thus developments that begin as a means of better understanding the material environment provide, in the end, a way of accessing less tangible meanings. Being able to handle these abstractions clearly constitutes a development in thinking, so it is fair to say that new developments in the linguistic potential have opened up new possibilities for thinking and learning.

At age four or five Stephen was only just beginning to grapple with abstract concepts and to use the resources of grammatical metaphor to do so. I am certainly not arguing that this is controlled by the time a child begins school. But I am arguing that the linguistic basis for understanding abstraction and for further developing metaphorical meanings is in place.

It may well be that in attempting to build school learning upon the child's early linguistic experiences we have tended to see the initial construction of the mother tongue taking place in the first three years of life as the whole story, and to assume that children lack the resources for building knowledge consciously. I would argue that we should take note of the fact that in the later pre-school years new resources for learning have developed, enabling new ways of thinking. I would also argue that the kind of experience that builds an orientation for literacy is not only a matter of encounters with print and with storying but involves a more general experience of being able to reflect on language, using the grammar in ways such as I have described.

## 5    The construal of events as generalisations

So far I have discussed the developments which occur in the realm of naming, classifying and defining, an area which involves that part of the grammar which allows language to become its own metalanguage – that is, relational clause grammar. But if we turn our attention now to the way events and 'goings on' are construed into language we can find parallel developments and fresh evidence of how the need to understand fuels linguistic developments which in turn fuel further developments in thinking. And we also see further the dialogue partner's role in guiding the learner towards the adult version of knowledge.

If we contrast some typical utterances from Stephen at about age 2;7 with others at about age 3;7, where he is using language to interpret ongoing events, we can see a parallel development to that illustrated by the classifying utterances. The examples are given in Table 3.2 below.

What distinguishes the later texts from the earlier examples is that each later one takes the here and now experience as a springboard from which to generalise. In 11a, (*He's throwing him cause he's a baddie*), it is in the familiar context of talking about what he is observing, but the additional clause *cause he's a baddie* only makes sense as an explanation if it is a characteristic of baddies as a class that they throw people. This kind of implicit generalisation first emerged at 2;7, but did not become routine until the fourth year. And to turn a running commentary into an implicit generalisation in this way necessitates a fresh development: a new deployment of external cause – to explain by classifying rather than in terms of affect (cf *I want it cause I like it*).

In examples 11b and 11c, the generalisations are made quite explicit. Long experience comparing and contrasting different individuals and their participation in various processes has enabled Stephen to form generalisations about categories of

**Table 3.2**  Stephen's use of language to interpret ongoing events 2;7 and 3;7

| Typical example of talk arising from ongoing observation/action | |
| --- | --- |
| Examples at approx 2;7 | Examples at approx 3;7 |
| 10a.  S:  (scribbling) I'm drawing | 11a.  (S explaining TV scene)<br>S:  He's throwing him<br>     'cause he's a baddie |
| 10b.  S:  Mummy's drinking coffee,<br>     Daddy's drinking coffee,<br>     Hal's drinking juice | 11b.  S:  What are you drinking?<br>M:  Wine<br>S:  Wine. Grown ups drink<br>     wine |
| 10c.  (out driving)<br>S:  The car's going faster | 11c.  (Watching riders in park)<br>S:  Do cars go faster than<br>     horses? |

participants. And the desire to construct those generalisations linguistically has required the development of nominal and verbal groups constructed without deixis,[2] so as to free the meaning from reference to a specific context of situation.

What is the further effect on Stephen's thinking of the repeated construal of such generalisations using these new linguistic possibilities? One effect is that he begins to try to shortcut the inductive process and to construe generalisations based on only a single observed instance. This can be illustrated by the following texts where a single observed experience is recalled and construed in language:

**Example 12**   Recalling specific incidents as generalisations

---

12a.   3;7   (The day after Hal blew up a plastic bag and then burst it)
        S:   You know you could pop shopping bags
        M:   Can you?
        H:   Mm, but they are hard to blow up

12b.   3;9   (Previous day at zoo, a caged lion had pounced onto some meat on a shelf)
        S:   Lions could jump up their things to eat
        M:   Lions could jump up their things to eat?
        S:   You know, at the zoo

---

These examples show that Stephen might now choose to reconstruct a single recalled incident not as a recount of that specific event – involving specific participants and events tied to specific past time – but as a general statement removed from any specific context of situation.

However, there are dangers in basing a generalisation upon a single observational instance, and the fact that Stephen was creating text in interaction with others meant that the conversational partner could alert him to this, as can be seen from Example 13:

**Example 13**   Overgeneralising in dialogue

---

13.   3;6   (S looking at a park from the car)
        S:   That can't be shut cause it hasn't got a gate (pause)
           All parks can't be shut cause they haven't got a gate
        M:   Well, *some* parks have gates. Centennial Park has gates

---

Here Stephen makes a comment on the park immediately in view and then immediately generalises from this to parks in general, underlining his shift in focus with the 'universal quantifier' *all*. The adult's response challenges the scope of Stephen's generalisation and draws his attention to a particular familiar example as a means of justifying this move.

Experience of this kind taught Stephen how to support and challenge generalisations with observational evidence. In Example 14, he himself cites an instance of experience to back-up the generalisation being negotiated.

**Example 14**    Supporting a generalisation

| |
|---|
| 14.    3;8    (S is playing with a white cockatoo feather)<br>        S:  Cockatoos can talk<br>        F:  Yes cockatoos can talk<br>        S:  And parrots can talk<br>        F:  Yes<br>        M:  (interrupts) *Some* parrots can talk<br>        S:  We went to school- we went to school and- and <u>I saw<br>            a parrot and he was blue and red and (?) lovely and-<br>            and- and he said hello to hi- and he said hello to me</u> |

And in Examples 15a–b he uses an observed instance as a challenge to the adult's statements:

**Example 15**    Challenging a generalisation

| |
|---|
| 15a.    3;8    S:  Can cars go faster than buses?<br>           M:  Oh yes cars go faster than buses<br>           S:  <u>Then how come that bus is beating us?</u><br><br>15b.    3;7    (F & S have noticed a sports car in the traffic)<br>           F:  And they [= sports cars] go fast, because they've<br>              got a big engine<br>           S:  <u>But that doesn't go faster than us. See?</u> We will go<br>              faster<br>           F:  He's not trying; if he was really trying he could go<br>              much faster than us<br>           S:  If he goes very fast he can – if he goes very fast he<br>              can beat us |

As far as the development of the linguistic system is concerned, this negotiation of generalisations in dialogue led to the development and use of the non-specific deictics *all, not all, every, only* and (stressed) *some*, as the inclusiveness of the categories participating in the processes was explored. It led to the meaning of *can* and *could* being extended from the negotiation of permission and ability between the dialogue partners to the negotiation of possibility and ability concerning third persons. And, indeed, there was an expanded use of usuality and modality generally. This dialogic construal of generalisations also provided an important context for extending the use of conditional links, as in 15a (*then how come...?*) – links which had originally developed in the negotiation of personal action.

With regard to the development of thinking, we have seen in these texts how, having begun generalising from a single example, his experience in creating text in interaction was teaching Stephen of the need to hedge such generalisations and of the value of citing particular observations to support them. And, as in Example 15b, he was learning to construct through language a context in which a disputed generalisation would be valid, as with the initial clause of the final utterance *if he goes very fast*. Thus, in the attempt to construe 'the facts' of experience in interaction, he was also gaining an apprenticeship in strategies for argumentation.

Playing out these strategies repeatedly in dialogue then produced a further development. The familiar pattern of dialogic interaction began to be taken over as part of Stephen's own way of formulating a problem. One way he did this was by incorporating some negotiating assessment into his initial generalisations, as when he asked a question like the following:

**Example 16**    Graded queries

| | | | |
|---|---|---|---|
| 16a. | 3;9 | S: | Can trains go faster than <u>most</u> cars? |
| 16b. | 3;11 | S: | Do <u>some</u> cats like dogs? |

Another way was for Stephen to problematise the relation between the already construed generalisation and the observed instance, in the form of a clause complex. This can be seen in an enquiry like the following which occurred in the fifth year:

**Example 17**    Constructing a problem monologically

> 17.   4;5   S:   How come that bus is beating us when cars go faster than buses?

The conditional relation which introduced earlier a challenging response to the addressee, as in Example 15a, is now created monologically. Thus practice in thinking through language in interaction with others has led to the ability to construct a problem solo; the problem in question being the need to reconcile the construed generalisation that should hold across specific contexts of situation (*cars go faster than buses*) with the current construal of an observation in the immediate context of situation (*that bus is beating us*).

## 6    Summary of developments

In sum, the various changes in Stephen's linguistic system and its use in the ways I have described can be interpreted in terms of a movement between poles of the kind shown in Table 3.3.

It is not of course that the child ceases to be concerned with the foci displayed in the left-hand column of Table 3.3, but rather that those of the right-hand column are new possibilities, and ones which are crucial to later school learning.

**Table 3.3**    Developments in language use between 2–3 years and 3–5 years

| Use of language at age 2–3 yrs | | Use of language at age 3–5 yrs |
|---|---|---|
| attend to observed material instance | and | attend to semiotic category |
| construe meaning in context | and | explore status of instance in terms of potential |
| build system from text | and | explore system with text |
| negotiate meaning in dialogue | and | negotiate meaning monologically |

I would suggest that this general characterisation of all the changes I have so far described in the use of the language over this period between 2;6 and 5 years of age concerns the register variable of mode. In his discussion of the three components of the context of situation, mode is discussed in the following terms by Halliday: 'If we are focusing on language, this last category of "mode" refers to what part the language is playing in the situation under considera- tion' (1978: 189). Martin (1992: 513) refers to mode in a similar way as 'the role language is playing in realising social action'. And when mode concerns the status of language with respect to the *ideational* dimension, he argues that 'mode mediates the semiotic space between action and reflection'. This, in general terms, is a matter of contextual dependency – 'the extent to which a text constructs or accompanies its field' (Martin 1992: 514).

In Figure 3.4 I have adapted and simplified Martin's mode network (1992: 527) into a continuum between 'action' and 're- flection', or the 'ancillary' and 'constitutive' (Halliday & Hasan 1985).

ANCILLARY —————————————— CONSTITUTIVE
accompany monitor observe reconstruct (shared)  (unshared) fictionalise generalise review theoretical

**Figure 3.4**   Mode: degrees of abstraction (after Martin 1992)

Even when concerning ourselves only with 'thinking' rather than 'doing' texts, we can suggest that in the process of making sense of material experience through the linguistic construal of single things or events, Stephen moved over time along this con- tinuum. That is, he initially created texts which were highly context-dependent, as phenomena were categorised and events described in the process of using language to accompany, moni- tor, observe and recall specific experiences. However, from about age three onwards, the texts created were more context-constitu- tive, as language was distanced from the specificity of experience. Or else where the immediate and specific phenomena of observa- tion were interpreted, it was in relation to the construal of things and events as 'potentials underlying and cutting across particular manifestations' (Martin 1992: 523).

According to Martin, mode also concerns the status of language with respect to the semiotic construction of interpersonal distance. This relates to the degrees of turn-taking, the self- consciousness of the composing process, the expectation of a response, and so on. In the most general terms, it can be regarded as relating to a continuum between more dialogic and more monologic construction of meaning, as in Figure 3.5.

DIALOGIC ————————————————————— MONOLOGIC

**Figure 3.5**   Mode: degrees of negotiation

Thus the internalisation of dialogic strategies to enable monologic formulation of assessment and problematising also constitutes a move in mode.

Moves along both these mode continua need to be seen in relation to the simplified classification of fields already discussed. We can then summarise by saying that on the one hand, in becoming prepared for the move to uncommonsense knowledge, the child must become experienced in moving along the mode continuum from monitoring, observing and reconstructing experience towards generalising it, and thus using language in a way that is relatively constitutive in mode, abstracted from specific contexts of situation. And on the other hand, in order to move towards the kinds of fields that are negotiated in written (and therefore more monologic) texts and through overt instruction, rather than by doing, experience in overt reflection on knowledge and in the monologic construction of meaning plays a crucial role.

# 7   Meaning systems as resources for learning

In what I have looked at so far – the general tendency towards generalisation, problematising the instance, 'proto'-abstraction and reasoning from text – I have noted developments across a whole range of linguistic systems, because my focus has been on learning *through* language. A more conventional approach to language development is to consider the acquisition of language *per se*, which means looking at developments within a particular linguistic system or systems. I would like in this section to suggest that to track individual linguistic systems can be regarded as a matter of exploring learning through language just as much as of learning language itself. That is to say, each major grammatical system, such as that of tense, modality, transitivity (Process-Participant relations), projection (quoting, reporting relations, etc) constitutes a resource for meaning and thus for thinking and learning. If we then follow developments within any single system we can track how that particular resource is used over time as a strategy for meaning.

I will turn now to a brief consideration of an individual language system in order to illustrate this and to make one further general point: when a system expands to allow for an additional major option, or when an existing option is extended into new contexts of use, the movement is very often from a more affective, interpersonal choice to a more objective, reflective one. Using a few further examples from the case study, I will sketch out an illustration of this move from an interpersonal source with respect to just one system, that of linking two clauses into a 'clause complex' by means of the logical-semantic relation of causality.

## 8   Development of causal links

Briefly the pattern of use is as follows. Stephen, like some other naturalistically studied children (see Hood & Bloom 1991), used hypotactic (dependent) clauses of 'reason' initially to negotiate action with the addressee, as in Examples 18a–c:

**Example 18**   Early examples of *because*: negotiating ongoing action

| | | | |
|---|---|---|---|
| 18a. | 2;6 | S: | Don't take it, cause I want it |
| 18b. | 2;6 | S: | Can't (refusing to comply with M's request) cause I'm too tired |
| 18c. | 2;7 | S: | (regarding caterpillar) Won't touch it, cause it might sting you |

It was only after some experience in enhancing the effectiveness of his refusals, statements of intention and commands, by adding a reason to justify them, that Stephen began to construct explicit causality outside the context of here and now negotiation with the dialogue partner. However, even then, the first moves involved topics in which Stephen's feelings were strongly engaged, such as the issue of his status as 'a big boy'. Examples 19a–b illustrate:

**Example 19**    Clause complexes with *because*: imbued with strong affect

---

19a.  2;8  S:    (busy with pen) I'm doing lots of names 'cause I'm a big boy

19b.  2;7  (S places drink carefully away from table edge)
　　　　　S:    Only *little* boys put on edge, 'cause little boys are naughty

---

Example 19a was different from the previous examples (18a–c) in being a 'running commentary' rather than a negotiation, while example 19b was the first recorded third-person example, quite exceptional at the time. In both cases, an issue central to Stephen's personal concerns provided the impetus for breaking new ground.

After this, *because*, as an external conjunctive link, gradually came to be used with respect to less emotionally charged topics. For example, to link two predictably sequential events:

**Example 20**    Later affect-neutral use of *because*

---

20.  3;5  S:    (observing traffic) A red tow truck pulling a car because it's engine has broken.

---

However, by the time hypotactic enhancement (with *because*) was used in this way, paratactic complexes (with *so*) were developing, and once again this was initially within an interpersonal context. Paratactic links with *so*, were always used when Stephen explicitly constructed the effect to follow the cause (i.e. there were no examples in the data of a hypotactic reason clause as 'marked Theme'). Initially, paratactic reason clauses were only used by Stephen to negotiate a request or refusal. For example, he found the structure a useful one when the effect was some non-compliant behaviour on his own part, as in Example 21:

**Example 21**    Early examples of *so*: negotiating action

---

21a.    3;10    H:    Mum, he won't stop calling me (?)

                S:    <u>He always says it to me so I always say it to him</u>

21b.    3;5    (M holding tissue to S's nose)

               M:    Big blow, big blow

               S:    I can't always do a big blow; big boys- big boys ... they do big blows; <u>I'm just a little boy so I do little blows</u>

---

What Stephen is doing here is making his refusals the obligatory conclusion to a factual generalisation. It is thus difficult to dispute the rightness of his account of his own behaviour without challenging the preceding 'fact'. So again, the new option for causal enhancement (that of a paratactic link) was initially available only in the context of certain speech functional moves.

But having been established for these interpersonal ends, the same kind of linguistically achieved logic can be coopted to construe a necessary relation between two impersonal facts, and by the fifth year, Stephen had begun to use linguistic reasoning of this kind to draw a conclusion. The following text, although still a second-person example, is removed from the context of negotiating action:

**Example 22**    Reflective reasoning

---

22a.    4;7    (S & M are discussing prices)

               S:    How about a house! A thousand! [i.e. dollars]

               M:    More than that

               S:    A million!!

               M:    Sometimes. Some houses cost that much.

               S:    <u>You haven't got that much, so you don't get another-</u> another thing- another house; but if you did, you could get a good house.

---

And in a final example, a third-person text shows Stephen drawing a conclusion from a clearly articulated premise:

**Example 22**    Reflective reasoning

| | | | |
|---|---|---|---|
| 22b. | 4;5 | S: | Mum, can bikes go faster than cars? Can bikes go faster than cars? |
| | | M: | You're always asking me that |
| | | S: | I can't remember |
| | | M: | They go the same |
| | | S: | What about vans? (ponders) <u>Vans go faster than cars so vans should go faster than motor bikes</u> |

Thus when tracking a single system like this, we observe the same tendency to shift in mode towards reasoning through text and towards the monologic construction – and indeed solution – of problems. But we can also see very clearly that even an archetypically ideational resource like causal enhancement – central for construing field and manifesting logical thought – has its origins ontogenetically in the interpersonal sphere, in the negotiation of action and/or the construal of affect-laden topics.

The pattern of a gradual move into ideational contexts for the deployment of a meaning option was not limited to the area of causal enhancement illustrated, but was apparent in other systems too, such as mental process projection, modality and conditional links. When it comes to mapping language development systemically therefore, a new option is initially very often fairly constrained. It may only be mobilised with respect to an area of field of special salience to the learner, or it may be available only alongside particular speech function choices or it may be mobilised only responsively in dialogue, and so on. Development of the linguistic system is not therefore just a matter of new choices, but of freeing the choices from various constraints.

From the above, it can be seen that in addition to the developments in mode that I have already described, this preschool period can be characterised in terms of a move from the interpersonal to the ideational, from the intersubjective to the objective, along the following lines:

**Table 3.4**    Building on interpersonal sources of meaning-making

| Original deployment of system | Later additional use |
|---|---|
| negotiating action (proposals) | negotiating information (propositions) |
| intersubjective | objective |
| affect-charged | affect-neutral |

Once again it is not a matter of one context of use or the other, but rather of building additional meanings from an interpersonal starting point.

And again, this development can be linked to the move from commonsense to uncommonsense knowledge. For example, the way that we use language initially to measure things is through the interpersonal systems of grading, with expressions like *The bag is very heavy, Today is hotter than yesterday*, and so on. Measurements within the scientific disciplines of uncommonsense knowledge, however, use objective scales of speed, temperature, mass, and so on. So as well as needing to use language systems in objective, affect-neutral contexts for science, learners will need to give preference to ideational rather than interpersonal ways of achieving a familiar goal, such as assessing some dimension.

Stephen appeared to be becoming attuned to this when he began occasionally to try out 'objective' assessments in his fifth year, as when he observed of a motorcycle accelerating past the car, *He's beating us by twenty-three metres*, rather than using the graded form, *He's going faster than us.*

Thus an appreciation of the interpersonal origins of many meaning choices suggests, on the one hand, where we should begin when intervening to develop learners' language, and on the other hand, clarifies the direction the deployment of language will need to take for learning within certain fields.

# 9   Conclusion

The approach I have adopted here arises from the theoretical axioms of systemic functional linguistics. Taking this perspective, I have suggested that learning needs to be seen in relation to language and that there is a dynamic relationship between learning through language and developing language itself. This linguistic model, which provides functionally grounded descriptive categories, has also permitted me to offer a broad characterisation of certain key developments in the early mother-tongue period, based on an examination of conversational interactions within the family.

In terms of the relation between language and learning, it is necessary to consider both what is learned and how it is learned. With regard to the *what* of learning, systemic theory has always argued that this be regarded as systems of meaning. Not only is language itself a system of meaning, but it has a special status because it is the major means for manifesting the 'higher' systems of meaning that constitute the social system – 'the social structure, systems of knowledge, systems of values, and the like' (Halliday 1975: 120).

One important consequence of seeing knowledge as semiotically constructed is to appreciate that even commonsense understandings are constructed. Because we come to much of our commonsense knowledge before the new ways of learning come to dominate, it is readily misunderstood as being natural and pre-given. Commonsense understandings, such as that people are creatures or that not all parrots can talk, seem to be unarguable facts about the world rather than constructions of meaning. But such 'facts' represent a semiotic construal of the world in which what counts as a creature, a parrot or as talking, what counts as 'all' of a class, and so on, has been negotiated between the newcomer and his meaning group, in order to construe a shared system of meaning within which these assertions count as valid. Such matters are not pregiven truths, waiting to be discovered by the observant.

Of course, at the same time as manifesting commonsense knowledge of the natural world, the snippets of talk we have seen here manifest particular values of the meaning group. This can be seen in the salience of the *little boys/big boys* distinction and the linkage of the latter to literacy in *I'm doing names because I'm a big boy*, the ethic of interpersonal relations visible in *he does it to me so I do it to him*, and so on. While it has not been my concern to explore the language from this perspective in this chapter, it is important to make the point that commonsense knowledge is no more neutral or natural than is educational knowledge.

In terms of *how* learning occurs, I have suggested two things: first, that there is a symbiotic relation between learning through language and developing language itself. That is, language develops as new options for meaning, as new grammatical realisations of existing options, as new configurations of options and as a new contextual deployment of existing options. And it develops to meet the current intellectual challenge. But having done so, experience in using the enriched language system may alert the learner to new possibilities for meaning.

The second point about how learning occurs is that it involves actualising the semiotic systems of knowledge and language into text and continuously reinterpreting the systems on the basis of new experiences in text. But because this actualisation into text occurs in dialogue, the reinterpretation that takes place and the new possibilities for meaning that arise, will depend on the nature of the texts children are enabled to create in interaction.

Obviously, precisely because knowledge is interpersonally constructed by parties to dialogue and because the dialogues manifest the higher-level social semiotic, the language-learning experiences of different children will not be uniform. The particular personalities of the dyadic relationships between caregiver and child, sibling and sibling, etc. are thus one aspect of variation, while the gender, position in the family of the child and social class and ethnicity of the family will be an even more important source of variation. (See Hasan 1986, 1992; Hasan & Cloran 1990 for discussion of semantic variation.)

This means that when it comes to the second object of my essay – the attempt to characterise the actual path of the development – the question immediately arises as to whether the description of Stephen's language development has any generalisability, and I will close with a few words on this point.

One aspect of this description of Stephen's language development concerns the lexico-grammatical options themselves: for example, the development of classifying clauses, defining clauses with metalinguistic verbs like *call* and *mean*, non-specific deictics, embedded clauses, generic and extended reference, modality, internal and external causal and conditional enhancement. Where children learning their mother tongue are concerned, both simple observation and evidence from the literature suggests that all normal children will have developed these by school age. But clearly there will be variation in the ways this meaning potential has been deployed and the frequency with which particular choices have been taken up.

This should not be interpreted as providing for any kind of 'deficit' theory, such as that the lexico-grammatical potential of all children is equally rich, but that the experience of actualising that potential may in some cases be deficient or impoverished. Hasan's work on semantic variation argues rather that variation in ways of meaning according to social class membership is interpretable not in terms of richer or poorer linguistic experience, but in terms of a linguistic experience which enables the learners, within the family, to construe the social system in a way adjusted to their social positioning (Hasan 1992).

The recognition of socio-semantic variation does not, however, prevent us from positing some general developmental patterns. For example, the use of relational grammar to construe meaning without reference to observational experience will clearly always be a later development than its signifying use. Similarly, the understanding of abstract concepts will always be a later development than the construal of tangible meanings. It also seems plausible that new meanings will often arise within the interpersonal sphere of speaker/hearer negotiation and affectual relations, as long as learning is taking place through spoken dialogic interactions with a small intimate meaning group.

I have described particular aspects of one child's learning history – moves to explore language as system, to learn from definitions, to privilege linguistic over observational construals, to deploy meaning in contexts distanced from their interpersonal sources, to reason monologically and to begin to handle abstraction. I believe Stephen's developmental history has a wider interest, however, in the fact that these developments are all characteristics of using language when learning educational knowledge. Thus, to the extent that any child moves in the direction of making symbol systems (like those of mathematics and written language) the object of study, moves from learning commonsense to uncommonsense bodies of knowledge, and moves towards accessing knowledge through written texts, then that child will arguably need to make similar moves in the way language is deployed for learning.

In these terms, data from this case study may serve to suggest the ways in which language must develop to accommodate the requirements of literacy and school learning, as well as illustrating the way developments in language enable developments in thinking.

# Notes

1   Constituency in Halliday's model is described in terms of a rank scale of grammatical units: morpheme, word, group/phrase and clause. Rankshift, or embedding, describes the phenomenon where a unit of one rank operates as a constituent of a unit at the same or lower rank.

2   The nominal group exemplifies 'generic reference', as in Martin (1992: 104). The verbal group is constructed with modality or else with

the marked tense choice of (simple) present so as not to situate the proposition in the here and now.

# References

Anglin, J.M. (1977) *Word, object, and conceptual development.* New York, Norton.

Anglin, J.M. (1983) 'Extensional aspects of the preschool child's word concepts'. T.B. Seiler & W. Wannenmacher (eds) *Concept development and the development of word meaning.* Berlin, Springer: 247–66.

Bates, E., L. Camaioni & V. Volterra (1979) 'The acquisition of performatives prior to speech'. E. Ochs & B.B. Schieffelin (eds) *Developmental pragmatics.* New York, Academic Press: 111–29.

Berger, P.L. & T. Luckmann (1966) *The social construction of reality.* Harmondsworth, Penguin.

Bernstein, B. (1975) *Class, codes and control* Vol. 3 *Towards a theory of educational transmissions.* London, Routledge & Kegan Paul.

Clark, E.V. (1973) 'What's in a word? On the child's acquisition of semantics in his first language'. T.E. Moore (ed.) *Cognitive development and the development of language.* New York, Academic Press: 65–110.

Clark, E.V. (1975) 'Knowledge, context, and strategy in the acquisition of meaning'. D. Plato (ed.) *Georgetown University round table on languages and linguistics, 1975.* Washington, Georgetown University Press.

Halliday, M.A.K. (1975) *Learning how to mean.* London, Edward Arnold.

Halliday, M.A.K. (1978) *Language as social semiotic: the social interpretation of language and meaning.* London, Edward Arnold.

Halliday, M.A.K. (1979) 'One child's protolanguage'. M. Bullowa (ed.) *Before speech.* Cambridge, Cambridge University Press: 171–88.

Halliday, M.A.K. (1981) 'Three aspects of children's language development: learning language, learning through language, learning about language'. Y.K. Goodman, M.M. Haussler & D.S. Strickland (eds) *Oral and written language development: impact on schools: Proceedings from the 1979 and 1980 IMPACT conferences.* International Reading Association & National Council of Teachers of English: 7–19.

Halliday, M.A.K. (1994) *An introduction to functional grammar.* Second edn. London, Edward Arnold.

Halliday, M.A.K. & Ruqaiya Hasan (1976) *Cohesion in English.* London, Longman.

Halliday, M.A.K. & Ruqaiya Hasan (1985) *Language, context, and text: aspects of language in a social-semiotic perspective.* Geelong, Vic., Deakin University Press (republished by Oxford University Press, 1989).

Hasan, Ruqaiya (1985) 'Meaning context and text – fifty years after Malinowski'. J.D. Benson & W.S. Greaves (eds) *Systemic perspectives on discourse* Vol. 1 *Selected theoretical papers from the 9th International Systemic Workshop* (Advances in discourse processes Vol. 15). Norwood, NJ, Ablex: 16–49.

Hasan, Ruqaiya (1986) 'The ontogenesis of ideology: an interpretation of mother child talk'. T. Threadgold, E.A. Grosz, G. Kress, M.A.K. Halliday (eds) *Language, semiotics, ideology* (Sydney Studies in Society & Culture, No. 3). Sydney, Sydney Association for Studies in Society and Culture: 124–44.

Hasan, Ruqaiya (1992) 'Rationality in everyday talk: from process to system'. Jan Svartvik (ed.) *Directions in Corpus Linguistics: proceedings of Nobel Symposium 82, Stockholm, 4–8 August 1991.* Berlin: Mouton de Gruyter.

Hasan, Ruqaiya & C. Cloran (1990) 'A sociolinguistic interpretation of every day talk between mothers and children'. M.A.K. Halliday, J. Gibbons & H. Nicholas (eds) *Learning, keeping and using language* Vol. 1: *Selected papers from the 8th World Congress of Applied Linguistics, 1987.* Amsterdam, Benjamins: 65–99.

Hood, L. & L. Bloom (1991) 'What, when and how about why: a longitudinal study of early expressions of causality'. L.Bloom (ed.) *Language development from two to three.* Cambridge, Cambridge University Press (reprinted from the Monographs of the Society for Research in Child Development, 1979, serial no. 181, Vol. 44).

Lee, B. (1987) 'Recontextualizing Vygotsky'. M. Hickmann (ed.) *Social and functional approaches to language and thought.* New York, Academic Press: 87–104.

Macnamara, J. (1982) *Names for things.* Cambridge, MA, MIT Press.

Martin, J.R. (1992) *English text: system and structure.* Amsterdam, Benjamins.

Nelson, Katherine (1974) 'Concept, word and sentence: interrelations in acquisition and development'. *Psychological Review,* Vol. 81: 267–85.

Oldenburg, J. (1987) 'From child tongue to mother tongue: case study of language development in the first two and a half years'. PhD thesis, University of Sydney.

Painter, C. (1984) *Into the mother tongue.* London, Pinter.

Painter, C. (1989) 'Learning language: a functional view of language development'. Ruqaiya Hasan & J.R. Martin (eds) *Language development: learning language, learning culture. Meaning and choice in language: studies in honour of Michael Halliday.* Norwood, NJ, Ablex: 18–65.

Painter, C. (1991) *Learning the mother tongue.* Second edn. Geelong, Vic., Deakin University Press.

Rescorla, L. (1980) 'Overextension in early language development'. *Journal of Child Language,* 7: 321–35.

Rosch, E. (1978) 'Principles of categorisation'. E. Rosch, B. Lloyd (eds) *Cognition and categorisation.* Hillsdale, NJ, Erlbaum: 28–48.

Trevarthen, C. (1980) 'The foundations of intersubjectivity: development of interpersonal and cooperative understanding in infants'. D.R. Olson (ed.) *The social foundations of language and thought.* New York, Norton.

Trevarthen, C. & P. Hubley (1978) 'Secondary intersubjectivity: confidence, confiding and acts of meaning in the first year'. A. Lock (ed.) *Action, gesture and symbol.* London, Academic Press: 183–229.

Tversky, Barbara (1990) 'Where taxonomies and partonomies meet'. S.L. Tsohatzidis (ed.) *Meanings and prototypes.* New York, Routledge.

Vygotsky, L. (1987) *Problems of general psychology.* N. Minick (trans) New York, Plenum.

# 4

## Making changes: developing an educational linguistics

### JOAN ROTHERY

## 1 Introduction

Curriculum documents in Australian schools foreground the role of language in education in a way never seen before in Australian educational contexts. Across a range of learning areas these documents state, not only that language is learned through use, but that it varies according to the context in which it is used. This approach to language development is in marked contrast to that of earlier decades where the school subject English, or Language Arts, was seen to have sole responsibility for language development which was conceived largely in terms of students mastering traditional school grammar through exercises of parsing and analysis. The role of language in learning was not addressed and it was assumed that learning traditional school grammar would equip students to meet their language needs on all occasions.

The current situation is, however, not without considerable irony. Whereas in decades past the language system was highly visible, this is no longer the case. The language system has completely disappeared from view in schooling and in most Australian preservice teacher education courses. So successful has this effacement of language knowledge been that students and educators alike have no idea what might be known about language. The invisibility of language has itself become invisible.

As a consequence teachers' comments about students' language use are general and subjective. They rarely, if ever, suggest positive strategies for helping students to use language effective for the context. As far as writing is concerned, the strategy of encouraging students to write frequently without any constructive teacher intervention tends to mean that some students continue to write the same kinds of text in the same ways. My research (Rothery 1990) has shown that classes frequently remain stratified by the teacher in terms of *good, average* and *poor* writers and, alarmingly, membership of these groups remains constant throughout the year.

These observations locate me as an educational linguist, a practitioner who is at home in two fields: education and linguistics. It might be granted that by virtue of professional qualifications and practice, the educational linguist has significant experience in both fields, affording distinct advantages for working in each field because of this duality of practice. Given the framework of a model with sociocultural orientation to meaning such as the systemic functional model, there exists the rich possibility for developing an alternative perspective on language and learning to the psychological one that dominates current educational theory and practice. I would therefore argue that the educational linguist has the capacity and opportunity to do more than make the language system visible as a resource for meaning in contexts which aim to promote language development. A strong and rich model of language description enables us to model the curriculum in terms of its literacy requirements, to map possible paths of development in literacy and learning and to develop criteria for assessment and evaluation. In short, it offers the opportunity to develop a language-based approach to learning.

Before saying more about the work of the educational linguist, let me step back and consider briefly the impact of educational linguistics on education in more general terms. Developing an alternative theoretical perspective on literacy and learning to the prevalent psychological one is an instance of critical literacy. One requirement for developing a critical literacy is to have a substantial understanding of competing theories and practices in a field in order to make assessments about the value of the contributions they make to teaching practice, curriculum development and so on. This brings me back to the importance of recognising the educational linguist as a professional practitioner in education and linguistics. As an educator, the educational linguist is likely to be sensitive to and knowledgeable about where the teacher is coming from in terms of an orientation to language and learning. This promises the possibility of agreement between the educational linguist and the teacher on the issue of teaching/learning goals, enabling them to negotiate the knowledge and practice required for achieving these goals. The educational linguist coming from a linguistic and educational perspective thus has the opportunity to open up radical changes in curriculum interpretation and pedagogy.

From a linguistic perspective the lexicogrammar and discourse semantic analyses of texts from educational contexts test and challenge the systemic functional model of language in constructive ways. Such analyses enable an ongoing dialectic between the realisation of system in text and the construction of system networks both in the lexicogrammar and discourse semantics and in the context of situation and culture. Educational linguistics is therefore a truly transdisciplinary study and practice. It crosses two fields, not simply in an applied sense, but in the sense of playing a role in the development of theories and practice in both.

## 2    Teachers and texts: the facilitating approach

Let me demonstrate how important this transdisciplinary perspective is in working with teachers. The following narrative, *The Fight*, is one I have often used in inservice work with teachers. I want to contrast the teachers' responses to it, which show 'where they are coming from', with those an educational linguist working within the systemic functional linguistics framework might make.

### Text 1    *The Fight*

> It all happened when I was walking home from school.
>
> Two kids from my class decided to pick on me. They started yelling stupid names like spazzo, pigface etc. I didn't mind this. I also didn't mind Kelly punching me in the shoulder. What I did mind was that Kelly kept me occupied while Matthew (better known as Roberts) rode my bike around the cul de sac of the street. This was harmless. But, still riding, he kicked off my bag and jumped off the bike leaving it to fall. This made me sore. I gave in to my temper.
>
> When Matthew saw this he took off. So it was me and David Kelly to battle it out. I chased him around and around the street. When I finally caught up to him I threw punches galore. Most of them missed. Kelly managed to escape and run home.
>
> I think I was the victor, but if I was, I don't think it was worth it.

Teachers value this text highly. The principal reason they give for this is that the writer makes a strong personal response to the experience written about, e.g. *I didn't mind this; What I did mind ...; This was harmless,* and so on. Understanding why teachers see these meanings as evidence of 'good story writing' requires knowledge of how preservice education prepares teachers of English for teaching literacy. The response made by the writer to the events written about in *The Fight* is seen by teachers to be evidence of the writer's exploration of the experience, an exploration likely to contribute to the writer's personal growth and development. In fact the last sentence, *I think I was the victor, but if I was, I don't think it was worth it,* is regarded as evidence of the writer learning and growing as a person through the exploration of experience.

The interpretation of this text is made in psychological terms and reveals the dominance of psychological and individualistic views of learning and language development in educational contexts. The 'personal growth' interpretation of learning through language focused strongly on the importance of narrative (Dixon 1967). In fact it was a psychological, psychoanalytic recontextualisation of the Leavisite approach to reading literature where such reading was seen to cultivate the finer sensibilities of human beings (Leavis 1976). In teacher education this view of the role of language in learning was linked to the linguistic insight that language was learned through use by claiming students would learn through language and develop language, including the ability to vary it according to context, through frequent and varied opportunities for use.

This individualistic interpretation of what was meant by learning language through use was made within a longstanding Western conception of learning, dating back at least as far as Rousseau (1966/1762). For Rousseau, learning was seen to occur when children were placed in situations that enabled their abilities to unfold and blossom. For educators in the last three decades this came to mean if children were placed in interesting, stimulating situations for language use, learning and language development would occur (Arnold 1982). The underlying assumption is that a person's identity and intellectual capacity have, in some sense, a separate existence from and are developed apart from participation in particular sociocultural contexts.

It has become apparent to many teachers that the facilitating approach to language development does not work. But they are powerless to challenge the current orthodoxy, or to enter into an informed debate about the relationship between language and learning, and what is meant by language variation according to context. The inability to participate in such debates is a direct consequence of language study having been removed from teacher education. Teachers do not have technical knowledge about the language system, the relationship between text and context, or of child language studies which document the adult's guiding, scaffolding role in adult/child linguistic interactions, a role which is crucial to children learning language and learning through language.

Another consequence of the view of learning exemplified in Rousseau's work was that social institutions and some relationships were seen to have a restrictive and inhibiting function on children's development so that the 'real' or 'natural' person could not emerge. Schools were in some sense 'artificial'. The theme is a familiar one in a range of Western discourses. It is summed up in a comment I heard in a radio discussion about the effects of schooling on children: *In flies a butterfly and out crawls a caterpillar.* These perceptions of the function of schooling make some teachers, perhaps many, ambivalent or uncertain, about their professional role. They do not see school education as a potentially empowering experience for their students.

Thus far I have given an educational linguist's assessment of 'where teachers are coming from', in respect of their education for teaching literacy. Let me now point out some of the consequences of the theoretical perspectives their teacher education has endorsed. One significant consequence is the reluctance of many teachers to engage with the literacy requirements of school subjects which are often considerable in respect of technicality and abstraction. The bodies of knowledge built up in disciplines such as Science, Geography, History, etc. are regarded by some teachers as 'second hand' knowledge for the student and therefore restrictive of their individual development. Somehow these bodies of knowledge have to be rediscovered by the students and made their own. In practice this means students are encouraged to use their 'own language' to learn a school subject. What this can mean for some is that their understanding remains at the level of everyday or commonsense knowledge. It does not proceed, for example, beyond the observable. It is acceptable, however, for so-called 'bright' students to 'pick up' the technical language of a subject and use it in their speech and writing but unacceptable for teachers to focus on it explicitly. Some students, as a consequence, write only texts about personal experience, copy out of books, or simply do not write at all.

Another serious consequence of the individualistic perspective of language development is apparent to the educational linguist working within the systemic functional linguistics framework. There is an inherent assumption in the facilitating approach to language development that students will draw similarly on a range of genres and registers to meet the requirements of school literacy. For students where there is a harmony between home and school language use this may occur. These students not only have access to a wide range of genres and registers, but also are able to make the generic and register choices that are highly valued in what Anne Cranny-Francis has called the institutional discourse of schooling (see this volume). For students from low socio-economic groups, non-English-speaking and Aboriginal backgrounds who do not have access to this range of choices and/or who do not 'read' which texts are valued in schooling, the facilitating approach is a failure.

At a Language in Education conference at Macquarie University, Sydney, in 1986 Michael Halliday said the following:

> To recognise static oscillation is to say that the something out there that is implied in terms like socialisation and language acquisition is not a homogeneous unity to which all have to conform. It is a complex structure full of divisions and discontinuities. On the linguistic side, it has its dialects and registers. It has subcultural distinctions that lie behind the dialects, and divisions of labour that lie behind the registers. At the very least, 'being socialised' means entering into and mastering a large number of discourses. Some of these may be sharply distinct from and indeed in conflict with each other. The different socialising agencies, the home, the neighbourhood and the school, may of course present discontinuities of this type; that is the point of Bernstein's discussion of home and school. They have somehow to be reconciled or at least transcended.
>
> (Halliday 1988: 7)

The facilitating approach cannot meet such challenges, since it offers teachers no means for identifying the genre and register resources or the coding orientations children bring with them to school.

As Bernstein points out, intra-organism theories of development acknowledge the role of social interaction in learning or developing competencies, but they see interaction as occurring

'with culturally non-specific others' (Bernstein 1990). The discon-
nection of the cultural from the social has been a major factor
in enabling the development and maintenance of facilitating
pedagogies.

## 3    A linguistic perspective on writing in the classroom

Let me now return to the narrative *The Fight* and consider its construction from a systemic functional perspective. Just as the focus
on social interaction failed to take account of the culturally
specific other, so the focus on the exploration of self through language fails to take account of text as a culturally specific object
which mediates the expression of experience and the response to
it. All the story genres foreground interpersonal meanings, often
in a stage of the generic structure. In narrative it is the Evaluation
stage (Plum 1988; Rothery 1990). These meanings give significance to the events under focus. This construction of story is
culturally determined. There is no way we can tell from the text
whether these meanings have a truth value in terms of the
narrator's response to experience.

In describing something of the structure of story genres I am
anticipating myself. This understanding of one aspect of the structure of story was part of seven years research into identifying the
genres of the primary school curriculum and their linguistic construction, which I undertook in collaboration with Jim Martin of
Sydney University's Linguistics Department. The perspective of
teachers on literacy and learning that I have referred to above,
together with the prevailing pedagogy of facilitation, gave Jim
Martin and myself the impetus to investigate literacy in the primary school from a sociocultural and linguistic perspective. It was
the first step in our efforts to develop a language-based approach
to teaching and learning.

In the first stage of our research we addressed three questions:

1. What text types, or genres, as Martin ultimately called them,
   were children writing in the primary school?
2. Which genres were important in learning the primary school
   curriculum?
3. How could we teach them so that students would be given
   the maximum opportunity for accessing and learning the
   curriculum?

We already had some ideas about the answer to the first question, as I had conducted a pilot study in which I analysed some hundreds of texts written by children in years 1–6 of the primary school. The pilot study reported on in Martin and Rothery (1980; 1981) identified a small group of agnate narrative-type genres – **observation/comment** (later called **observation**), **recount** and **narrative** – and also a factual strand: **report, exposition** and **literary criticism**. Observation lists events, there is no temporal sequence. The events are given significance through expressions of attitude, and reaction. Recount deals with a sequence of events. Generally speaking, it is about how the participants 'get from point A to point B'. For example, students typically write recounts about school excursions. Narrative is about the disruption of usuality in a sequence of events, which, as a consequence, create a problem for those involved in them. The participants confront the problem and attempt to overcome it (Rothery 1990). The report genre describes 'the way things are' according to the principles of Western science. Exposition argues a case for or against a thesis while literary criticism evaluates another text. It is important to note, because it is often overlooked by some critics of genre-based literacy work, that the texts were distinguished on the basis of distinctive differences in lexicogrammatical and discourse semantic choices which construct the function of the stages of the genres. The function label given to a generic structure stage serves to identify succinctly the meanings constructed linguistically. The results of the pilot study showed that observation and recount were the narrative types written most frequently but narrative, when it occurred, was more highly valued than other narrative types or scientific reports.

The large-scale study of The Writing Project, which commenced in 1983, resulted in the collection and generic structure analysis of more than 2,000 texts from a Sydney primary school (Martin 1984; Martin & Rothery 1984). Similar results to that of the pilot study emerged also from the analysis of this data, shown in Table 4.1.

Narrative types constituted a little over 77 per cent of the sample. Moreover, the only story genre all students gained experience in writing was observation, the least valued of the story genres. Factual types constituted 18 per cent (rounded figure). Nevertheless, the fact that some children were choosing to write scientific reports from the first years of schooling challenges the

**Table 4.1**   Types of writing in primary school: results of a genre analysis (after Martin & Rothery 1984)

|  | picture description genre | Story genres | | | Factual genres | | |
|---|---|---|---|---|---|---|---|
|  |  | observation | recount | narrative | report | procedure | exposition/ explanation |
| *N* | 113 | 1020 | 540 | 229 | 367* | 32 | 17 |
| Per cent | 4.87 | 44.00 | 23.29 | 9.87 | 15.83 | 1.38 | 0.73 |

Total texts examined: 2,318

[Description = 4.87%; Story = 77.16%; Factual = 17.94%]

\* Although in all there wre 376 reports, it is interesting to note that over 30 per cent of these were written by just one Year 3 male pupil. So the true picture is nearer 90 per cent story genre of one kind or another.

hypothesis by Britton, Burgess, Martin, McLeod and Rosen (1975) that factual writing develops from what they call the expressive writing, a type that seems close to observation in its structure.

The results of these studies were illuminating, not only because of the information they gave about what students were writing but also because of the information we received from teachers about the role of literacy in learning the curriculum. It was apparent from discussions with the teachers that they identified texts mainly as 'stories' and 'reports' but there was no consistency about what was included in these categories, nor could they give criteria for distinguishing them. Different types of story were not explicitly recognised although narrative was the most highly valued. This meant the classroom situation for writing was potentially a confusing one for students as they might be told to write 'a story' or 'a report' in different areas of the curriculum without having a clear understanding of what type of writing was required or of its role in learning.

The privileging of story in literacy was an important finding, as was the valuing of narrative within 'story'.[1] Writing in the primary school meant mainly writing stories. This focus was a consequence of the influence of both the personal growth model (Britton 1970; Dixon 1967) and the process approach advocated by Graves (1979, 1981, 1983). Regardless of the curriculum area, there was a focus on writing about and exploring personal experience as a means for learning. As a consequence, reading and writing genres that were important in learning Science and Social Science, for example, were largely ignored. Even if teachers wished to pursue developing literacy in these fields, they had no knowledge of the generic and register demands of the subjects to inform their classroom teaching.

The valuing of narrative above observation and recount was well documented not only in the pilot but also in the two large-scale studies which I undertook later for my own postgraduate research (Rothery 1990). In all three studies observation and recount were more frequent than narrative but when narrative occurred it was more highly valued. The same hidden curriculum for story writing in junior secondary English was revealed by Rothery and Macken (1991) when they analysed a set of sample texts written in response to the Writing Task of the 1987 English Reference Test, a public examination for Year 10 students in New South Wales. The task gave students a choice of topics and asked them to write about one in any form they chose. Story genres, particularly narrative, received the top gradings even though there were well-written factual texts. Perhaps the hidden curriculum was most obviously revealed in the examiner's comment about an advertisement: according to this examiner, the advertisement 'lacked plot and characterisation'.

## 4   A generic perspective on *The Fight* as a narrative

If we examine the generic structure of narrative as exemplified in *The Fight* we can develop some understanding of why it is given such a high status, not only in school writing but in novels and films in the broader community.

The stages of *The Fight* are Orientation^Complication/ Evaluation^Resolution^Coda. (Coda is an optional stage in narrative as are Abstract and Synopsis.) In *The Fight*, Evaluation is interspersed with Complication, shown by the '/' notation. Evaluation can also occur as a discrete stage. Lexicogrammatical and discourse semantic analyses show clearly that narrative can be identified as a distinct story type on the basis of changing patterns of linguistic choices in different parts of the text. The first stage, Orientation, is an 'orienting' one where, usually, characters are introduced and settings established. This is followed by a stage, Complication, in which a usual pattern of events is disrupted in some way, thus causing a problem for one or more of the

**Table 4.2**    The schematic structure of *The Fight*

|  | ***The Fight*** |
|---|---|
| **Orientation** | It all happened when I was walking home from school. |
| **Complication/ Evaluation** | Two kids from my class decided to pick on me. They started yelling stupid names like spazzo, pigface etc. I didn't mind this. I also didn't mind Kelly punching me in the shoulder. What I did mind was that Kelly kept me occupied while Matthew (better known as Roberts) rode my bike around the cul de sac of the street. This was harmless. But, still riding, he kicked off my bag and jumped off the bike leaving it to fall. This made me sore. I gave in to my temper. |
| **Resolution** | When Matthew saw this he took off. So it was me and David Kelly to battle it out. I chased him around and around the street. When I finally caught up to him I threw punches galore. Most of them missed. Kelly managed to escape and run home. |
| **Coda** | I think I was the victor, but if I was, I don't think it was worth it. |

participants involved in them. Then follows a stage where the 'unusuality' of the events is evaluated to give them significance. (As noted previously, Evaluation can be interspersed with Complication.) The next stage, Resolution, usually the final one, is where the main character/s confront the problem and attempt to overcome it. The Coda gives a retrospective overall evaluation of the narrative's events. Although Labov and Waletzky (1967) give no functional explanation for their choice of labels, the labels seem appropriate ones for the meanings constructed in each of the narrative stages. Hence I adopted them in my analysis of narrative texts.

In Western cultures we learn to regard events whose outcome is problematic for the participants as entertaining and intriguing. There is a sense of suspense we find enjoyable in reading to find out 'how it all ends'. But narrative has a powerful instructional message which distinguishes it from other story genres. It teaches us, as individuals, to confront problems and attempt to overcome them. Life, it tells us, is always likely to take unexpected turns in respect of the pattern of events we are involved in. But we need to be motivated to address the problems such changes cause for us and attempt to return events to a state of usuality as we understand it in our culture. Narrative, in other words, embodies an ideology which focuses strongly on the role of the individual in society and the power of the individual to shape the course of events s/he is involved in. It is, of course, an ideology that is central to Western capitalist cultures. It is little wonder, therefore, that among the story types outlined narrative is so highly valued in school and community.

## 5   Making changes in the pedagogic scene

To get to this point in our research was exciting because the possibilities for making significant changes that would benefit students' learning were becoming apparent. To actually begin to make changes was another matter. Clearly, the next phase of our work was 'action research' where I needed to work with teachers in their classrooms to identify 'across the curriculum' literacy requirements and to develop a pedagogy that would enable students to access them. I am indebted to Geoff Williams of the University of Sydney, without whose assistance this stage would almost certainly have taken much longer to organise. Luckily, with his help I was able to work with two teachers in a Sydney primary school for two to three days a week for almost a year.

Some crucial policy decisions were made before the classroom work began about the direction of this research stage. The first was that the focus of the in-class work would be on curriculum goals and the role of literacy in achieving them. The curriculum focus was, and is, attractive to teachers because it places educational concerns at the centre of the work. This is particularly important, as teachers need to feel that their work and their students' learning will benefit from a literacy focus.

The second decision was that the literacy focus would be on texts and their generic structure. The genre focus was also attractive to teachers because it involved working with whole texts. Teachers, like most of us, have a sense of the semantic unity of written texts, usually in terms of a staging such as Introduction, Body and Conclusion. We capitalised on this understanding but, through the functional language model, gave it sociocultural dimensions in terms of social purpose achieved through the function of stages. Thus the text was given a functional role in learning the curriculum and its role in the wider community was identified. For example, expositions argue a case for or against a thesis. This way of arguing is important in learning in a number of curriculum learning areas and is also important for participating in the community whether for writing a letter of complaint about a service, for example, or taking up a position about environmental issues in a submission to a government agency. At present many students in schools designated as disadvantaged[2] do not see themselves as being able to participate successfully in the school or community in these ways. All in all, genre was a productive category for teachers and students to work with.

There were also practical decisions to be made about how to work with the teachers in the classroom. Again, I had made some decisions in advance. The first was that I would spend several weeks in the classrooms as an observer/assistant. The importance of the observation stage cannot be overestimated. Using the systemic functional linguist framework, the educational linguist can assess and evaluate how language is used for learning and for regulating student behaviour. Some of the assessment is made on the basis of text analysis. Some is made informally, on the run, so to speak. Some of the questions I addressed were:

- What genres and registers are students reading and writing?
- How do the teachers prepare students for writing?
- What is the role of 'the oral rehearsal' of text as part of the preparation for writing?
- How are interpersonal meanings used to negotiate teacher/ student relationships in the classroom and in the school?

Overall the first stage was one of information gathering which provided input for the planning and teaching stages. It was also a time for gaining the trust of teacher and students so the educational linguist's participation in classroom activities is accepted and welcomed as a constructive contribution.

On the first occasion of my classroom work the teachers readily saw the value of this stage and asked me to give them feedback on my observations regarding their teaching strategies and the texts their students wrote. In subsequent work, particularly in the secondary school, it has sometimes been difficult to convince teachers of its worth. This, in itself, is significant. It seems to indicate that teachers are unaccustomed to reviewing their classroom practice reflectively and analytically. Again, this is likely to stem from a lack of tools enabling them to take up a reflective role, in particular tools provided by knowledge about language, which would enable them to monitor and reflect on their own and their students' language use in contexts where teachers and students are working towards the achievement of particular learning goals (Macken & Rothery 1991). This analysis and reflection is crucial for assessing and planning classroom work. It may, for example, lead to a choice for 'backtracking' to consolidate learning that students are having difficulty with, perhaps using different materials and strategies. There are many different decisions that could result from this reflective practice. Without it, however, teachers are reduced to saying, *That didn't work, but I don't really know why*, or *That did work, so I'll forge ahead*. They are working intuitively rather than with finely honed analytic tools. So, in a very practical way, here we come up against some of the serious pedagogical consequences that have arisen from rendering language invisible in educational contexts.

The second decision I made was that the teacher would decide on the area of the curriculum she wished students to work in and I would work cooperatively with her to plan and teach the literacy she thought important in learning that part of the curriculum. The role I would take in the classroom would be guided by her decision. It could be an observer, a team teacher, a small group or class teacher. In the course of a unit of work all of these might be incorporated.

The third decision Jim Martin and I made was that we would develop an interventionist pedagogy, where the teacher would have a well-defined teaching role. We saw such a pedagogy as the means for giving all students the maximum opportunity to access the curriculum. The implementation of this decision in our pedagogic program has led to some educators making some unwarranted assumptions. For some, a teaching role is synonymous with an authoritarian stance in the classroom where students are passive recipients of 'teacher talk'. There seems to be no justification for this assumption, either from the pedagogy's research base or its classroom implementation. Our decision was based on the insights gained from child language studies (Halliday 1975; Painter 1985) where the adult caretaker typically takes up various roles to assist children in learning language and learning through language. Adults frequently and regularly take up a 'telling' role with children, where, simultaneously, knowledge is presented linguistically and genres are modelled.[3] They also guide and scaffold adult/child linguistic interaction by asking questions and making comments about shared experiences so that texts are produced as a joint construction, a strategy which is also a modelling one as it 'leads' children into the production of genres without having to take sole responsibility for the production of text. It seemed to us these pre-school pedagogical practices provided a sound basis for the development of a classroom pedagogy (Rothery 1986).

The intervention stage was one of trial, error and reflection. Both teachers wanted to work on various types of factual writing, as well as narrative. They were well aware that literacy, even in Grade Two, had a crucial part to play in learning Science and Social Science but they were unsure about what generic goals were relevant and how they could teach them to students. For some of the literacy tasks we could identify generic goals. For others we were not sure what genre or genres the students would write. Jim Martin and I closely examined the texts written by the pupils. We grouped and re-grouped them as we sought to identify the social purpose of the texts and the function of their stages through lexicogrammar and discourse semantic analyses.

On the basis of these analyses, we ultimately identified **procedure**, **report**, **explanation**, **exposition** and **discussion** as genres important in learning across the curriculum in the primary school. Procedure, the genre that enables us to do or make things, is important in learning Science and Social Science and makes possible students' participation in activities in the Creative Arts area, Physical Education, etc. Reports describe 'the way things are' according to Western scientific principles. Explanations explain how natural and technological phenomena come into being. Reports and explanations are important in learning Science and Social Science. Exposition and discussion are genres of persuasion and are written across the curriculum. In exposition a case is argued for or against a thesis. In discussion arguments are presented from more than one point of view about an issue. The students found the writing interesting and challenging. One was overheard saying: 'It makes you feel grown-up doing writing like this.' In the course of the classroom work teacher and students built up a metalanguage for talking about texts and the function of their stages.

During the course of the classroom work I was operating on two levels. At one level I was engaged in the planning and implementation of the classroom activities aimed at developing literacy and learning in a given part of the curriculum. At another level, using the systemic functional linguistic framework I was tracking and reflecting upon the way classroom activities were developing: the way the field was being opened up; the nature of the student participation; the type and suitability of texts available for student reading; the negotiation of the build-up of field knowledge; the movement of students from the oral to the written mode in their oral rehearsal of what they intended to write. On each occasion I was in the classroom the teacher and I would spend some time reflecting on the pedagogy in this way and also, if applicable, on the texts the students were writing or had completed. The teacher was thus guided into using language that would enable her to reflect on her implementation of the teaching/learning strategies which she could use when the educational linguist was no longer present.

This activity was most productive for both parties. On one occasion we were puzzled by a set of texts that included procedures and explanations. The intended literacy goal was explanation, the genre which enables us to account for natural and technological phenomena according to Western scientific knowledge. In fact, some students wrote procedures, texts which instruct about how to do or make something. We had asked students to investigate how a machine of their choice worked. It was a demanding task for primary school students, but they were carefully guided and scaffolded into building their field knowledge. Nevertheless, some students, when it came to writing, wrote about how to work the machine. As we looked back on the activities it became apparent that we had not clearly distinguished 'how it works' from 'how to work it'. It is a significant step for teachers to locate the most likely cause of the literacy problems in the pedagogy rather than in the students' cognition.

## 6   The schematic structure of pedagogic intervention

The pedagogy the teachers and I developed to enable students to access the curriculum has remained central to our work, although it is still evolving. We have always represented it as a circle (see Figure 4.1) to indicate there are different points of entry for students according to their development in learning and literacy. We have always shown the possibility for recursion so that, for example, after jointly constructing a text with the teacher, students may do more work on deconstruction before undertaking another joint construction. The teacher will make this decision, not on the basis of so-called student 'failure' but on the basis of her/his assessment of what students need to learn in order to work on a joint construction more successfully.

The stages of the cycle as shown in bold on the circumference of Figure 4.1 are:

1. Negotiating Field
2. Deconstruction
3. Joint Construction
4. Independent Construction

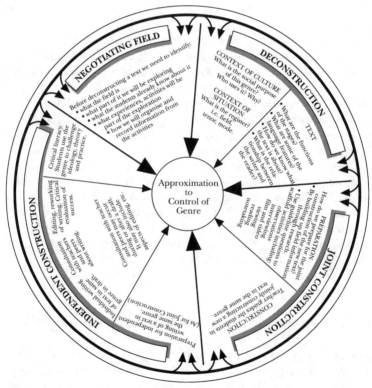

**Figure 4.1**    The teaching cycle

The labelling of the stages of the cycle gives teachers and students a metalanguage for the pedagogy. The metalanguage enables both parties to make explicit the part played by each stage in achieving the literacy goal of a given unit of work. In the stage called **Negotiating Field** the teacher and students' exploration of the field would be from a specific end-point in mind. For example, if students are going to write an exposition about whether or not animals should be kept in zoos, they need to build up knowledge about how some of the animals found in zoos live in their natural habitat. However, before they come to this, their initial exploration is likely to be a sharing of knowledge about the behaviour of pets they are familiar with. In the course of exploring the field there will, thus, be a movement from everyday to educational knowledge. The extent of this movement will vary according to the knowledge students already have of the field. Generally, however, the field focus will become narrower and sharper as the teacher prepares the students for reading a model text. Bernstein's (1971) concepts of classification and framing are useful for mapping the changing emphases in this stage. Initially, weak classification will be involved in the field exploration as the students will need to range widely to build up knowledge about animals. However, the classification will become stronger as students build up biological knowledge about animals' behaviour. Similarly, initially, the framing is expected to be weak while students choose the areas they are going to explore, but as the work progresses the teacher will need to take a more strongly guiding role in pointing students towards types of texts and areas of knowledge relevant to understanding the text or texts students need to read in the Deconstruction stage. It is clear that throughout the Negotiating Field stage teacher and students will be cooperatively building up a shared knowledge of the field. This is tantamount to saying that at the same time the students will be learning the language of the field, since the two are inseparable: we cannot know the field unless we know the language of the field.

The **Deconstruction** stage is designed to introduce the students to model texts of the genre dealing with the field that the students have already explored: the aim is to familiarise them with the genre so that they can 'read' it and deconstruct it. The students learn how the genre works to achieve its social purpose through the function of its stages. Just as they have built up some technical language about the field, so they now build up a metalanguage about text and language. With the teacher's assistance students also explore the role of the genre under focus in school learning and in the life of the community.

The Deconstruction stage makes possible the **Joint Construction** by providing, through the metalanguage, a scaffolding for teacher and students to use in jointly constructing a text. However, before students embark on a joint construction they need to build up the field knowledge they will draw on in jointly constructing a text. In the early stages the students need to be taught research strategies such as locating sources of information, notemaking and summarising. Questions to scaffold the research are essential. Once this preparation is complete teacher and students are ready for the Joint Construction.

As I have already remarked (see section 5), this stage was developed on the basis of our understanding of how pre-school children develop language through interacting with adult caregivers. The adult's guiding, scaffolding role in the context of shared experience enables the child to contribute to the construction of the text. Here are two examples both from Painter (1986: 76 and 77, respectively):

**Text 2    The moth** [Child 29 months, talking to mother]

H:    I break a moth. I find a moth. I break it all up.
M:    Where did you find it?
H:    In the laundry. I found it in the laundry.

**Text 3    Visit to the beach** [Child 27 months, talking to father]

F:    What have you been doing today?
H:    All sorts of things.
F:    Where did you go?
H:    On the beach.
F:    Did you find straws and cups and things (as usual)?
H:    Yes … (pause) … not cups.
F:    What else did you do?
H:    Erm, run around. Go in the water; with Mummy. Mummy and Hal.
F:    Was it cold in the water?
H:    Yeah!!

In text 2, the mother's question *Where did you find it?* elicits additional information about place. Grammatically, Hal's response specifies a Circumstance of Location: place. Through exchanges of this kind, he comes to realise what kind of information is relevant to talking about the events one may be recounting. In text 3, Hal's father asks him about an outing with his mother, a type of outing Hal's father has often been involved in himself. Again, the father's questions prompt the child's responses and 'teach' him about the kind of information worth talking about. Notice the focus on what was different – *Was it cold in the water?* – as well as on usuality – *Did you find straws and cups and things?*.

In the Joint Construction stage the teacher is expected to take up a similar role with the the whole class, or with a small group. Her questions would thus guide and scaffold the students' responses to construct the meanings of the genre. (The students will already have built up class notes which they could refer to during this stage.)

The teacher, while accepting the students' offerings, may still need to ask for additional information, just as the parent does with the child. In the classroom, however, one aim will be to engage as many students as possible in the joint construction. The teacher will also have another role, that of guiding children into the language of the written mode. This is likely to involve her in rewording some of the students' contributions, and thus modelling for them the language of written texts. Here is a short section of a transcript of a recording of the joint construction of an exposition about whether children should go to school, which illustrates how the teacher guides students to shift from the oral to the written mode:

**Text 4    From speaking to writing** [From a Year 6, Joint Construction stage]

T.   What will you tell me? How could you start it for me? Oh you've already written an introduction.
     Well, you start for me. Looking at those, remember we've got the introduction there, we've got some ideas: instead of being bored at home, free education, and what was the other thing we've got included? And parents don't have to look after you while you are at school. Phillipa.

S:   *I strongly believe that children should go to school so they can learn a wide range of subjects, so they can get a job so they can support a family.*

T:   Right. Who can expand on that? Lisa.

S:   *I strongly believe that children should go to school for these main reasons: um, and I'm going to list them all.*

T:    Sorry, keep going again.
S:    *For these main reasons.*
T:    *For these main reasons.* Who can think of a different word other than main? Who can think of another word?
S:    For these reasons shown here.
T:    For these reasons written here.
      OK. Who thinks *main reasons?* Hands up, quick! A show of hands. *Main? These listed?* I've forgotten what the other ones were. *Following?* OK. Looks like *following.*
      *For the following reasons.*

Phillipa's offering for the opening sentence of the exposition is 'very spoken' with its succession of consequential conjunctions:

> I *strongly believe that children should go to school so they can learn a wide range of subjects, so they can get a job so they can support a family.*

She has, however, presented her thesis and introduced the arguments to be developed at greater length. Her use of the consequential conjunctions makes it difficult to develop an ordering of arguments by using internal conjunctions in the paragraphs to follow. To do this smoothly the writer needs to use grammatical metaphor. The teacher accepts Phillipa's response but asks for an expansion which is given by Lisa:

> I *strongly believe that children should go to school for these main reasons: um, and I'm going to list them.*

Lisa uses a grammatical metaphor *reasons*, but then shifts into language closer to the oral mode, *and I'm going to list them.* By using *reasons* rather than a succession of conjunctions, the way is open to list a number of arguments and then deal with each in turn through internal conjunctions such as *first, secondly* and so on. The teacher then focuses on alternative choices for the Classifier *main* in the nominal group *main reasons.* (The students in this Year 6 were familiar with these 'metalinguistic' terms from previous work they had already done on exposition.) Finally, the class votes on the choice of Epithet, and by consensus *for the following reasons* is favoured.

This short excerpt from a thirty-page transcript exemplifies another aspect of this pedagogy. It is time consuming when students are learning in a field new to them and working with a given genre for the first time in the written mode. But the time spent on stages in the teaching/learning cycle, and the choice of stages will change as students move towards becoming confident, independent learners. Gradually, the scaffolding will be removed as students undertake their own research and are able to move into the final stage of the cycle, Independent Construction, without working through the Deconstruction and Joint Construction stages. Clearly, students are likely to progress at different rates so we are not looking at a 'lock-step' sequence in the cycle. Some students may need to do more work than others on Deconstruction before moving on to the Joint Construction stage. Others may need to do more than one Joint Construction. Meeting the students' needs for different rates of progression requires flexibility and highly developed skills of classroom organisation on the part of the teacher.

The final stage of the pedagogic cycle is **Independent Construction** where students, after undertaking field research (if it is required), write their own texts. During this stage there is the opportunity for consultation with teacher and peers before the final draft is written.

The conception of the pedagogy just described has been adopted by teachers in many schools in different states of Australia. Teachers have tested it in their practice and found that it provides strategies for planning, teaching and assessment which enable them to work productively with students to promote development in language and learning. Although the cycle foregrounds literacy, in fact students are talking and listening as well as reading and writing. There is thus an integration, as syllabuses recommend, of what they describe as the four modes of language use.

In terms of literacy and learning in the primary school, the research has had far-reaching implications. We have been able to demonstrate that, with good teaching, students are able to write factual genres such as report and exposition which have traditionally been considered beyond the abilities of primary school children. We have also been able to give a balance to literacy and learning in the primary school curriculum which had previously been lacking. Science and Social Science had not been sites for developing literacy in the sense of identifying the literacy crucial to learning in those areas. With the changes introduced by this pedagogy, story still has an important place in the curriculum, but it is no longer foregrounded, or treated as the only kind of writing to be undertaken regularly, as was previously the case.

The results of the primary school research were reported at the

Australian Reading Association Conference in Perth in 1986 in two papers written by Martin and myself.[4] The papers caused some controversy at the conference, but they placed genre-based pedagogy on the educational linguistics agenda. One important consequence was that the Disadvantaged Schools Program in the Metropolitan East Region of Sydney decided to introduce the 'genre-based' approach to literacy into inservice programs for primary schools in their region. The literacy and learning needs of students in DSP schools, many of whom are from non-English-speaking backgrounds, are urgent and teachers in these schools are often acutely aware of how ill-equipped they are to address them effectively. In view of this it was not surprising for this program to conclude that we had much to offer teachers and students. The DSP Centre at Erskineville in Sydney has now become a major site for developing language-based approaches to learning.

## 6.1    Continuing research in educational linguistics: junior secondary years

The second phase of research into students' development of learning and literacy has taken us into the junior secondary years of schooling. Again, after some initial pilot research and intervention in classrooms, mainly in English and Science, a major research project, 'Write it Right', was set up by the Disadvantaged Schools Program and the Education Training Foundation of New South Wales. Its brief was to research the literacy requirements of the key learning areas of English, Science, Mathematics, Creative Arts, Technology and Applied Studies, and Human Society and its Environment in the junior secondary years (7–10). The products of this research are expected to appear in the form of a book describing the literacy requirements for each learning area, including units of work for classroom use and a video to introduce teachers to 'the package'. The units of work are developed and trialled by teachers in conjunction with the researcher so the pattern of cooperative action research established in the primary school has been carried through into the secondary school phase. Ultimately, the products will be an inservice package for teachers.

A new dimension was added to the project by including a brief to research literacy in workplaces[5] where links could be made between the workplace literacy and specific areas of school literacy. This explicit sociocultural focus on literacy is a phenomenon of the late twentieth century. It has largely come about because of rapid and marked changes in approaches to 'skilling' and promotion in the workforce, changes which have brought a new awareness of the role of both oral language and literacy in the professional development of all employees from the factory floor upwards.

At the moment of writing this chapter, the research into the literacy requirements of school English and Science is complete, as is the industry-related research for Science. Research into the other school learning areas and their industry-related areas is under way, and it would be premature to attempt a report on these projects. Let me, however, comment briefly on some of the findings for secondary school literacy; I will do this after a discussion of some more general issues regarding educational linguistics in the secondary school.

Subject, or learning areas, in the secondary school are defined as discrete bodies of knowledge. In Bernstein's (1971) terms there is a strong classification of knowledge. This definition is apparent from the division of the school day into time periods allocated to different learning areas and from the roles of secondary teachers who teach subjects in which they have specialised during their own tertiary education. The generic focus, although still vital in articulating learning and literacy requirements, is insufficient for identifying what is involved in using literacy to learn the various subjects included in the secondary school curriculum. To tackle this task effectively the researchers had to examine closely the language of the field and the various modes students were expected to employ as part of learning a subject, for example, graphs and diagrams in Science and Social Science. In English particularly, we had to examine how tenor relationships were constructed in language as these are vital for positioning the reader to read the message or theme of a narrative text in a particular way. In other words, in the terms of Martin's stratified model of context (Martin 1992), our involvement with secondary school literacy involves exploring both the registers of secondary school subjects as well as their genres.

During this stage of our research, what we did by characterising curriculum goals in terms of genre and register was to identify these bodies of knowledge as socially constructed. For example, one aspect of learning science in the Western tradition involves explaining how natural phenomena come into being through a sequence of cause-and-effect relationships. Another aspect is classifying living and non-living matter according to taxonomic principles. Yet another is carrying out experiments within the framework of scientific method, through the steps of a procedure. Scientific knowledge is not static but evolving, and, as is the case with most disciplines in our culture, it is the site for competing theories for explaining the phenomena with which it deals. Thus, arguably, we can view Science as a set of texts which students must be able to access, according to the stage they are at in their learning, in order to learn the discipline. This perspective is important because it again highlights the crucial role of pedagogy. In taking up this perspective with all school subjects, we are involved in shifting the culture of schooling from a psychological to a sociocultural orientation. As educators, as well as linguists, we are concerned with characterising school subjects in ways that will help us teach students to learn them effectively.

## 6.2  *Junior secondary English and the story genres*

With these general remarks as a preface, let me now turn to junior secondary English where my own research took place, both exemplifying some matters already raised about the way the educational linguist characterises the curriculum, and also presenting another dimension to the secondary school research. Through deconstructing the New South Wales Syllabus for English 7–10, classroom observation, and through the analysis of student texts – particularly the sample ones published to exemplify gradings in the state-wide English Reference Test – we identified a set of key genres for English. These are shown in Figure 4.2.

Clearly story and response are at the heart of English, although the persuasive writing of exposition and discussion is rapidly becoming more important as new syllabuses in the senior school focus on community issues in relation to literature and popular culture (a distinction still made in the majority of New South Wales school English faculties). For teachers, the distinction of different types of story (Plum 1988; Rothery 1990, 1993) was new, as was the identification of four response genres. Yet these genres 'exist' in the culture, and, most importantly, some are more highly valued than others. As noted already, narrative is more highly valued than observation and recount among the story genres.

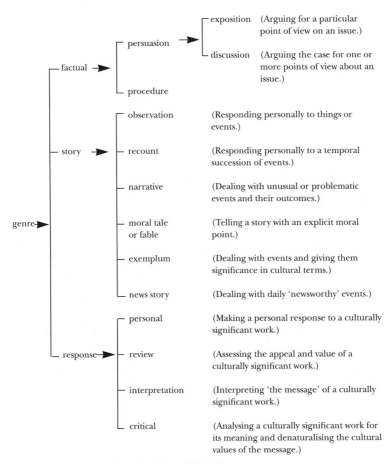

**Figure 4.2**   Genres in school English 7–10

Among the response genres, interpretation is more highly valued than personal response and review. In identifying the story and response genres in terms of their staging and some aspects of their linguistic construction, we were articulating some of the literacy requirements of junior secondary English in ways that enabled teachers to teach them.

My discussions with teachers of junior secondary English revealed that they felt unsure about planning for development in literacy across Years 7–10. They were very conscious of a gap between the literacy requirements of junior and senior English.

To address the issue of development we took into account field and tenor choices as well as the generic choice. This approach to development will be exemplified by examining a possible path of development for writing narrative, the most highly valued of the story genres (Figure 4.3).

| Genre | Register | |
|-------|----------|--|
| | *Field* | *Tenor* |
| **Subversive narrative** ↑ | Two fields in tension, cultural values denaturalised through tension. | Writer/reader relationship:<br>– Challenging reader to become involved in the intersection of familiar and unfamiliar fields. |
| **Thematic narrative** ↑ | Two fields in tension, (not projected) cultural values naturalised through tension. | Writer/reader relationship:<br>– Inviting readers to become involved in the intersection of familiar and unfamiliar fields.<br>– Reconciling evaluation of field disruption with a naturalising meta value or message. |
| **Projecting narrative** ↑ | Two fields related by projection: commonsense projects technical/fantasy/historical. | Writer/reader relationship:<br>– Guiding the reader in the semiotic construct of alternative realities.<br>– Challenging the reader to evaluate the present with respect to possible fields of activity. |
| **Science fiction narrative** ↑ | Specialised, technical science fiction/fantasy. | Writer/reader relationship:<br>– Challenging reader to develop consciousness of community relations.<br>– Disturbing reader with disruption of familiar behaviour by alien community. Constructs a need for participants to intervene to redress disruption. |
| **Narrative** | Commonsense: actual, potentially actual. | Writer/reader relationship:<br>– Sharing experience.<br>– Sharing response to disruption of field events and their problematic outcome. Constructs a need for participants to intervene to redress disruption. |

**Figure 4.3**   Paths of development: from narrative to subversive narrative

The point of mapping a possible path of development is to show accessible starting points for writing and to show how other choices build on these so that students develop their writing abilities in a cumulative fashion. This pattern of a spiral curriculum development is closely associated with the American educator Jerome Bruner (1963, 1968), who saw effective learning as a process of students building on previous knowledge in a way that enabled them to advance to different levels of understanding. For Bruner, age and readiness were not the crucial factors, but rather how students were introduced to new learning in a way appropriate for their stage of understanding and how this could be effectively built on.

A readily accessible starting point for **narrative** is writing about actual or potentially actual everyday experience. Students can draw on their own everyday experience to construct the field. Familiarity with the field allows them to concentrate on manipulating the activity sequence and the role of participants in the sequence to construct the Complication and Resolution stages. The tenor relationship between writer and reader is one of solidarity constructed through assumptions about everyday experience being shared and the response to that experience, as foregrounded in the Evaluation stage, also being shared.

From writing narratives with fields of actual experience students can move to narrative where to handle the field successfully they may have to undertake some research. **Science fiction**, for example, is a popular choice of reading among junior secondary students. If the students are already comfortable with the generic structure of narrative, they can pay more attention to fields which require research to handle them convincingly. Science fiction can have a subversive element as it has the potential to challenge the application of scientific knowledge by foregrounding the possible future negative outcomes which may result from present practice. The tenor positions the reader to feel disturbed by the events. Patterns of familiarity are disrupted in extremely unusual ways so the reader is both conscious of what is taken for granted in the present and how alienating life could become in the future. Science fiction is thus a potential site for critical literacy in narrative through its potential to challenge cultural values and practice.

The **projecting narrative**, where two fields are interwoven, challenges the writer linguistically. One field, usually that of everyday experience, projects another, invariably a world of the past, fantasy or the future. Two principal resources are mental and relational Processes (Rothery & Macken 1991). The tenor relationship positions the reader to compare the fields so that the present is evaluated in respect of the activities of another field. It is likely the linguistic resources deployed for writing the projecting narrative are similar to those drawn on for writing review, interpretation and critical response. In these genres two fields are interwoven, one of literary criticism, the other of the text written about. For many young writers, the interweaving of fields is demanding. Identifying the linguistic resources at risk and giving students experience in using them will stand them in good stead across a range of genres in English.

**Thematic narrative** embeds a message in the text. It does so by bringing two fields into tension and through this tension 'naturalises' particular cultural values which constitute the message of the text. Naturalising the cultural value is achieved through the tenor, the reader is positioned to see the values associated with the representation of one field as 'better' or 'worse' than the other. The short story *Click*, which students were asked to write about in the 1987 New South Wales English Reference Test, presents the message that one should confront reality, not hide from it. The main character, Jenny, is represented as an obsessive television viewer, a prisoner of the box! The negative values accorded television come largely from Jenny's mother's comments about her daughter's viewing and from Jenny's reactions to a TV commercial she is engrossed in. Through the attitudes of the characters, television is presented as the world of illusion. Jenny's viewing is interrupted by the sound of a police siren. When she goes outside to investigate what has happened she sees a young girl dead on the street. When she returns to her television viewing the events and characters seem phony and unreal. She turns the set off with an emphatic *Click*. In the short story a tension is set up between the world of television and that of the street accident. Television represents an illusory world while the street accident represents reality. Jenny's experiences in both and her reactions to them are the means for placing a higher value on the events of the 'real' world.

For as many students as possible to learn to 'read' the message of a thematic narrative, and to write such a text, they must understand how it is constructed to position the reader to accept the message. The deconstruction enables the reader to understand the social construction of the text. The values endorsed are not 'natural', they are socially constructed. The reader is thus in a position to challenge them if s/he so desires.

In writing a **subversive narrative** the student is constructing a thematic narrative where again two fields are in tension, but values are denaturalised through the tension. The writer is thus building on her/his prior knowledge about the construction of a thematic narrative. For example, given the values generally accepted in our culture, to construct a narrative in which the world of television was more highly valued than that of 'real life' would be regarded as subversive.

The path of development outlined for narrative is not prescriptive. Obviously, students in the junior secondary school will be at different stages in handling narrative. But it gives teachers and students a progression that opens up challenges in narrative writing and gives the teacher a way of building up narrative abilities on the basis of what students already know and can do. The generic structure of narrative is constant throughout. But the writer is involved in more complex construction of fields and of tenor relationships as s/he moves on from writing about actual experience. At the same time s/he is developing an explicit awareness of how texts are 'value laden' and how readers are positioned to see the values, in most cases, as 'natural'. In other words, what the student is learning is that the school subject English inducts her/him into mainstream cultural values in subtle and powerful ways. In developing an awareness of this a critical literacy is opened up.

In the introduction to this chapter, I pointed to the fact that the educational linguist has the potential for testing and challenging in constructive ways the model of language with which s/he is working. Our work with secondary school English provides an actual example of this. My own research into story writing in primary school had already made it clear that much more research was needed on how interpersonal meanings position the reader in relation to the events of the story genres. The research into junior secondary English made me realise that the need was even more pressing at this stage as it became obvious from my analyses and classroom intervention that the interpersonal meanings were the principal resource for naturalising or denaturalising the cultural values embedded in story genres. They were also the ones students were least conscious of, so strong was the focus on text in terms of experience. On the basis of these analyses, Martin began to write a network, ultimately identified as APPRAISAL (Martin 1993) which was tested through the analysis of texts, revised, tested and so on.[6] This dialectic between theory and practice was fruitful as the educational linguists developed a better understanding of the role of interpersonal meanings in texts, not only in school English but in History, Visual Arts, and the media, while their concern with interpersonal meanings in texts in the pedagogic sites led to the development of a general descriptive framework which is a contribution to linguistics.

## 7    Genre-based pedagogy and critical literacy

In section 1, I made a claim that a truly language-based approach to learning is an instance of critical literacy. In this section, I wish to elaborate on this statement. But before directly addressing this issue, I will first offer a view of what reading with understanding means. This is very closely related to my earlier comment that a well-informed educational linguist has the opportunity to evaluate prevailing psychological theories of literacy and learning by contrasting them with theories that are socioculturally based and language oriented, as for example the systemic functional linguistic framework is. Let me exemplify what I mean by a language-based approach making a critical difference to how one approaches the problem of literacy in the classroom. The following is a procedure that a Year 8 class was asked to act on in order to carry out a scientific experiment.

### Text 5    Seed experiment

- Collect 2 petri dishes.
- Place a thin layer of soil in one dish and some cotton wool in the other dish.
- Label the dish with soil 'soil' and the other dish 'no soil'.
- Next, place about 20 seeds in each petri dish.
- Spray each dish with water until it is damp to touch.
- Finally, put the dishes in a warm sunny spot in the classroom.

Science teachers in several schools participating in the Disadvantaged Schools Program complained that students could not 'read' scientific procedures. If the teacher demonstrates the actions the students could proceed, but they could not work directly from the text. Robert Veel[7] and I worked with a class on text 5 to 'unpack' its social purpose, that of enablement, through the language of the text. Using an overhead projector we focused on the 'action words' – i.e. verbs – that come first in most clauses. Students participated by identifying and circling these words. We also focused on *next* and *finally* as words ordering the sequence of events. From there we focused on the implicit temporal succession conjunctive relation between the first and second clauses, the second and third and the fourth and fifth clauses. From this language focus the students could see this text was one to act on and that the actions were sequenced. They were clear about its social purpose. They were now much more confident about carrying out the experiment. The procedure had not been demonstrated but some crucial language features had been made explicit. In a subsequent lesson I worked with the students in helping them organise their experiments. I became aware that some students were treating both dishes in the same way. When I pointed this out to the teacher she said she thought it was because they did not understand 'the concept of scientific method'. When I looked at the text again I saw her explanation in a different light. There was a crucial area of the language we had not worked on and that was how reference was deployed to inform the reader how each dish should be treated. In the first clause *2 petri dishes* are introduced. In the second the two dishes are separated as *one dish* and *the other dish*. In the next clause *one dish* is tracked as *the dish with soil* and the second as *the other dish*. In the third and fourth *the dishes* are referred to as *each petri dish*. Finally, the participants are brought together as *the dishes*. Instead of blaming the students' scientific method, I would argue that those students doing the same thing to each petri dish were not successfully 'keeping track' of the participants in the text as different choices were made for identifying them. The teacher who wrote the text deliberately focused on short, simple sentences to make the text easy to understand. Without a metalanguage she had no way of knowing what linguistic demands she was constructing in them, and hence could not identify the sources of difficulty students were encountering in reading that text. Her explanation in terms of students' lack of scientific method is obviously less than helpful where the students themselves are concerned.

It seems reasonable to suggest that critical literacy presupposes reading with understanding. To do this, however, one must have developed high levels of literacy which demands induction into what we can call mainstream literacy. There is a tendency in discussions of critical literacy to take this familiarity with the mainstream literacy as 'a given'. What I want to argue here is that many students in our schools, at all stages of schooling, are battling to develop a literacy that enables them to work successfully with basic syllabus requirements. Students are now faced with very uncertain employment prospects, even with high levels of literacy. With lower levels of mainstream literacy their opportunities are obviously even more diminished.[8] To ignore the significance of mainstream literacy in the workplace is to abrogate our responsibilities as educators.[9]

For teachers and students working within the systemic functional linguistics framework, there is no sudden move at any specific point from mainstream to critical literacy. There is throughout students' schooling a gradually developing critical orientation as they work with a range of texts in different genres and registers. To some extent this was demonstrated earlier in describing a possible path of development for reading and writing narrative. A first step in developing this orientation is understanding that texts are socially constructed; that they are interrelated in respect of genre and register; and that the texts with which students work are functional within the mainstream culture.

For students to make use of these understandings practically in their own work, they need to understand how context shapes text, and this in turn requires a metalanguage. Through understanding, texts are socially constructed, and having a metalanguage to talk about them, students position themselves differently in relation to texts in comparison to a view of texts as individually created constructs. For example, knowledge of narrative generic structure, as described in the discussion of *The Fight*, makes it possible for students to see how this structure helps induct readers into patterns of highly valued behaviour. At the same time knowledge of grammatical structures from a functional perspective enables students to understand how texts position readers, thus opening up the potential to challenge their meanings. Writing about grammatical metaphor, this is what Martin (1985: 32) has to say:

> Children need to learn to read texts which are full of grammatical metaphors if they are to access the information contained in them. Children need to learn to produce grammatical metaphors if they

are to write convincing Expositions. And most important, children need to learn about grammatical metaphors if they are to defend themselves from perverse ideologies masquerading as fact and truth.

It is important to recognise that language is more than a way of expressing, that in fact it creates that very thing which is to be expressed. For instance, Halliday (1991) has shown how the ideology of economic 'growthism' is constructed by certain features of the grammar of English. He notes that resources of the earth, such as air, water and soil, are not countable in the grammar and thus tend to be thought of as without limits, and so inexhaustible; that in transitivity the entities that take part in material processes are arranged by the grammar along a continuum according to their potential for initiating such processes. Human beings come at the most active end of the pole with inanimate objects located at the other. The grammar does not present inanimate objects as doers, certainly not in ongoing, constructive or conservational processes. These features of the language makes it hard for us to take seriously the notion of an inanimate nature as an active participant in events. As a consequence, we don't talk or write about what forests do in the environment, thus making their contribution to the well-being of humanity invisible. He also points out the distinction made by the grammar of mental processes where the participant is always a conscious being thus, ultimately, imposing a strict discontinuity between ourselves and the rest of creation (Halliday 1991: 27). This kind of deconstruction, which the systemic functional framework enables, opens up the possibility of challenging ideologies which so often seem 'natural' in the culture.

The ability to read closely – to deconstruct – need not necessarily construct an alternative perspective. I would argue, however, that it predisposes readers not only to challenge meanings but actively to search for alternatives. To promote alternative perspectives, in any context, without deconstructing the mainstream, may not have the outcome educators hope for. The encouragement of the personal response to literature in English in preference to a traditional literary criticism response is a good example. The personal response is not an alternative response for students who do not know what they are taking an alternative response to. The personal response does not enable students to see how texts in English 'naturalise' values. Indeed, the personal response, valuable as it may be for the reader/writer, also serves to naturalise values. It is an alternative perspective but not a critical response. I would argue strongly that if we wish readers to have the opportunity to challenge current ideologies and endorse or develop alternatives, we must focus closely on language. Halliday (1991: 17) sums it up thus:

> If language merely 'reflects' our experience of what is out there by correspondence with the categories of the material world it is hard to see how we could threaten or subvert the existing order by means of working on language. But this is what we are doing when we plan the grammar in order to combat sexism. That this makes sense is because language does not correspond, it construes.

The message is clear for educators. If we want our students to develop high levels of literacy and a critical orientation, we must engage them, at all levels, in an explicit focus on language. Not just language, but explicitness about how language works to mean, is at the heart of educational linguistics.

## Notes

1 [See, however, Carter this volume for an alternative perspective. Editors.]
2 Schools in Australia are classified as disadvantaged if the majority of parents' incomes fall within the bottom 15 per cent of the income scale on a state basis. In many areas this group coincides with people coming from non-English-speaking and Aboriginal backgrounds.
3 For a more detailed  discussion of this perspective see Painter in this volume.
4 For some of the same and/or similar issues, see Martin and Rothery (1986b, 1986c).
5 Cf Carter, this volume, on the need to focus on language in the workplace. See also Solomon, this volume, who reviews the Plain English approach to language in the workplace.
6 For a related discussion of the interpersonal, see Martin this volume; also for story reading in secondary schools, see Cranny-Francis this volume.
7 At this stage Robert Veel was a Senior Research Officer with the *Write it Right* project.
8 [See Luke this volume for an alternative view. Editors.]
9 [With specific reference to the views expressed by Rothery and those expressed by Luke in this volume, see also Carter's wry classification of left-wing positions! Editors.]

# References

Arnold, R. 1982. 'Writers, learners and self-esteem', *English in Australia* **62**, pp. 37–44.

Bernstein, B. 1971. 'On the classification and framing of educational knowledge', in Michael F.D. Young (ed.) *Knowledge and Control: New Directions for the Sociology of Education.* Collier-Macmillan: London. pp. 47–69.

Bernstein, B. 1990. 'The social construction of pedagogic discourse', in *Class, Codes and Control,* Vol. 4: *The Structuring of Pedagogic Discourse.* Routledge: London.

Britton, J. 1970. *Language and Learning.* Penguin: Harmondsworth.

Britton, J., Burgess, T., Martin, N., McLeod, A. & Rosen, H. 1975. *The Development of Writing Abilities* (11–16). Macmillan Education: London.

Bruner, J.S. 1963. *The Process of Education.* Alfred Knopf and Random House: New York.

Bruner, J.S. 1968. *Towards a Theory of Instruction.* W.W. Norton & Company Inc.: New York.

Dixon, J. 1967. *Growth through English.* National Association for the Teaching of English and the Oxford University Press: London.

Graves, D. 1979. 'What children show us about revision', *Language Arts* **56**.

Graves, D. 1981. *Donald Graves in Australia: Children Want to Write* (edited by R.D. Walshe). Primary English Teaching Association: Rosebery, New South Wales.

Graves, D. 1983. *Writing: Teachers and Children at Work.* Heinemann Educational Books: Exeter, NH.

Halliday, M.A.K. 1975. *Learning How to Mean: Explorations in the Development of Language.* Edward Arnold: London.

Halliday, M.A.K. 1988. 'Language and socialisation: home and school', in L. Gerot, J. Oldenburg & T. Van Leeuwen (eds) *Language and Socialisation: Home and School, Proceedings of the Working Conference on Language in Education, Macquarie University, Sydney, 17–21 November, 1986.* pp. 1–12.

Halliday, M.A.K. 1991. 'New ways of meaning: a challenge to applied linguistics', *Journal of Applied Linguistics* **6**, Special Issue. Greek Applied Linguistics Association. pp. 7–36.

Labov, W. & Waletzky, J. 1967. 'Narrative analysis: oral versions of personal experience', in J. Helm (ed.) *Essays in the Verbal and Visual Arts.* (American Ethnological Society – Proceedings of Spring Meeting, 1966). University of Washington Press: Washington, DC. pp. 12–44.

Leavis, F.R. 1976. *The Common Pursuit.* Penguin Books: Harmondsworth.

Macken, M. & Rothery, J. 1991. *Developing Critical Literacy: A Model for Literacy in Subject Learning. Issues in Education for the Socially and*

*Economically Disadvantaged Monograph 2*. Metropolitan East Disadvantaged Schools Program, Erskineville, New South Wales.

Martin, J.R. 1984. 'Language, register and genre', in Deakin University Production Unit (ed.) *Children Writing: A Reader.* Deakin University Press: Geelong, Vic. pp. 21–30.

Martin, J.R. 1985. *Factual Writing: Exploring and Challenging Social Reality.* Deakin University Press: Geelong, Victoria.

Martin, J.R. 1992. *English Text: System and Structure*. Benjamins: Amsterdam.

Martin, J.R. 1993. 'Grammar and feeling: a systemic approach to the semantics of affect'. Paper presented at the Australian Systemic Linguistics Conference, Adelaide, January 1993.

Martin, J.R. & Rothery, J. 1980. 'Writing Project Report Number 1', *Working Papers in Linguistics*, Department of Linguistics, University of Sydney.

Martin, J.R. & Rothery, J. 1981. 'Writing Project Report Number 2', *Working Papers in Linguistics*, Department of Linguistics, University of Sydney.

Martin, J.R. & Rothery, J. 1984. 'Choice of genre in a suburban primary school'. Paper presented at the Annual Conference of the Applied Linguistics Association of Australia, Alice Springs, August 1984.

Martin, J.R. & Rothery, J. 1986a. 'What a functional approach to the writing task can show about "good writing"', in Barbara Couture (ed.) *Functional Approaches to Writing: Research Perspectives*. Frances Pinter: London. pp. 241–65.

Martin, J.R. & Rothery, J. 1986b. 'Genres and language learning: writing as a social process in an infants school'. Plenary paper given at the Twelfth Annual Congress of the Australian Reading Association on Text and Context, held at the Sheraton Hotel, Perth, 2–5 July 1986.

Martin, J.R. & Rothery, J. 1986c. 'Exploring and explaining: factual writing in a primray school'. Keynote paper given at the Twelfth Annual Congress of the Australian Reading Association on Text and Context, held at the Sheraton Hotel, Perth, 2–5 July 1986.

New South Wales Department of Education, Studies Directorate. 1987. *Writing K-12*. Government Printer: Erskineville, New South Wales.

New South Wales Department of School Education. 1992. *The Action Pack: Animals*. Metropolitan East Disadvantaged Schools Program: Erskineville, New South Wales.

Painter, C. 1985. *Learning the Mother Tongue*. Deakin University Press: Geelong, Victoria.

Painter, C. 1986. 'The role of interaction in learning to speak and learning to write', in C. Painter & J.R. Martin (eds).

Painter, C. & Martin, J.R. (eds) 1986. *Writing to Mean: Teaching Genres Across the Curriculum*. Applied Linguistics Association of Australia, Occasional Papers No. 9.

Plum, G. 1988. 'Text and Contextual Conditioning in Spoken English: A Genre-Based Approach'. Unpublished PhD thesis, University of Sydney.

Rothery, J. 1986. 'Teaching writing in the primary school: a genre based approach to the development of writing abilities'. (Writing Project Report). *Working Papers in Linguistics* **4**. Department of Linguistics, University of Sydney.

Rothery, J. 1990. '"Story" writing in primary school: assessing narrative type genres'. Unpublished PhD thesis, University of Sydney.

Rothery, J. 1993. *Exploring Literacy in School English*. Metropolitan East Disadvantaged Schools Program: Erskineville, New South Wales.

Rothery, J. & Macken, M. 1991. *Developing Critical Literacy: An Analysis of the Writing Task in a Year 10 Reference Test. Issues in Education for the Socially and Economically Disadvantaged: Monograph 1*. Metropolitan East Disadvantaged Schools Program: Erskineville, New South Wales.

Rousseau, J.J. 1966. *Emile*. (Trans. Barbara Foxley) (first published 1762). Dent: London.

# 5

---

# Evaluating disruption: symbolising theme in junior secondary narrative

## J.R. MARTIN

## 1 Background

This chapter will report on ongoing research into the system and structure of narrative genres. This work draws in particular on PhD research by Plum (1988) and Rothery (1990), who were in turn building on foundational linguistic analyses by Labov and Waletzky (1967) and Hasan (1984). (A useful overview of the most relevant analyses of narrative is provided in Toolan 1988.) The special focus of this ongoing research has been on writing and responding critically to narrative in English classrooms in Australian junior secondary schools, as part of the Sydney Metropolitan East Region Disadvantaged Schools Program.

## 2 Narrative system and structure

Working closely with Rothery, Plum (1988) distinguished a number of spoken story genres by looking carefully at their overall staging and the role played by interpersonal meaning in developing their impact. For example, he contrasted **recounts**, which relate a relatively unproblematic sequence of events with an ongoing prosody of comment, with **anecdotes**, which relate an out-of-the-ordinary experience in order to share a reaction. Both of these story genres Plum contrasted with **exemplums**, which relate a culturally significant incident and proceed to offer a moralistic interpretation, and with the more familiar **narratives of personal experience**, as introduced by Labov and Waletzky (1967). An overview of Plum's staging for these genres is presented in Table 5.1. Note that the genres share opening and closing stages, that they

**Table 5.1**  Divergent staging patterns for some story genres
(after Plum 1988)

| | open | experience | comment | experience | close |
|---|---|---|---|---|---|
| | | | staging | | |
| *genres* | | | | | |
| **recount** | (Orientation) | Record | [prosodic] | – | (Coda) |
| **anecdote** | (Orientation) | Remarkable event | Reaction | – | (Coda) |
| **exemplum** | (Orientation) | Incident | Interpretation | – | (Coda) |
| **narrative** ... | (Orientation) | Complication | Evaluation | Resolution | (Coda) |
| *&* ... | ... | ... | ... | ... | ... |

differ in the kind of comment offered the reader, and that only
the narrative of personal experience displays a classic 'quest' narrative structure with a frustrated hero overcoming something
going wrong in order to restore equilibrium.

The narrative intertextuality highlighted in Table 5.1 can be
reformulated systemically in order to bring out more clearly the
interrelationships among these four of Plum's story genres. The
network in Figure 5.1 opposes recount to the other genres on the
basis of the relatively unproblematic experience they relate. Then
the notion of overcoming disequilibrium is taken into account to
distinguish narratives (of personal experience) from anecdotes
and exemplums (which tend not to resolve explicitly their compli-
cating events). Finally, anecdotes, which attempt to share a
reaction to unusual events, are contrasted with exemplums, which
deal moralistically with culturally significant incidents. The network is a first step towards a 'grammar' of story genres. Note that
it construes genre along Saussurian principles as a semiotic system
– as a connotative semiotic realised through language in
Hjelmslev's terms; in systemic functional linguistics, this amounts
to theorising genre as a dynamic open system, following Lemke
(1984, 1990, 1992).

For reasons of space, it will be possible to illustrate here just one
of the story genres reviewed above (for further exemplification,
see Plum 1988; Martin 1992a; Rothery 1993). The genre selected
is an anecdote, which instantiates the features [expectancy, −frus-
tration, reaction] from Figure 5.1. As such, it begins with an
Orientation, setting the story in time and space; this is followed
by Remarkable event, in which the noteworthy event is related;

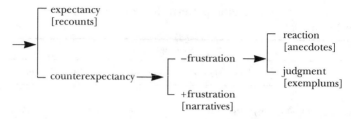

**Figure 5.1**    Story genres as system (towards genre agnation)

subsequently the reader is explicitly instructed to react empatheti-
cally. For spoken anecdotes the Reaction stage is typically less
coercive, with narrators counting on their listeners to react in solidary ways.

**Text 1**    Anecdote

---

**Orientation**

While jogging through leafy East Killara at 6:38 yesterday morning,
Barry McCrea was entranced by a rare romantic sight.

**Remarkable event**

A tall young man double-parked his station wagon beside a car in
Wentworth Avenue, got out, and under the windscreen wiper of
the car placed a red rose.

**Reaction**

All together ... aaaaaah.

---

[Column 8; *Sydney Morning Herald*, August 6, 1991:1]

## 3    Genre as social context

As presented in section 2 above, genre theory was developed as a
theory of social context – as a theory of the social processes constituting a culture when viewed from the perspective of language
(alongside the complementary perspectives of alternative denota-
tive semiotics such as music, image, dance, etc.). The model treats

the relationship between language and social context in terms of **realisation**; this means that language is interpreted as symbolically construing, construed by and reconstruing (over time) social context (i.e. genre). In Australian junior secondary schools, this model has to be elaborated somewhat to account for the way in which highly valued modernist narratives are read as tokens of an underlying message or 'theme':[1] the text as a whole is treated as a kind of metaphor, with the story itself projecting a deeper level of meaning – a level of meaning which students are expected to unpack in critical responses to literature (see Rothery & Macken 1991) and to embed in the narratives they write on their own. The symbiotic relationship between language and social context, in general, and in the context of Australian junior secondary English classrooms is outlined in Figure 5.2.

The holistic perspective on genre, assumed to this point, is close to that developed by Bakhtin. Note the way in which he, in the quotation below, uses the concept of speech genre to integrate what he refers to as thematic content, style and compositional structure. The parallels with Hallidayan metafunctions, the ideational, the interpersonal and the textual, and systemic notions of text in context, are striking (cf. Halliday 1978; 1994).

> All the diverse areas of human activity involve the use of language. Quite understandably, the nature of forms of this use are just as diverse as are the areas of human activity. … Language is realised in the form of individual concrete texts (oral and written) by participants in the various areas of human activity. The texts reflect the

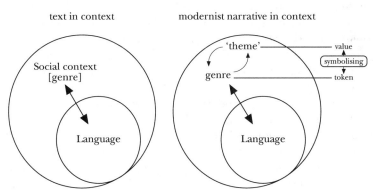

**Figure 5.2**   Language in relation to genre as a theory of social context

specific conditions and goals of each such area not only through their content (thematic) and linguistic style, that is the selection of the lexical, phraseological, and grammatical resources of the language, but above all through their compositional structure. All three of these aspects – thematic content, style, and compositional structure – are inseparably linked to the whole of the text and are equally determined by the specific nature of the particular sphere of communication. Each separate text is individual, of course, but each sphere in which language is used develops its own relatively stable types of these texts. These we may call speech genres. [Bakhtin (1986: 60), writing in 1952–53; the term *text* has been substituted for *utterance* throughout.]

# 4    A stratified model of context

In fact, in order to account for the way in which modernist narratives project their 'theme', the model of language and social context presented in Figure 5.2 can be usefully elaborated by stratifying social context into two levels which will be referred to here as genre and register.[2] The level of register is metafunctionally organised into field, mode and tenor variables, reflecting the intrinsic functional organisation of language itself (Martin 1991).

Following Martin (1992a), **field** refers to what is going on, where this is interpreted in terms of a set of activity sequences oriented to some global institutional purpose; **mode** refers to the role language is playing, both in terms of feedback (the monologue through dialogue continuum) and abstraction (the language in action, language as reflection dimension); and **tenor** refers to interlocutor relations (see Poynton 1984, 1985/1989, 1990), with respect to both status (equal/unequal) and contact (involved or distant) – corresponding to the simultaneous dimensions of power and solidarity introduced by Brown and Gilman (1960).

Below, one of the modernist narratives used to apprentice students into an appropriate reading position for public examinations will be examined closely from the perspectives of field and tenor in order to determine how these register variables work together to construct the genre and project its theme. As far as field is concerned, the critical parameter has to do with disruptions to the everyday unfolding of the intersecting activity

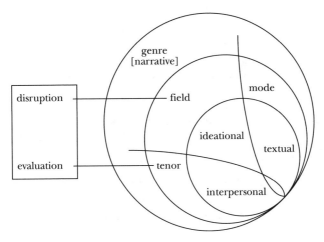

**Figure 5.3**   Disruption and evaluation in relation to metafunction, register variables and genre in a stratified model of social context

sequences in the narrative. As for tenor, the critical parameter has to do with the ongoing evaluation of these disruptions, and the intense amplified evaluation of one disruption in particular. The theoretical place of this concern with disruption and evaluation is outlined in Figure 5.3.

## *4.1   Field and disruption*

For the most part narrative genres involve disruptions to commonplace unfoldings of the activity sequences constituting particular fields. Readers' expectations about what will happen next are challenged, as something unusual intervenes. In the modernist narrative under consideration here, *The Weapon* by Fredric Brown (1984) (see Appendix), the story opens with Dr James Graham sitting alone, thinking about his work. Once this activity sequence is established, ideal readers make ongoing predictions about what will usually happen next, expecting all the while that given the genre something untoward will soon occur. The opening sequence of *The Weapon* is, in fact, broken by an intruding mental activity – namely that of Dr Graham worrying about his mentally arrested son. The disruption unfolds as follows, with the work activity interrupted by the domestic one:

---

work activity

The room was quiet in the dimness of early evening. Dr James Graham, key scientist of a very important project, sat in his favourite chair, thinking. It was so still that he could hear the turning of pages in the next room as his son leafed through a picture book.

Often Graham did his best work, his most creative thinking, under these circumstances, sitting alone in an unlighted room in his own apartment after the day's regular work. ...

[EXPECTING: and tonight he was working on a particularly interesting problem ...]

---

interrupted by domestic activity

... **But** tonight his mind would not work constructively. Mostly he thought about his mentally arrested son – his only son – in the next room. The thoughts were loving thoughts, not the bitter anguish he had felt years ago when he had first learned of the boy's condition. The boy was happy; wasn't that the main thing? And to how many men is given a child who will always be a child, who will not grow up to leave him? Certainly that was a rationalization, but what is wrong with rationalization when it ... **[clause broken off]**

[EXPECTING: ... makes it possible to live with something that would be otherwise unbearable ...]

---

In this example the disruption is explicitly grammaticalised through the concessive conjunction *but*. This is just one of a variety of devices for marking counter-expectation, which are signalled in bold face throughout the analysis of the rest of the narrative below. In addition, the text has been annotated below with suggestions at each point of disruption as to how the established activity sequence might have predictably continued had it not been interrupted. Note that what interrupts an activity sequence is the intrusion of another one (or closure of one so that another can begin); it is this pattern of intersection that creates the potential for conflict both within and between individuals in narrative genres. Analysis of disruption in the text continues as follows:

---

interrupted by service activity

... – The doorbell rang.

Graham rose and turned on lights in the almost-dark room before he went through the hallway to the door. He was not annoyed; tonight, at this moment, almost any interruption to his thoughts was welcome.

He opened the door. A stranger stood there: he said, 'Dr Graham? My name is Niemand; I'd like to talk to you. May I come in a moment?'

Graham looked at him. He was a small man, nondescript, obviously harmless – possibly a reporter or an insurance agent.

But it didn't matter what he was. Graham found himself saying, 'Of course. Come in, Mr Niemand.' A few minutes of conversation, he justified himself by thinking, might divert his thoughts and clear his mind.

'Sit down,' he said, in the living room. 'Care for a drink?'

Niemand said, 'No. thank you.' He sat in the chair; Graham sat on the sofa.

The small man interlocked his fingers; he leaned forward. He said, ...

[EXPECTING: 'Dr Graham, it's a pleasure to be here this evening. Thank-you very much for agreeing to talk with me' ...]

---

interrupted by political activity

... 'Dr Graham, you are the man whose scientific work is more likely than that of any other man to end the human race's chance for survival.'

A crackpot, Graham thought. Too late now he realized that he should have asked the man's business before admitting him. It would be an embarrassing interview – he disliked being rude, yet only rudeness was effective.

'Dr Graham, the weapon on which you are working – '... **[clause broken off]**

[EXPECTING: ... has the potential to end life on this planet several times over ... ]

interrupted by domestic activity

… The visitor **stopped** and turned his head as the door that led to a bedroom opened and a boy of fifteen came in. The boy didn't notice Niemand; he ran to Graham.

'Daddy, will you read to me now?' The boy of fifteen laughed the sweet laugh of a child of four.

Graham put an arm around the boy. He looked at his visitor, wondering whether he had known about the boy. From the lack of surprise on Niemand's face, Graham felt sure he had known.

'Harry' – Graham's voice was warm with affection – 'Daddy's busy. Just for a little while. Go back to your room; I'll come and read to you soon.'

'*Chicken Little*? You'll read me *Chicken Little*?'

'If you wish. Now run along …

[EXPECTING: '… and hop into bed and I'll be along in a little while.']

interrupted by service activity

… **Wait**. Harry, this is Mr Niemand.'

The boy smiled bashfully at the visitor. Niemand said, 'Hi, Harry,' and smiled back at him, holding out his hand. Graham, watching, was sure now that Niemand had known; the smile and the gesture were for the boy's mental age, not his physical one.

The boy took Niemand's hand. For a moment it **seemed that he was going to** climb into Niemand's lap, …

[EXPECTING: … and Niemand reached out warmly and sat the boy on his knee.]

interrupted by domestic activity – which closes (temporarily)

… and Graham pulled him back gently. He said, 'Go to your room now, Harry.'

The boy skipped back to the bedroom, not closing the door.

Niemand's eyes met Graham's and he said 'I like him,' with obvious sincerity. He added, …

[EXPECTING: 'Such a happy good-natured child.']

political activity resumes – and closes (apparently)

… 'I hope that what you're going to read to him will always be true.'

Graham didn't understand. Niemand said, '*Chicken Little*, I mean. It's a fine story – but may Chicken Little always be wrong about the sky falling down.'

Graham suddenly had liked Niemand when Niemand had shown liking for the boy. Now he remembered that he must close the interview quickly. He rose, in dismissal.

He said, 'I fear you're wasting your time and mine, Mr Niemand. I know all the arguments, everything you can say I've heard a thousand times. Possibly there is truth in what you believe, but it does not concern me. I'm a scientist, and only a scientist. Yes, it is public knowledge that I am working on a weapon, a rather ultimate one. But, for me personally, that is only a by-product of the fact that I am advancing science. I have thought it through, and I have found that that is my only concern.

'But, Dr Graham, is humanity *ready* for an ultimate weapon?'

Graham frowned, 'I have told you my point of view, Mr Niemand.'

Niemand rose slowly from the chair. He said, 'Very well, if you do not choose to discuss it, I'll say no more.' He passed a hand across his forehead. "I'll leave, Dr Graham. …

[EXPECTING: and he walked towards the door.]

---

service activity resumes – and closes

… I wonder, **though** … may I change my mind about the drink you offered me?'

Graham's irritation faded. He said, 'Certainly. Will whisky and water do?

'Admirably.'

Graham excused himself and went into the kitchen. He got the decanter of whisky, another of water, ice cubes, glasses.

When he returned to the living room, Niemand was just leaving the boy's bedroom. He heard Niemand's 'Good night, Harry,' and Harry's happy 'Night, Mr Niemand.'

Graham made drinks. A little later, Niemand declined a second one and started to leave.

Niemand said, 'I took the liberty of bringing a small gift to your son, doctor. I gave it to him while you were getting drinks for us. I hope you'll forgive me.'

'Of course. Thank you. Good night.'

Graham closed the door;

---

domestic activity resumes

he walked through the living room into Harry's room. He said, 'All right, Harry. Now I'll read to –' ...

[EXPECTING: '... you. Where's that book got to?]

---

interrupted by political activity

... There was **sudden** sweat on his forehead, but he forced his face and his voice to be calm as he stepped to the side of the bed. 'May I see that, Harry?' When he had it safely, his hands shook as he examined it.

He thought, *only a madman would give a loaded revolver to an idiot.*

---

As Joan Rothery has stressed to me, one further point about field that should perhaps be highlighted at this stage is the choice of out-of-the-ordinary goings on to establish activity sequences. In *The Weapon* the key elements are the choice of a mentally arrested son in the domestic sequences, the selection of a scientist working on an ultimate weapon in the work sequences, and the use of a radical subversive in the political sequences. These selections mean that the narrative is loaded with points of impact as the extraordinary fields collide.

## 4.2   Tenor and evaluation

Like Labov (1972, 1982), Plum and Rothery have been particularly concerned with the role played by interpersonal meaning in shaping narrative genres. Here one aspect of this interpersonal inflection will be examined in detail – namely, the realisation of AFFECT. Apart from seminal work by Poynton (1985/1989) on AFFECT and VOCATION, there is very little systemic analysis in this area to draw on. Accordingly, a provisional framework for analysing emotion in narrative will be briefly developed here, based on Martin (1992a).

The key areas of the lexicogrammar at issue here involve 'qualities' and 'processes'. Emotive qualities may describe (Epithet) or be ascribed to participants (Attribute[3]); they can also be used to characterise the attitude in which a process is undertaken (Circumstance of manner). In addition, affective mental processes can be used to construe the reactions of participants; agnate to these are behavioural processes which express the physiological manifestation of inner feelings. These various realisations of affect are exemplified in Table 5.2.

In the framework developed here, an attempt will be made to map out the major dimensions of feeling assumed by members of the culture as part of their unconscious socialisation into its ways of meaning. The ways in which feelings are manifested by social subjects is, of course, strongly conditioned by gender, ethnicity, generation and class – as shown below (see section 5). In addition, institutions such as religion, psychology and psychiatry typically develop and prescribe uncommonsense theories of affect and its manifestation which will be set aside here.

1. 'POLARITY' – The contrast here is between good feelings and bad ones,[4] in the context of a question like *How are you?*. Bad feelings provoke a query like *What's wrong?* – and to parry this, everybody has to lie.

   | positive affect | the boy was HAPPY |
   | negative affect | the boy was SAD |

2. 'PROCESS TYPE' – The opposition here is between a surge of emotion manifested through behavioural processes (expressing feelings) versus an ongoing predisposition or mood as manifested through mental processes (feelings as inner states).

   | behavioural surge | the boy LAUGHED |
   | mental disposition | the boy LIKED the present |

**Table 5.2**    Key lexicogrammatical regions realising AFFECT

| 'qualities' | | |
|---|---|---|
| – describing participants | a HAPPY boy | Epithet |
| – attributed to participants | the boy was HAPPY | Attribute |
| – manner of processes | the boy played HAPPILY | Circumstance |
| 'processes' | | |
| – affective mental | the present PLEASED the boy | Process |
| – affective behavioural | the boy SMILED | Process |

3. 'PERSON'[5] – The distinction here is between relatively contained emotion, where something is felt but it's not clear what the source or cause of the feeling is (e.g. 'What's wrong? – I don't know.') and relatively directed reaction towards someone or something going on (e.g. 'What's wrong? – That guy is driving me crazy.'). Thus *I'm angry at you* but not *\*I'm sad at you*; *I'm wary of you* but not *\*I'm restless of you*; and so on.

| | |
|---|---|
| feeling in self | the boy was <u>HAPPY</u> |
| reaction to other | the boy <u>LIKED</u> the present |

4. 'VALUE' – Like many other interpersonal resources (generalised as systems of APPRAISAL below; see Martin 1992b), AFFECT can be graded by degree. As a first step, these can be divided into outer (low/high) and median values, as with MODALITY.

| | |
|---|---|
| low | the boy <u>LIKED</u> the present |
| median | the boy <u>LOVED</u> the present |
| high | the boy <u>ADORED</u> the present |

5. 'TYPE' – Finally there is the issue of the kind of feeling involved. The framework used here divides feelings into three types: satisfaction, security and accomplishment. Positive and negative values for these types are exemplified below. With **satisfaction**, this opposes sadness to happiness; with **security**, anxiety is opposed to confidence; and with **accomplishment**, exasperation is contrasted with preoccupation.

| | |
|---|---|
| satisfaction | the boy was <u>SAD</u>/<u>HAPPY</u> |
| security | the boy was <u>ANXIOUS</u>/<u>CONFIDENT</u> |
| accomplishment | the boy was <u>FED UP</u>/<u>ABSORBED</u> |

It is not clear at this time by what criteria a framework of this kind can be semiotically motivated. Informally, I might simply note in passing that between the ages of one and two, my son periodically descended into temper tantrums during which he hollered cyclically for *bopple* (his bottle), *baggy* (his blanket) and *Mummy/Daddy*; when any one of these was provided, it was immediately rejected and the yelling cycled on to the next of the three needs. These primal screams are associated with satisfaction (feeling full), security (being warm) and accomplishment (doing with) in Figure 5.4, which outlines a discourse semantics system for AFFECT. The column headed 'the grammarian' displays where

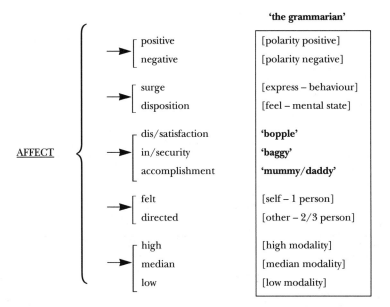

**Figure 5.4**    AFFECT systems (discourse semantics, interpersonal metafunction)

possible the grammatical systems which inspired the oppositions constituting the AFFECT network. The paradigm generated by this network is presented in Figure 5.5.

As a first step in applying this framework, one reading of *The Weapon* is provided below in which lexicogrammatical items taken as realising affect are highlighted – with a distinction drawn between mental states (small capitals) and affective behaviour (courier font). Mental states are realised through qualities of participants and processes,[6] and mental processes; affective behaviour is realised through material and behavioural processes reflecting a mental state. In order to clarify the presentation, the material and behavioural processes taken as realising affect on this reading of the text are listed below (in courier font), alongside the emotion they were taken as manifesting (mental states are not formatted in small caps in this list). In *The Weapon* most of the affective behaviour manifests the positive feeling of caring (between parent and child; between host and guest).

|  | SURGE (of behaviour) | PREDISPOSITION |
|---|---|---|

NEGATIVE AFFECT

**discord**

| misery<br><br>[felt] | wimper<br>cry<br>wail | down      [low]<br>sad      [median]<br>distraught      [high] |
|---|---|---|
| antipathy<br>[directed] | rebuke<br>tell off<br>bawl out | dislike<br>hate<br>abhor |

**insecurity**

| disquiet | restless<br>twitching<br>shaking | uneasy<br>anxious<br>freaked out |
|---|---|---|
| apprehension | flinch<br>wince<br>cower | wary<br>fearful<br>terrorised |

**frustration**

| ennui | fidget<br>yawn<br>tune out | bored<br>fed up<br>exasperated |
|---|---|---|
| desire | ask<br>urge<br>plead | aspiring<br>envious<br>craving |

POSITIVE AFFECT

**satisfaction**

| desire | chuckle<br>laugh<br>rejoice | cheerful<br>buoyant<br>jubiliant |
|---|---|---|
| care | shake hands<br>hug<br>embrace | like<br>love<br>adore |

**Figure 5.5**   A provisional framework for the analysis of AFFECT

**security**

| confidence | declare<br>assert<br>proclaim | together<br>confident<br>assured |
|---|---|---|
| trust | delegate<br>commit<br>entrust | trusting<br>dependent on<br>reliant on |

**fulfilment**

| engagement | attentive<br>busy<br>flat out | interested<br>absorbed<br>engrossed |
|---|---|---|
| engagement | compliment<br>honour<br>laud | valuing<br>admiring<br>revering |

**Figure 5.5** (*cont.*)    A provisional framework for the analysis of AFFECT

| | |
|---|---|
| [care] | 'Care for a drink?' |
| [engagement] | The small man interlocked his fingers; |
| [engagement] | he leaned forward. |
| [care] | he ran to Graham. |
| [care] | 'Daddy, will you read to me now?' |
| [happiness] | The boy of fifteen laughed the sweet laugh of a child of four. |
| [care] | Graham put an arm around the boy. |
| [care] | I'll come and read to you soon.' |
| [care] | You'll read me *Chicken Little?*' |
| [care] | The boy smiled bashfully at the visitor. |
| [care] | Niemand said, 'Hi, Harry,' and smiled back at him, |
| [care] | holding out his hand. |
| [care] | the smile and the gesture were for the boy's mental age ... |
| [care] | The boy took Niemand's hand. |
| [care] | ... it seemed that he was going to climb into Niemand's lap, |
| [apprehension] | and Graham pulled him back gently. |
| [happiness] | The boy skipped back to the bedroom, |
| [ennui] | He passed a hand across his forehead. |

| | |
|---|---|
| [care] | may I change my mind about the drink you offered me?' |
| [care] | 'I took the liberty of bringing a small gift to your son ... |
| [care] | I gave it to him |
| [care] | while you were getting drinks for us. |
| [care] | Now I'll read to –' ... |
| [disquiet] | There was sudden sweat on his forehead, |
| [apprehension] | his hands shook as he examined it. |

This reading of the text has been annotated with glosses designed to capture the affectual inflection of each phase of activity in the text. The first phase, for example, is glossed as a 'precious moment of work activity', in line with the prosody of positive feelings of engagement accumulating through this mental activity. This activity is interrupted by a rather differently inflected phase of worry over domestic activity, glossed in terms of 'un/ reconciled anguish'. Unfortunately, appropriate apologies for these glosses cannot be formulated at this preliminary stage of our research.

---

PRECIOUS MOMENT (**engagement**) of work activity [The room was QUIET in the DIMNESS of early evening. Dr James Graham, KEY scientist of a VERY IMPORTANT project, sat in his FAVOURITE chair, thinking. It was SO STILL that he could hear the turning of pages in the next room as his son leafed through a picture book. Often Graham did his BEST work, his MOST CREATIVE thinking, under these circumstances, sitting ALONE in an UNLIGHTED room in his own apartment after the day's regular work.]

---

interrupted by UN/RECONCILED ANGUISH (**misery**) of domestic activity [ ... But tonight his mind would NOT work CONSTRUCTIVELY. Mostly he thought about his MENTALLY ARRESTED son – his only son – in the next room. The thoughts were LOVING thoughts, not the BIT-TER ANGUISH he had felt years ago when he had first learned of the boy's condition. The boy was HAPPY; wasn't that THE MAIN THING? And to how many men is given a child who will always be a CHILD, who will not grow up to leave him? Certainly that was a rationalization,[7] but what is wrong with rationalization when it ...]

interrupted by WELCOME INTERLUDE (**engagement**) of service activity [The doorbell rang. Graham rose and turned on lights in the ALMOST-DARK room before he went through the hallway to the door. He was NOT ANNOYED; tonight, at this moment, almost any INTERRUPTION to his thoughts was WELCOME. He opened the door. A stranger stood there: he said, 'Dr Graham? My name is Niemand; I'd like to talk to you. May I come in a moment?' Graham looked at him. He was a SMALL man, NONDESCRIPT, OBVIOUSLY HARMLESS – possibly a reporter or an insurance agent. But it DIDN'T MATTER what he was. Graham found himself saying, 'Of course. Come in, Mr Niemand.' A few minutes of conversation, he <u>justified</u> himself by thinking, might DIVERT HIS THOUGHTS and CLEAR HIS MIND. 'Sit down,' he said, in the living room. `Care for a drink?' Niemand said, 'No. thank you.' He sat in the chair; Graham sat on the sofa. The SMALL man `interlocked his fingers`; he `leaned forward`. He said]

interrupted by EMBARRASSING INTRUSION (**antipathy**) of political activity ['Dr Graham, you are the man whose scientific work is more likely than that of any other man to end the human race's chance for survival.' A CRACKPOT, Graham thought. TOO LATE now he realized that he should have asked the man's business before admitting him. It would be an EMBARRASSING interview – he DISLIKED being RUDE, yet only RUDENESS was <u>effective</u>. 'Dr Graham, the weapon on which you are working –']

interrupted by PLEASANT RELIEF (**care**) of domestic activity [The visitor stopped and turned his head as the door that led to a bedroom opened and a boy of fifteen came in. The boy didn't notice Niemand; he `ran to` Graham. 'Daddy, will you `read to` me now?' The boy of fifteen laughed the SWEET laugh of a child of four. Graham `put an arm` around the boy. He looked at his visitor, wondering whether he had known about the boy. From the LACK OF SURPRISE on Niemand's face, Graham felt sure he had known. 'Harry' – Graham's voice was WARM WITH AFFECTION – 'Daddy's busy. Just for a little while. Go back to your room; I'll come and `read to` you soon.' '*Chicken Little*? You'll read me *Chicken Little*?' 'If you wish. Now run along ...]

interrupted by CONSTRAINING MITIGATION (**disquiet**) of service activity [Wait. Harry, this is Mr Niemand.' The boy smiled BASHFULLY at the visitor. Niemand said, 'Hi, Harry,' and smiled back at him, holding out his hand. Graham, watching, was sure now that Niemand had known; the smile and the gesture were for the boy's mental age, not his physical one. The boy took Niemand's hand. For a moment it seemed that he was going to climb into Niemand's lap,]

interrupted by PLEASANT RELIEF (**care**) of domestic activity – which closes (temporarily) [and Graham pulled him back GENTLY. He said, 'Go to your room now, Harry.' The boy skipped back to the bedroom, not closing the door. Niemand's eyes met Graham's and he said 'I LIKE him,' with obvious SINCERITY. He added]

ANNOYING INTRUSION (**ennui**) of political activity resumes – and closes (apparently) ['I hope that what you're going to read to him will always be <u>true</u>.' Graham didn't understand. Niemand said, '*Chicken Little* , I mean. It's a FINE story – but may Chicken Little always be <u>wrong</u> about the sky falling down.' Graham suddenly had LIKED Niemand when Niemand had shown LIKING for the boy. Now he remembered that he must close the interview quickly. He rose, in DISMISSAL. He said, 'I FEAR you're WASTING YOUR TIME AND MINE, Mr Niemand. I know all the arguments, everything you can say I've heard a thousand times. Possibly there is <u>truth</u> in what you believe, but it does NOT CONCERN me. I'm a scientist, and only a scientist. Yes, it is public knowledge that I am working on a weapon, a rather ULTIMATE one. But, for me personally, that is only a by-product of the fact that I am advancing science. I have thought it through, and I have found that that is my only CONCERN. 'But, Dr Graham, is humanity *READY* for an ULTIMATE WEAPON?' Graham frowned, 'I have told you my point of view, Mr Niemand.' Niemand rose slowly from the chair. He said, 'Very well, if you do not choose to discuss it, I'll say no more.' He passed a hand across his forehead. "I'll leave, Dr Graham.]

WELCOME INTERLUDE (**trust**) of service activity resumes – and closes [I wonder, though … may I change my mind about the drink you offered me?' Graham's IRRITATION FADED. He said, 'Certainly. Will whisky and water do? 'ADMIRABLY.' Graham excused himself and went into the kitchen. He got the decanter of whisky, another of water, ice cubes, glasses. When he returned to the living room, Niemand was just leaving the boy's bedroom. He heard Niemand's 'Good night, Harry,' and Harry's HAPPY 'Night, Mr Niemand.' Graham made drinks. A little later, Niemand declined a second one and started to leave. Niemand said, 'I took the liberty of bringing a small gift to your son, doctor. I gave it to him while you were getting drinks for us. I hope you'll FORGIVE me.' 'Of course. Thank you. Good night.' Graham closed the door;]

---

PLEASANT RELIEF (**care**) of domestic activity resumed [he walked through the living room into Harry's room. He said, 'All right, Harry. Now I'll read to –' …]

---

interrupted by TERRIFYING INTRUSION (**apprehension**) of political activity [There was sudden sweat on his forehead, but he forced his face and his voice to be CALM as he stepped to the side of the bed. 'May I see that, Harry?' When he had it SAFELY, his hands shook as he examined it. He thought, *only a* MADMAN *would give a loaded revolver to an* IDIOT.]

One of the most fundamental problems with a reading of this kind lies in the fact that while AFFECT is frequently 'denoted' using the resources outlined above, it is frequently 'connoted' as well – with ideational tokens standing for emotions of various kinds.[8] For example, to say that Dr Graham's room was *quiet* is in one sense simply to describe its low level of noise – a physical property of Graham's environs. At the same time, items like *quiet, dimness, still* and *unlighted* in some sense **stand for** feeling: they connote, from the reading position of a university academic, an emotion of engagement – a mood of fulfilment through absorption in thought. The first two phases of *The Weapon* are re-analysed below, distinguishing between direct realisations of emotion and ideational tokens; classifications of the latter are prefaced *t-* (for token).

---

PRECIOUS MOMENT (**engagement**) of work activity The room was QUIET [t-engagement] in the DIMNESS [t-engagement] of early evening. Dr James Graham, KEY [respect] scientist of a VERY IMPORTANT [respect] project, sat in his FAVOURITE [care] chair, thinking. It was SO STILL [t-engagement] that he could hear the turning of pages in the next room as his son leafed through a picture book. Often Graham did his BEST [respect] work, his MOST CREATIVE [respect] thinking, under these circumstances, sitting ALONE [t-engagement] in an UNLIGHTED [t-engagement] room in his own apartment after the day's regular work.]

---

interrupted by UN/RECONCILED ANGUISH (**ennui**) of domestic activity [... But tonight his mind would NOT work CONSTRUCTIVELY [t-ennui]. Mostly he thought about his MENTALLY ARRESTED [t-disquiet] son – his only son – in the next room. The thoughts were LOVING [care] thoughts, not the BITTER ANGUISH [misery] he had felt years ago when he had first learned of the boy's condition. The boy was HAPPY [happiness]; wasn't that THE MAIN THING [respect]? And to how many men is given a child who will always be a CHILD [t-care], who will not grow up to leave him? Certainly that was a rationalization, but what is wrong with rationalization when it ...]

---

Pursuing this point, it appears that AFFECT can be either directly **inscribed** in text, or indirectly **evoked** by ideational tokens. This [inscribe/evoke] distinction is not unrelated to the more traditional notions of connotation and denotation. The contrast between inscription and evocation is highlighted below by providing alternative realisations for the selections actually taken up by Brown in *The Weapon* (Brown's choices are in small capitals below). Where attitude is inscribed, it can be viewed as constructing a reading position for compliant readers; where it is invoked, this reading position is more negotiable. The interplay between the coercion and negotiation of AFFECT is an important variable in narrative rhetoric.

| inscribe attitude | evoke attitude |
|---|---|
| tranquil | QUIET |
| calm | DIMNESS |
| KEY | high ranking |
| VERY IMPORTANT | long standing |
| FAVOURITE | newly upholstered |
| peaceful | SO STILL |
| BEST | publishable |
| MOST CREATIVE | inductive |
| unharassed | ALONE |
| serene | UNLIGHTED |
| properly | NOT … CONSTRUCTIVELY |
| retarded | MENTALLY ARRESTED |
| LOVING | paternal |
| BITTER ANGUISH | sleepless nights |
| HAPPY | healthy |
| THE MAIN THING | number 1 on the agenda |
| adorable | CHILD |

This dialectic can be highlighted by rewriting the opening phases of *The Weapon*, with AFFECT either entirely denoted, or entirely connoted. The selections transformed from the original to accomplish this are highlighted in bold face below:

**EVOCATION: experiential resources** (as tokens of attitude)

work activity [The room was QUIET in the DIMNESS of early evening. Dr James Graham, **HIGH RANKING** scientist of a **LONG STANDING** project, sat in his **NEWLY UPHOLSTERED** chair, thinking. It was SO STILL that he could hear the turning of pages in the next room as his son leafed through a picture book. Often Graham did his **PUBLISHABLE** work, his **INDUCTIVE** thinking, under these circumstances, sitting ALONE in an UNLIGHTED room in his own apartment after the day's regular work.]; domestic activity [… But tonight his mind would NOT work **PROPERLY**. Mostly he thought about his **MENTALLY ARRESTED** son – his only son – in the next room. The thoughts were **PATERNAL** thoughts, not those responsible for the **SLEEPLESS NIGHTS** he had endured years ago when he had first learned of the boy's condition. The boy was **HEALTHY**; wasn't that **NUMBER 1 ON THE AGENDA**? And to how many men is given a child who will always be a CHILD, who will not grow up to leave him? Certainly that was a rationalization, but what is wrong with rationalization when it …]

**INSCRIPTION: interpersonal resources** (construing attitude)

---

work activity [The room was TRANQUIL in the CALM of early evening. Dr James Graham, KEY scientist of a VERY IMPORTANT project, sat in his FAVOURITE chair, thinking. It was so PEACEFUL that he could hear the turning of pages in the next room as his son leafed through a picture book. Often Graham did his BEST work, his MOST CREATIVE thinking, under these circumstances, sitting UNHARASSED in a SERENE room in his own apartment after the day's regular work.]; domestic activity [... But tonight his mind would NOT work CONSTRUCTIVELY. Mostly he thought about his RETARDED son – his only son – in the next room. The thoughts were LOVING thoughts, not the BITTER ANGUISH he had felt years ago when he had first learned of the boy's condition. The boy was HAPPY; wasn't that THE MAIN THING? And to how many men is given a child who will always be ADORABLE, who will not grow up to leave him? Certainly that was a rationalization, but what is wrong with rationalization when it ...]

---

Systemically it would appear that the AFFECT network presented in Figure 5.4 above needs to be supplemented with systems allowing for this choice between inscription and evocation. This opposition is introduced in Figure 5.6. In addition, evoking realisations are divided into those which **invite** a reaction and those which **provoke** one through the use of lexical metaphor (metaphors in other words are treated as demanding an interpersonal connotation). Sample realisations are provided in Figure 5.6.

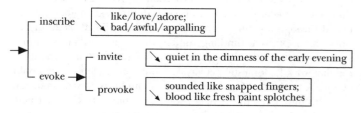

**Figure 5.6**    Choices for direct and indirect realisation of AFFECT

# 5   Subjectivity and reading position

In section 4 above, one relatively mainstream reading was provided for the affectual inflection of intersecting phases of activity in *The Weapon*. Before proceeding to base an interpretation of the way in which this modernist narrative projects its theme on this reading, it is important to relativise the reading with respect to divergent subjectivities in the culture. For example, the reading given to the first two phases of activity was glossed in terms of a 'precious moment of work activity interrupted by the un/reconciled anguish of domestic activity'. If we assume the reading position of a mature, anglo, middle-class, male academic with young children, then this reading seems quite natural. For this kind of social subject, what could be more precious than a quiet moment alone to collect one's thoughts, with children preoccupied elsewhere and other (female) relations (e.g. wife, daughter) notably absent?

Contrast, however, the reading position that might be taken up by migrant, adolescent, female, working-class students. For these subjects, tokens such as *quiet, dimness, still, alone,* and *unlighted* might well connote negative feelings than positive ones – for example, loneliness; and relatively powerless subjects of this kind might well be very disturbed by the mentally retarded son. Indeed, as Cranny-Francis (this volume) documents, the interpretation that one group of social subjects of this kind provided for the text was that Niemand had given the son the gun so that he could kill himself to put himself out of his misery. From this reading position then, a more likely gloss for the first two phases of the narrative would involve a 'lonely period of inactivity aggravated by the ongoing anguish of domestic activity'.

Alternatively, we might consider another non-mainstream position – but this time a critical one: that of a mature, feminist subjectivity. Read resistantly, from this kind of reading position, one might gloss the two phases under consideration here in terms of 'indulgent disengagement from domestic activity interrupted by cowardly rationalisation of domestic responsibility'.

The possibility of these and other complementary readings are of extreme significance in a number of respects. Theoretically, they demonstrate the need for further stratification of social context, with register and genre contextualised by a further layer of ideology. This makes room in the model for consideration of the uneven distribution of meaning potential in the culture and for analysis of the implications of divergent social subjectivities for reading position. Halliday comments on the issue of 'bifurcated' contexts as follows; the problem of overlapping meaning potential is outlined in Figure 5.7.

> I would interpret the power relations in a particular situation, when we represent that situation in terms of field, tenor and mode, by building into our representation the fact that the situation may mean different things for different interactants. The total picture is obviously going to bring in all angles; but in any typical context of situation in which there is a power relationship of inequality, then the configuration embodied in that situation is different from the way it is seen from either end. This means, of course, that the register that is being operated by the interactants will be bifurcated, although we may choose to characterise the register of the situation as a whole by building in both strands.
>
> [Thibault 1987: 620–1.]

Viewed from the perspective of teachers and students in Australian junior secondary English classrooms, the pressing issue posed by divergent subjectivities is that when it comes to public examination procedures, only one reading position is highly valued – namely that of mature, anglo, middle-class subjects with modernist sensibilities. Reading interpersonal meaning is especially problematic in this respect, since, as noted above, a good deal of AFFECT is evoked ideationally rather than interpersonally

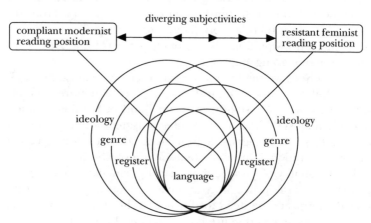

**Figure 5.7**    Divergent subjectivity, meaning potential and social context

inscribed. And beyond this, the manifestation of AFFECT, if not the basic AFFECT parameters themselves, are strongly conditioned by generation, class, ethnicity and gender. To take just one example, consider the realisations of a surge of antipathy in Figure 5.5. The [rebuke, tell off, bawl out] options are far more open to powerful subjects than less powerful ones, who are more likely to [ignore, avoid, shun] in contexts where anger is expressed. The challenge for secondary English teachers lies in striking a balance among: (i) teaching students to provide valued readings in appropriate contexts; (ii) recognising alternative readings where they arise and dealing with them in non-dismissive ways; and (iii) introducing students to the possibility of resistant readings, which challenge the mainstream reading positions naturalised by modernist narrative. For a range of productive teaching strategies along these lines, see Rothery (1993).

## 6   Genre, disruption and evaluation

In section 4.2 above, disruption and evaluation in *The Weapon* were considered in some detail. It is now appropriate to step back one level of abstraction in the model and consider how these field and tenor patterns interact to construct the genre. Here we will draw on Rothery's interpretation of the text's staging, as outlined below. In this reading, Rothery makes use of Labov and Waletzky's categories for the analysis of narratives of personal experience.

According to Rothery (personal communication), the first two phases of the narrative comprise its Orientation – setting the story in time and place, and introducing the chief protagonist. Activity in this stage of the narrative is mental rather than physical. This makes it easy to draw the line between Orientation and Complication at the point where mental activity is interrupted by physical activity, and the story's antagonist is introduced.

Rothery included the next five phases of activity in the Complication: Niemand's arrival, his first political attack, Harry's entry, Harry's introduction to Niemand and Harry's return to his room. Rothery considers Niemand's first attack a potential Evaluation stage – physical activity is suspended and replaced with verbal activity (debate); but Graham and Niemand are unable to consummate their contestation because of Harry's interruption. It is only once Harry has returned to his room that matters can be followed through in earnest.

In the next phase of the narrative things do come to a head. Again, physical activity is supplanted by verbal jousting. Niemand puts his position and Graham replies; the phase concludes with Niemand suggesting he take his leave. Instead, however, the story continues with a Resolution comprised of a return to host/guest (taking drinks, gift-giving) and parent/child (bed-time story) relations. In the narrative's final phase, its Coda, the theme of the story is driven home as Graham discovers the nature of the gift Niemand has left with Harry, and himself performs a very shallow reading of its significance.

This reading of the interaction among field disruption, tenor evaluation and generic staging is outlined below. From the perspective of field, note that activity sequences interrupt each other abruptly up to the Evaluation; thereafter the closure of each phase is more natural, negotiated among participants – up to the Coda when the gun arrives quite unexpectedly on the scene. This interplay of interruption and closure helps construct a textual wave, which builds the story up to its Evaluation and then winds it down – setting up the punchy surprise Coda at the end.

**Orientation** [staging courtesy of Joan Rothery]

> PRECIOUS MOMENT (**engagement**) of work in/activity

> interrupted by reflection on UN/RECONCILED ANGUISH (**misery**) of domestic situation

**Complication**

> interrupted by WELCOME INTERLUDE (**engagement**) of service activity

[potential Evaluation!]

> interrupted by EMBARRASSING INTRUSION (**antipathy**) of political activity

> interrupted by PLEASANT RELIEF (**care**) of domestic activity

> interrupted by CONSTRAINING MITIGATION (**disquiet**) of service activity

> interrupted by PLEASANT RELIEF (**care**) of domestic activity – which closes (temporarily)

**Evaluation** (peak of appraisal, resonating with Orientation, Coda)

> ANNOYING INTRUSION (**ennui**) of political activity resumes – and closes (apparently)

**Resolution**

> WELCOME INTERLUDE (**trust**) of service activity resumes – and closes

> PLEASANT RELIEF (**care**) of domestic activity resumed

**Coda**

> interrupted by TERRIFYING INTRUSION (**apprehension**) of political activity

Figure 5.8 maps out the interaction among field disruption, tenor evaluation and generic staging in schematic terms. Of particular interest is the way in which field disruption is associated with a swing from positive to negative AFFECT from one phase to another throughout the text. Only in the Resolution do we find two phases of positive AFFECT in a row, which works in harmony with field disruption to foreground the apprehension of the story's final phase.

Rothery and Plum, following Labov and Waletzky, characterise the Evaluation stage as an intense stage of interpersonal inflection. And in *The Weapon* this is certainly true. A more delicate analysis of AFFECT in this phase of the narrative is provided below (assuming a mainstream reading position); the mood constructed

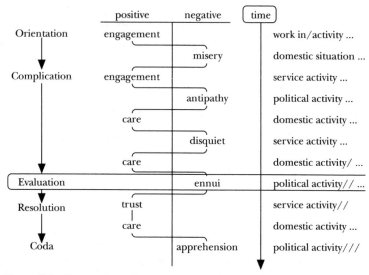

**Figure 5.8**   Interaction of genre, tenor (affect) and field (disruption) in *The Weapon*

is profoundly negative, involving all of discord, insecurity and frustration. In addition, three judgements (*true, wrong, truth*) are classified.

Evaluation – AFFECT: frustration, insecurity, discord; JUDGEMENT: truth

ANNOYING INTRUSION (**ennui**) of political activity resumes – and closes ['I hope that what you're going to read to him will always be <u>true</u> [judgement:truth].' Graham didn't understand. Niemand said, '*Chicken Little*, I mean. It's a FINE [satisfaction:care] story – but may Chicken Little always be *wrong* [judgement:truth] about the sky falling down.' Graham suddenly had LIKED [satisfaction:care] Niemand when Niemand had shown LIKING [satisfaction:care] for the boy. Now he remembered that he must close the interview quickly. He rose [t-frustration:ennui], in DISMISSAL [t-frustration:ennui]. He said, 'I FEAR [insecurity:apprehension] you're WASTING YOUR TIME AND MINE [t-frustration:ennui], Mr Niemand. I know all the arguments, everything you can say I've heard a thousand times. Possibly there is <u>truth</u> [judgement:truth] in what you
(*Continued*)

(*Continued*)
believe, but it does NOT CONCERN [frustration:ennui] me. I'm a scientist, and only a scientist. Yes, it is public knowledge that I am working on a weapon, a rather ULTIMATE [t-insecurity:disquiet] one. But, for me personally, that is only a by-product of the fact that I am advancing science. I have thought it through, and I have found that that is my only CONCERN [fulfilment:engagement].' 'But, Dr Graham, is humanity *READY* for an ULTIMATE WEAPON [t-insecurity: apprehension]?' Graham frowned [discord:misery], 'I have told you my point of view, Mr Niemand.' Niemand rose slowly [t-discord:antipathy] from the chair. He said, 'Very well, if you do not choose to discuss it, I'll say no more.' He passed a hand across his forehead [t-frustration:ennui]. 'I'll leave, Dr Graham.]

Beyond this a number of other APPRAISAL systems are deployed to intensify the interpersonal inflection of this stage of the narrative. These involve MODALISATION (of probability and usuality), INTENSITY and MEASURE (see Martin (1992b) for a survey of APPRAISAL resources). Realisations of these systems are highlighted in bold face below and analysed for high, median or low values; throughout the Evaluation extreme values (high and low) predominate.

Evaluation – APPRAISAL: extreme usuality, amount, intensity, modality

ANNOYING INTRUSION (**ennui**) of political activity resumes – and closes ['I hope that what you're going to read to him will **always** [high usuality] be <u>true</u>.' Graham didn't understand. Niemand said, '*Chicken Little*, I mean. It's a FINE story – but **may** [low obligation] Chicken Little **always** [high usuality] be <u>wrong</u> about the sky falling down.' Graham **suddenly** [immediate time distance] had LIKED Niemand when Niemand had shown LIKING for the boy. Now he remembered that he **must** [high obligation] close the interview **quickly** [median time distance]. He rose, in DISMISSAL. He said, 'I FEAR you're WASTING YOUR TIME AND MINE, Mr Niemand. I know **all** [high amount] the arguments, **everything** [high amount] you **can** [low ability] say I've heard **a thousand times** [high amount]. **Possibly** [low probability] there is <u>truth</u> in what you believe, but it does NOT CONCERN me. I'm a scientist, and **only** [low intensity] a
(*Continued*)

(*Continued*)
scientist. Yes, it is public knowledge that I am working on a weapon, a **rather** [median intensity] ULTIMATE one. But, for me personally, that is **only** [low intensity] a by-product of the fact that I am advancing science. I have thought it through, and I have found that that is my **only** [low amount] CONCERN.' 'But, Dr Graham, is humanity READY for an ULTIMATE WEAPON?' Graham frowned, 'I have told you my point of view, Mr Niemand.' Niemand rose slowly from the chair. He said, 'Very well, if you do not **choose** [low inclination] to discuss it, I'll say **no more** [low amount].' He passed a hand across his forehead. "I'll leave, Dr Graham.]

Intense interpersonal comment of this kind foregrounds the Evaluation as a pivotal stage in the interpretation of the narrative. In modernist narratives which unfold as tokens of an underlying message, we can thus expect the Evaluation, reinforced by the Orientation and Coda, to play a critical role in projecting the story's theme.

# 7    Projecting theme

As far as we have been able to determine, prestigious readings of *The Weapon* involve the following key ingredients, listed below along with their critical instantiations in the text:

1.  Description of nature of Graham's work, in Evaluation:

    'I am working on a weapon, a rather ultimate one ...'

2.  Niemand's objection to Graham's work, in Evaluation

    'But, Dr Graham, is humanity READY for an ultimate weapon?'

3a. Niemand's intervention, as implied by Coda (disruption):

    [Niemand gives loaded revolver to Harry]

3b. Graham's evaluation of Niemand's action, in Coda (evaluation):

    He thought, *only a madman would give a loaded revolver to an idiot.*

The narrative instructs compliant naturalised readers to read

Graham's own work as an instance of a madman giving a loaded revolver to an idiot; and thus to see that the point of the narrative (its 'theme', following Hasan (1985/1989: 97–9), or message) is that humanity is not ready for an ultimate weapon. How does it do this? As noted above, the interaction of Orientation, Evaluation and Coda should be critical; so let's review them together here.

---

**Orientation**
 – (thoughts of son) stop Graham's work
 – Graham rationalises son's condition

---

PRECIOUS MOMENT (**engagement**) of work in/activity [The room was QUIET in the DIMNESS of early evening. Dr James Graham, KEY scientist of a VERY IMPORTANT project, sat in his FAVOURITE chair, thinking. It was SO STILL that he could hear the turning of pages in the next room as his son leafed through a picture book. Often Graham did his BEST work, his MOST CREATIVE thinking, under these circumstances, sitting ALONE in an UNLIGHTED room in his own apartment after the day's regular work.] interrupted by UN/ RECONCILED ANGUISH (**misery**) of domestic situation [ ... But tonight his mind would NOT work CONSTRUCTIVELY. Mostly he thought about his MENTALLY ARRESTED son – his only son – in the next room. The thoughts were LOVING thoughts, not the BITTER ANGUISH he had felt years ago when he had first learned of the boy's condition. The boy was HAPPY; wasn't that THE MAIN THING? And to how many men is given a child who will always be a CHILD, who will not grow up to leave him? Certainly that was a <u>rationalization</u>, but what is <u>wrong</u> with <u>rationalization</u> when it ...]

---

**Evaluation**
 – Niemand instructs reader on symbolic power of narrative
 – Niemand fails to stop Graham's work on weapon
 – Graham rationalises his work

ANNOYING INTRUSION (**ennui**) of political activity resumes –
and closes ['I hope that what you're going to read to him will always
be <u>true</u>.' Graham didn't understand. Niemand said, '*Chicken Little*, I
mean. It's a FINE story – but may Chicken Little always be <u>wrong</u>
about the sky falling down.' Graham suddenly had LIKED Niemand
when Niemand had shown LIKING for the boy. Now he remembered
that he must close the interview quickly. He rose, in DISMISSAL. He
said, 'I FEAR you're WASTING YOUR TIME AND MINE, Mr Niemand. I
know all the arguments, everything you can say I've heard a
thousand times. Possibly there is <u>truth</u> in what you believe, but it
does NOT CONCERN me. I'm a scientist, and only a scientist. Yes, it is
public knowledge that I am working on a weapon, a rather ULTIMATE
one. But, for me personally, that is only a by-product of the fact that
I am advancing science. I have thought it through, and I have
found that that is my only CONCERN.' 'But, Dr Graham, is humanity
*READY* for an ULTIMATE WEAPON?' Graham frowned, 'I have told you
my point of view, Mr Niemand.' Niemand rose slowly from the
chair. He said, 'Very well, if you do not choose to discuss it, I'll say
no more.' He passed a hand across his forehead. "I'll leave,
Dr Graham.]

**Coda**
   – son given metaphorical power to stop Graham's work on weapon
   – symbolism initially (at least) lost on Graham

interrupted by TERRIFYING INTRUSION (**apprehension**) of political activity [There was sudden sweat on his forehead, but he
forced his face and his voice to be CALM as he stepped to the side of
the bed. 'May I see that, Harry?' When he had it SAFELY, his hands
shook as he examined it. He thought, *only a MADMAN would give a
loaded revolver to an IDIOT.*]

Note that in each stage, the issue of Graham stopping work is
raised. In the Orientation, his son Harry succeeds in stopping him
(for an evening); Niemand fails in the Evaluation; and then in the
Coda Harry has been given the symbolic power to stop him for

good. In each stage Graham in a sense rationalises away the challenge: in the Orientation he reasons that Harry's condition serves him better in some respects than that of normal children, in the Evaluation he argues that it is the science and only the science that matters, and in the Coda he interprets Niemand's gift as an act of madness rather than political subversion. In addition, each stage is loaded with negative feelings (misery, ennui and apprehension), underscoring the fact that all is not well. In general terms then, modernist readers are positioned to read the story as globally concerned with Graham stopping dangerous work.

## 7.1    Disruption and theme (field)

As noted during the consideration of field above, *The Weapon* draws on other-than-everyday activity sequences, with a high potential for disruption. Beyond this, we suspect that modernist readers are accustomed to keying into anything out of the ordinary. They learn to ask why it is there, as opposed to everyday experience (which is the stuff of recounts rather than narratives). Out-of-the-ordinary 'trigger' elements in *The Weapon*, as introduced above, involve Graham's work on an ultimate weapon, his mentally arrested son and Niemand's fears for humanity:

**extraordinary work activity**
    key scientist of a very important project;
    I am working on a weapon, a rather ultimate one

**extraordinary domestic activity**
    mostly he thought about his mentally arrested son – his only son;
    the smile and gesture were for the boy's mental age, not his physical one;
    only a madman would give a loaded revolver to an idiot

**extraordinary political activity**
you are the man whose scientific work is more likely than that of any other man to end the human race's chance for survival;
is humanity ready for an ultimate weapon?

Another aspect of field that stands out for modernist readers is the presence of loose ends. The modernist reader knows that everything in the text is there for a reason; and that everything not there is not there for a reason too. By keying in on unexplained presences and absences the modernist reader gains important insights into the constructedness of the text. In *The Weapon* the key loose ends have to do with Niemand's name (German for 'no man', i.e. everyman), Niemand's familiarity with Harry (which Graham tracks from low modality to high – *possibly, wondering whether, felt sure, was sure now*), and Graham's unexpectedly hospitable reaction when Niemand changes his mind about a drink (*... may I change my mind about the drink you offered me?' Graham's irritation faded ...*). The key passages from *The Weapon* instantiating these loose ends are reviewed below (with developing modalisation in bold face):

> A stranger stood there ... My name is Niemand [= no man!] ... He was a small man, nondescript, obviously harmless – **possibly** a reporter or an insurance agent ... He looked at his visitor, **wondering whether** he had known about the boy. From the lack of surprise on Niemand's face, Graham felt **sure** he had known ... Graham, watching, was **sure** now that Niemand had known; the smile and the gesture were for the boy's mental age, not his physical one ... '... I wonder though, ... may I change my mind about the drink you offered me?' Graham's irritation faded. He said, 'Certainly ...' When he returned to the living room, Niemand was just leaving the boy's bedroom ... Niemand said, 'I took the liberty of bringing a small gift to your son, doctor. I gave it to him while you were getting drinks for us. I hope you'll forgive me.'

Realist readers will never know if Niemand is Niemand's real name, how he came to know about Harry or why Graham agreed to have a drink with his enemy (*a crackpot*). That's not the point. What matters is the way in which the loose ends help the narrative project its theme.

## 7.2   Evaluation and theme (tenor/ideology)

As far as evaluation is concerned, probably the most important thing to note from a modernist reading position is the source of the APPRAISAL in the narrative. As far as AFFECT is concerned, the source of most evaluation is Dr Graham; generally it is his reactions that are directly inscribed, and so condition the interpretation of indirect evocations. The story in other words is told from Graham's point of view. There is only a little evaluation from Niemand's perspective, mainly affective behaviour evoking a reaction, and a little positive evaluation of Harry and negative evaluation of Graham's work – as follows:

The small man `interlocked his fingers`; he leaned forward ...
Niemand said, 'Hi, Harry,' and `smiled back at him, holding
out his hand` ... Niemand's eyes met Graham's and he said 'I LIKE
him,' with obvious sincerity. He added, 'I hope that what you're
going to read to him will always be <u>true</u>.' ... Niemand said, '*Chicken
Little*, I mean. It's a FINE story – but may Chicken Little always be
WRONG about the sky falling down.' ... 'But, Dr Graham, is humanity
READY for an ULTIMATE weapon?' ... He `passed a hand across
his forehead` ... Niemand said, 'I took the liberty of `bringing a
small gift` to your son, doctor ... I hope you'll FORGIVE me.'

This makes the Coda all the more striking in its shift of perspective from Graham to Niemand, and since Niemand is no man, to
the reader:

He (`who else?, we are supposed to ask`) thought, *only a madman would give a loaded revolver to an idiot.*

All of a sudden we are invited to re-read the narrative from
Niemand's point of view[9] – to empathise with his feelings throughout, and possibly before and after his meeting with Graham. The
modernist reader has to shift from the compliant solidarity
with Graham constructed by the story to a resistant solidarity with
Niemand and his attempted subversion of Graham's ethos.

## 7.3   Genre and theme

The 'sensitive' modernist reader of modernist narrative has to tie
everything together. S/he knows and has faith in the overall constructedness of the text, which repays close reading by revealing
its telos. Somehow, disruption and evaluation have to be reconciled – in terms of the staging of the genre, and ultimately in
terms of its underlying theme. *The Weapon* constructs the compliant modernist reader in such as way that s/he has in fact to
re-read the story in light of its Coda, which dynamically reconstrues the narrative from Niemand's point of view.

Consider then the re-reading of disruption and evaluation in
*The Weapon* from Niemand's, instead of Graham's, perspective –
most of which has to be supposed, since it is neither inscribed nor
evoked:

---

**Niemand's disruption & evaluation**
anxious moment of service activity [gaining entrance]
leading to determined undertaking of political activity [challenging Graham]
interrupted by uneasy intrusion of domestic activity [meeting Harry]
returning to exasperating resumption of political activity [pressing Graham]
leading to anxious return to domestic activity [procuring drink]
enabling fearful completion of political activity [giving Harry the gun]
allowing anxious return to domestic activity [having drink and leaving]

---

Disruption and evaluation of this kind construct a very different story – a quest narrative starring Niemand, as he might render it to his fellow subversives after the event. In Niemand's narrative, the main point of Evaluation would almost certainly have taken place in Harry's bedroom. And what finer Coda for this reconstrual than his *I hope you'll forgive me* (for bringing a gift to Harry), Niemand knowing what he knows. Compliant modernist construals and reconstruals of *The Weapon* are outlined in Table 5.3.

## 7.4   Projecting theme

This brings us to the theme of *The Weapon*, having looked at disruption (field) and Evaluation (tenor) in detail, and considered the effect of the Coda on the re/construal of the genre. One point that should be brought out here is that *The Weapon* is an apprenticing text, especially designed to induct adolescents into a modernist reading position. As far as the content form is concerned, note the way in which Niemand explicitly guides students into looking for a deeper meaning with his *Chicken Little* allusion:[10]

> 'I hope that what you're going to read to him will <u>always be true</u>.'
>
> Graham didn't understand. Niemand said, '*Chicken Little*, I mean. It's a fine story – but may Chicken Little <u>always be wrong</u> about the sky falling down.'

Table 5.3

|  | CONSTRUE<br>(story structure from<br>Graham's perspective) | RECONSTRUE<br>(story structure from<br>Niemand's perspective) |
|---|---|---|
| Orientation | sitting at home | [before setting off … ] |
| Complication | visitor arrives and<br>challenges research | getting gun to boy alone in<br>his bedroom |
| Evaluation | research rationalised | [… reaction in bedroom …] |
| Resolution | drinks and leave-taking | drinks and leave-taking |
| Coda | 'only a madman would<br>give …' | 'I hope you'll forgive me' |

To spell this out, Niemand suggests that *Chicken Little* and Graham's work are intertexts; and that the one comments on the other. Niemand hopes that Chicken Little will always be wrong, thereby implying that he might be right – that Graham's work may well render the world a token of the value Chicken Little cried. Niemand's semiotic message is: read one activity sequence as a token of another (i.e. make one activity give value to another).

Apprenticeship is reinforced in *The Weapon*'s expression form, through the use of italics. Italics foreground: (i) the semiotics lesson outlined above; (ii) Niemand's next to direct rendering of the story's theme; and (iii) Graham's own too shallow reading of the gun:

> '*Chicken Little?* You'll read me *Chicken Little?*' … '*Chicken Little,* I mean.'
> 'But, Dr Graham, is humanity READY for an ultimate weapon?'
> He thought, *only a madman would give a loaded revolver to an idiot.*

This is all, of course, crude bludgeoning for trained readers; but for many novices it is scarcely explicit enough.

The text then is dripping with clues. Key elements have been graphologically foregrounded. Niemand has told us to read one activity sequence as token of another. Now what? What's the semiotic process that gets us from the story to its theme? What's the recipe?

As far as ingredients are concerned, the following four pieces of activity are critical:

1.   'I am working on a weapon, a rather ultimate one ...'
2.   'But, Dr Graham, is humanity READY for an ultimate weapon?'
3a.  [Niemand gives loaded revolver to Harry]
3b.  He thought, *only a madman would give a loaded revolver to an idiot.*

How do we mix together and stir? The difficulty here lies in reading beyond the linear unfolding of the activity to get at why one activity follows another and eventually to get at how one activity stands for another. One promising dialectic in this regard is to challenge the co-occurrence of critical ingredients with the question 'why?'. This dialectic is worked through in steps below, focusing on the relation between Graham's work and Niemand's gift. The relationship between these two events is reworked in terms of addition, then temporal sequence, then cause, until the two are seen as instantiations of madmen giving lethal weapons to an idiot (Graham's ingredient above), which is pushed a step further as instantiating the theme that humanity cannot be trusted with the possibility of its own destruction (Niemand's ingredient above). The dialectic reconstrues temporal sequence as symbolisation (reworks story as meaning, to put this another way round).

| a and b | [addition] | Graham works on weapon; Niemand gives revolver |
|---|---|---|
| **why?** | | |
| a then b | [time] | Graham works on weapon then Niemand gives revolver |
| **why?** | | |
| a so b | [cause] | Graham works on weapon so Niemand gives revolver |
| **why?** | | |
| a^b/c | [realisation] | Graham works on weapon so Niemand gives revolver/as instance of madman giving lethal weapon to idiot |
| **why?** | | |
| a^b/c//d | [realisation] | Graham works on weapon so Niemand gives revolver/as instance |

of madman giving revolver to idiot
as//instance of humanity can't be
trusted with the possibility of its own
destruction

The critical step involves reworking Graham's own evaluation of Niemand's action as an abstract interpretation of both Niemand's actions and (perhaps more to the point) Graham's own:

| | Tokens | Value |
|---|---|---|
| Actor | Dr Graham/Niemand | = a madman |
| Process giving | | |
| Goal | ultimate weapon/ loaded revolver | = a [lethal weapon] |
| Recipient | to humanity/to Harry | = to an idiot |

It is then a small step to ask why the narrative sets up this particular relationship of signification; Niemand's query (... *is humanity ready for an ultimate weapon?*) ties this up neatly for compliant readers. The dialectic is rendered schematically in Figure 5.9 below (for a detailed discussion of the grammar of Token and Value and its semiotic significance, see Matthiessen (1992)).

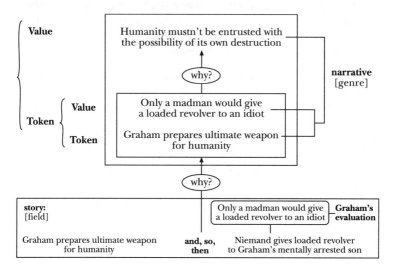

**Figure 5.9** Asking 'why?' as a dialectic for interpreting the way in which *The Weapon* projects its theme

Generalising from this example, when reading modernist narrative we might, as a first step, treat the goings on of the story as a collection of incidents, with no redundancy among events. Some students do read stories tactically in this way, even under examination conditions; they react to just a part of what is going on, ignoring the rest (see Cranny-Francis, this volume). A next step involves reading the story's goings on as temporally redundant; students often respond to stories in this way by simply recounting what happened, without explaining why. Asking why pushes readings a step further to causal redundancy; at this level students try to explain why Niemand is angry with Graham, why Niemand leaves the gun, why Graham is angry with Niemand, and so on. To get beyond this level of interpretation readers have to move from relations of addition, time and cause to relations of symbolisation – from redundancy to metaredundancy. Here students treat events as giving value to each other, as token of some underlying theme. This step needs to be repeated until everything in the narrative is tied together as projecting the point of the story – its ultimate and unifying theme. The procedure is outlined below, with levels of interpretation closely tied to grading during public examinations. Using an A to E marking scale, in Australia, reading narrative as a collection of events gets E (outright failure), as a linear sequence of events gets D, as a causal sequence of events gets C, as symbolically related to one another gets B, and as symbolically unified under an overriding theme gets A. The social consequences of the different levels of reading are thus severe.

| | | | |
|---|---|---|---|
| a and b | [addition] | collection [no redundancy] | E |
| **why?** | | | |
| a then b | [time] | [temporal redundancy] | D |
| **why?** | | | |
| a so b | [cause] | [causal redundancy] | C |
| **why?** | | | |
| $a^\wedge b/c$ | [realisation] | [metaredundancy] | B |
| **why?** | | | |
| $a^\wedge b/c//d$ | [realisation] | [meta-metaredundancy] | A |
| **why?** | | | |

– until narrative tied together ...

# 8 Reprise

Following Labov, Plum and Rothery have drawn attention to the significance of interpersonal meaning in the construction of a range of narrative genres. This chapter has outlined one of the ways in which a stratified model of context (Martin 1992a) within a systemic functional linguistics framework can be used to show the way in which interpersonal meaning (especially AFFECT) inflects experiential meaning to give shape and significance to the generic staging of one junior secondary school text. In addition the model has been used to explore the ways in which this modernist narrative projects an underlying message or theme, which students are expected to uncover when responding critically to narrative in public examinations.

Adopting a reading position which uncovers these underlying themes is critical to success in English in Australian schools. In light of this, the major challenge facing research of this kind lies in generalising procedures which make this reading position publicly available to students whose subjectivity does not naturally position them to respond critically to text in valued ways. At present, in Australia, it is a challenge that is more than exacerbated by widely held reservations about the wisdom of: (i) using the technical discourse of linguistics, social semiotics and/or contemporary critical theory to talk about narrative; and of (ii) making mainstream reading positions available to students from non-mainstream backgrounds (for fear that their native subjectivities will be devalued or perhaps even destroyed in the process[11]). For an invaluable response to this challenge, see Rothery (1994) – a package of materials which introduces secondary English teachers to relevant understandings about language and context, with a view to expanding the reading positions that can be taken up by their students if, when and where they so choose.

## Notes

1  The term 'theme' will be preferred here because of its currency in Australian junior secondary school classrooms; it is not, of course, to be confused with the grammatical function Theme, which following systemic conventions begins with an upper case graph, distinguishing

it from theme as underlying message. (The term theme is also used by Hasan 1985/1989.)

2    The level of register is traditionally referred to as context of situation in systemic theory, with the term register restricted to the effect of field, mode and tenor choices on meanings at risk. Following Martin (1992a), this chapter opposes register to genre as complementary and stratified perspectives on social context.

3    More precisely, Epithets in nominal groups functioning as Attribute in attributive relational clauses (following Halliday 1994).

4    In labelling these feelings 'positive' and 'negative' I am not attempting to **evaluate** the feelings concerned as good or bad, or as worthy of expression or suppression, but simply to label the feelings as they are generally viewed in the culture.

5    This distinction might also be related to PROCESS TYPE, since mental processes are typically directed (e.g. *I fear it/it frightens me*), whereas relational processes lend themselves to inexplicitness as far as the direction/source of the feeling is concerned (e.g. *I'm frightened, I'm fearful*).

6    Qualities may, of course, be realised in nominalised form, e.g. *anguish*.

7    Underlined items realise JUDGEMENT rather than AFFECT, and are concerned with moral evaluation in terms of fate, capacity, resolve, truth and ethics rather than emotive reactions (see Iedema et al. 1994 for discussion).

8    This problem was glossed over above when material processes such as *interlocked his fingers, leaned forward,* and *passed a hand across his forehead* were included as tokens of affective behaviour.

9    Environmentally conscious readers may already have begun this shift earlier in the text, out of sympathy for Niemand's 'green' politics, which point emphasises the close connection between text interpretation and reading position.

10   It is thus a very serious problem for apprenticing readers if this allusion simply passes over their heads, as it would certainly do for a variety of Australian subjectivities.

11   Martin (1993) takes up this reservation in the context of an overview of relevant Australian initiatives in educational linguistics.

# References

Bakhtin, M.M. 1986 The problem of speech genres. In M.M. Bakhtin *Speech Genres and other Late Essays* [translated by V. McGee]. Austin: University of Texas Press, pp. 60–102.

Barthes, R. 1966 Introduction to the structural analysis of narratives.

*Communications* 8 [reprinted in R. Barthes 1977 *Image, Music, Text.* London: Fontana, pp. 79–124].

Brown, F. 1984 The Weapon. In P. Forrestal & Jo-Anne Reid (eds) *The Brighter Side of School.* Melbourne: Thomas Nelson.

Brown, R. & A. Gilman 1960 The pronouns of power and solidarity. In T. Sebeok (ed.) *Style in Language.* Cambridge, MA: MIT Press, pp. 253–76.

Cranny-Francis, A. 1990 *Feminist Fiction: Feminist Uses of Generic Fiction.* Cambridge: Polity Press.

Cranny-Francis, A. & J.R. Martin 1991 Contratextuality: The poetics of subversion. In F. Christie (ed.) *Social Processes in Education: Proceedings of the First Australian Systemic Network Conference, Deakin University, January 1990.* Darwin: Centre for Studies of Language in Education, Northern Territory University, pp. 286–344.

Halliday, M.A.K. 1976 *Halliday: System and Function in Language* (G. Kress ed.). London: Oxford University Press.

Halliday, M.A.K. 1978 *Language as Social Semiotic: The Social Interpretation of Language and Meaning.* London: Edward Arnold.

Halliday, M.A.K. 1982 The de-automatization of grammar: from Priestley's 'An Inspector Calls'. In J.M. Anderson (ed.) *Language Form and Linguistic Variation: Papers Dedicated to Angus MacIntosh.* Amsterdam: Benjamins, pp. 129–59.

Halliday, M.A.K. 1994 *An Introduction to Functional Grammar.* 2nd edn. London: Edward Arnold.

Hasan, Ruqaiya 1984 The nursery tale as a genre. *Nottingham Linguistic Circular* 13 (Special Issue on Systemic Linguistics), pp. 71–102.

Hasan, Ruqaiya 1985 *Linguistics, Language and Verbal Art.* Geelong, Vic.: Deakin University Press [republished London: Oxford University Press, 1989].

Iedema, R., S. Feez & P. White 1994 *Media Literacy: Write It Right Literacy in Industry Project, Stage Two.* Sydney: Metropolitan East Region's Disadvantaged Schools Program.

Labov, W. 1972 The transformation of experience in narrative syntax. *Language in the Inner City.* Philadephia: Pennsylvania University Press, pp. 354–96.

Labov, W 1982 Speech actions and reactions in personal narrative. In D. Tannen (ed.) *Analysing Discourse: Text and Talk* (Georgetown University Round Table on Language and Linguistics 1981). Washington, DC: Georgetown University Press.

Labov, W. & J. Waletzky 1967 Narrative analysis. In J. Helm (ed.) *Essays on the Verbal and Visual Arts* (Proceedings of the 1966 Spring Meeting of the American Ethnological Society). Seattle: University of Washington Press, pp. 12–44.

Lemke, J.L. 1984 *Semiotics and Education.* Toronto: Toronto Semiotic Circle (Monographs, Working Papers and Publications 2).

Lemke, J.L. 1990 *Talking Science: Language, Learning and Values.* Norwood, NJ: Ablex (Language and Ecuational Proceses).

Lemke, J.L. 1992 New challenges for systemic-functional linguistics: dialect diversity and language change. *Network* 18, pp. 61–8.

Martin, J.R. 1991 Intrinsic functionality: implications for contextual theory. *Social Semiotics* 1.1, pp. 99–162.

Martin, J.R. 1992a *English Text: System and Structure.* Amsterdam: Benjamins.

Martin, J.R. 1992b Macroproposals: meaning by degree. In W.A. Mann & S.A. Thompson (eds) *Discourse Description: Diverse Analyses of a Fund Raising Text.* Amsterdam: Benjamins, pp. 359–95.

Martin, J.R. 1993 Genre and literacy – modelling context in educational linguistics. *Australian Review of Applied Linguistics* 13.

Matthiessen, C.M.I.M. 1992 Language on language: the grammar of semiosis. *Social Semiotics* 1.2, pp. 69–111.

Plum, G. 1988 *Textual and Contextual Conditioning in Spoken English: A Genre-based Approach.* PhD thesis, Department of Linguistics, University of Sydney.

Poynton, C. 1984 Names as vocatives: forms and functions. *Nottingham Linguistic Circular* 13 (Special Issue on Systemic Linguistics), pp. 1–34.

Poynton, C. 1985 *Language and Gender: Making the Difference.* Geelong, Vic.: Deakin University Press [republished London: Oxford University Press, 1989].

Poynton, C. 1990 *Address and the Semiotics of Social Relations: A Systemic-Functional Account of Address Forms and Practices in Australian English.* PhD thesis, Department of Linguistics, University of Sydney.

Rothery, J. 1990 *Story Writing in Primary School: Assessing Narrative Type Genres.* PhD thesis, Department of Linguistics, University of Sydney.

Rothery, J. 1994 *Literacy in School English (Write it Right Resources for Literacy and Learning).* Sydney: Metropolitan East Disadvantaged Schools Program.

Rothery, J. & M. Macken 1991 *Developing Critical Literacy: An Analysis of the Writing Task in a Year 10 Reference Test.* Sydney: Metropolitan East Region Disadvantaged Schools Program.

Thibault, P. 1987 An interview with Michael Halliday. In R. Steele & T. Threadgold (eds) *Language Topics: Essays in Honour of Michael Halliday, Vol. 2.* Amsterdam: Benjamins, pp. 599–627.

Toolan, M.J. 1988 *Narrative: A Critical Linguistic Introduction.* London: Routledge (Interface Series).

## Appendix: The Weapon, by Fredric Brown

The room was quiet in the dimness of early evening. Dr James Graham, key scientist of a very important project, sat in his favourite chair, thinking. It was so still that he could hear the turning of pages in the next room as his son leafed through a picture book.

Often Graham did his best work, his most creative thinking, under these circumstances, sitting alone in an unlighted room in his own apartment after the day's regular work. But tonight his mind would not work constructively. Mostly he thought about his mentally arrested son – his only son – in the next room. The thoughts were loving thoughts, not the bitter anguish he had felt years ago when he had first learned of the boy's condition. The boy was happy; wasn't that the main thing? And to how many men is given a child who will always be a child, who will not grow up to leave him? Certainly that was a rationalization, but what is wrong with rationalization when it – The doorbell rang.

Graham rose and turned on lights in the almost-dark room before he went through the hallway to the door. He was not annoyed; tonight, at this moment, almost any interruption to his thoughts was welcome.

He opened the door. A stranger stood there: he said, 'Dr Graham? My name is Niemand; I'd like to talk to you. May I come in a moment?'

Graham looked at him. He was a small man, nondescript, obviously harmless – possibly a reporter or an insurance agent.

But it didn't matter what he was. Graham found himself saying, 'Of course. Come in, Mr Niemand.' A few minutes of conversation, he justified himself by thinking, might divert his thoughts and clear his mind.

'Sit down,' he said, in the living room. 'Care for a drink?'

Niemand said, 'No, thank you.' He sat in the chair; Graham sat on the sofa.

The small man interlocked his fingers; he leaned forward. He said, 'Dr Graham, you are the man whose scientific work is more likely than that of any other man to end the human race's chance for survival.'

A crackpot, Graham thought. Too late now he realized that he should have asked the man's business before admitting him. It would be an embarrassing interview – he disliked being rude, yet only rudeness was effective.

'Dr Graham, the weapon on which you are working –'

The visitor stopped and turned his head as the door that led to a bedroom opened and a boy of fifteen came in. The boy didn't notice Niemand; he ran to Graham.

'Daddy, will you read to me now?' The boy of fifteen laughed the sweet laughter of a child of four.

Graham put an arm around the boy. He looked at his visitor, wondering whether he had known about the boy. From the lack of surprise on Niemand's face, Graham felt sure he had known.

'Harry' – Graham's voice was warm with affection – 'Daddy's busy. Just for a little while. Go back to your room; I'll come and read to you soon.'

'*Chicken Little*? You'll read me *Chicken Little*?'

'If you wish. Now run along. Wait. Harry, this is Mr Niemand.'

The boy smiled bashfully at the visitor. Niemand said, 'Hi, Harry,' and smiled back at him, holding out his hand. Graham, watching, was sure now that Niemand had known; the smile and the gesture were for the boy's mental age, not his physical one.

The boy took Niemand's hand. For a moment it seemed that he was going to climb into Niemand's lap, and Graham pulled him back gently. He said, 'Go to your room now, Harry.'

The boy skipped back to the bedroom, not closing the door.

Niemand's eyes met Graham's and he said, 'I like him,' with obvious sincerity. He added, 'I hope that what you're going to read to him will always be true.'

Graham didn't understand. Niemand said, '*Chicken Little*, I mean. It's a fine story – but may Chicken Little always be wrong about the sky falling down.'

Graham suddenly had liked Niemand when Niemand had shown liking for the boy. Now he remembered that he must close the interview quickly. He rose, in dismissal.

He said, 'I fear you're wasting your time and mine, Mr Niemand. I know all the arguments, everything you can say I've heard a thousand times. Possibly there is truth in what you believe, but it does not concern me. I'm a scientist, and only a scientist. Yes, it is public knowledge that I am working on a weapon, a rather ultimate one. But, for me personally, that is only a by-product of the fact that I am advancing science. I have thought it through, and I have found that that is my only concern.'

'But, Dr Graham, is humanity *ready* for an ultimate weapon?'

Graham frowned, 'I have told you my point of view, Mr Niemand.'

Niemand rose slowly from the chair. He said, 'Very well, if you do not choose to discuss it, I'll say no more.' He passed a hand across his forehead. 'I'll leave, Dr Graham. I wonder, though ... may I change my mind about the drink you offered me?'

Graham's irritation faded. He said, 'Certainly. Will whisky and water do?'

'Admirably.'

Graham excused himself and went into the kitchen. He got the decanter of whisky, another of water, ice cubes, glasses.

When he returned to the living room, Niemand was just leaving the boy's bedroom. He heard Niemand's 'Good night, Harry,' and Harry's happy ''Night, Mr Niemand.'

Graham made drinks. A little later, Niemand declined a second one and started to leave.

Niemand said, 'I took the liberty of bringing a small gift to your son, doctor. I gave it to him while you were getting the drinks for us. I hope you'll forgive me.'

'Of course. Thank you. Good night.'

Graham closed the door; he walked through the living room into Harry's room. He said, 'All right, Harry. Now I'll read to –'

There was sudden sweat on his forehead, but he forced his face and his voice to be calm as he stepped to the side of the bed. 'May I see that, Harry?' When he had it safely, his hands shook as he examined it.

He thought, *only a madman would give a loaded revolver to an idiot.*

# 6

## Technology and/or weapon: the discipline of reading in the secondary English classroom

### ANNE CRANNY-FRANCIS

## 1  Introduction

Jim Martin's chapter addressed a very crucial problem in the reading of the story, *The Weapon*[1] which was, basically, how to do it in a socially and institutionally empowering way. As Martin recounted, this story was problematised by the inability of one group of junior secondary students to produce the reading he has described for you. The class teacher had presented the class with the story, *The Weapon*, and asked the students to read and then discuss the story in groups. The aim, as she put it, was that students should try to discover 'what the story is about'. This is a very conventional way of teaching English: students collaborate on a reading which they then expand, explicate and/or modify after input from the teacher. The teacher was very disturbed in this instance to find that the class did not produce a reading which in any way resembled her expected reading; furthermore, she found that the reading they did make was totally inexplicable by reference to the text. After a similar experience with another text (students were again unable to produce the conventional, institutionally approved reading) the teacher enlisted the help of a literacy consultant employed by the State Department of Education. The literacy consultant also found the students' reading difficult to account for and so, in turn, enlisted my help as a literary theorist and tertiary teacher to explicate the reading that these students had produced. The students' reading was basically as follows: it is better to be dead than to be intellectually impaired. The environmentalist gave the boy the gun so that he could kill himself; it was a kindly act by the environmentalist.

The aim of this chapter is to explore how and why the students might have made that reading, in terms of the discourses – institutional, disciplinary, and pedagogical – operating in the secondary English classroom. In doing so I shall be delineating a theoretical positioning which makes sense of that reading – a positioning which can also assist students to situate their own reading in relation to the demands of the discipline and of the institution in which they are participating. This theoretical positioning holds that the meaning or meanings of a text cannot be decoded or interpreted simply by analysis of the textual manipulation or realisation of one or more semiotic systems. Instead, the theory holds that meaning-making is a complex operation, involving not only the reader (whose accumulated social and cultural capital gives her/him different kinds of access to readings), but also a number of interrelated textual and contextual (if such a division be permitted for reasons of analysis) features: first, textual semiosis or the 'poetics' of the text (how choices made in the production of the text – for example, genres used, intertextual referencing, language choices – contribute to the production of meaning); secondly, the institutional setting within which the reading takes place (which might range from classroom to schoolyard, each a site with particular discursive and material demands); and thirdly, the material practice constituting the text (that is, the technology involved in the constitution of the text with which readers may be more or less familiar).

Another fundamental premise of the theoretical position delineated in this chapter is that, as a consequence of this conceptualisation of meaning-making practice, texts are seen as potentially productive of a great number of meanings, not just one. However, this does not mean that every one of these meanings or readings has the same value, socially and institutionally. Basically, it means that for any text, at a particular time and place, there will be one or more readings which is/are institutionally approved and validated. These approved meanings or readings are produced when an approved methodology or way of reading is used to activate meanings which accord with the basic discursive practice of the institution within which the reading takes place. Within the institution of education, for example, this means using an approved methodology (discussed further below) to activate meanings which accord with the discursive practice of the institution, which is fundamentally liberal humanism informed by, for example, some feminist and anti-racist discourses. Other meanings may be produced either by using a different methodology or reading practice and/or by reference to a different discursive positioning; however, in many instances, these readings will be rejected by that institution – as 'misreadings', 'partial readings' or simply as 'wrong'.

These other readings are of great interest for a number of reasons. Some of these non-approved readings will proceed from methodological practices which the institution does not currently approve, but which may be a part of the everyday experience of students. Such readings may well represent future directions for the institution. Other readings will be produced by students whose own discursive positioning is very different from that assumed by the approved reading(s), and again may indicate necessary developments for the institution; that is, they may constitute meanings which the institution itself must learn to validate. Other readings again may be symptomatic of the failure of the institution to make accessible to students the genres and discourses which its main purpose is to teach. In this last case, the exact nature of the readings can tell us a great deal about the reasons for this institutional failure.

In this chapter the non-mainstream reading of the short story, *The Weapon*, produced by one secondary English class is examined in order to explore the reasons for its production. The questions asked of that reading concern the kinds of methodology the students employed; how their own discursive positioning impacted on their reading practice; the institutional status of the reading they did make; and the potentially deconstructive nature of their reading. Finally, consideration is given to the status of that reading and the need for students to have access to the theoretical and methodological skills which will enable them to produce not only their original reading, but also to analyse and criticise that reading, and also to produce the institutionally approved reading(s) and to analyse and criticise that/those reading(s).

## 2    Reading *The Weapon*: literacy in the English classroom

At first hearing the students' reading of *The Weapon* seemed inexplicable, which is revealing in itself. The students' reading was inexplicable to a relatively more sophisticated (and differently positioned) reader because or if she/he tends to produce automatically the institutionally approved reading of the text. In other words, conventional expectations about the reading and the students' predicted response may confound the attempt to understand their particular reading. Michel de Certeau's work on *tactical* responses to institutional demands deals with precisely this kind of situation; using his terminology, the students' reading can be seen as an example of a *tactical* reading.[2] That is, the students produced a reading of the text which expressed their own interests and concerns, rather than the interests and concerns of the institutional site in which they are involved.

For de Certeau, the powerful institutions of our society are able to demand particular behaviours, thoughts and responses from us as individuals. He discusses the coercive power of these institutions as a 'calculus of force-relationships' or a *strategy*. Individuals do not always comply with these institutions, however. For a variety of reasons, ranging from incompetence to unwillingness to outright critical resistance, they reject the demands placed on them institutionally and instead operate according to their own desires, in a way which presents itself to them as personally empowering. This calculus of force-relationships, devoid of institutional backup or reinforcement, is what de Certeau calls a *tactic* (de Certeau 1984: xviii–xx).

Institutions have the power to act *strategically*, to make demands on the individual with which she/he supposedly must comply in order to be part of that institution. Individuals may resist that institutional positioning and instead act *tactically*, in a way which seems more relevant to them and their desires. In acting tactically, however, individuals may well position themselves outside the institution they are negotiating – and that can have a range of negative consequences for them. On the other hand, their distance from institutional demands may be empowering, enabling them to analyse and manipulate their institutional positioning. It is a highly ambiguous situation.

In this particular classroom situation the tactical reading is more likely to have had negative than positive consequences. The students had produced a reading that the teacher knew was 'wrong' but she did not understand how they had made it. And the students had no idea why it was 'wrong' and no idea how to make a 'right' reading. It was a tactical reading, but in what sense was it empowering? After all, one must consider the nature of their reading: a belief that to be intellectually impaired is worse than death. It is doubtful, however, that this is a belief which educators would set out to encourage in young adults. This reading is empowering in the way that racism and sexism is empowering; in that it makes the individual feel important and powerful by allowing her or him feel better off (in terms of status or power) than someone else. The students were not critical of this reading. They did not see it as problematic. The teacher did, but had difficulty intervening because of her highly understandable confusion about how and why they had made this particular reading in the first place.

One immediate response to this reading of the story might be that these students were identifying with a person about their own age and that, as young adolescents, they are terribly afraid of seeming to be different. To be intellectually impaired is to be different; they would rather be dead. That might well be the basis of their response. However, it is important to challenge the perception of it as 'obvious'. A great deal of methodological and theoretical complexity is elided by that 'obviousness'.

First, it elides the totally experiential character of the students' reading; their response deals only with the character who is approximately their own age. The reading does not take account of the development of the narrative or of any other aspect of the poetics of the text. Strictly speaking, it is also not proficient in its dealing with this experiential function of the text since it not only decontextualises the one character on which the reading is based, but it also fails to take into account the interweave of interpersonal and textual elements involved in the constitution of this character. In other words, this is a very selective experiential reading: the isolation of one character from the story of which he is a part, an element, and an assessment of him based on the students' own fears and desires.

Why would the students make such a reading? In answering this question we can start to trace the theoretical and methodological influences on them.

## 3   The English class: a discursive analysis

The reasons for this highly individuated and individualised reading lie in a particular combination of the discourses which operate in the English classroom, most commonly a Leavisite critical methodology combined with a version of child-centred pedagogy.

For F.R. Leavis the key to literary criticism lay in a finely honed critical sensibility, a quality of mind and character which enabled a highly sensitive reader to understand, seemingly intuitively, what the writer was about in constructing a text. Leavis was totally opposed to theoretical knowledge which he believed would blunt critical sensibility.[3] You might argue that Leavis was presenting the case for a high degree of semiotic awareness, even if unself-conscious, and certainly that is essentially how the successful Leavisite critics functioned. However, Leavis's hostility to theory meant that his methodology was read as a call for acute sensitivity to the story and the moral dilemmas it addressed – not to the theoretical construct motivating the story and its sociocultural meanings. Story was fetishised to the exclusion of story-telling, and the only apparent way of appreciating that story was by feeling it intensely in yourself; feeling the characters' lives as though they were your own. If you could not do that, then you could only conclude that you were an insensitive soul who was unfit for the fine works with which you came in contact.

Since Leavis's time, many critics have questioned the basis of his work, pointing out that there are barriers of class, gender and ethnicity (among others) against many individuals making the prescribed sensitive readings of the prescribed sensitive texts. (See, for example, Belsey 1980; Eagleton 1983; Widdowson 1982.) Nevertheless, Leavis's ideas dominate commonsense responses to texts, like the mainstream discourses which those responses commonly encode. Since those of us who grew up any time earlier than the 1980s were mostly raised as realist readers, on texts which concealed rather than flaunted their constructedness and intertextuality, it is second nature ('commonsense') for us to feel with the characters, even if the character is unashamedly a piece of rubber, like ET, the main character of Stephen Spielberg's film of that name, whose imminent death was constituted so tragically by the filmmakers that as many adults as children were reduced to tears. That response is still very commonly voiced in the media. So, for example, Brett Easton Ellis's book about a psychopath, *American Psycho*, was held up as a responsible piece of writing because of the insight it gave us into the mind of a psychopath(!). In years to come, if not already, it is clear that the book gives us some insight into the collective unconsciousness – or consciousness – of a society obsessed with violence and of a writer prepared to exploit (and just possibly deconstruct) that, but that what it tells us about psychopaths (whomever that category actually covers) is probably minimal. This Leavisite understanding of the process of reading not only dominates common sense and the media, it is also still one of the dominant discourses in English Literature classrooms.

One might consider, for example, the New South Wales Syllabus documents (Board of Senior School Studies 1982) defining the goals of 2/3 Unit Higher School Certificate English – two years on from the students whose reading formed the basis of this analysis. Under the heading 'The study of texts' is the following opening sentence: 'Any sophisticated concept of "literary criticism" is here unhelpful' – the Leavisite position clearly defined. Interestingly, like Leavis, this Syllabus document identifies poetry as 'the most demanding [and] ... potentially the most rewarding' textual form for analysis. The following instructions about what constitutes the study of poetry are again extremely illuminating in terms of their theoretical source. In a paragraph which rails against students using any kind of theoretical apparatus to read poetry, the document establishes its legitimacy in **moral** terms: so the student '*may be tempted* to collect information about poets and their "periods", about the characteristics of genres ... they *may be tempted* to catalogue the devices that a poem may employ ... they *may be tempted*, finally, to go to "the critics" in order to learn, and then repeat, what they take "the accepted view" of a poem or poet to be' (my italics). This language of temptation and fall, of sin, is used to legitimate the concluding instructions about how to study poetry: 'Biographical, descriptive, and critical information is often, of course, illuminating and valuable, and it may guide or support a personal response: but such "information" is not acceptable as a **substitute** for personal response. For it is particularly in the reading and study of poetry that students need to go beyond the mere acquisition of "information" and nerve themselves to say something on their own accounts.' (My stress.)

These documents demand a detailed analysis in themselves, but several features of the fragments quoted might be noted. First, Leavisite theory is clearly delineated, with its emphasis on personal response rather than theoretical awareness; indeed, in a classic Leavisite strategy, theory is denounced as useless. Secondly, in the passages recounted, terms such as 'information' and 'the critics' are consistently apostrophised, with the implication that they are less than respectable and somehow inimical to the process of learning. Thirdly, the moral imperative used in the passage above reproduces a view of English derived from Matthew Arnold and continued by Leavis, which sees English as the saviour of 'civilisation' without ever defining or deconstructing what that 'civilisation' might be. Later deconstructions have in fact shown that the notion of civilisation that has traditionally been encoded in writings on English has been a consistently Anglocentric, bourgeois and patriarchal one.[4] It is also worth noting here that students who accept literally this demand to give a personal response, at either General Reference Examination (Year 10) or Higher School Certificate level, are doomed to failure because the Leavisite demand for 'personal response' is not the commonsense language it appears superficially. Rather, it is a highly coded technical language meaning something quite different, as Joan Rothery's examination of sample GRE English marks demonstrated (Rothery 1991).[5]

Of course, teachers do not slavishly follow the dictates of syllabus documents, which often combine several different methodologies (for example, the HSC syllabus documents quoted above combine Leavisite and New Critical methodologies). However, a reading of them does help us specify the discourses operating in the discipline of English. The students who were attempting to read *The Weapon* were Year 9 students, so not as sophisticated as the students whose work is described by the HSC documents. Nevertheless, these documents contribute significantly to the establishment of English as a discipline within the institution of education. And what makes the influence of the Leavisite methodology even more profound is its combination with a particular version of a child-centred pedagogy.

It is important to be aware that 'child-centred' has many interpretations. It might mean anything from a critically informed Social Literacy pedagogy[6] to the emotional terrorism of a John Keating, the teacher characterised in *Dead Poets' Society*.[7] The version of this child-centred pedagogy I am concerned about here might be characterised (and I hope, not caricatured) in the following terms: an individualistic relationship (along the lines of Bernstein's personal coding) is established between teacher and student, supposedly in an attempt to inspire the student (with the teacher's concern?); the student is asked to 'experience' texts in a Leavisite way, which often conflicts fundamentally with the cultural and social capital or resources of that student; the student is given texts about people of the same age group in an attempt by educators to produce this empathetic response demanded by Leavisite theory.

The result of this practice is that students are sensitised to only one aspect of the text – the story – resulting in a totally experiential or representational reading practice. Further, students have been schooled by years of being given books about people their own age to look for the person about their own age to empathise with – their one conscious intertextual experience, you might say – so that this is almost inevitably going to be the focus of their reading. Interestingly, of course, in *The Weapon* the same age character is not the focus of the story, but rather an element in the construction of an argument. If the students had been very proficient in understanding narrative and story, they might well have recognised that character's role in the institutionally approved reading. Note that the reading or meaning that the proficient students might have made is not necessarily the 'correct' or 'right' meaning, but is the institutionally approved one. It is only 'correct' or 'right' in that it is likely to be rewarded by teachers and examiners – which is why all students have to be able to produce that reading – but there is no transcendent correctness or rightness about that reading of the story.

The less proficient students, whose reading we are studying, are dependent on the overt expression of the discourses, disciplinary and pedagogical, to which they have been exposed. The key term which governs those discourses, and which unites them, is 'personal response', which these students read non-technically and literally. The elided technical demands of 'personal response' involve an implicit understanding about semiosis (dismissively categorised as 'information' in the documents discussed) and about the institution in which they are positioned (which might be metonymically represented by the figure of the 'critic', and which basically is about knowing the right thing to say at the right time).

## 4    Reading as a discursive weapon

The student readers of *The Weapon* said very much the *wrong* thing. They presented a reading of the text which was not 'correct' institutionally, and which showed an apparently callous disregard for the intellectually impaired members of society. Returning to my starting point: the reading they made, might be obvious (given their age, perhaps) but why they said it, *in this institutional setting*, is not. Recall the reading these students made of the story: that the environmentalist gave the boy the gun so that he could kill himself, because he (the boy) was intellectually impaired. A concern which was expressed about the reading was that it was an expression of prejudice and intolerance which is not socially acceptable (it would also not gain them a sympathetic reading by any examiner in a public examination). So why are these students so apparently antisocial?

The probable answer is that these students are not actually anti-social; that, in fact, they are expressing the mainstream practice of their society. In a sense, they are too honest. The strategy that these students have not learned – and this is where they fail institutionally – is to reproduce in their reading the liberal humanist rhetoric of both the (majority of) the middle classes and the educational (and other) institutions in their society. They have not learned that there is a difference between what a society does and what it says. Their reading is a deconstruction of social attitudes and rhetoric in that it *tells it like it is*, not how it might or should be. The students' reading might be a very useful starting point for a deconstruction of contemporary attitudes to intellectual impairment (and perhaps other kinds of socially unacceptable positionings) and of the way in which unequal social practices are elided or hidden by philanthropic statements about the very people injured by these practices. That is, this reading might become part of a critical learning experience for these students.

Again, this reading must be contextualised institutionally: one of the problems for these students was not only that they produced a reading which was not institutionally powerful (in that it showed no ability to read, in the institutionally approved way, the narrative with which they were presented), but also that they produced a reading which showed a complete insensitivity to the mainstream rhetoric of their society. Learning that mainstream rhetoric is actually part of the process of learning English as a semiotic system. Of course, many would also argue that that rhetoric should be taught critically; that is, that these students should be taught not simply to repeat that rhetoric, but to deconstruct it – take it apart, analyse the values in which it is grounded. It is also worth noting here, however, that the successful students of English are not necessarily critical at all. They learn the semio-sis of English; they learn the liberal rhetoric of their society; and they repeat both in a sometimes disturbingly cynical fashion in their essays and examinations. These successful students may never have to deconstruct their prejudices, since they will have them so successfully concealed by liberal rhetoric.

Of course, that is a worst possible scenario; many successful students are doubtless also critical readers. The crucial point for this analysis is that English studies may censure those students who are lacking proficiency *semiotically* for having exactly the same values as those students who are proficient, and that this censure will be expressed in *moral* terms. This makes the point very clearly that in learning a semiotic system, one is learning language in use. Students who have not learned how to express their values or beliefs in socially acceptable rhetoric may find that their implicitly deconstructive readings of their society (via its texts) are taken as proof of *their* moral bankruptcy. The successful students whose mainstream liberal rhetoric elides their own practice of exactly the same values will not be censured, but rather rewarded. Put in the most unadorned way: the conservative middle-class student who has learned the liberal rhetoric of her/his society – probably at home from middle-class parents – can do very well in a system concerned not with *critical literacy*, but simply with literacy *per se*. That liberal rhetoric will not be challenged and she/he will be able to maintain all kinds of conservative values into adult life and practice, so preserving the society in which she/he will be power-ful and successful. On the other hand, the working-class student or the student whose ethnic background is different from that which dominates the society, who does not have that background training in the manipulation of institutional discourses (which is essentially what is involved in learning to use the right rhetoric in the right situation) and who is sometimes also less than fully profi-cient semiotically will find that her/his institutional naivety, when combined with the same uncritical approach to social issues as the middle-class student, results in her/him being perceived as not only less intelligent but also less morally aware.

This brings us back to Leavis's notion of 'higher feelings' and to the personalised version of child-centred pedagogy with which I started. When that pedagogy is practised in association with Leavisite methodology in the English classroom, the combina-tion works effectively to constitute the stereotypical view of the working-class or non-Anglo student as deficient. The deficiency might be classed as semiotic, but of course matters of semiosis or textuality are elided by Leavisite theory. So the deficiency is evaluated in other terms, as moral bankruptcy or insensitivity, and this judgement functions as a powerful technology for the maintenance of a particular class and its ideology since it attacks the self-confidence and drive to self-expression and autonomy of those from any other social positioning. Working-class students and/or those from non-Anglo racial or ethnic backgrounds can be made to feel *personally* lacking, insensititive and incapable of higher feelings.

In the reading of *The Weapon* with which we began, and its institutional evaluation, we are witnessing the way in which English as a discipline can be used as a weapon – against those who do not fit the profile of the successful social subject (that is, Anglo middle-class). This is not the only function of English, of course; English is also a powerful technology for living successfully in this society. However, we can only understand the power of English when we understand its institutional practice, which is both intensely conservative *and* potentially radical and/or revolutionary.

This can be related to reading practices in a very concrete way. I began by acknowledging that the students whose reading of *The Weapon* I was studying did not produce the institutionally successful and powerful reading Martin discussed in his chapter (this volume). We can understand the practice of English by conceptualising, in Bakhtinian terms, that this institutionally successful reading is only one of a proliferation of meanings which might be produced from that text. Another fundamental premise of this analysis is that the institutionally approved reading is not the only reading or the right reading or the correct reading. Instead, the process of meaning-making has to be understood as constituted not only textually but also by the institutional discourses defining the site at which the reading takes place and by the material practice involved in text production and consumption.

I have dealt at some length with the institutional discourses operating in the secondary English classroom – pedagogical and disciplinary discourses which define the reading practice at that site. Material practice is also a major concern, and by this I mean the students' proficiency with the medium in which the text is constituted. We often forget that literature of all kinds is a specific material practice, a technology with its own history. One of the reasons we do forget that lies with the methodologies and theories which govern its use, which effectively blind us to it as a material practice, concealing the fact that we do have to learn this technology just as we have to learn about computers and video equipment.

In relation to the students' reading of *The Weapon* the material practice involved is actually a major consideration: why did the student readers of *The Weapon* look for the significance of the story in the final scene? The language in which the question is posed, in fact, indicates the answer. One possible reason is that they looked at the final scene because their literacy is primarily visual;[8] because they read verbal texts as a series of scenes, like a film or television program. Furthermore, many of the programs the students are most familiar with – popular film, MTV and soap operas – do not have the same kind of cumulative teleology as the conventional quest narrative. Rather, the final scene is the source of meaning proliferation – of conjecture, not resolution. These postmodern students with their postmodern literacy skills find it difficult, not surprisingly, to learn the modernist reading skills required of them in the secondary English classroom – skills they certainly do need to have, just as they need their postmodern reading skills. This postmodern poetics is most familiar to these students from texts in different media, involving completely different material practices, and the students whose reading we are analysing may have read the short story in terms of that different practice. This is not surprising: after all, many skilled modernist readers attempt to read television in the same terms that they read literary texts.

## 5    Meaning production and institutionalised readings

This case study of one reading of a short story illustrates a number of issues about meaning production; primarily, that it is not a matter of locating one transcendent meaning in a text. Meaning is not simply a grammatical construct. It is constituted by a number of related practices: the semiotics of the text (the entire set of meaning potentials[9] constructed in and by a text, through the mobilisation of its intertextual resources) as inflected by the institutional discourses operating at the site where meaning is to be made, and by the reader's proficiency with the material practice by which the text is constituted. In other words, meaning is not a singular condition of any text. This seems to be in total contradiction to most structuralist readings of texts, which usually locate one particular reading of any text as that which explains its function and structure. In one sense it is contradictory, but looked at from another perspective what this means is that the reading located by structuralist analysis as the right or correct or most likely reading of a text is not the only reading, but it *is* the reading which is most predicted when the text is placed within its usual institutional setting. In other words, the structuralist readings elide these matters of institutional positioning – and, of course, to that extent they may also comply with the most conservative institutional positioning of a text. What a structuralist analysis locates as the coercive positioning of the reader by the text (by specifying the way the text works as a meaning-making practice) is probably just that, *when* the text is read within its contemporary institutional and disciplinary site. So, for example, reading D.H. Lawrence's novels as extraordinarily perceptive accounts of interpersonal relationships is probably still very acceptable in most institutional and disciplinary sites. The reader can then relate what she/he sees as key aspects of the text to this reading – and note that these key aspects are highlighted for that reader by her/his acceptance of that particular reading. In another context, however, perhaps a feminist seminar, readers might not make the same reading of D.H. Lawrence's work. They might read Lawrence's texts as patriarchal constructions of interpersonal relationships as seen from a particularly masculinist perspective. They may well locate the more conservative reading as that which is most apparent to members of a patriarchal society who are compliant with, and essentially blind to, its patriarchal discourse. Their feminist reading will then be placed as an alternative reading practice which deconstructs this patriarchal discourse. They, too, will locate key aspects of the text which support their own analysis. The point is that the institutional and disciplinary context of the reading is not an adjunct to, but is *fundamentally constitutive of*, the reading of a text. D.H. Lawrence's texts have not changed over the last five or six decades; the readings of them have.

Critical analysis of a text is not a matter of locating a specific meaning but of proliferating meanings or meaning potentials from the text. When those meaning-potentials are considered in relation to the discourses operating in or defining a particular (institutional and disciplinary) setting or context, the mainstream reading at that particular site can be located.

# 6    Reading strategies and kinds of literacy

The student readers of *The Weapon* were not successful institutionally for a number of reasons. First, they were not able to read the poetics of the text effectively. They did not understand the narrative structure of the story and so were unable to place the final scene of the story in context and then move to a more abstract or metaphorical reading of the text. Secondly, they did not understand the methodology of the discipline in which they are involved, reading 'personal response' in commonsense, not technical terms. Thirdly, they did not understand the politics of the institution in which they are working (the education system) with its liberal rhetoric, which meant that they did not censor the illiberal reading they made. Instead, the students produced a tactical reading of the story, motivated by their own fears and desires, reflecting contemporary social practice, rather than its rhetoric. It is also a reading which is likely to have been prompted by the experiential bias of their critical practice, produced out of a combination of disciplinary and pedagogical discourses. This reading might also be seen as a product of a postmodern poetics learned implicitly by the students from the popular texts (soap opera, music video, popular film) of their society.

Successful student readers would make the kind of reading Martin discussed in his chapter (this volume). In this successful reading the liberal politics of the institutional site aligns with the liberal politics of the text to validate a reading produced by an orthodox reading of the narrative: the story is about environmentalism, about an environmentalist demonstrating to a scientist the need to take responsibility for his own scientific research and its powerful technological applications. This reading demonstrates the technological power of literacy itself: the reader has been positioned to make the step from specific example to abstract reasoning which is the motive power behind most reading practices; a way of abstracting information from texts which enables them to be dealt with quickly and efficiently. Note, however, that when the successful reading is made, the exploitative discourse expressing a rejection of the intellectually impaired is ignored; it is not even seen or recognised. It is not a choice necessarily recognised or enacted by the successful student, despite her/his otherwise powerful reading practice. An institutionally successful reading is not necessarily a critical reading.

Another reading is that the story is about a man who gives a mentally impaired boy a gun so that he can kill himself. Again, this is not a critical reading, nor does it accord with either the liberal politics of the text or the institution in which the reading was made. This reading is not produced by an institutionally approved reading of the text; by an orthodox reading of the narrative and of the intertextual references which inform that narrative. It also demonstrates lack of awareness of the liberal politics of the pedagogical, disciplinary and institutional discourses by which the students are positioned. Furthermore, it suggests a readership uncomfortable with this medium as a material (and discursive) practice.

A critical reading of this text might well address issues raised by the tactical reading. For example, a critical reading might ask why a story written for adolescents employs a character their own age who is intellectually impaired? Is this, in fact, an exploitative use of intellectual impairment which conveys exactly the kind of contempt for intellectual disability the student readers fear? This may mean that these students are extremely sensitive to what is going on in this text, and how it enacts contemporary social practice. However, they do not have a metalanguage for discussing their reading, which is fixated on the experiential. Without an overt discussion of text as social practice, which means specifically addressing the semiotics of the text and their own institutional positioning, these students are not able to articulate the basis of their fears other than by an illiberal reading of the story which is institutionally transgressive.

In summary, then, the points I want to draw from this analysis are the following: first, that meaning is not a singular attribute of any text, to be accessed by textual analysis (grammatical and/or discursive) alone; secondly, that meanings proliferate from any text but the successful or powerful meanings at any given site will be determined by the complex of institutional discourses operating at that site along with the material practice which defines the individual's interaction with that text; thirdly, that meanings or readings that seem to be wrong or misguided may be the result of a range of difficulties experienced by a student in operating in a particular institution, not just – or not only – semiotic or grammatical difficulties, as well as of differences between the discursive positioning of the student and that assumed by mainstream readings; finally, that working with a more comprehensive understanding of how and why particular readings are made of texts can be enormously enriching not only in terms of textual analysis itself (for example, by enabling deconstructive readings) but also in terms of understanding students' positioning within institutions. In this way, reading may be, for these – and all – students, not a weapon used to regulate them socially, but a technology by which they may achieve the maximum range of choices in all facets of their lives.

## Notes

1   This story is contained in the Appendix to the chapter by Martin, and is the focus of the grammatical analysis in that chapter.

2   See Michel de Certeau (1984) for detailed descriptions of the notion of 'tactical resistance'; also Fiske (1989) for descriptions of the use of this term 'tactic' in relation to reading practices.

3   See, for example, F.R. Leavis (1976).

4   See for example, Chapter 1, 'The Rise of English', in Eagleton (1983); Brian Doyle (1982).

5   Rothery's examination of the sample questions, answers, marks and examiner's comments on a Year 10 English paper showed that the answers which were given the lowest gradings consistently read a request for personal response as just that, an individuated, idiosyncratic and personal response to the text. The highest marks were given to answers which recognised the request for personal response as a demand that the student locate the institutionally approved reading position of the text and use a particular combination of structuralist and Leavisite methodologies in constructing an answer.

6   That is, a pedagogy which utilises an analysis of the individual's social positioning in the learning process; see, for example, Mary Kalantzis and Bill Cope (1989).

7   Analysis of the film demonstrates that Keating uses a control tactic based on emotional manipulation of the students in his classes (Cranny-Francis & Martin 1991). If this is a valid depiction of a child-centred pedagogy, 'good teaching' can be seen as, among other things, a matter of individuated emotional policing.

8   The notion that the literacy skills of contemporary students are

primarily visual rather than verbal is rapidly becoming an interest for theorists, particularly in the area of cultural studies. One recent detailed analysis of the relationship between verbal and other literacies is McKenzie Wark (1992).

9 Note that the term 'meaning potential' is used in a literary critical sense to refer to the notion that texts are the source of many different meanings, when such factors as differences in the positioning of readers, the institutional setting of the particular reading, and the intertextual references activated in particular readings are taken into account.

# References

Bakhtin, M.M. (1981) *The Dialogic Imagination: Four Essays.* Trans C. Emerson & M. Holquist. Ed. M. Holquist. Austin: University of Texas Press.

Bakhtin, M.M. (1986) *Speech Genres and Other Late Essays.* Trans Vern McGee. Ed. C. Emerson & M. Holquist. Austin: University of Texas Press.

Belsey, Catherine (1980) *Critical Practice.* London: Methuen.

Bernstein, Basil (1971) *Class, Codes and Control. Vol. 1: Theoretical Studies towards a Sociology of Language.* London: Paladin.

Bernstein, Basil (1990) *The Structuring of Pedagogic Discourse. Vol. IV: Class, Codes and Control.* London & New York: Routledge.

Board of Senior School Studies (1982) 'English Syllabus Years 11 and 12'. North Sydney: Board of Senior School Studies.

Cranny-Francis, Anne & J.R. Martin (unpublished paper) 'In/visible education: class, gender and pedagogy in *Educating Rita* and *The Dead Poets' Society*'. Paper delivered at the Second Australian Systemic Linguistics Conference, University of Queensland, 11–13 January 1991.

Cranny-Francis, Anne. (1992) 'The value of 'genre' in English Literature teaching', *English in Australia*, 99: 27–48.

de Certeau, Michel. (1984) *The Practice of Everyday Life.* Trans Steven Rendall. Berkeley: University of California Press.

Doyle, Brian (1982) 'The hidden history of English studies'. In Peter Widdowson, ed., *Re-Reading English.* London: Methuen, pp. 17–31.

Eagleton, Terry (1983) *Literary Theory: An Introduction.* Oxford: Basil Blackwell.

Fiske, John (1989) *Understanding Popular Culture.* Boston: Unwin Hymans.

Kalantzis, Mary and Bill Cope (1989) *Social Literacy: An Overview.* Sydney: Common Ground.

Leavis, F.R. (1976) *The Common Pursuit.* Harmondsworth: Penguin.

Rothery, Joan (1991) 'Developing critical literacy through systemic functional linguistics: an analysis of the "hidden" curriculum for writing in junior secondary English in New South Wales'. Paper delivered at the Second Australian Systemic Linguistics Conference, University of Queensland, 11–13 January 1991.

Wark, McKenzie (1992) 'After literature: culture, policy, theory and beyond'. *Meanjin*, 51(4): 677–90.

Widdowson, Peter ed. (1982) *Re-reading English*. London: Methuen.

# 7

## Learning to think like an historian: the language of secondary school History

ROBERT VEEL and CAROLINE COFFIN

## 1 Introduction

There is perhaps no exaggeration in the claim that the nature of human knowledge as we know it depends on our ability to use language. This is not to claim that there is nothing else to knowledge; simply to affirm the central role of language in the creation and maintenance of knowledge. If this is so, it seems beyond dispute that language would occupy an important position in schooling. This chapter is concerned with an exploration of this claim. By focusing on the language of history as encountered by students in their schooling, we will explore the way language works to construct particular forms of knowledge as well as particular ways of knowing. Our major hypothesis with regard to the language of history is that it represents a wide range of genres,[1] beginning with a variety which appears fairly close to ordinary everyday language use and extending through to a stage which is very far removed from such use, thus implicating other-than-ordinary everyday social processes.

In exploring the language of school history it is further suggested that in order to succeed in this subject, students must develop certain ways of meaning that are specific to the genres of history and that this development of meaning potential requires gaining control of an increasing range of genres. In order to do this students need to follow a path of language development whereby knowledge gained at an earlier point in their studies is reformulated in increasingly abstract ways at later points. In this way students develop new forms of consciousness, new ways of knowing about the past. Successive forms of consciousness both assume and subsume earlier forms of consciousness; each form stands on the shoulders of the preceding one, both developing and re-interpreting the social order it represents. An understanding of the linguistic path along which students travel, combined with appropriate pedagogical intervention, would seem important for educators, since it cannot be assumed that all students come to school with control of the entire range of the genres of history, particularly those which are not likely to occur outside educational contexts.

Although the teaching of history involves both oral and written language, it is the written language of history that is of crucial importance in differentiating students. Our investigation of reading and writing practices reveals a fairly predictable and stable pattern in the way particular types of meaning are valued at different points in the study of school history. Stated in general terms, this pattern means that students' ability to 'record', 'sequence', 'list', etc. has a privileged status earlier on in schooling, whereas the ability to 'make generalisations', 'determine cause and effect', 'develop a logical argument', etc. is privileged in later years.[2] It is this pattern of privileged and privileging meanings that determines the linguistic path of school history, since these meanings are embodied principally in the language of history as a school subject. This chapter is a contribution towards identifying some of the characteristic features of language which construe and are construed by this pattern. A description of these features would seem an urgent task, for they are generally not explicated in any way in official syllabi, nor are they given much attention in pre-service teacher training (Christie et al. 1991).

Before engaging in an analysis of representative history texts, we will provide the background of the present research (section 2); we will then contextualise our investigations by saying a few words about the language of history in the New South Wales curriculum (section 3). Following the analysis of texts in section 4, we move on to question the validity and status of the pattern of privileged and privileging meanings in the current practice of school history (section 5), especially in light of alternative views of the nature and role of history. Finally, we look at how a 'critical orientation' to literacy can contribute to our understanding of the language of school history.

## 2    Background to present research

The information presented in this chapter is based on research conducted by the Disadvantaged Schools Program in the Metropolitan East Region of Sydney, through a project known (for better or worse) as *Write It Right*. The Disadvantaged Schools Program (DSP) was established across Australia in 1974 in order to specifically and exclusively address the educational disadvantages faced by students from low socio-economic backgrounds. The aims and activities of the DSP have varied over the years, but more recently there has been an emphasis on curriculum reform; on changing both the content of the curriculum and the approach taken to teaching, assessment and evaluation. The DSP in the Metropolitan East Region of Sydney has devoted itself to language and literacy education in particular, conducting large-scale research projects and developing teaching resources.

Since the mid-1980s the DSP has been using genre theory and systemic functional grammar to underpin its language and literacy work in schools. Initially, this work concentrated on the primary school,[3] and was based on research by Martin and Rothery (1980, 1981, 1986; Martin 1986). Since 1991, however, it has been researching the literacy demands of a range of junior secondary school subjects through the *Write It Right* project. Using this research, the project is also developing training materials and classroom resources to assist teachers to recognise and explicitly teach about the language of their subject (Rothery 1993a, 1993b; Veel 1993a, 1993b).[4]

Over the ten years or so since the genre-based work was first introduced to classrooms, there has been considerable evolution in the theory itself. This has been a result of both the attempts to account for written language in an ever-widening range of educational contexts and of critical response to genre theory from academic colleagues. This evolution in theory is reflected in part in the work being reported here. Whereas the DSP's research and materials development for the primary school, in line with Martin's initial theorising, tended to focus on a more global description of the way written genres function across social contexts within a culture, the work of the *Write It Right* project has concentrated on the way language works within the bounds of individual school disciplines. Many factors have made this shift in emphasis inevitable. Labour, time and space are all divided and organised very differently in the secondary school; teachers in the secondary school have very different professional biographies from their colleagues in the primary school; and the discourses which influence and shape secondary school education (academic disciplines, the priorities of industry and commerce, etc.) are very different from those which influence primary school education (discourses of child development, individual creativity, the psychology of learning, and so on).

Another factor leading to a shift away from 'global' descriptions of genres was the criticism that such descriptions are unacceptably 'totalising' in the way they describe both language and society. Thus the claims being made about written genres by the *Write It Right* project are, on the whole, more modest. Descriptions of written genres relate to language practices *within* specific subject areas *within* the institution of schooling. Although there are links in the language used across school subjects (e.g. many school subjects make use of recounts) and between schooling and other institutions (e.g. both research science and school science use experimental reports), the configuration of genres in relation to one another varies enormously from subject to subject, as does their relationship to syllabus design and assessment. In short, the descriptions of language use offered by *Write It Right* are much more grounded in the particular contexts of school subjects than previous descriptions of genres.

Over the course of *Write It Right* a protocol has emerged for analysing the literacy demands of a school subject, and linking these demands to the syllabus demands of the subject. In other words, an explicit link is being made between the types of learning expected in a subject area and the types of language which embody that learning. The protocol includes the following stages:

1. Analyse the range of written genres encountered by students in their *reading* practices and required of students in their *writing* practices. A detailed consideration of both reading and writing practices is needed to build a picture of the learning demands of a subject. In the *Write It Right* project, about 4,500 texts written by students in a range of school disciplines (English, Geography, History and Science) were collected and analysed for their generic structure and a range of indexical lexicogrammatical features. Of these about 1,000 texts were in the area of history. In order to analyse student reading practices and

access to any 'model' texts for writing, a range of textbooks and other classroom materials were also collected and examined.

2. Locate the genres in relation to the syllabus, outcome statements, public examinations, school programs, school assessment and classroom practice. As well, broader academic and public debates about the nature and role of disciplinary knowledge, and of the pedagogical practices surrounding the use of a written text, need to be taken into account.

3. Analyse register shifts (field, tenor, mode) in genres across subject area. Link these to broad aims and rationales in syllabuses.

4. Analyse lexicogrammatical shifts in genres across subject area. Link these to specific learning outcomes in syllabi.


# 3   Secondary school history

Before looking at a small range of texts used in school history, it is worthwhile first to consider briefly two important factors which influence the range and types of written language which students encounter when they study history in New South Wales. These factors, the design of the New South Wales *History 7–10* syllabus itself, and competing theories about the nature of history and the way it should be taught have a profound influence on the way students learn to interpret and respond to the written texts of history.

In Australia, on the whole school syllabi are designed in a way which renders language invisible as a medium for learning about and acting on the world, even though it is through written language that students are most frequently assessed. In New South Wales, for example, school syllabi tend to function as 'guideline' documents only. Aims, objectives and outcomes are very broad and it is expected that each school will devise a program which covers the aims, objectives and outcomes of the syllabus in its own way. The content of the New South Wales *History 7–10* syllabus (published in 1992) is similarly broad and, although it is organised around 'mandated focus questions' (e.g. 'What have been the major influences on how Australians regard themselves today?', 'What have been the significant relationships between Australia and other countries over the last two centuries?' etc.) and highlights important problems and issues to investigate, it does not prescribe any 'body of facts' which is to be learned by students. The syllabus does not contain any specific reading and writing outcomes, making it very difficult for teachers to determine what meanings and what modes of expression will be most valued.

Despite the lack of detail in the *History 7–10* syllabus, it is not uninformed in its approach to history. Indeed, it would be inaccurate to read the lack of detail in the syllabus as implying a *laissez-faire* view of the discipline. Patterns in assessment practices indicate that both teachers and examiners do have in mind, often unconsciously, quite specific views of the kinds of written texts which best construct particular kinds of meanings in history.[5] What this situation implies is that the main criteria by which students are deemed successful or otherwise in history, namely the kinds of language used, are largely invisible in the syllabus. The invisibility of linguistic criteria often has the effect of marginalising those students (and teachers) who cannot read the implicit messages in the syllabus and cannot 'naturally' develop the reading and writing abilities expected by the syllabus. If the literature on educational success and failure is to be credited, it is highly probable that the consequences of this invisibility will be worse for socio-economically disadvantaged students, since they are less likely to have access to privileged meanings from sources outside school, and are therefore less likely to be able to 'read between the lines' and determine what is expected of them in school assessment.[6]

Another problem with the New South Wales *History 7–10* syllabus worth raising at this point is that it fails to contextualise itself sufficiently with regard to competing philosophies about the nature of historical knowledge and competing views about teaching and learning history. Our discussions with people at all levels in the education system indicates that there is often a considerable mismatch between the way history teachers were themselves taught to interpret and respond to history and the aims of the new syllabus whose writers had in mind a very different conception of the nature of history. The failure to state explicitly the philosophical, ideological and pedagogical underpinnings of the syllabus, and to differentiate these underpinnings from other approaches, has led to varied, and often incompatible, interpretations of the syllabus in classroom practice.

On a philosophical level, the tension is between 'grand narrative' conceptions of history and the post-structuralist conceptions of history, heavily influenced by the work of Michel Foucault (1972, 1978). The 'grand narrative' model gives emphasis to things such as cause-and-effect links between events; notions of continuing, unending development over time; unitary, *en masse* explanatory principles (i.e. recurrent themes or motifs in history) and the segmentation of chronological time into historical periods.

In his writing, Foucault develops an elaborate alternative to this view, which emphasises the multiplicity of views of the world which operate at any one time and sees a need to look beyond 'official' history to understand the complex networks of social relations operating in social contexts over time. One of the approaches to school history adopted in *History 7–10* appears particularly to have been influenced by Foucault's so-called 'archaeological approach'. Foucault's often complex arguments have been succinctly sum- marised in a study guide published by Deakin University (Deakin University Production Unit 1985). The guide describes the archae- ological approach in the following way:

> Archaeology, instead of searching for lineages, continuous lines of development, and progress within particular knowledges, looks instead at the spaces between different but interlocking domains ... he sought out lateral and indirect influences and relations rather than chronological connections.
>
> The archaeological method attempts to avoid traditional explana- tory concepts ... Foucault wishes to be guided, not by a pre-conceived grid, but to remain open to the specific details and connections that historically particular knowledges develop. The rules of formation of knowledges are not generalisable, but always remain contextually specified ...
>
> Instead of referring to 'great texts', 'grand discoveries' or 'master thinkers' to substantiate his arguments, Foucault instead relies on archives, texts of minor officials, texts that are usually neglected in political analyses, as the raw materials of his investigations.
>
> (Deakin University Production Unit 1985: 77–8)

The Foucaultian conception of history is a challenge for many history teachers, who would have been schooled in the 'grand narrative' manner of dealing with the past. Critics of this approach claim that history risks losing its status as a separate dis- cipline by being moulded into the post-structuralist conception. Post-structuralists would argue that this may not be a bad thing; neither history nor any other discipline should be arbitrarily seg- regated from other types of knowledge.

Competing pedagogical theories, most notably those of

progressive vs traditional teaching are another factor which directly influences the type and range of written texts encountered by students, and the way they are taught to respond to these texts. Like the competing theories of history, these competing pedagogical theories are not addressed explicitly in the *History 7–10* syllabus, leaving it to the teacher to 'read between the lines' in interpreting the document. The implications for classroom practice of these competing theories will be familiar to people working in the field of education. Progressive initiatives in the area of history, for example, opened the way for the teaching of more 'social history' – where the texts of 'ordinary people', usually in the form of recounts, are used to supplement the grand narrative texts.[7] Rather than write 'logical' analyses of historical texts, students in the progressive classroom are often encouraged to respond 'personally', to state what they felt rather than what they thought. Debates over the merits of progressive education in junior secondary history have much the same dimensions as other areas of education. On the one hand, progressive classroom practice has done much to give students a voice in classroom learning, to make teachers 'start from where students are at' – as the expression runs – and to make the educational knowledge of school history connect with everyday experiences. On the other hand, it risks leaving students with little more than their everyday experience and often reduces complex and valuable understandings to statements of dubious value in any context. The following excerpt from a recent history textbook exemplifies this: 'The migration of people from many other countries has made Australian culture diverse and colourful. Now Australia is a multicultural society and our identity has changed again.' (Pyne et al. 1994: 45). The lack of explicit reference to theory – either historical or pedagogical – in the *History 7–10* syllabus only serves to make the document more difficult for teachers to make sense of, and more difficult for marginalised students to profit from.

These difficulties can be seen on a daily basis in the classroom. The orientation of many progressive teachers towards the emotional response of the individual student, for example, has lead to some significant misreadings of those elements of the syllabus which are legitimated by post-structuralist theory. This is particularly so in the area of 'empathetic understanding', a perspective on history which runs right through the syllabus. A member of the History Syllabus Committee, whom we interviewed, explained empathetic understanding in post-structuralist terms. It is seen as a combination of 'the cognitive with the affective'. In working towards an empathetic understanding, students should interrogate sources, both official and unofficial, in order to understand how marginalised social subjects may have reacted to and felt about historical events. This might lead, for example, to a critique of the way mainstream, Anglocentric Australian history deals with Australian Aborigines – an empathetic understanding of the Aborigines' perspective on events. This, in turn, might lead to critical or even resistant reading of official or 'traditional' interpretations of history. According to a post-structuralist view of history, empathetic understanding is thus a potentially subversive activity. In classrooms with a progressive orientation, however, 'empathetic understanding' has often resulted more in bathos than in pathos. Students are asked to use their *imagination*, rather than any informed reading of historical archives, to empathise with historical subjects. The result of this interpretation of empathetic understanding is often a loosely conceived imaginative task (e.g. 'Imagine you are a slave in ancient Greece', 'A day in the life of a medieval village'), to be completed with little, if any, investigation of historical sources. It is not our intention to deny that perspectives of the type intended by 'empathetic understanding' are valuable if they actually succeed in encouraging students to question taken-for-granted attitudes and values. But it is certainly our claim that there has been no systematic effort to understand how one inculcates such enlightened attitudes over the course of teaching to 11–18 year olds. The vacuum created by the absence of such pedagogic understandings, in explicit terms, is naturally filled by other means. For example, viewed specifically, an approach of this kind is appealing to teachers of students who find the language of school history difficult and therefore shy away from tasks requiring extensive reading and critical interrogation of sources. Thus, ironically, emphasis on 'empathetic understanding' translates itself into indifference to enquiry, refusal to explore alternative accounts, and a celebration of subjectivism, all of which appears to be sanctioned by the syllabus. The consequences of this misreading for disadvantaged students, however, can be very serious indeed. Having been trained to produce a personal response as a way of showing empathetic understanding, these students are less likely to produce more favoured kinds of analytical response in contexts such as public examinations; they thereby risk official failure in the education system.[8]

# 4    Some school history genres

The four texts which are discussed in this section illustrate just some of the *reading* demands placed on secondary school history students. They have been selected to show the kinds of shift in language which are required for the increasingly abstract interpretations of history expected of these students. Although they are texts which students are required to read, they have been selected because they are also indicative of the kinds of understandings and interpretations which (according to the syllabus and on the evidence of school and public assessment practices) students are expected to express through their writing. Taken in the sequence in which they are presented, the four texts vary linguistically from the relatively everyday 'spoken' grammar and small-scale time sequence of text 1 to the dense, abstract 'written' grammar of text 4. The texts come from a number of sources including more traditional 'grand narrative' text books (texts 2, 3 and 4) and progressive 'primary sources only' books (text 1). The linguistic patterns described in these four texts are typical of patterns to be found in the over 100 texts from school textbooks which we have examined, and are also to be found in the even larger number of student written texts we have collected and analysed.

The sequence of texts presented here is not meant to suggest a staged or 'lock-step' interpretation of school history, where students who have mastered the knowledge at one level of the syllabus then abandon these understandings to progress to a higher level. Nor is it meant to suggest that 'autobiographical recounts' or 'historical recounts' are only ever encountered at the lowest levels of school history. What is important to consider is the different ways in which texts are treated at different points in the syllabus. 'Autobiographical recounts', for example, occur at all levels in the study of history. They are the raw materials of history, the source documents which historians act upon. However, it is unlikely that junior secondary students will be expected to interpret and write about autobiographical recounts in the same way as a university historian. The junior secondary student is unlikely to have the same breadth of historical context into which to place the text, and, in any case, would be actively discouraged from doing so by a school system which privileges less sophisticated kinds of readings. However, as students study more and more history their interpretations and responses to source documents are expected to approximate more and more those of the professional historian. Thus the texts presented here are evidence of increasingly sophisticated ways of interpreting and responding to historical sources.

It should also be noted that the four texts have been extracted from chapters of school history textbooks, and thus tend to be 'bleeding chunks' or fragments of much longer texts; they should not really be seen as standing independently. Nonetheless each extract does have some integrity. Text 1 stands on its own in the textbook from which it is drawn, marked off from the rest of the book by a border, and with no accompanying commentary text. The other texts are sections from chapters of textbooks, separated from other sections of the book by headings, illustration and spacing.

Each text has been analysed from a number of perspectives, using a few of the analysis techniques available from within systemic linguistics (Halliday 1985a; Martin 1992; Matthiessen 1995; Halliday & Martin 1993). Ideally, each text should be considered thoroughly at a number of 'levels' of organisation in the linguistic system: generic structure, register and lexicogrammar, as analysis at each of these levels will reveal different things about how different forms of historical consciousness are constructed through text.[9] However, for reasons of space, the main focus here is on lexicogrammatical patterns in each text, with a few comments only about generic structure and register. The analyses used include:

(1) *Generic structure*:
The division/divisibility of the text into identifiable stages, each of which performs a distinct function in achieving the overall purpose(s) of the text. A discussion of generic structure is useful here in so far as it allows us to draw relationships between texts across different contexts. It allows us to say, for example, that the structure of one text in one context, resembles that of another text in another context, and may be therefore more or less easy for a student to recognise and make sense of.

(2) *Register*:
In discussing the register of written texts we are really projecting backwards from the grammatical evidence given to us through the texts to speculate about the kind of educational context in which

the text was conceived. This can be useful in drawing our attention to the kinds of choices that have been made in the text *vis-à-vis* the overall meaning potential of the language system.

    (a)  Field: The things and events being talked about in a situation, and the relationships between things and events constructed in a situation; what is done, who/what does it, to/for whom/what, etc. Of particular concern in the context of the research presented here is the relative 'everydayness' or 'abstractness' of things and events – how 'commonsense' or 'uncommonsense' a field is.[10]

    (b)  Tenor: The way social relations between reader and writer are construed in the texts, and the way social relations among participants in the text are construed. Here we are particularly concerned with the role constructed for student readers of history texts. Are they treated as novices or experts? Thinkers or feelers? Adults or children?

    (c)  Mode: The way the language system itself influences the nature of the text. Of particular concern here is the relative 'spokenness' or written nature of the text, and whether the overall structure of the texts derives from the way events unfold over time or, alternatively, from the need to develop a logical argument.

(3) *Lexicogrammar*:

The lexicogrammatical features used for analysis and discussion here have been selected to highlight the kinds of changes that occur in the grammar of written historical texts as one moves from relatively everyday/commonsense construals of history to more uncommonsense/educational renderings. They need to be considered both singly and collectively, as 'syndromes' of features which, taken together, realise kinds of texts. For example, all of the texts discussed in this chapter display grammatical features for sequencing events in time (conjunctions, circumstances of time, 'phased' verbal groups, enhancing clauses, etc.), yet each text deploys these features quite differently; the features occur in quite different grammatical environments and thus have a quite different *valeur*. The description and glosses given to grammatical features here are necessarily brief. More detailed discussions and analyses can be found in Halliday (1985a) and Martin (1992).

The features analysed and discussed in this section are enumerated below:

(a) *Abstraction*:

To what extent participants and places in the text are referred to as singular, tangible entities, close to the lived experience of the writer, or, alternatively, in terms of their political or social roles, in a kind of 'pseudo-objective' semiotic space. For example, the difference between referring to 'my mates Jack and Bill' versus 'soldiers in the company' marks a difference in abstraction.

(b) *Grammatical metaphor*:

To what extent the qualities, events and things of history are represented through 'incongruent' grammatical categories in the text. Writing about grammatical metaphor, Halliday states:

> This is like metaphor in the usual sense except that, instead of being a substitution of one *word* for another, as when you say 'you're talking tripe' instead of 'you're talking nonsense' it is a substitution of one grammatical structure, by another; for example, *his departure* instead of *he departed*. Here the words (lexical items) are the same; what has changed is their place in the grammar. Instead of pronoun *he* + verb *departed*, functioning as Actor plus Process in a clause, we have determiner *his* + noun *departure*, functioning as a Deictic plus Thing in a nominal group ...
>
> What is the nature of this rewording? One way of thinking of it is by imagining the age of the reader, or listener. In talking to a 9 year-old, we would never say *in times of engine failure*, we would say *whenever the engine fails* ... What we are doing, when we reword in this way, is changing the grammar by making it younger.
>
> (Halliday & Martin 1993: 79)

Besides linking grammatical metaphor to the age of the writer/speaker or imagined reader/listener, Halliday (1985b: 95) also points out that more complex forms of grammatical metaphor are 'particularly characteristic' of written language. Martin (1993b: 226–8) has taken discussions of grammatical metaphor into the area of school history, arguing that it is an essential tool for building abstract discourse and for allowing 'internal reasoning' in history. Martin gives the following example of grammatical metaphor at work in this way in history (grammatical metaphors shown in italics): 'The *enlargement of Australia's steel making capacity* and of chemicals, rubber, metal goods and motor vehicles owed something to *the demands of war*'. (Martin 1993b: 227). In examining the comparative use of grammatical metaphor in these texts we are thus looking at the assumptions made about readers' age, and experience with written texts, together with the level of abstraction in the text and the degree of internal reasoning.

(c) *Temporality*:

How and to what extent the text uses grammatical resources to organise events into a time sequence. Resources for construing temporality deployed in these texts include Circumstances of temporal location (e.g. *in the morning*), enhancing clauses (e.g. *when he died, it began to disintegrate* ...), conjunctions (e.g. *next, then, after* ...) and phased Processes (e.g. *began to disintegrate*).

(d) *Causality*:

How and to what extent the text uses grammatical resources to construct cause-and-effect links between things and events. The degree and kind of cause-and-effect links in a text is usually closely associated with the occurrence of grammatical metaphor. Resources for construing causality include conjunctions (e.g. *because, so, therefore* ...) and Circumstances (e.g. *because of their ability as soldiers* ...), and, more subtly, through transitivity structures (e.g. *the success of some encouraged others* [which may be re-worded as 'caused others to act'] ...).[11]

(e) *Unexpectancy 'buts'*:

To what extent the text explicitly constructs relationships of unexpectancy between events, using the conjunction *but* or a comment adjunct such as *suddenly* or *unexpectedly*. The use of such a feature indicates an attempt to imbue the text with a narrative flavour.

(f) *Nominal groups*:

The relative complexity with which participants in the text are represented through nominal groups. Nominal groups can vary from very simple structure (e.g. *we, Turks*) to structures which are long and dense (e.g. *possible American domination of post-war settlement in the pacific*). Nominal group structure is closely linked to the use of grammatical metaphor and is a good indication of how 'spoken' or 'written' a text is.

In the discussion of the four texts, we will first present the text, with the stages in its generic structure indicated in parentheses.

We will then proceed to discuss its register. For our first text, an autobiographical recount, a discussion of each of the linguistic features mentioned above is given. For texts 2, 3 and 4 only the grammatical features which contrast with those deployed in previous texts are discussed. When all four texts have been described we will make some comparisons between the texts and try to draw some conclusions about overall patterns of linguistic features across the texts.

## 4.1   Text 1: an autobiographical account and its description

The first text to be produced below is an **autobiographical account** of a war experience. The generic structure stages of the text are given in brackets, following which the part of text considered to construe that stage is produced.

### Text 1: Into action

*[Orientation]*
   On the night before the attack on Gallipoli we were all lined up on board our ship.

*[Record of events]*
   We were issued with three days' rations and ammunition. They told us not to talk, smoke, or load any of our rifles. About 4 am. they loaded us into big open boats and began towing us inshore. We were told not to hang around on the beach but to go inland as far as we could. We weren't the first to hit the beach. It was nearly full light when we arrived. There was lots of shooting but not many were wounded or dead on the beach. We didn't lose any men as far as I remember. There wasn't much order on the beach; we just ran across to the steep cliff and began climbing.
   At first it was pretty easy, no Turks, but soon we were beginning to cop it. It was like shooting rabbits. One would pop up and you had to be quick. Other times you were the rabbit. I joined a few other blokes from the 10th Battalion and we made the first ridge.
   I got 'knocked' about 9 am. I learned later I got shot clean through one lung. When I came to, I was under a bush. I kept passing out all day. I wasn't found until next morning and carried back to the beach. They took a mob of us out on a barge to a hospital ship. From there we were taken to Cairo Hospital where I recovered. I was no good to them with only one lung so they sent me back home. I was in the Anzac March on 25 April 1916.

*[Re-orientation]*
Most of my mob didn't survive the war. The wounded ones like me
lived to tell the tale but all of my mates got wiped out later in France.

(Sawyer 1984: 31)

**Discussion of text 1**

The **generic structure** of text 1 is that of a recount
(Orientation^Record of events^Re-orientation). Recounts are a
genre familiar to most students, both because they occur in writing in a range of school subjects (e.g. Recounts of personal
experience in English, recounts of experimental procedures in
Science) and because they also occur (with some variation) in oral
language in both educational and non-educational contexts
(Labov & Waletzky 1967; Plum 1988). Students' familiarity with
the structure of this text will make it easier for them to comprehend and interpret.

The **field** construed by the text is very much an 'everyday' one,
in which the things referred to in the text can be seen and
touched, and the goings on witnessed or heard (i.e. the text is
fundamentally about 'concrete' kinds of experience). The human
participants are typically unique individuals or groups, referred to
by their speech relationship to the narrator, through the use of
personal pronouns (e.g. *we* and *they*), rather than by their institutional roles (*the leader, the troops*, etc). Places are also referred to by
their spatial relationship to the narrator – how close or how far
away they are from the narrator (e.g. *inshore, on the beach, inland,
the first ridge*), rather than through any more 'objective' carto-
graphical reference (*in the south, two miles away*, etc). In keeping
with the 'everyday' nature of the field 70 per cent of the Processes
represented in the text are material or verbal, referring to the
physical acts and locutions of participants (e.g. *issued, told, ran,
arrived*).

The **tenor** of the reader/writer relationship construed by the
text is one of relative solidarity. This solidarity is achieved through
a combination of the 'storytelling' nature of the generic structure
with the conversational use of speech roles to refer to participants
(e.g. *we, I, you, us, one*) and the use of colloquial lexis (e.g. *to hang
on, blokes, like shooting rabbits*). Among participants, tenor relationships vary from the solidary, inclusive *we* used to refer to the

soldiers, the adversarial *they* used to refer to officers, and the more institutional *Turks* to refer to cultural others.

The **mode** construed by the text is very much that of spoken language. The lexical density (number of lexical items per clause)[12] is 2.46, relatively low for written language. As well, the organisation of the text accords with the order in which the events recounted in the text themselves unfolded; i.e. the text time unfolds parallel to field time. **Nominal groups** are relatively short and simple:

> *They* told *us* not to talk, smoke or load *any of our rifles.*

**Abstraction** in the text is low (see 'field' above). There is relatively little **grammatical metaphor** to be found, and when used it is relatively commonplace (e.g. *the war, shooting*) and would not pose problems for most readers. The events related in the text are not reasoned about in any way and so there is hardly any use of **causality**.

**Temporality** is an important feature of the text. While the greater part of temporality is carried by the fact that the text's structure reflects that of the order of events themselves, the text is also located in 'real time' through the use of Circumstances of temporal location, as the following examples show:

> *On the night before the attack on Gallipoli,* we were all lined up on board our ship.

> *About 4 am.* they loaded us into big open boats ...

The use of a number of *buts* highlights the speaker's opinion of the unusuality of events recounted in the text, and his attempts to narrativise events.

> At first it was pretty easy *but* soon we were beginning to cop it.

This is a common feature of many narrative-type texts (Rothery 1990) and adds to the storytelling flavour of the text.

## 4.2 Text 2: an historical recount and its description

Text 2 is an instance of the genre of **historical recount**. Its stages and description are given as for text 1.

## Text Two: The spread of Islam

*[Background]*

When Mohammed started spreading his new religion in Mecca, he
became most unpopular with the city authorities. In 622 he was
forced to flee to Medina where he converted the Jewish inhabitants
and became their leader. Six years later, he was strong enough to
attack Mecca which fell in 630. Mohammed was then master of all
Arabia. In 632 Mohammed died.

*[Record of events]*

Because of their ability as soldiers and their religious mission to convert others to a new religion, the Arabs rapidly expanded their
territory and their forces pushed into north Africa, south west Asia,
and most of Spain. But in 732 Charles Martel finally stopped the
Moslems at Poitiers. This was one of the most important battles in
history for it determined whether Europe would remain Christian or
become Moslem.

Between 786 and 809, a strong ruler, Harun-al Raschid, held the
Mohammedan Empire together. But when he died, it began to disintegrate till raids by Mongol tribes in the thirteenth century finally
destroyed it. But the Moslem faith continued and spread through
Africa along the trade routes.

*[Judgement]*

Wherever the religion was established, it was accompanied by some
of the most beautiful art, pottery and architecture in the world. In
medicine, mathematics and literature the Moslems contributed
much to civilisation.

(Coupe & Jenkins 1980: 95)

## Discussion of text 2

Linguistically, text 2 marks a substantial move away from the
spoken, tangible nature of text 1. In some ways the **generic structure** of the text (Background^Record of events^Judgement) is
similar to that of the autobiographical recounts; particularly the
'record of events' stage is common to both texts. However, the
structure is also significantly different. Rather than providing a
setting in space and time to events and introducing the central
participants as one might expect in an Orientation, the
Background stage introduces the text by providing a telescopic
summary of the events which have led up to the events focused
upon in the Record stage (here the *spread* of Islam, not

Mohammed's life). The Judgement stage at the end of the text also marks a development. It functions to give an explicit evaluation of the significance of the events recounted in the texts in terms of institutional categories such as 'medicine', 'mathematics', 'literature' and 'civilisation'. We may see this stage in the text as providing a model of the process of historical interpretation for students. It gives the events in the text a significance which is quite different from that in the Re-orientation stage of text 1.

The **field** of text 2 is also significantly less 'everyday'. This can be seen in clauses such as:

> But in 732 Charles Martel finally stopped the Moslems at Poitiers

where Participants are groups defined by their institutional status (e.g. *the Moslems*) or individuals with significant institutional roles (e.g. *Charles Martel*, who acts as an agent of history, not a unique individual – presumably Charles Martel did not stop the Moslems single-handedly!) and places are referred to by their geographical position (*at Poitiers*) rather than by their relationship to individuals. As well, the Processes represented in the text are at a more 'general' level, referring not to single actions affecting individual Participants but to large scale events involving large, institutional groups of people. These features place the text at a distance from the flow of everyday life as we experience it on a day-to-day basis and thus renders the text more **abstract** than text 1. The people, places and events in text 2 do not refer to the narrator's direct experience, but to a 'removed' construction of the past.

The **tenor** of text 2 is more overtly pedagogical, with an expert/learner relationship between writer and reader being implied. The comparatively abstract nature of the text also places greater social distance between the text and both reader and writer.

**Temporality** is a major feature of the text. On average 75 per cent of the clauses have some kind of temporal marker, a much higher percentage than the other texts being discussed here. This is not to say that the other texts are atemporal – simply that the passing of historical time is much more explicitly foregrounded in this text. The main resources used to sequence the text are Circumstances of temporal location and 'phased' Processes. Many of the Circumstances of temporal location (e.g. *In 622, Between 786* *and 809*) are given special prominence by being placed in marked Theme[13] positions at the beginning of clauses and paragraphs:

> *Between 786 and 809*, a strong ruler, Harun-al-Raschid, held the Mohammedan Empire together.

Some of the Processes in the text are 'phased', giving added emphasis to the time dimension of events:

> When Mohammed *started spreading* his new religion in Mecca ...

Some adjuncts and conjunctions also emphasise the temporality of the text:

> But in 732 Charles Martel *finally* stopped the Moslems at Poitiers.

Like text 1, there is little **causality** expressed in text 2 (on average only 12 per cent of clauses in the text have some kind of causal marker). The use of **grammatical metaphor** is significantly greater than in text 1 (an average of 0.29 grammatical metaphors per clause, up from 0.06 in text 1), but this is still relatively low. *Buts* are also used, giving the text a narrative flavour.

## 4.3   Text 3: an historical account and its description

Unlike texts 1 and 2, text 3 is not a *re*count – it is an account. Its generic structure and description are provided below.

### Text 3: The feudal system

*[Background]*
> For almost five hundred years the Romans provided strong, effective government over much of Europe, western Asia, and north Africa. Orders issued in Rome were put into effect by governors and enforced by the Roman armies.

*[Account]*
> But the power of the empire declined gradually and it became more and more difficult for Rome to exert its authority. So the outlying tribes revolted, broke away, and set up governments of their own. The success of some encouraged others and gradually the strong, centralised Roman system gave way to many petty chiefs who emerged, each controlling a small area of land. Of course these rulers were unable to defend their territories adequately if a strong

enemy attacked them. And this frequently happened after the Roman armies could no longer keep the peace. Therefore the rulers had to seek the help of stronger neighbours to protect them. Naturally some payment was expected for this service and so the system of feudalism began.                  (Coupe & Jenkins 1980: 89)

## Discussion of text 3

Like text 2, text 3 marks another move away from the everyday spoken nature of text 1. The overwhelming feature of the text in comparison to the previous examples is the use of **causality** to construct logical relations of cause and effect between events. The Record of events stage has been renamed Account to indicate the shift away from simply recording a sequence of events towards an attempt to provide an explicit, logical explanation for the unfolding of events. On average 30 per cent of the clauses in text 3 have some form of causal marker. Causality is achieved through the use of explicit causal conjunctions (e.g. *so, therefore, and [so]*) and through the use of **grammatical metaphor**. Grammatical metaphor allows events to be represented as things (e.g. *power, success*) and so enables events to be placed in a cause-and-effect relationship to one another, as the following example shows:

> The success of some encouraged others and [so] gradually the strong, centralised Roman system gave way to many petty chiefs ...

Rewritten to show the cause-and-effect relationship explicitly, this sentence could be paraphrased as:

> Some were successful. This *caused* others to act in the same way. All this combined *to cause* the Roman system to give way to many petty chiefs ...

An analysis of the linguistic features of causality reveals the following cause-and-effect sequence in text 3:

1. The power of the empire declined *and so* ...
2. Rome was unable to exert its authority *and so* ...
3. the outer tribes revolted
4. The successful revolution *caused* others to revolt.
5. Many revolutions *caused* many petty chiefs to emerge
6. The petty chiefs could not protect themselves *and so* ...

7. they needed the help of a powerful neighbour
8. The powerful neighbour expected payment *and so ...*
9. the feudal system began

The **nominal groups** in text 3 are noticeably more dense and lengthy than for texts 1 or 2. This shift appears to arise from the use of grammatical metaphor which frequently needs to be qualified in some way (e.g. the power *of the Empire,* the success *of some*), or to be judged (e.g. the *strong,* centralised Roman system, *strong, effective* government).

Like text 2, this text makes use of a number of **temporal markers** to sequence events in the text (on average 0.55 per clause, down from 0.75 in text 2). With the exception of the opening sentence, however, they are not foregrounded nearly so much as in text 2. This is a good example of the way lexico-grammatical features work in 'syndromes' to realise meaning in texts. In text 2 it is the presence of temporal marker **in marked Theme position**, together with the relative **absence of causal markers**, which gives the text its 'recount' status. In text 3, however, the same feature occurs in a different grammatical environment, with an altogether different effect.

Causality, grammatical metaphor and dense nominal groups all have the effect of pushing the **field** construed by the text further away from one of 'everyday' knowledge developed through our experience of the physical world and into a form of knowledge which is much more clearly 'educational' in nature. These features also render the **mode** of the text relatively 'written'; it is grammatical features such as cause and effect which push the text forward, rather than the unfolding of events in the field.

## 4.4   *Text 4: an evaluative exposition and its description*

The last text to be discussed here is an instance of the genre known as evaluative exposition. Its generic and lexicogrammatical description is given below.

### Text 4: Evaluative exposition

*[Judgement]*
　　How equal was the United States–Australia relationship? It was no more an equal relationship than had been Australia's relationship with Britain.

*[Evidence]*

The opening of United States and Australian government wartime files during the 1970s has allowed historians to construct a more accurate picture of the relations between the two nations than was previously possible. These files have revealed that there was conflict as well as co-operation. As the dominant partner in the alliance, the United States had little need to compromise, but was more able than Australia to pursue its specific national objectives and interests.

Wartime censorship and the need for wartime diplomacy to be kept secret ensured an image emerged of warm relations between the alliance partners, but it is now clear that relations were often strained. The Australian government was frequently critical of the priorities of American strategy during the war. The Roosevelt administration in the United States often sought to gain permanent political and economic advantages from Australia in return for wartime aid and, despite Australian objections, the United States devoted as much of its resources as possible to an early victory in Europe. At the same time, it tried to maintain total control of operations against Japan and tried to ensure that it would dominate the post-war settlement in the Pacific.

By 1943 Curtin was calling for closer consultation between members of the British Empire. After 1944 the Chifley government was seeking continued defence co-operation with the United States, but on Australia's terms and those terms were rejected by the Americans. During the transition to peace, Labour became concerned about possible American domination of the post-war settlement in the Pacific, and so the Australian government reaffirmed its links with Britain.

The main benefit of the American alliance for the Australian government was that MacArthur, unlike his own government and that of Britain, shared Australia's view of the importance of defeating Japan rather than Germany first. What most Americans did not realise was that MacArthur's main ambition was his own triumphant return to the Philippines. And there is no doubt that MacArthur used his wide powers over censorship and publicity to glorify his own achievements and to belittle those of the Australians who did most of the ground fighting in the region until 1944.

(Darlington 1990: 344)

## Discussion of text 4

Of all the texts we have examined, text 4 is the one most removed from the everyday spoken language of most school students. The grammar of the text is more 'written-like' than any of the other texts and all aspects of the register are more abstract.

The **generic structure** of the text is that of an evaluative exposition (Judgement^Evidence), whose overall purpose is to persuade readers about a proposition. This is not to say that the text does not recount historical events (most historical argument depends upon recounts and/or accounts for evidence), merely that recounting is not the main organising principle of the text. The persuasive purpose of the text is clearly indicated in the opening sentence:

How equal was the United States–Australia relationship?

The opening stage is called Judgement because it contains an explicit interpretation of historical events, leaving the reader in no doubt as to the writer's opinion:

It was no more an equal relationship than had been Australia's relationship with Britain.

The major section of the text – the Evidence stage – offers historical information selected to support the judgement made in the opening stage. Unlike the various stages in the foregoing texts, this stage of the text is not organised around a time sequence, but around a series of points, which support the assertion made at the beginning. Roughly speaking these points are as follows:

1. The opening of files (1970s) has given us new information as to the true nature of the US–Australia relationship.
2. Censorship during the war (1942–45) meant that strains in the US–Australia relationship were not made public.
3. During the war and the transition to peace (1943–49?) the Labour government moved closer to Britain.
4. It was only because of MacArthur's personal ambitions that the US–Australia alliance was beneficial for Australia.

The **field** of discourse construed by the text is highly abstract. The world being constructed here is one of abstract historical and political entities (e.g. r*elationship, interests, priorities*) rather than tangible things and people. **Grammatical metaphor** is the main resource used to create these entities, and so the text has a much higher proportion of grammatical metaphor than the other texts (an average of 1.57 per cent per clause). The non-metaphorical Participants, however, are also removed from our everyday experience of the world. Places, for example, are referred to by their geo-political role (e.g. *Japan, Europe, the United States*). The field is also less oriented to an activity sequence than the other texts. Many of the Processes describe and define states and intentions rather than actions:

It *is* now clear that relations *were* often strained

the United States *had little need* to compromise

The **mode** of the text is very much that of a written one. The lexical density of the text is 7.30 items per clause – much higher than in any of the other texts we have examined. Beside the frequent use of grammatical metaphor, there are a large number of dense **nominal groups**, including the following examples:

Wartime *censorship* and the need for wartime diplomacy …

The *priorities* of American *strategy* during the war …

… total control of *operations* against Japan

… possible American *domination* of the post-war *settlement* in the Pacific …

Nominal groups which include grammatical metaphors, such as the above examples, are used frequently by writers of persuasive texts. They provide resources for compressing and reifying complex sets of events into single things. This then allows these things to be succinctly reasoned about, judged and used as evidence in exposition, without recourse to lengthy and distracting recounts of events. Consider, for example, how the succinct nature of the argument in the following extract

Wartime censorship and the need for wartime diplomacy to be kept secret ensured an image emerged of warm relations between the alliance partners, but it is now clear that relations were often strained

might have become diffuse without the resources of grammatical metaphor and the nominal group. Here is a less metaphorical rendering of the extract:

During the war many official documents were censored and diplomats were forced to negotiate secretly. Because of this most people believed that Australia and the United States got on well together. But it is now clear that often they did not get on well at all.

Grammatical metaphor and dense nominal groups also allow texts to be 'internally' rather than 'externally' structured. In other words, they allow writers to muster up historical events and order them as arguments according to principles other than that of historical time sequence (i.e. external structuring). The use of grammatical metaphor and the nominal group means that sequences of events in history can be turned into 'arguments', each of which can be clearly signalled in the text. The following example shows this:

> The main benefit of the American alliance for the Australian government was ...

This completes our somewhat hurried discussion of the four texts. In the following sub-section, we will attempt to present a synthesis of this analysis.

## 4.5   Putting it all together: syndromes of features

In the introduction to this chapter (see section 1) it was asserted that in studying school history 'successive forms of consciousness [realised in language] both assume and subsume earlier forms of consciousness; each form stands on the shoulders of the preceding one, both developing and re-interpreting the social order it represents'. Having looked at a representative sample of history texts we can now examine overall patterns and see how this pattern of 'assuming and subsuming' works.

Table 7.1 summarises overall patterns of change in some of the grammatical features we have been discussing. Total occurrences of each feature in the text are given in the plain rows. The average occurrence per clause of each of these features is then given in bold. It is these averages which provide us with a basis for comparison between texts and thus makes it possible to see patterns across the texts.

### Lexical density

There is a progressive increase in the average number of lexical items per clause across the four texts. Following Halliday (1985b: 63–7), we can take this to indicate that the texts become increasingly 'written like' in their grammar. It would appear from these texts that in school history students are *gradually* apprenticed into

**Table 7.1** Summary of total and average occurrences of selected grammatical features.

|  | Text 1 Auto-biographical recount | Text 2 Historical recount | Text 3 Historical account | Text 4 Evaluative exposition |
|---|---|---|---|---|
| **No. of clauses** | **47** | **24** | **20** | **26** |
| No. of lexical items | 116 | 96 | 80 | 190 |
| **Lexical density** | **2.46** | **4.00** | **4.00** | **7.30** |
| Personal/individual participants | 37 | 9 | 0 | 4 |
| **Average per clause** | **0.78** | **0.37** | **0.00** | **0.15** |
| Abstract/institutional participants | 8 | 26 | 20 | 29 |
| **Average per clause** | **0.17** | **1.08** | **1.00** | **1.15** |
| Temporal markers | 13 | 18 | 11 | 11 |
| **Average per clause** | **0.27** | **0.75** | **0.55** | **0.42** |
| Causal markers | 1 | 3 | 6 | 5 |
| **Average per clause** | **0.06** | **0.13** | **0.3** | **0.19** |
| Grammatical metaphor | 3 | 7 | 14 | 41 |
| **Average per clause** | **0.06** | **0.29** | **0.7** | **1.57** |

increasingly dense written texts. The increasing lexical density is shown in Figure 7.1.

**Grammatical metaphor**

In commenting on individual texts, it was noted that grammatical metaphor occurred when there was a need to construct cause-and-effect links or to organise historical events into arguments. Martin (1993b) has also shown how it is used to construct abstract historical concepts. Grammatical metaphor is thus a good indicator of how 'abstract' a text is for students; how removed from the everyday experience of events. It has also been argued by Halliday (1985b: 95) that grammatical metaphor is a feature associated with more mature writing and is one way of achieving high lexical density in a text.

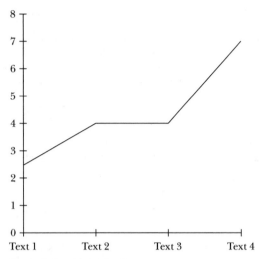

**Figure 7.1**    Lexical density in the four texts

If all this is so, then our analysis confirms a tendency to increasing abstractness across the four texts we have examined. This is shown in Figure 7.2. Moreover, the increase in grammatical metaphor *co-occurs* with increasing lexical density, confirming that these two features are indeed related in the language of school history. Note, however, that between texts 2 and 3, the level of grammatical metaphor increases without any increase in lexical density. The increase in grammatical metaphor here is most probably due to the move from the historical recount genre, with its emphasis on sequence, to historical account, with its emphasis on cause and effect.

### Moving from the personal to the institutional

As students learn the discourse of school history, the privileging of individuals as the subject matter of history which occurs in text 1, rapidly gives way to more *en masse* kinds of representations, where it is more frequently groups of people who act and react. Similarly, the privileging of proximate, personal relationships between narrator and the events s/he is narrating, gives way to more distant, 'objective' relationships where the narrator takes on the guise of the 'historian' – an observer of history – rather than a participant

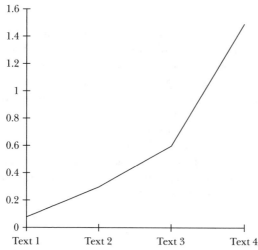

**Figure 7.2**   Average grammatical metaphors per clause

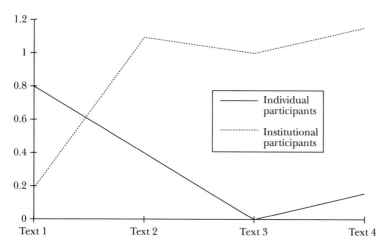

**Figure 7.3**   Average individual vs institutional participants

in history. On the basis of these texts, it would seem that the progressive educational notion of the personal voice receives short shrift in school history. (See Figure 7.3.)

## Causality and temporality

Here we have the clearest indication of the 'assume and subsume' tendency in apprenticeship into the language of history. The grammatical features which are introduced and foregrounded across the texts (e.g. temporality in text 2 and causality in text 3), although dissipating somewhat, still play a significant role in subsequent texts. Thus an historical account (text 3) combines temporal markers developed in the historical recount (text 2) with causal markers. Text 4 develops things further by combining both of these features with increasing use of grammatical metaphor and increased lexical density; it assumes and subsumes the lexicogrammar of previous texts. (See Figure 7.4.)

## The syndrome

Collapsing the categories of features shown separately above into one graph, one can see how these features work *together* to realise progressively new kinds of meaning. In Figure 7.5, the average number of linguistic features increases from text 1 to text 4. Text 4, the text with the greatest number of selected features, uses a *combination* of features to realise the 'uncommonsense' meanings of the text. Indeed, it is because of the combination of all these features, compressed into dense nominal groups, that text 4 has a much higher lexical density than the other texts. Put simply, it

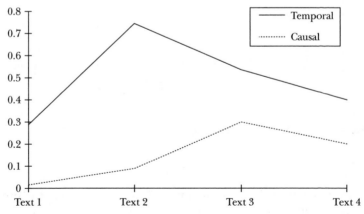

**Figure 7.4** Average temporal vs causal markers

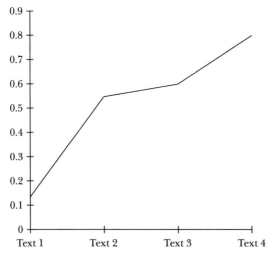

**Figure 7.5**   The 'syndrome' of features: average institutional participants, temporal markers, causal markers and grammatical metaphors per clause

packs in more information and more logical relationships. Because of this, it is likely to be more difficult for students to read and interpret.

## 5   So what's the problem?

When introducing these texts we mentioned that, linguistically speaking, they represent a typical sequence which apprentices students into the abstract, written discourse of history. So far we have presented this sequence of texts as if it were the only one possible, as if it were somehow God-given or 'natural'. Looked at from other perspectives, however, this sequence of texts may be problematic: what sort of picture of the world do these texts paint? Whose interests do they represent?

Texts 2 and 3, for example, represent the grand narrative tradition of history. The work of Foucault and others has shown us the limitations of this type of grand narrative. Often they do not admit 'non-official' historical documents to complement or challenge the canon of official historical texts, resulting in unproblematic, and often inaccurate, accounts of the past.

From some points of view, text 2 'The spread of Islam' might seem to construct a highly Christianocentric view of European history. The fact that the Moslems are *finally stopped* is judged as *one of the most important battles of history for it determined whether Europe would remain Christian or become Moslem.* Historically significant individuals, such as Mohammed and Harun-el-Raschid, are situated only in the context of their role in spreading Islam (compare this with the way an English monarch might be treated by a similar text). They simply act without thinking, reasoning or judging. The sequence of events recounted in the texts is presented unproblematically, with no space given for alternative interpretations. The patronising nature of the final stage of the text confirms the mono-cultural perspective of the text:

> Wherever the religion was established, it was accompanied by some of the most beautiful art, pottery and architecture in the world. In medicine, mathematics and literature the Moslems contributed much to civilisation.          (Coupe & Jenkins 1980: 95)

The 'truthful' and 'logical' status of texts such as text 3 has been criticised by Foucault and others. Because it fails to consider alternatives, the logical cause-and-effect sequence in text 3 appears as if it is a complete and somehow inexorable account of human history. The text suggests a kind of inevitable flowing on between the collapse of the Roman system and the rise of the medieval system, brought about by shifts in military power, which themselves seem to flow logically. Yet it is possible to construct an equally plausible, equally 'logical' and equally truthful account of the same events simply by attributing the same events to a different set of causes. The following text, which is also an account of the transition from the Roman system of government to feudalism, demonstrates this possibility. It comes from another grand narrative account of the medieval period, and offers economic rather than military explanations for the emergence of the feudal system in Western Europe.

### Feudal society

> To escape the rapacity of the Roman tax collector, peasants in the latter days of the Roman empire often put themselves under the protection of the biggest of the local landowners. In return for the title to the peasant's land, the landowner guarded the civil interests of his client and as far as possible shielded him from taxes. This seems a

hard bargain from the peasant's point of view, for he surrendered his freehold and became a tenant whom the landlord could evict at will; and it is a telling measure of the burden of taxation that in the last century of the Western Empire the freeholding peasantry voluntarily liquidated itself. The landlord gained all round. He tended to take his increasing rent in produce where possible, for the less money there was about, the less the tax gatherer took. It became necessary for him to live on his land and not in a distant town, and he soon came to administer the everyday life of his estate and its practically rightless peasantry as though the central authority did not exist.

(McEvedy 1961: 8)

Examining the texts from other perspectives, such as a Foucaultian one, we can see that, while the sequence of texts we have examined may be sound from a linguistic point of view, they may not be at all satisfactory from an historical point of view. This creates something of a dilemma for history teachers. How does one modify the teaching of history in a way that is linguistically responsible, that ensures students access to the language of history?

One linguistically irresponsible response to this situation has been to remove or substantially diminish the role of texts such as texts 2 and 3 in the teaching of history. Students are simply given a range of source documents and are expected to write abstract, evaluative expositions on the basis of the source documents. This is an unsatisfactory response. Having analysed the language of text 4 and compared it with other texts, it is clear that it would not be an easy text for many students to read or write. Nevertheless, access to this kind of text would seem most important. Because they enable writers to critique popular views of the past and offer alternative interpretations, they are of significant value in any approach to the field. Moreover, evaluative expositions such as text 4 have clear applications outside the field of school history. They are powerful ways of discussing issues and advocating change in a range of contexts. Making the function and organisation of this sort of text accessible for students may have to take place over a number of years and may involve the reading and writing of a great number of 'mediating texts', such as texts 2 and 3. If our aim as educators is to make as much of the meaning potential of history, along with other discourses, available to as many students as possible, then it would seem essential that we take whatever steps are necessary to ensure that all students participate in the specialised discourse of history.

Presenting texts like text 4 to students without careful planning, or expecting students to write texts such as text 4 simply on the basis of the inspection of a number of primary sources (as often occurs today in school history in Australia), has the potential for the most pernicious kind of educational inequity. One possible outcome is that some groups of students may simply learn to ape this genre in an uncritical, purely reproductive way. James Gee has memorably described this kind of writing as 'mushfake' (Gee 1990: 157). An even less desirable outcome is that many students risk not even learning to make an approximation of the genre, and remain 'semiotically stranded' in less abstract, less socially powerful genres such as picture descriptions or personal responses.[14]

There is a tension in history education, therefore, between the need to prepare students adequately to read and write expository texts, which challenge commonly held views, and the need to view the use of grand narrative texts with a degree of suspicion. This tension creates a dilemma for teachers and teacher educators. Texts 2 and 3 seem to be valuable ways of building up shared field knowledge and of apprenticing students into the resources we use to construct abstract, evaluative knowledge which has the potential to force a re-consideration of dominant views of history. At the same time one should not have to teach students to reproduce dominant discourses simply in order to deconstruct that reproduction. Nevertheless, text 4 risks being unapproachable for many students if not planned for and anticipated in school curricula.

## 6    Critical orientation to literacy – a possible alternative

Allan Luke has referred to the dilemma outlined above – between the need to reform the nature of knowledge and the need to keep on teaching – as the 'Gordian knot' of literacy education (Luke 1990: viii). In this part of the chapter we will argue that shared knowledge about language between teachers and students, and the explicit use of this shared knowledge in history to deconstruct and learn to write historical texts, may be a positive step towards untying the knot. If you have read the descriptions of history texts in this chapter, then you already share some knowledge about the language of history with the writers and with other readers. We contend that it is knowledge such as this that allows students to read and write history better, but also to view historical texts as socially constructed, and therefore 'problematic' in regard to their truthfulness and accuracy.

There is now considerable evidence as to the viability and successful outcomes of explicit teaching about the specialised language of schooling. This includes substantial anecdotal evidence from teachers and students as well as more empirically based work by researchers and evaluators (e.g. Walshe et al. 1990; Kamler 1992).[15] Three things have been shown clearly. First, of course, that students' reading and writing abilities in a specific range of genres do develop as a result of genre-based approaches being used in the classroom. Secondly, that students of all ages, including those from low socio-economic backgrounds and/or language backgrounds other than English, have the capacity to learn a functional 'language for talking about language' (i.e. a functional *metalanguage*) and that they can use this metalanguage to learn to read and write the written texts of schooling. Thirdly, that a functional metalanguage has the capacity to change the way students approach written texts. Explicit, shared knowledge about the way language works helps to break down barriers between learners and texts. Students begin to see that written text as 'constructed' and therefore open to either imitation or challenge. This change in orientation towards written text not only helps students to become better readers and writers, it opens up the terrain for challenge and renovation. Programs can and have been devised in a number of subject areas which not only give students access to the meaning potential of a range of written genres via an explicit examination of the language used to construct those genres, but which also throw light on the very methods in which ways of thinking and acting are constructed through school knowledge.

In this way, knowledge about language engenders what we shall call a **critical orientation** to literacy. Such an orientation should be a necessary (if not sufficient) component of any critical literacy we seek to promote in schools. A critical orientation to literacy, based upon a functional understanding of text, gives us a way in to the meanings and linguistic resources of these texts, but also allows us to see these texts as nothing more than cultural constructs. With a critical orientation it may even be possible to expose how the mainstream thinks, even to appropriate the meaning potential of the mainstream, without necessarily being co-opted by these discourses. This claim needs careful examination, for it is not without risks. However, these risks may well prove worth taking. Certainly, it is preferable to the 'benevolent inertia'[16] which has permeated so much educational practice in the last decades.

There is no doubt that 'critical literacy' – the ability to reflect on, challenge and change the constructed nature of discourse – is an important aspect of any language education program. For school knowledge to both advance and remain socially responsible, it is necessary constantly to challenge the way knowledge is constructed and to question the way knowledge and the material practices derived from that knowledge impact on our world. There is little chance of this happening if students are trained unthinkingly to reproduce knowledge and practice. In school history, it is necessary for us not only to introduce students to 'official' versions of history, but also to give students the resources to scrutinise these versions closely and challenge them if necessary. We hope that if the examination of the language of history in this chapter has shown anything, it has shown that this is not a straightforward task, nor one which can be performed by students instantaneously.

Too often 'critical literacy' is seen simply as the ability to offer a topic- (or field-) based critique of current practice. If a student can write an exposition or discussion criticising what the products of Western thought have done to the environment, or issues of gender or ethnicity, they are seen to *possess* critical literacy. This is a limited view of critical literacy, and also one potentially as 'reproductive' as any other approach to literacy. Students are restricted to particular ways of criticising texts ('mushfake') and, often, to familiar 'sanctioned' topics. This is not to say that the ability to critique in these ways is not a valuable skill, simply that it is inadequate as a description of critical literacy. Critical literacy is a practice, not a possession. It is what you do with a text, not the kind of texts you own or choose to read.[17]

## 7    Conclusion

A 'critical orientation' to literacy is based on shared knowledge about language. It attempts to expose the constructed nature of discourse in school subjects. By teaching about *how* discourses are constructed through choices in the resources of the linguistic system, one is not only ensuring that students have access to socially powerful meanings and practice at making these meanings, but also changing the way students view these meanings. By this we mean a simultaneous understanding that powerful meanings, while often being powerful for very good reasons, are in no way 'natural' meanings – they are constructed by particular groups of people for particular reasons. Just as these meanings have been constructed, so too they can be deconstructed and reconstructed for new purposes. A critical orientation to the language of history is not just about making students effective readers and writers of history; it is also about making them into good historians.

It is also hoped that the examination of language in this chapter has shown that knowledge about language gives us a powerful tool for critically evaluating the way school curricula are constructed and students assessed. A linguistically informed critique of curriculum is more than simply a matter of questioning what topics are covered, the teaching techniques used or whether or not students are taught to critique particular topics in particular ways. Rather, it is a matter of seeing how school curricula construct particular forms of consciousness for students through language, how learning is viewed, what types of learning are valued and, most importantly, why some groups of students succeed in learning the language of school history and some do not. Moreover, it gives us a resource for challenging and changing school practices, and for intervening in the process of students' language development.

In building this model of a critical orientation to literacy, we have tried to demonstrate the usefulness of a functional model of language in describing the links between language and ways of thinking which are taught to students in schools. There is still much more that can be done with systemic functional linguistics to understand what we teach and how we teach it. But we cannot, nor ought we to try to, use any model of language, or any philosophy of knowledge – post-structuralism included – to try to *determine* the kinds of social subjects our school system produces. To demand blithely that students acquire 'critical literacy' without first building a critical orientation to literacy, and without building an understanding of language, is to do just that.

# Notes

1  'Genre" here is being used as a technical term to refer to functional varieties of text with a recognisable social purpose within a cultural context, and with recognisable stages within the text. See Martin (1992: 546ff).

2  The terms 'privileged' and 'privileging' come from Bernstein who states: 'Privileged refers to the priority of meanings within a context. Privileging refers to the power conferred upon the speaker as a consequence of the selected meanings' (1990: 16).

3  This work, going under the name of 'Language and Social Power' project, has published a number of materials for teachers: *A Brief Introduction to Genre* (1989), *Teaching Factual Writing* (1988), *The Report Genre* (1989), *The Discussion Genre* (1989), *The Recount Genre* (1991), *Assessing Writing* (1991), *The Action Pack* (1992). All published by the Disadvantaged Schools Program, Metropolitan East Region, NSW Department of School Education.

4  For a synopsis of the evolution and current state of genre-based work in Australia, see Martin (1993a).

5  See, for example, the 'Sample answers' and examiners' comments published each year for the Higher School Certificate examinations in New South Wales.

6  Bernstein's (1977) discussion of 'invisible pedagogies' sets out the risks of implicit demands in schooling. It is one of the motivations for the argument here that school literacy should be made explicit.

7  Unlike the Foucaultian approach, however, social history, at least initially, was not used to challenge grand narrative interpretations of history. It is only really since the arrival of post-structuralism in History that the potential of the texts of social history to challenge mainstream interpretations has been taken up, and that the use of such texts has been seen to have deep philosophical and ideological consequences. It is only *very* recently that this potential has been advocated in school history.

8  The class-based difference in response to educational tasks being asserted here has been explored in detail by Bernstein (1977, 1990) under the rubric of 'coding orientation' and has been confirmed in research by Holland (1981) and others.

9  'Genre', 'register' and 'lexicogrammar' are here being referred to as strata in the linguistic system, following Martin (1992), with 'register' being used as a collective term for the contextual variables field, tenor and mode. This is quite different from the value given to the term 'register' by other systemic linguists (e.g. Halliday & Hasan 1985).

10  These terms have been adopted here from Bernstein (1977: 99).

11  This is achieved through grammatical metaphor, where a nominalised process acts on another process and thereby 'causes' it to happen. The causal relationship is therefore buried in the transitivity structure of the clause. This phenomenon is discussed by Martin (1992: 264–5).

12  [For a discussion of lexical density, see Halliday in this volume. Editors' note.]

13  For marked Theme, see Halliday (1994: 42ff).

14  'Personal responses' are described in detail in Rothery (1993a).

15  In England, the recently published *Language in the National Curriculum* materials (Carter 1990) have also discussed and demonstrated the value of knowledge about language, often drawing on Australian research by Rothery and others.

16  This expression was first used by Halliday (1974) to describe well-meaning but ineffectual educational programs. Nearly twenty years later, it still seems applicable.

17  Compare Hasan's notion of 'reflection literacy' in this volume.

# References

Bernstein, B. 1977. Class and pedagogies: visible and invisible. In *Class, Codes and Control, Vol. III*. London: Routledge.

Bernstein, B. 1990. *The Structuring of Pedagogic Discourse. Vol. IV: Class, Codes and Control*. London: Routledge.

Carter, R. (ed.) 1990. *Knowledge about Language and the Curriculum: The LINC Reader*. London: Hodder and Stoughton.

Christie, F., B. Devlin, P. Freebody, A. Luke, J.R. Martin, T. Threadgold and C. Walton 1991. *Teaching English Literacy: A Project of National Significance on the Preservice Preparation of Teachers for Teaching English Literacy, Vols 1–3*. Department of Education, Employment and Training. Darwin, Centre for Studies of Language in Education, University of the Northern Territory.

Coupe, S. and B. Jenkins 1980. *Progress of Man*. Adelaide: Rigby.

Darlington, R. 1990. *Land of Hopes and Illusions*. Sydney: The Shakespeare Head Press.

Deakin University Production Unit 1985. *Feminist Knowledge as Critique and Construct: Study Guide*. Geelong, Vic.: Deakin University Press.

Disadvantaged Schools Program 1988. *Teaching Factual Writing*. Sydney: Disadvantaged Schools Program, Metropolitan East Region, NSW Department of School Education.

Disadvantaged Schools Program 1989a. *A Brief Introduction to Genre*. Sydney: Disadvantaged Schools Program, Metropolitan East Region, NSW Department of School Education.

Disadvantaged Schools Program 1989b. *The Report Genre*. Sydney: Disadvantaged Schools Program, Metropolitan East Region, NSW Department of School Education.

Disadvantaged Schools Program 1989c. *The Discussion Genre*. Sydney: Disadvantaged Schools Program, Metropolitan East Region, NSW Department of School Education.

Disadvantaged Schools Program 1990. *Assessing Writing: Scientific Reports*. Erskineville, NSW: NSW Department of School Education.

Disadvantaged Schools Program 1991. *The Recount Genre*. Sydney: Disadvantaged Schools Program, Metropolitan East Region, NSW Department of School Education.

Disadvantaged Schools Program 1992. *The Action Pack: Activities for Teaching Factual Writing*. Sydney: Disadvantaged Schools Program, Metropolitan East Region, NSW Department of School Education.

Foucault, M. 1972. *The Archaeology of Knowledge*. Trans A.M. Sheridan Smith. New York: Pantheon.

Foucault, M. 1978. *Introduction: The History of Sexuality, Vol. 1*. Trans Robert Hurley. Harmondsworth: Penguin.

Gee, J. 1990. *Social Linguistics and Literacies: Ideology in Discourses*. London: Falmer Press.

Halliday, M.A.K. 1974. *Language and Social Man*. London: Longman/Schools Council.

Halliday, M.A.K. 1985a. *An Introduction to Functional Grammar*. London: Edward Arnold.

Halliday, M.A.K. 1985b. *Spoken and Written Language*. Geelong, Vic.: Deakin University Press (republished in 1989 by Oxford University Press).

Halliday, M.A.K & R. Hasan 1985. *Language, Context and Text: Aspects of Language in a Socio-semiotic Perspective*. Geelong, Vic: Deakin University Press (republished in 1989 by Oxford University Press).

Halliday, M.A.K & J. Martin 1993. *Writing Science*. London: Falmer Press.

Holland, J. 1981. Social class and changes in orientations to meanings. *Sociology* **15**(1): 1–18.

Kamler, B. 1992. There's no such thing as free topic choice: the social construction of gender in written text. *Opinion* **21**(1): 18–33.

Labov, W. & J. Waletzky 1967. Narrative analysis. In J. Helm (ed.) *Essays on the Verbal and Visual Arts: Proceedings of the 1966 Spring meeting of the American Ethnological Society*. Seattle: University of Washington Press.

Luke, A. 1990. Series editor's introduction. In J. Gee *Social Linguistics and Literacies: Ideology in Discourses*. London: Falmer Press, pp. vii–ix.

Martin, J. 1986. Intervening in the process of writing development. In J. Martin & C. Painter (eds) *Writing to Mean: Teaching Genres Across the Curriculum*. Applied Linguistics Association of Australia, Occasional Papers No. 9.

Martin, J. 1992. *English Text: System and Structure.* Amsterdam: Benjamins.

Martin J. 1993a. Genre and literacy – modelling context in educational linguistics. *Annual Review of Applied Linguistics* **13**: 141–72.

Martin, J. 1993b. Life as a noun: arresting the universe in science and humanities. In M.A.K. Halliday & J. Martin *Writing Science.* London: Falmer Press.

Martin, J. & J. Rothery 1980. *Writing Report No. 1.* Department of Linguistics, University of Sydney.

Martin, J. & J. Rothery 1981. *Writing Report No. 2.* Department of Linguistics, University of Sydney.

Martin, J. & J. Rothery 1986. *Writing Report No. 4.* Department of Linguistics, University of Sydney.

Mattheissen, C. 1995. *Lexicogrammatical Cartography: English Systems.* Tokyo: International Language Sciences publishers.

McEvedy, C. 1961. *The Penguin Atlas of Medieval History.* London: Penguin.

New South Wales Board of Studies 1992. *History 7–10.* Sydney: NSW Board of Studies.

Plum, G. 1988. *Textual and Contextual Conditioning in Spoken English: A Genre-based Approach.* PhD thesis, Department of Linguistics, University of Sydney.

Pyne, M., C. Anderson, B. Clark, A. Hewitt, S. Moore and C. Dunshey 1994. *Checkpoint. Vol. 2.* Melbourne: Longman Cheshire.

Rothery, J. 1990. *Story Writing in Primary School: Assessing Narrative Type Genres.* PhD thesis, Department of Linguistics, University of Sydney.

Rothery, J. 1993a. *Exploring Literacy in School English.* Erskineville, NSW: Disadvantaged Schools Program, Metropolitan East Region, NSW Department of School Education.

Rothery, J. 1993b. *The Narrative in Video: A Unit of Work for Junior Secondary English.* Erskineville, NSW: Disadvantaged Schools Program, Metropolitan East Region, NSW Department of School Education.

Sawyer, R. 1984. *Speaking of History.* Melbourne: Nelson.

Veel, R. 1993a. *Exploring Literacy in School Science.* Erskineville, NSW: Disadvantaged Schools Program, Metropolitan East Region, NSW Department of School Education.

Veel, R. 1993b. *Plants and People: A Unit of Work for Junior Secondary Science.* Erskineville, NSW: Disadvantaged Schools Program, Metropolitan East Region, NSW Department of School Education.

Walshe J., J. Hammond, G. Brindley & D. Nunan 1990. *Evaluation of the Metropolitan East Disadvantaged Schools Program's Professional Development Program for Primary Teachers, Focussing on Teaching Factual Writing.* Prepared by The National Centre for English Language Teaching and Research, Macquarie University. Sydney: Disadvantaged Schools Program, Metropolitan East Region, Department of School Education.

# 8

## Literacy and learning across the curriculum: towards a model of register for secondary school teachers

### MARY MACKEN-HORARIK

## 1  Introduction

For many students, junior secondary school is a difficult and confusing experience. In the move from primary to secondary school,
they face unfamiliar timetabling arrangements, a host of new
teachers and a learning environment divided into different subjects. Gone are the days when they could explore a topic or theme
across a range of core learning areas with the help of one classroom teacher. Now, learning becomes a stop-start business in
which, at the end of a forty-minute period, students 'down tools'
and move to a new room, with a new teacher to take up work in
another subject. But what does it mean to learn a subject? And,
just how do students learn to read and write the texts by which
they 'get into' these subjects? Across the span of these years,
generally speaking, students work on without a clear sense of
direction or guide posts to their level of achievement in each subject.

For many of their teachers, also, the junior secondary years pass
without any distinctive rhythm or focus. The head of faculty may
hand them a list of topics, themes or set texts which students are
to 'cover' from year to year, but these lists are hardly a guide to the
kind of progression or development expected from students in
each year, much less across four years. The syllabus documents for
the different subjects or disciplines provide teachers with little
assistance when it comes to articulating and setting goals for
learning, establishing an environment which promotes this and
estimating the degree to which learners have achieved these goals.

When it comes to relating learning to the different literacy demands of each subject, teachers are expected to rely on their own good sense and professional judgement as they plan for, promote and assess their students' learning over a unit of work, a term or a year. For many students, these are the four 'dead years' of schooling, as one teacher put it, unrelated to what has gone before in primary school and an inadequate preparation for the academic pressures of senior school which are to come.

I want to locate myself, as a secondary school teacher, within this educational problem and to sketch out a metalanguage for thinking and talking about learning in secondary school, what it means to engage with discipline knowledge, to become an expert in various areas of enquiry and to do so through written language. Learning can be regarded as a semiotic phenomenon if we conceptualize it as an ability to access and utilize a new meaning potential. *Register* is an important notion in this project. In the systemic functional model, the term refers to the fact of language variation, forming part of the theoretical metalanguage, although there is a diversity within the SF model in the conceptualization of the notion of register, as indicated by Matthiessen (1992). But the term has also entered the common parlance of many secondary school teachers. In the current English 7–10 syllabus for New South Wales schools, register is defined as 'the variation by a writer or speaker in the use of language for a particular task so that the language selected is appropriate for the purpose, the situation and the intended audience' (Board of Secondary Education, 1987).

But, what does it mean to say that language varies according to the context in which it is used? What do we mean by *context*? And, how do we understand and represent the influence of contextual pressures such as 'purpose, situation and intended audience' on language? Teachers, and the curriculum documents that guide their practice, readily acknowledge that students need to deal with wide varieties of language use. But how do they integrate their intuitive and often idiosyncratic perspectives on language variation with their understandings about literacy, in particular, and with learning overall? Above all, how do they draw on these understandings to promote learning across the curriculum?

This chapter reports on research which aims to give a greater theoretical coherence and practical usefulness to the notion of register – building on the model of language in context, as it is developed by Halliday (1991). In order to be relevant to all junior secondary school teachers, the contextual model needs to be broad enough to encompass learning in different subjects and general enough to indicate the level of difficulty students face in any learning situation. Such a description takes us beyond an *ad hoc* specification of *field* (as topic), *tenor* (as audience) and *mode* (as spoken or written) in using the notion of register. It takes us into a model of context which acknowledges the challenge central to all educational learning: a challenge which involves, at a primary level of specification, engaging with specialized forms of knowledge, learning to take up 'expert roles' in different disciplines and gaining control of written discourse.

Systemic functional theory provides a rich and inclusive model of language in context. And because it is a theory which has always been eminently suited to application, its resources can be 'mined' and reworked in the interests of those whose primary expertise lies in other fields. The contextual model outlined in this chapter was developed as a result of trialling 'genre-based approaches to teaching literacy' in a number of secondary school classrooms, through reflection on what happened in these classrooms and through dialogue with other educational linguists, like Joan Rothery. Joan has worked, as have I, for a number of years applying systemic functional theory to the solution of educational dilemmas in both the primary and secondary school context. Teachers often request assistance with the literacy problems their students experience in schooling. Working across the disciplines as teacher-linguists, we apply aspects of systemic functional theory to these issues and then develop models which we test, with the help of interested teachers, in the classroom. This experience forces us to re-think both the theory and our use of it and so the process goes on.

In this chapter, I want to present four figures which attempt to model the context-text relationship from the point of view of educational learning. The model of context draws on the context-text relationship as outlined by Halliday and Hasan (1985), a paper by Halliday on commonsense and educational learning (Halliday 1988), and some recent work by Rothery and Martin on commonsense and technical knowledge (Martin and Rothery 1991). The understandings I have developed over the years are, in large measure, a result of an ongoing dialogue with these texts and, occasionally, the producers of them.

Following a brief exposition of this model, I will take up two of its dimensions (field and mode) and show how they illuminate teaching practice in a Year 10 Science and a Year 10 English classroom. I have chosen Science and English because they are both crucial to success in secondary school learning but represent distinctive areas of the curriculum. What students learn and the kinds of reading and writing they do in these two subjects are easily distinguished. Nevertheless, as disciplines of educational learning in junior secondary school, Science and English are equivalent. And articulating the nature of the commonalities shared by all secondary school subjects can only be accomplished if we work from a comprehensive model of the school as a cultural domain. From the point of view of the cultural context, the school system imposes a more or less identifiable instructional and regulatory regime on young people and it is as well to be clear-eyed about the extent to which the school operates as an important agent of social control in most societies.

However, I will not attempt to deal with the regulatory side of the school experience here, but will concentrate on the learning task young people face if they are to succeed in junior secondary schooling. This task is multi-faceted and constitutes a profound challenge for young learners. The theoretical issues are detailed in the first part of the chapter and then exemplified in some case study material which focuses on how two teachers and their students negotiated this task in Science and English. In the final sections of this chapter, I will comment on the pedagogic practices of these teachers and isolate some of the implications of the contextual model for education more generally.

## 2  The contextual model

What is distinctive about school learning? How does it relate to learning which goes on in other domains? Figure 8.1 outlines three domains in which learning occurs: the **everyday**, the **specialized** and the **reflexive**. These terms attempt to capture the distinguishing characteristic of the learning that goes on in each 'place'.

The term 'everyday' is self-explanatory. It is the world of the home and the community into which children are born and which provides them with their primary formation. But the everyday

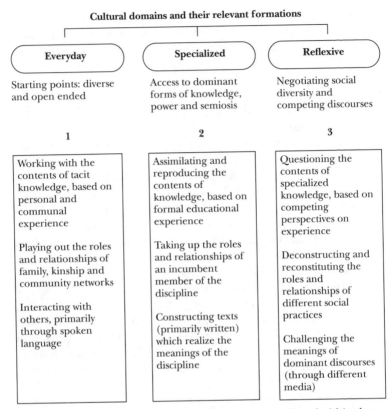

**Figure 8.1**    A view of the practices and meanings privileged within three domains

world is not uniform. In multi-cultural societies like those of Australia or Britain, children's starting points *vis à vis* schooling are diverse and open-ended. They may learn in a language other than English and develop different expectations of what life offers them depending on their gender, their ethnic origin, their class or their religion.[1]

In domain 2 – specialized learning – people train in or devote themselves to a particular area of study, occupation or activity. In the complex societies in which schools function, young people will not gain access to dominant forms of knowledge, power or meaning-making without formal education in the disciplines. Educational learning in disciplines such as Science, Social Science, Mathematics and so on, orients young learners to specialist areas of expertise on which different professions are based. This term attempts to capture the relationship between specialized knowledge within formal education and its function in occupations in the wider society.

The term 'Reflexive', referring to domain 3, draws from linguistics itself. As a technical term in linguistics, it identifies the subject and the object of a verb or pronoun. In a sentence like *She fancies herself*, the pronoun *herself* refers back to the subject of the sentence, *She* and is also the object of *fancies*. Similarly, with the reflexive verb, in the sentence *He was shaving*, the verb implies that the subject *He* was doing something to himself. In this domain, the learner begins to reflect on and question the grounds and assumptions on which specialized knowledge rests. The neat distinction between the knower and the known disappears. We begin to realize that in a socially diverse world, every subject has a vested interest in maintaining a particular view of the object of his or her reflections. It is a world of competing discourses, and in the final analysis, there is a strong relationship between who I am, in the social order of things, and what I 'know': all forms of knowledge are enmeshed with the value systems of the knowers.

Each of these three domains is a site in which all members of a culture participate to some degree and which privileges certain kinds of learning. I will attempt to present a synoptic (albeit idealized) picture of the everyday, the specialized and the reflexive domains from the point of view of how participants behave in each.

## 2.1 Domain 1: the everyday

In everyday communication around the home and community, much is taken for granted. Language is a part of reality. People coordinate material practices and enact the social relationships that go with these largely through spoken dialogues. In the roles and relationships typical of life in family and community settings, 'the self' is constructed as a member of a particular cultural group. In small communities, social closeness is assumed – or, at least, familiarity with the values and role expectations of members of the group is. For caregivers and children, in home and peer settings, commonsense knowledge serves to get most things done. People learn as they were taught, through the wisdom and experience of those who went before them, through observation and a good dose of trial and error. For example, in caring for the young, caregivers typically draw on the 'know how' which their own parents gained through their experience of parenting. They may consult an outside specialist but only in situations in which the help of immediate kin is inadequate. In general, people learn and work together against a background of shared understandings and tacit knowledge as they play out the roles and relationships assigned them in the life of the family and community and interact with others largely through spoken language. Learning in these contexts comes about 'by doing' alongside 'significant others' – that is to say, through a pedagogy of participation. And even when an adult explicitly teaches the child something, the child usually has some discretionary control over what is learned and how long it takes to do so.

### 2.2  Domain 2: the specialized

Educational learning initiates students into forms of knowledge that run parallel to those of commonsense. Although their domains do overlap at some points, children can no longer rely on the classifications and tacit understandings they developed as a result of learning at home or in the community. The forms of knowledge in academic subjects like Science or English are systematically organized. As Halliday points out, students now 'have to construe, from technical and often highly metaphorical written texts, generalizations that they must recognize as relating to but systematizing their own previous everyday experience' (1991: 22–3).

In the domain of specialized learning, students have to assimilate and reproduce the contents of knowledge as they learn to make meanings explicit: to read and write texts which build up all information necessary to their interpretation. Language is no longer a taken-for-granted part of a 'sensuous reality' (Hasan 1988), learned by mapping its meanings on to more or less familiar situations of use. It is the reality.

Within specialized domains, in education as in the wider society, the 'self' is constructed as objective and relationships are marked by a social distance. Furthermore, these roles and the texts through which students play these out are largely learned through conscious design and intervention – for which the teacher has a primary responsibility. In this domain we come to expect a pedagogy of instruction as teachers induct students into the rigours of mainstream educational discourses.

## 2.3 Domain 3: the reflexive

Representing the contexts of educational learning as specialized encourages a static view of learning and a conservative view of the prevailing social order. But, at the same time as it inducts students into hegemonic orders of knowledge, school learning can also serve to induct students into discourses which seem to contradict these, not least because the social processes that generate schooling are themselves conflict-ridden.

In the reflexive domain, we are dealing with the intersection of the everyday and the specialized in a society which is culturally diverse and in which power is distributed unevenly. And it is here that we can see how value-laden both discipline and common-sense knowledge are. Scientific knowledge, for example, presents itself as empirically sound, objective and impersonal, interested only in verifiable truth. But the scientific paradigm is itself under challenge from within and without the discipline. The question of who is 'mother' in in-vitro fertilization or surrogacy programs, for example, is a pressing issue for those affected by new developments in reproduction technology. And the issue of gene therapy is scientifically and ethically fraught for scientists at the leading edge of change in the field. In this third domain, knowledge is considered as a social construction – open to scrutiny, challenge and change.

In moving between everyday and specialized perspectives on a field like reproduction, students are forced to confront their experience and understandings from at least two points of view (e.g. science and personal experience). Knowledge is no longer fixed or monolithic and students are forced to come to terms with its socially contingent nature, even if only at a rudimentary level. The 'self' is constructed as mediating varied perspectives on knowledge. And the language through which knowledge is explored reflects these contradictions. Students now need to learn to construct texts that deal with controversial and competing points of view on issues. This demands not only a knowledge of the meanings of the discipline but also an ability to negotiate a path through competing discourses on these meanings.

The written and spoken texts for negotiating social contingency and cultural diversity are learned again explicitly through conscious design – although the pedagogical strategies for developing them will be characterized by openness, by discussion and by greater variation in modes and media of communication (e.g. the use of videos, newspapers, and radio programs). It will be more a pedagogy with a dialectic view, encouraging learners to move between competing perspectives and to learn to critique and synthesize these views for a range of purposes. An outline of this dialectic is provided in the following subsection.

## 2.4    *Synthesizing the three domains of learning*

Figures 8.2 and 8.3 appropriate the categories of *field, tenor, mode* and *genre* from different perspectives on 'register and genre theory' within SF linguistics and map them on to these three cultural domains. Field, tenor and mode provide a multi-functional perspective on the contexts of each domain. As Halliday has pointed out, these are the 'three significant components of the context of situation: the underlying social activity, the persons or "voices" involved in that activity, and the particular functions accorded to the text within it' (1991: 10). The field (Halliday's 'social activity') is inextricably linked with the knowledge/content dimension of learning across three domains. The tenor (Halliday's 'persons or "voices" involved in that activity') is captured along the role/relationships dimension. Mode ('the functions accorded to the text') is part of the semiotic dimension of the learning environment.

This representation of context and meaning draws on Halliday's thesis about the 'hook up' between contextual categories and metafunctions (e.g. Halliday and Hasan 1985) which argues that the categories of field, tenor and mode are well motivated theoretically because they correspond to three principal types of meaning in any text. In this thesis, the field of discourse activates experiential meaning selections, the tenor of discourse activates interpersonal meaning selections and the mode of discourse activates textual meaning selections in a text. In early formulations of register theory, field, tenor and mode together defined the context of situation and register was identified as a semantic category: the configuration of meanings associated with a given situation type.

There is no reason why the wider context of culture cannot also

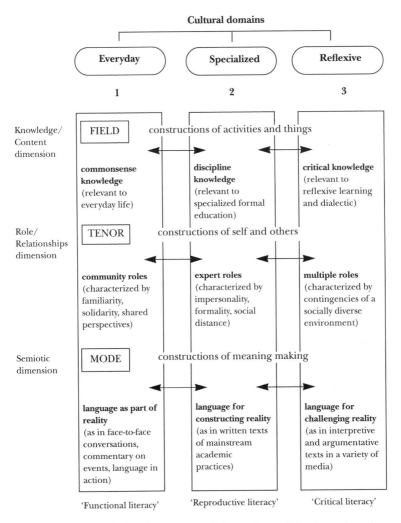

**Figure 8.2**  Articulating the contextual dimensions of the three domains

be represented from the point of view of these three kinds of function. Hence, whatever domain we are in, along the field dimension, learners will view meanings in terms of constructions of activities and things. Along the tenor dimension, they will deal with constructions of self and others and, along the mode dimension, they will be involved with constructions of semiosis whether in spoken or written language. Every context and every text has these three dimensions to their construction although the kind of construction will vary according to which cultural domain we are in or which reading of a situation we make.[2]

In the first domain, for example, the everyday world is a combination of related (or agnate) situation types which evoke particular registers. The cultural domain is the context in which language functions and the language system is the meaning potential through which we construe the culture. *A register is the meaning potential privileged within a particular cultural domain.* Hence, in the process of learning in their local environment, children build up a tacit knowledge of the registers which are sanctioned in different situations. In other words, they learn to recognize the meaning requirements of particular situations and to realize these in the texts they produce.

But, different situation types do not always elicit the same kinds of texts from learners. Some groups of children may not share the same expectations about the meaning requirements of a situation as others. The specialized domain is the foundation on which school learning rests. The registers privileged in these contexts depend on disciplined knowledge, assume the role of an incumbent 'expert' on the topic and are realized in language modelled on the written style. This means that, whether the mode is spoken or written, students need to engage with language which is often lexically dense, technical and highly nominalized. That is why it is useful, for analytical purposes, to separate situation from register, rather as Halliday does.

Much work has been done on the mismatch between the semantic styles of some groups of children and the semantic styles evaluated positively by the school. (Bernstein 1973, 1975, 1986; Hasan 1985, 1989). How do teachers confront the dilemma of the educational failure of so called 'disadvantaged students'? Faced with such a wide gap between the registers in which learners operate outside school and those which they need to control for successful academic achievement, many of them conflate educational learning with everyday learning and thereby reduce the options which they expect their students to take up in school learning. In terms of the contextual model, while such teachers seek to make school learning relevant to students, their notion of relevance is a limited one: they tend to explore fields of knowledge in commonsense terms, to recreate community roles (with expectations of familiarity and solidarity) in classroom interaction and restrict students to the kinds of language they are already familiar with through everyday life. The texts students meet and produce are largely those which are close to immediate experience. Reconstituting education as a variant of everyday learning, however, denigrates the functional value of this kind of learning in its cultural context, and effectively strands students in a school version of commonsense knowledge.

Assigning the right register to any task is made even more difficult where the syllabus documents and public examinations downplay the specialized demands of educational learning. In New South Wales, there is only one public examination for junior secondary education – a Reference test in Mathematics, Science and English. In part C of the English Reference test, all students are given an open-ended writing task and invited to write 'a story, a speech, a newspaper article, a film or television script or any other form you choose'. An analysis of specimen papers and examiners' comments for previous papers indicates, however, that the majority of students who produce 'A' range responses write very traditional narratives. Those who choose to write in another genre, like an advertisement, for example, are penalized for failing to consider matters like 'character and plot' (Rothery and Macken 1991). Their failure in this case is not one related to ability in English. Nor is it a failure to understand the situation or task. It is a failure to recognize the hidden register of the assessment task (i.e. not everyday but specialized) and to realize this reading in a text of an acceptable genre. And, because the junior secondary syllabus prioritizes matters of 'the personal response' and 'relevance', it is in large measure failing to orient students to the registers valued by examiners in junior and senior secondary assessment tasks.

In Figure 8.2, educational learning in the second domain is the instructional task for all teachers, whether their brief is that of Science, English or Mathematics education. They have to help their students to operate successfully in the academic registers of these disciplines. As a first step, this means helping the learners to distinguish the meaning requirements of everyday learning and educational learning. But, in order to do this, they have to see specialized learning as having an interface with learning in the world beyond the classroom. As the later case studies will show, students have developed understandings of phenomena (like situation comedies or sexual reproduction) and bring these to bear on any task their teacher sets them in the classroom. The point is to bring these understandings – the known – out into the open so as to better negotiate a path into specialized knowledge – the unknown. And, when it comes to moving into the reflexive domain, teachers need to view specialized learning as 'problematic' and to highlight these readings of the context – i.e., the possible – at various points in a teaching learning sequence.

Thus in Figure 8.2, along the three dimensions of the model, the arrows between the domains attempt to show that learning in any domain is a product of the relationship with the one adjacent to it. Students build up the meaning potential of specialized learning contexts – its registers – on the basis of the prior learning they have done in the everyday world. And they begin to move into reflexive learning by challenging the understandings they have established in the specialized domain. Learning can be represented semiotically as a shunting between two readings of a context.

Each domain can also be probed for the kinds of literacy it promotes. In domain 1, written texts like signs, labels and warnings are part of the environment: they serve a pragmatic function. As such, they can be associated with the rudimentary 'functional literacy' programs offered to adults in 'Survival English' courses. In domain 2, we are increasingly dealing with texts which construct and disseminate knowledge. Further, knowledge is built up and modelled through the language of the written style. In this task, students have to reproduce the understandings of mainstream academic practices in order to prove themselves acceptable to the gatekeepers of the discipline. Students who question the self-understandings promoted by a discipline in an examination, by writing critiques or subversive texts, will usually be penalized for their troubles. 'Critical literacy' - associated with the registers of domain 3 – is most often practised by those who are already on top of the specialized demands of an academic discourse or who are viewing it from the point of view of a marginalized discourse. It is the reading and writing through which people challenge the meanings of dominant discourses and posit alternative viewpoints on the *status quo*.

There is an implicit sequencing in the arrangement of the domains (moving from left to right). I assume that, as a general principle, when they are first learning something, people move from everyday, into specialized and then into reflexive learning. The effectiveness with which they can problematize and critique a field depends on how thoroughly they have engaged with it as a specialized area of knowledge. The case study material revealed an implicit sequencing principle at work in the pedagogic practices of the two teachers. These involved, first, helping students to shunt between the understandings developed previously either in their everyday world, or through earlier classroom work, and those relevant to the field as construed in the discipline. Secondly, more critical perspectives were encouraged (*vis à vis* reading and writing) once these same students were familiar with these specialized knowledge requirements and could draw on them in a consideration of contemporary issues surrounding the field of study.

At a primary degree of delicacy this contextual model offers teachers a common perspective on what it means to teach 'language across the curriculum'. Whether the subject is English, Science, Mathematics, Art, History or Geography, each discipline is a specialized area of knowledge; each imposes a recognizable set of roles on the learners and demands an increasing facility with written language across a range of media (Macken and Rothery 1991).

More delicately, each subject is a particular kind of speciality. The syllabus documents, textbooks, processes of enquiry, analysis, argumentation and proof, are emblematic of the representation each subject makes of itself as a domain of knowledge. And because the categories of field, tenor and mode can themselves be differentiated at increasing degrees of delicacy, each subject can be represented as a combination of integrated field, tenor and mode values. Furthermore, these values are reconstituted as students move into more reflexive perspectives on their subject. And domains 2 and 3 can be viewed from the point of view of the social, academic and pedagogic practices which students need to learn in the process of formation. Figure 8.3 revisits each learning domain, synoptically, from the point of view of the genres which each one privileges and which, in turn, the genres evoke.

Figure 8.2 was biased towards the situational perspective on context, while Figure 8.3 leans towards the textual perspective. The text types in each domain are agnate, since they construct a related kind of context: for example, instruction, observation, anecdote, personal response and commentary are agnate genres

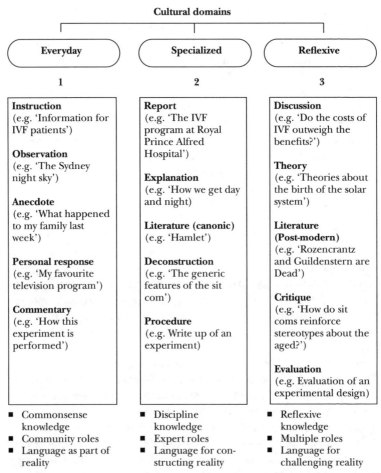

**Figure 8.3**   Genres and their typical context of use (Science and English)

as they all stay close to immediate experience – to the deictic centre of consciousness. Similarly, report, explanation, literary text, deconstruction and procedure are agnate genres because they all construct a reality which re-configures experience, as discipline knowledge tends to do: these genres distance us from experience via written semiosis. Discussions, theories, post-modern narratives, critiques and evaluations project a view of reality as something to be questioned and even subverted.

Different genres can be identified in terms of the function they serve within the process of learning.

I have attempted to keep the field constant along the horizontal dimension of the model and to show something of the development in generic complexity which occurs as educators move learners along the contextual continuum away from the 'here and now of you and me'. In learning about in-vitro fertilization, for instance, students typically deal first with texts which are close to immediate experience, as in *Information for IVF patients*. Later, they move into texts which generalize across a set of experiences, for instance *The IVF program at Royal Prince Alfred Hospital*, and then into texts which explore issues raised by contradictory experiences of the IVF program, e.g. *Do the costs of IVF outweigh the benefits?*.

A parallel development occurs in English. In learning about the structure of situation comedies (or *sit coms*, for short), students often begin by considering their own responses to these programs e.g. *My favourite television program*. Later, with assistance from their teacher, they move into text types which generalize across a range of sit coms, as in *The generic features of the sit com*. Then, through thinking about the covert messages of the genre and discussing these with others, they can begin to produce text types which critique these messages, e.g. *How do sit coms reinforce stereotypes about the aged?*.

## 2.5   A dynamic view of learning

Figure 8.2 has represented learning as a development in register – in the ability to handle the meaning requirements of situations which are increasingly abstract and complex – while Figure 8.3 took a generic perspective – the ability to interpret and produce text types appropriate to these contexts. Figure 8.4 takes two contextual dimensions of learning in each domain to develop some of the implications of this approach for pedagogy. The underlying hypothesis is that any learning environment can be explored from the point of view of its field, its tenor or its mode.

In Figure 8.4, I want to show what it means to build up knowledge of a field and what it means to enhance control of the written mode. The pathways to critical knowledge take learners from common sense through discipline knowledge. Learners can use language to challenge reality effectively only after they can control the language for constructing reality. Development along

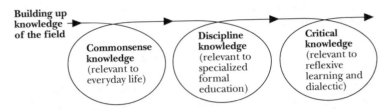

**Questions to consider**

- What is the nature of the speciality into which I want to initiate my students?
- What steps do I take to move students into understanding privileged within the discipline?
- How do I help my students to use this knowledge base to dialogue with other discourses and to view knowledge construction as open to question?

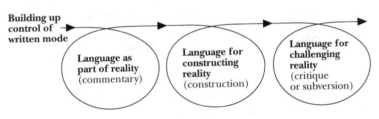

**Questions to consider**

- Which modes and media do we need to utilize at different stages of this work?
- Which genres are going to help students move into both specialized and reflexive perspectives on this subject in this unit of work?
- What metalanguage do students need to control at different stages of this work?

**Figure 8.4**  Contexualizing development (field and mode)

the mode dimension involves more than simply learning to move from spoken to written language. Some kinds of written language are more demanding than others and the more wordy construal of the mode dimension is an attempt to capture the nature of the semiotic challenge facing students in each domain. Furthermore, it will be obvious that there is a proportionality for field and mode (and tenor) in each domain. Commonsense knowledge is typically mediated via language which is 'part of reality', i.e. spoken language; discipline knowledge is construed and constructed via written language, or language modelled in the 'written style'; and critical knowledge is communicated via language which 'challenges reality' – and this is a feature of, say, television documentaries which are multi-modal media. As Halliday has suggested on a number of occasions, there is a strong association between field and mode (Halliday 1988). Furthermore, when it comes to the classroom practice, one may draw usefully on the proportionalities within each contextual domain and on the relationships which obtain between them. They will influence the kinds of questions which teachers can ask as they think through the pedagogical implications of these three domains. With Figure 8.4, I have taken the field and mode dimensions of the model and tried to highlight some of the questions pertinent to planning a unit of work.

Along the *field* dimension, in the first instance, teachers need to consider the nature of the speciality they want the students to engage with. This requires that they think through the learning goals for the unit of work they are planning. In the process of introducing students to the field, they will need to ascertain where the learners 'are at' already with respect to the specialized knowledge demands of the discipline. If their goals for learning include a more critical focus, they will need to explore issues surrounding the field and its applications with their students. Planning for learning involves setting goals which are relevant to all three domains and then deciding how to realize these in the learning activities chosen at each stage.

There is an implication for pedagogy if learning goals include both discipline and critical knowledge. A pedagogy of benevolent inertia has no place in the application of this contextual model. Teachers take on the responsibility for actively initiating students into the mainstream knowledge of a discipline, and for helping them to engage with more reflexive perspectives on this knowledge at various points in the teaching learning sequence. The success with which their learners can engage in analysis, discussion and critique will depend on how well they have engaged with the field as a specialized domain in the first place. For students who have not had the good fortune to build up this knowledge in other domains, the classroom work will be of vital importance here.

Along the *mode* dimension, because learners build up the meaning potential of the discipline through *texts*, teachers have to make considered decisions about which modes, media and genres students will need to utilize at different stages of the classroom work. Certain modes are typically associated with certain kinds of learning. Establishing what students in a class already know about a topic or issue is something teachers often do though classroom talk, although other modes are also relevant to this task. Engaging with technicality and abstraction – the linguistic technology of discipline knowledge – is a task which depends on reading and writing. More critical perspectives are opened up in text types which encode different discursive positions or voices. As the case studies show, media texts like newspaper reports, magazine articles and video programs commonly raise issues and problematize the assumptions on which discipline knowledge is based. In short, pedagogical choices for different modes, media and genres will differ depending on whether students are engaging with a specialized 'field' for the first time, are already into it or are beginning to question some of the assumptions on which it is based.

There are other pedagogical implications of the model. I shall return to these after a detailed description of the work of two teachers who make use of this contextual model in their classroom practice.

## 3   Two case studies: introductory remarks

In this section I want to describe the strategies that two teachers used to 'open up' the field of study for their students during the course of a unit of work. Along with this, I want to approach their classroom work from the point of view of the *mode* dimension and to highlight the steps each teacher took to initiate their students into the written genre(s) through which the field is constructed. Both units of work were intended to improve students' writing while they engaged with a new area of knowledge.

The questions outlined in Figure 8.4 serve as organizing principles for my account of Bill Simon's work in English and of Margaret Watt's in Science. I have selected a number of emblematic texts from the corpus collected over the period during which I participated and observed in each classroom. These texts represent the kinds of writing and reading done by the class at critical stages of the classroom work. For each text, I will attempt to bring out something of the situation in which it was used or produced and something of the development it reveals.

### 3.1   *Case study 1: Bill Simon and Year 10 English*

Bill Simon is an experienced English teacher in Sydney's Inner city west. He has taught for many years in schools classified as disadvantaged. At present, he is teaching in a High School for girls, most of whom come from non-English speaking backgrounds. The teachers are attempting to boost the girls' academic performance through high levels of literacy. The funding made available through the Disadvantaged Schools Program has been used to inservice the teaching staff in genre-based approaches to teaching literacy and to incorporate these into a language across the curriculum program, which is school-managed. When I began to visit Bill Simon's classroom, terms like *genre, narrative structure, field, tenor* and *mode* were already part of our common metalanguage. The students, whose progress we were monitoring, had also become familiar with these terms over a period of three years. For Bill, as for many of the teachers at this High School, learning about language is an important pathway to discipline knowledge.

The classroom work being described here was done over a ten-week period in 1992. The unit centred on the situation comedy – the 'sit com', a well known television genre popular with most of the class. Bill wanted to introduce his class to the sit com as a genre of popular culture, to enable them to identify the features of the genre and, later, to deconstruct a number of sit coms using the metalanguage cooperatively developed during this period. This meant that the students would watch a number of sit coms as a class, read and talk about how these sit coms were constructed and identify features of the genre in each program they watched. Following this, he wanted students to write essays deconstructing the sit com genre. As part of this project, they would consider programs from different countries – *Mother and Son* (Australian), *The Golden Girls* (American), and *Fawlty Towers* (British), trying to identify features in common to these as examples of the sit com genre.

But, as well as deconstructing the sit com, Bill wanted the class to make a critical appraisal of the genre. In his own words, he wanted them *to identify how prejudice manifests itself in contemporary society and how the Arts can challenge these perceptions.* Once his students were able to understand the structure of the sit com, he wanted them to consider how the genre serves to naturalize a particular view of old people (and, as a possibility, to challenge 'ageist stereotypes').

The final, long-term goal was that students produce their own sit com, so they had to become actively involved in all processes of producing a situation comedy (scripting, pre-production, performance, production and post-production). The specialist discipline into which he wanted to apprentice his students was more like a 'semiotics of popular culture' than the traditional field of school English, with its focus on literary texts or on reconstructions of personal experience, more common in junior secondary years.

As a way into the field, he gave small groups a list of sixteen television shows – including comedies, soapies, current affairs programs and variety programs – and asked the students to divide the shows into four categories using any criteria they felt were useful. They sorted the shows according to different criteria. Some groups classified them according to the country in which they were produced, some according to their viewing time slot or the channel on which they were shown. These criteria were often mixed with other more generic ones, as some students had already done some classroom work on television soapies in previous years.

The process of building up knowledge of the field involved, as a first step, establishing what prior experience and understanding students had of the sit com. Text 1 and 2 are excerpts from a lesson transcript of early work on the sit com genre. In this lesson, Bill was working through an essay he had written about *Mother and Son* as an exemplary Australian sit com. As the class read through this text, he would stop at the end of each paragraph and review any unfamiliar words with his students. He elaborated the meaning of words like *motif* or *status quo* in commonsense terms which made them more immediate as in text 1, or readily imaginable as in text 2.

## English text 1

| | |
|---|---|
| Bill: | Any other words? Motifs? Oh OK. Good. Right. Now have a look around you in this room; top to bottom, the ceiling, the walls. Have a look at Harry, her jumper, the chair she's sitting on. OK. Is there any motif in this room? |
| Student: | They're all blue. |
| Bill: | They're all blue. OK. So a motif ... we can say that in this room we have a blue motif. |
| Student: | Surroundings? |
| Bill: | Not quite. |
| | [Students make other suggestions; utterances not intelligible]. |
| Bill: | Yes, it's a thing that's repeated: maybe a colour or an idea or some sort of symbol or image. |
| Student: | 'Indeed'? |

Bill:        (laughing) 'Indeed' is one of my verbal motifs – yes, indeed, a recurring motif.

## English text 2

Bill:        OK. Any words in that paragraph? Which one Heidi?
Heidi:      'Status quo' Sir.
Bill:        Sonya?
Sonya:      The position things are in.
Bill:        Yeah, it's the way of the world; how society operates … um the normal way of things before it gets complicated. Girls, let me give you a very interesting example. So, suddenly, if Irene was to organize all her friends, Connie etcetera, etcetera to go and storm the principal's office, kill a principal and install herself as principal of the school and threaten everyone with death if they don't obey, that would change the 'status quo' in the school … change the normal way the school operates. OK?

What is going on here, semiotically speaking? Through the spoken mode, Bill is enabling students to draw on the meaning potential they have developed in their everyday lives to interpret abstract terminology. This was a frequent strategy he used to move students into the specialized register, of which his essay was an instance.

After early class discussions and the first exercise where they attempted to sort a range of television shows using self-developed criteria, students began work on the sit com more systematically. Now they learnt that, as the class handout pointed out, the sit coms were:

… programs which operate on a simple enough premise, a situation which is obvious to the audience and is never changed. For example, the shipwreck of a band of people on a deserted island ('Gilligan's Island'), a group household ('The Golden Girls'), the running of a hotel ('Fawlty Towers'), the goings on at a television station ('Mary Tyler Moore' as well as 'Murphy Brown'), the trials and tribulations of a son with his old, dithering mother ('Mother and Son'), the cohabitation of an astronaut and his genie ('I Dream of Jeannie'), the goings on at the political office ('Yes Minister') or the fortunes of a fallen aristocrat ('To the Manor Born').

They learnt also that sit coms fall into two broad categories: *The ones based around the home and the ones based around work – with some examples which manage to combine the two settings* (Class handout).

Their first formal writing exercise asked them to decide on and describe the situation or premise of a number of sit coms. Students worked in small groups to build up a portfolio of summaries. Text 3 is a good example of the kind of work produced:

**English text 3:** *Acropolis Now*

> Jim Stephanidis is a greek cafe owner who was forced to take over his father's business when he left for Greece. Merno, Suzanna, and occasionally Effie (Jim's cousin), help Jim run the cafe. Jim has had no previous experience in running a business, so he always seems to do something that won't benefit the cafe, and Suzanna is always left to worry about solving the problem and, in some instances, saving the cafe. All the cast are stereotypical Greeks who have strong Greek accents, love Monaros and going to discos.
>
> [Angelique & Stephanie]

Text 3, produced by Angelique and Stephanie, two members of the class, is a good example of the writing produced at this stage. The language of the text places it within the second domain for English, but only just. It is self-contextualizing, written language and students are drawing out the basic situation operating beneath each episode, and are thus classifying the episode as an instance of a genre. But the text is largely congruent with commonsense knowledge describing the ongoing situation in a way which meshes with the experience of any regular viewer. It renders the basic situation of *Acropolis Now* in experiential terms as a problematic which different characters – Jim, Merno, Suzanna and Effie – have to solve.

After introducing the class to a broad range of sit coms, Bill narrowed the focus and began work on three programs in particular: *Mother and Son, Fawlty Towers* and *The Golden Girls.* Students worked in groups analysing an episode of the Australian sit com *Mother and Son*, contrasting the relationships between the principal characters, describing the visual gags used in the show and its setting, and imagining the kind of audience for which it was intended. During this time, they also read background material about how Geoffrey Atherden, chief script writer for *Mother and Son*, developed the series.

Bill wanted students to write their own 'brief' for an episode of *The Golden Girls.* However, before they did so, they analysed one episode of the show in detail, producing character profiles for the main characters, looking at the narrative structure of the episode and describing the camera angles used at different stages of the narrative. It should be noted that students in this class had already been introduced to narrative structure[3] in previous years: analysing the chief complication of the episode and different characters' evaluations of this gave them a useful way into the structure of the sit com. The students spent about two weeks considering and writing about the structure of individual episodes. Now Bill pulled back from this and asked students to develop a broader, more genre-based analysis of the sit com. At this time, he played a more instructional role, working actively to induct students into a new metalanguage for describing the ingredients – or essential elements – of a sit com. They worked on the essential elements of the genre like *inversion, sets of contrasting characters, recurring gags, use of a plausible plot, naturalist filming* and *traditional narrative structure*. They applied elements to the three sit coms, finding examples and testing the criteria against their own viewing experience.

As preparation for their first major essay on the sit com genre, the class read and deconstructed an essay, written by their teacher on *Mother and Son*. Following this, they wrote an essay, based on Bill's model, in which they evaluated the extent to which the American program *The Golden Girls* could be considered a successful American sit com. They drafted their essays in pairs and completed a final draft independently. Here is Filippa's essay, as submitted:

**English text 4**

> The television show The Golden Girls is indeed a successful sit com because it employs the basic elements which are common to all sit coms. Its plot is plausible, it uses the technique of inversion, sets of contrasting characters, recurring gags and both its filming and it's structure can be described as naturalist. Furthermore, the setting, the accents used and the allusions used in the show make it uniquely American.
>
> All sit coms employ a similar set of elements; a formula which has been very successful in the past. This could be one reason to explain the proliferation of these genre of television shows. One of the basic elements is the plausibility of their situation. The Golden Girls is indeed very plausible, since parents often do become the responsibility of their children. The daughter, who is played in the show by

Bea Arthur, bears the burden of taking care of her forgetful but cunning mother, played by Estelle Getty. Part of the show's success depends on this realistic plot device.

Another common element of sit coms is the inversion it uses. This refers to when the 'normal' situation is reversed and consequently produces humour. Parents are expected in society to take care of their children and to continually provide their support. In the show, however, it is the child that takes care of the mother. Furthermore, to complicate matters even more, Sophia in the show does imagine that she is still the main carer in the family. Dorothy, however, is not the only child Sophia has; she is mother of Gloria, who is Sophia's favourite and a direct contrast to Dorothy. Unlike her sister, she is more successful in her relationships and lives away from her mother. Dorothy loves her sister very much but she is never there to help her look after Sophia cause she is often too busy. The effect of this contrast between the two characters is also another contributing factor for the show's success. Moreover, the constant arguing that takes place between mother and daughter is one of the recurring motifs or gags in the show.

These recurring motifs is something that aims to create intimacy and familiarity between the show and its targeted audience and, not surprisingly, the viewers come to expect them. If Sophia, for example, was to suddenly become a humanitarian character, the premise for the sit com would be destroyed. Other motifs employed by The Golden Girls include Blanche, a room mate and friend, whose lust for men overtake her, Rose, another house sharer, with her St. Olef's stories, Sophia's stories of Sicily and Sam, Dorothy's ex-husband, who tries anyway he can to get Dorothy jealous or back again.

Finally, the way the show is filmed resembles naturalist drama because it attempts to make viewers feel like old friends and that they are indeed part of the action. Naturalist filming does not try to alienate the audience nor does it try to dazzle them with any creative filming techniques. For these kinds of shots will destroy the intimacy created between the show and the people who are comfortably watching in their lounge rooms.

Another element that sit coms share with naturalist drama (soapies) is the reliance on traditional narrative structure. At the beginning of each episode, something happens to threaten the status quo of the situation. This, of course, is quickly dealt with, a resolution takes place and the characters undergo a quick evaluation of their relationship. In The Golden Girls, Sophia usually involves herself in some humorous schemes, involving outsiders, Dorothy interferes and stops impending disasters from eventuating and the show concludes with the two of them re-affirming their love for each other.

It is evident that The Golden Girls employs all the traditional elements of the sit com genre and this can account for its success in America. Another reason is the fact that it is a uniquely American show. The characters are recognisably middle class Americans by the way they speak. Furthermore, the references to political and social events as well as institutions and individuals are indeed American.

[Filippa]

Filippa, like the others in her class, has produced a text in a specialized register – that of semiotics or, perhaps, media criticism. She has utilized the abstract categories of her new metalanguage to deconstruct *The Golden Girls*, and to view it as a typical instance of the genre. For Filippa, as for others in her class, the sit com is now a term with implications for the construction of a text rather than simply a commonsense way of classifying different television comedies. It is a construct with elements which can be identified and used to deconstruct any number of generic instances. In other words, she is able to apply abstract categories like *inversion, recurring gags, plausible plot* and *naturalist filming* to a range of sit coms and to use these as principles for comparing and contrasting the sit coms. Terms like *motifs* and *status quo*, which had been unknown to her, she can now utilize to describe and exemplify aspects of the structure of the genre.

It is important to note just how derivative students' written work had been up to this point. With the exception of the sit com brief, which required that students imagine and write a treatment for a new episode of *The Golden Girls*, their work was heavily scaffolded by teacher models and produced by group effort, on most occasions. Learning to take up expert roles with respect to media criticism meant, initially, that they assimilate and reproduce the understandings sanctioned within the discipline. As time went on, however, and the class began to take a reflexive perspective on what they had learned, Bill handed over more responsibility to the class, asking them to decide for themselves how they researched the next issue and what approach they would take to it in their writing. Finally, of course, when it came to developing their own sit com, Bill made a decision to take his hands 'off the wheel completely'. They eventually wrote treatments for, scripted, filmed and produced their own sit com without any teacher intervention.

After approximately six weeks on this aspect of the sit com genre, Bill directed students' attention to some of the issues surrounding media representations of both young and old people. He intended that they use the knowledge base they had built up already to *dialogue with other discourses surrounding age* and, in the course of this, *to view knowledge construction as open to question*. He wanted them to examine critically the representation of old people in sit coms like *Mother and Son* and *The Golden Girls*, the picture of ageing presented there, and whether it accorded with the experience of people they knew. Also, students were to do some research into discrimination against people on the basis of their age. Further, students were asked to draw these two strands together in a feature article for a popular magazine. There follows the specific instructions given in a class handout from which the students were to work:

> Write a feature article on ageism (discrimination on the basis of age), using elements discussed in the previous lesson.
> Remember:
> 1. Make sure you know the structure and language features of the feature article.
> 2. You must write on ageism.
> 3. You will need an eye-catching heading.
> 4. You must make reference to how old people are presented in the sit coms, especially 'Mother and Son' and 'The Golden Girls'.
> 5. Decide who is your audience and use the appropriate register.
> 6. Make sure you use facts, quotes and personal commentary.
> 7. You may like to consider only one manifestation of ageism; e.g. relationships, work, rights, health, etc.

Students were now ready to tackle the issue of ageism in media representations of old people. For example, in one discussion I witnessed, girls were picking out the foibles of the principal female characters in *The Golden Girls*. They talked about Blanche's image as a 'sexy' woman and why they were amused by the idea of older people being interested in sex. One member of the group claimed it was unnatural for an old woman to be into sex. Another challenged her, asking why we see it as strange or funny. She herself had grandparents who still enjoyed sex ... and so on. These discussions were not wasting time. Talking about such issues was actually taking them into the domain of media critique because they were beginning to deconstruct the ageist discourse operating beneath the seemingly innocent narratives of the popular culture.

The 'hard research' involved investigating the facts of age discrimination in Australia. Students found information on this from the New South Wales Anti-Discrimination Board. On the day I visited, they were listing the legal ages when people can begin to drink, drive, vote and when men and women are supposed to retire and so on. Students also worked in small groups on the feature article as a magazine genre, although I did not observe any explicit classroom work on its structure. They read some feature articles in magazines like *Cleo, Dolly* or *Cosmopolitan,* deconstructing them by using class notes on the features of the genre which Bill had prepared.

This final writing task initially proved onerous for the students, or so it seemed to me as one who observed their initial drafting of their feature article. With only four weeks to go until end of term, students were under pressure to finish this task, but to do this, they had to research the field (ageism in contemporary society) and also to learn to write in a new genre (the feature article) in a short space of time. As a general rule, Bill asks his students to tackle only one aspect of the learning context at a time: they did not work on a new field at the same time as attempting to produce written text in an unfamiliar genre. It is difficult to concentrate on language 'as an object' at the same time as using it 'as the instrument' of learning something new. Nevertheless, the written work produced independently by students at the end of term was of a consistently high standard, with the following representing one of the best efforts.

### English text 5: *'What's age got to do with it?'*

In these so-called 'modern' times, it seems everyone is trying to bring about a stop to every sort of discrimination. Racism is regarded as the worst form of cruelty, while the 'new age sensitive man' is trying to abolish sexism. But what most people don't realise is that a new unknown form of discrimination occurs everyday – Ageism.

To find the definition of ageism, I ventured towards my friendly dictionary and was somehow not surprised to discover that even in my trusty 7th edition of the Oxford dictionary, ageism was nowhere to be found ... But ageism, just like it sounds, is basically discrimination on the basis of age. How many times have your parents said to you: 'No, you can't do that – you're too young'? Well, that is a minor case of ageism!

Other forms of ageism arise in the workplace, by government laws and even in the media. For example, many young people, such as yourself, are fortunate enough to have part-time work. Many employers prefer to hire younger workers, in order to save money, and this could be regarded as a more serious case of ageism against more 'expensive' employees.

Cathy is 15 and works at a local supermarket. Her opinion: 'It's really obvious what employers do. Even though the 18 and 19 year old workers are a lot more experienced, I find that the younger workers like myself are always hired to work longer hours and days like public holidays (when double time is paid.)'

So, is there anything these younger employees can do about it ? Is there an anti-ageism discrimination agency? No, unfortunately not.

But ageism is not just discrimination against the young. Older members of the community (who incidentally, young people are told to respect), are treated to the worst cases of ageism, particularly by the media. Top rating situation comedies such as 'The Golden Girls' and 'Mother and Son' earn their incomes through the use of this discrimination against the elderly. I'm sure everyone has seen an episode of 'The Golden Girls' and while many regard the humour as very clever, not many consider the image of the elderly it portrays. In this show, old people are portrayed as either eccentric (Rose), cheap and desperate (Blanche), lonely (Dorothy) or just plain cruel. Also, the Australian show 'Mother and Son' uses the same concept of humour arising from the actions of the elderly, to boost ratings. Maggie, played by Ruth Cracknell, is the protagonist who is rather old and seems to be living in the past, due to her lack of memory. She is portrayed as innocently devious (because her lack of logic prevents her from realising what she is doing is cruel!) particularly to her son, whom the audience is made to feel sorry for, because she is such a 'burden.' Perhaps her character's semi-madness is humiliating and insulting to other elderly.

Ageism is also reflected in many state and federal laws, mainly discriminating against young people and limiting their activities. Teenage boys and girls are told, through legislation, that they are permitted to have sex at 16, yet they cannot marry until they are 18. Teenagers are not allowed to drive until they are 17, they cannot buy cigarettes or alcohol, or watch 'R' rated films or even vote in elections until they are 18. The government does not realise that certain teenagers are mature enough to make sensible decisions, such as voting in elections and so these laws are limiting those teenagers who want to contribute to today's society ... Many teenagers also feel that these laws are actually insulting because they classify all young people as 'too immature' to make up their mind about important issues. Even minor things like the age a child can enrol in school can be classified as a type of ageism because it might suggest a child is not intelligent enough (!), which, like the case for teenagers, might apply to many youngsters but not all. Amazing, isn't it?

This case of ageism cannot be considered as very significant by most, but Sue Clambert, keen believer in the abolishment of ageism, is trying to set up an anti-ageism board. She believes everyone, no matter how old they are, deserves equal rights and feels that 'an organisation such as this is essential in these times because people need to have equal rights and there really isn't anyone to turn to at the moment.'

Well, some may argue that 'ageism' is used as just a good way to gain attention, but many people, like myself, do indeed believe that any sort of discrimination is cruel and should be stopped immediately.

What's age got to do with it anyway ?

[Sonya]

The language of English text 5 places it within the registers of the reflexive domain. Sonya has produced a coherent text which draws on and integrates all she had learned about age discrimination in society and about the portrayal of the aged on television in a feature article for a teenage magazine. This text shows that Sonya is able to negotiate multiple roles in her enactment of this task. She moves from the role of an informed authority: *But ageism, just like it sounds, is basically discrimination on the basis of age;* to that of a chatty feature writer: *To find the definition of ageism, I ventured towards my friendly dictionary and was somehow not surprised to discover ...;* to that of a teenage peer: *How many times have your parents said to you: 'No, you can't do that – you're too young'? Well that is a minor case of ageism.*

From the point of view of the field, she is now able to view the sit com as a value-laden construct, to 'read' the stereotype behind the way *old people are presented* and to imagine other ways of presenting them. She writes, for example, that Maggie is *portrayed as innocently devious* and that *Perhaps her character's semi-madness is humiliating and insulting to other elderly.* Sonya is using the language of critique to challenge the meanings of dominant discourses and, in doing this she is entering the territory of critical literacy.

In the following term, the class began work on their own sit com and Bill claims that it was here that their earlier experience of deconstructing the genre really paid off. In making their own sit com, the students became palpably aware of the constructedness of television narratives and they reported that the process of making a situation comedy made them more critical of the programs they watched in their nightly television viewing.

## 3.2   Case study 2: Margaret Watts and Year 10 Science

Let me turn now to a unit of work in another classroom to show how the model can be used to explore the relationship between literacy and learning in a different subject. Like Bill Simon, Margaret Watts has participated in inservices on genre-based approaches to teaching literacy over a number of years as a teacher in a disadvantaged school and she has been very adventurous in seeking to learn about and apply genre to the literacy problems her students bring with them to her classroom.

This unit focused on writing explanations and the field of study was reproduction technology. This was to cover elementary principles of human reproduction, inheritance and the use of reproduction technologies like in-vitro fertilization and genetic engineering. As will be seen, however, these 'base-level understandings' were 'contextualized' in alternative (contradictory) ways as Margaret introduced the class to reproduction in the context of medical ethics, social issues and media treatments of reproduction technologies. In this way, students learned to take up a range of perspectives on the field, which served to problematize their knowledge about reproduction, in scientific, technological and social terms.

Students at Margaret's current school do not, on the whole, come from disadvantaged socio-economic backgrounds. Margaret is an experienced head teacher of Science and, generally speaking, students settled down to work fairly quickly and stayed 'on task' for most of the period. The students in this class accept that they will be challenged at a fairly high level in terms of written work, engagement with the field of knowledge and problems relating to the application of scientific knowledge to technology and society.

Margaret and I worked cooperatively around the metalanguage of genre and register and shared perceptions about the value of modelling and joint negotiation of meaning with students. My impressions of 'what' students learned and 'how' they learned it are based on classroom observations at regular intervals, consultation with her and fairly detailed scrutiny of students' work in longer pieces of writing and in the test which they completed at the end of the unit of work.

Over this ten-week unit, Margaret planned to introduce her students to the explanation genre as an essential part of their work on human reproduction and its technologies. As such, she was going to focus on language 'as object' for a period of time while students deconstructed and then learnt to write the explanation genre. She planned that they would write explanations about how the sex of a child is determined, how the IVF process works, and later, how the material of inheritance can be changed. Moreover, they would do these tasks in writing. This meant that students needed to be thoroughly inducted into the field, as biologists understand it, if they were going to be able to construct scientific explanations of these processes.

When it came to more critical reflection on the field, Margaret wanted students to debate these issues with a 'good science base'. Students could not discuss the ethical and social issues surrounding the IVF program without a thorough grasp of the actual procedure and they could not understand this if they hadn't first built up adequate understandings of how babies are conceived and develop. Similarly, in order to 'explain to the woman in an IVF program why the child she is carrying may not look like her', they would have to draw on both their earlier work on human reproduction and IVF and their new understandings about inheritance and how it works. In other words, Margaret 'built up' the field in a cumulative way, so that work on each new topic proceeded on the basis of already established understandings. What follows is an account of the steps she took to move her students from their current understandings to those privileged within the discipline.

Students' commonsense knowledge of human reproduction was mediated by individual experiences in their everyday lives and certainly would not have been uniform. At any rate, these students had already done some introductory study of reproduction, so Margaret began by reviewing what they had already learnt and establishing a common knowledge base for the lessons to follow. A complete account of the work done in this initial period is beyond the scope of the present chapter. However, I will select examples which demonstrate the direction which classroom work took and the kind of development students made as a result. Margaret reviewed what students had already done on the topic of reproduction in earlier years by asking students to complete exercises such as labelling diagrams. Students labelled diagrams of the male and female reproductive organs, naming each part with its technical name. Incidentally, by focusing on the diagrams, Margaret was sensitising the class to the interplay between non-linguistic and linguistic modalities of semiosis – how pictures and words together make meanings. The diagrams re-present the familiar world of sexual organs but enforce a new perspective. Students were considering the body – the most materially immediate context of early learning – from the point of view of biological processes. In a very physical sense, they were now 'shunting' from commonsense to discipline knowledge, as Margaret endeavoured to establish base-level understandings about human reproduction.

As well as labelling diagrams of the male and female sexual organs, students completed cloze passages on the female reproductive system, on fertilization and on pregnancy and birth. Science text 1 is the first of these.

### Science text 1: The female reproductive system

When a girl is born, she has thousands of undeveloped eggs in each _____. These eggs are also called _____. Once puberty begins, these eggs will be released and travel down the _____ _____ to the thick, muscular _____ where a baby can develop. The large tube leading from the uterus is called the _____. The folds of skin around the entrance to the vagina are called ____.

Somewhere between the ages of 10 and 15, some of the eggs in a girl's ovaries develop. One egg is released from an ovary about every ____ weeks. This tiny egg moves along the oviduct (also called a _____ _____) towards the _____. While the egg is developed, released, and moving down the tube, a thick _____ continues to develop in the uterus.

If the egg is not fertilized, part of the lining, together with liquid and some blood, comes out through the ____ during _____. This 'period' usually lasts ___ days. The whole cycle usually takes about ___ days and is controlled by ____.

Once they knew the technical name for each body part, students could assign it to its relevant place in a cloze passage. Each part of the human reproductive system now became functionally linked with others in a dynamic process. Margaret supported students by orally rehearsing the activity sequences with them before they began work on diagrams, flow charts and cloze exercises of these kind. Moreover, they completed these as part of whole-class or group interaction and student roles were largely those which operate in informal learning situations. The reading and writing they did at this time was akin to functional literacy contexts where language is part of what is going on, and readers can rely on extra-linguistic cues to help them decode the text.

As the English texts 1 and 2 show, learners expand their meaning potential outwards from the 'here and now of you and me'. This meaning potential is developed during this time primarily through spoken language or through written texts which move between commonsense and discipline knowledge. Science text 1 intersects with a world familiar to most girls by Year 10. But, it takes them beyond their localized experience of sexual organs and a monthly period into the biological meaning of menstruation. Once they are familiar with these new technical terms and the taxonomies and activity sequences from which the terms are drawn, they can then use them as a foundation for further learning.

Margaret narrowed the field focus earlier than Bill, who gave the students more discretionary power to determine the pace of their classroom work on the sit com genre. Students wrote an initial explanation about how the sex of a child is determined and then worked on the different stages of 'egg development'. They were asked to draw up a table which summarized the events from 0 hours to 12 days after conception (i.e. fertilization). One student, Laurent, used a timeline to outline the stages in the development of the egg as shown below:

**Science text 2: Egg development**

| TIME | EVENTS |
| --- | --- |
| 1.5 days | Zygote splits into 2 cells |
| 2 days | Zygote splits into 4 cells |
| 3 days | Ball of 16–32 cells is formed |
| 4 days | Hollow ball of 64–128 cells |
| 4–5 days | Embryo still free in uterus |
| 6–7 days | Embryo attaching to wall |
| 11–12 days | Embryo embedded |

This was an important prerequisite to understanding the in-vitro fertilization procedure (more commonly known as IVF). At this point, Margaret showed a video program on IVF to the class and asked them to write a short account of the process based on the notes they made during this program. Science text 2 is Laurent's version of the IVF process at this point:

### Science text 3: *What is IVF? (video)*

> The IVF procedure is carried out by a male ejaculating for a specimen of his sperm. The woman then has her egg removed and the sperm and the egg are then introduced to each other in a test tube. 48 hrs after fertilisation has begun, the fertilised egg is then injected into the womb. Normal growth of cells then continue.
>
> As a team of 23 scientists at Monash University discovered, the procedure is not easy, and in one year of collecting eggs, the success rate was 50–60%. In Australia, there are 2–3000 operations done each year, costing $1,500 to the parents and only $45–50 per child to the community.
>
> Though this program is successful, there are still many ethical problems that arise. These problems include high cost and success rate.
>
> [Laurent]

Margaret pressed on with the business of writing an explanation of IVF as a clinical and biological process, rather than stopping to consider in a detailed way its associated financial and ethical problems. It was at this point that she stopped work on 'science' and asked students to focus on an important text type through which it is constructed: the explanation. So the genre became the field of study now. How did she do this?

Because the students had had no explicit guidance about the structure and nature of written genres in Science, Margaret introduced them to some key text types like explanations, reports, procedures, expositions and discussions. It should be noted here that the term 'genre' and 'text type' were used interchangeably during classroom applications of genre-based approaches at this time. Each student read an example of the genre and then decided on its 'social purpose'. They discussed some of the differences between the genres. Then Margaret asked students to focus in particular on the contrast between explanations and reports. Some of them observed that causal connectors were more common in explanations and that they are more about 'things in action' (processes) than 'things in place' (taxonomies).

A few days after this, as part of their early work on IVF, Margaret structured the students' first effort at writing an explanation. Using an overhead projector, she analysed the task *Explain the in-vitro fertilization process*, breaking it down into its component parts and the technical verbs necessary to explain the IVF sequence.

Processes like *ovulate, removal, placing, masturbating, transfer* and *mixing* are critical to reconstructing IVF procedure in its first phases. She modelled the use of these processes using the following framework, which reproduces her Board notes:

**Task: Explain the in-vitro fertilization process**

1. Define IVF
2. Outline situation: people who need IVF
    (e.g. fertilize, block, transfer, travel)
3. Explain procedure
    (e.g. ovulate, masturbate, removal, transfer, place, mix)
    ......................... Embryo Implantation
    ......................... Return of embryo
    (e.g. insert, implant, remove, wait, menstruate)

Students then worked in small groups to construct jointly their own explanation. The final draft of the first writing task, produced by Beth, one of the more competent students, shows how students build on both knowledge of the field (its activity sequences and technical terminology) and the genre (its purpose and staging) in any successful writing activity.

### Science text 4: *Explanation of how IVF works*

IVF involves fertilization of the egg outside the woman's body.

Participants are infertile couples, where either the woman has a damaged fallopian tube or the man has a low sperm count, wishing to have a child.

When the man produces the sperm, it is mixed with the egg that has been removed from the woman's ovary. Fertilization occurs on the petri dish.

Two or three days later, the embryo is placed into the uterus by way of a long thin tube. At about this time the egg would be arriving from the fallopian tube in normal circumstances.

Four or five days after the insertion of the egg, it should start to attach itself to the wall of the womb. If this occurs successfully, the embryo embeds and continues to develop.

[Beth]

The language of this text places it in the second domain for Science: it is a coherent explanation of in-vitro fertilization, sequenced both temporally and causally so that the reader can easily reconstruct the procedure on the basis of what is written.

Beth has drawn on earlier work on the technical names for sexual organs and their function and on the phases of development from conception onwards and she has integrated these in a text which displays her understanding of both a biological (fertilization) and a clinical process (IVF).

Again, as with all the texts students produced on human reproduction and its technologies, the writing was heavily scaffolded and significantly 'reproductive' at this stage of their work. Margaret played a primarily instructional and guiding role as she inducted the learners into unfamiliar territory of this field. She did not expect them to write 'original' material in an unfamiliar genre without her assistance at this point in their learning.

There is neither time nor space to describe all the activities and the writing students did during this ten-week period. But if we consider the three explanations they produced after being introduced to the genre, we can see how each subsequent writing task builds on the knowledge base already established in prior lessons:

Task 1:   Explain the process of in-vitro fertilization.
Task 2:   Write a letter to a couple who have embarked on the IVF program. Explain to the woman why it is that the child she is carrying may not look like her.
Task 3:   Explain how the material of inheritance may be changed.

In order to do each task, students had to draw on the knowledge they had accumulated to this point and then explain it in coherent written discourse. There was no way they could write a good explanation without a thorough grasp of the field. The explanations varied somewhat according to the ideational complexity of the task – moving from the more temporally sequenced ones about the IVF process in early work to more theoretical ones about changes in the material of inheritance.[4] But the increasing complexity of the writing tasks involved the interpersonal dimension also. Explaining the process of inheritance and bringing out its implications for IVF parents, for example, called on a technical understanding of the field of IVF and of inheritance and an ability to re-formulate this knowledge so as to make it explicit for a lay audience. Thus, even within the contexts of the second domain, as students were challenged to 'talk from within the discipline out', they were learning to take alternative perspectives on a process – those of the scientist with a specialized knowledge of inheritance and those of the layperson with a commonsense understanding of how children come to be like their parents.

From the point of view of mode, the learners were reading and writing texts which were increasingly distant from immediate experience. In the early days they drew heavily on diagrams, flow charts and observations of illustrated or filmic treatments of the topic in order to move into the field. But knowledge of this specialized domain is modelled primarily through written language which is typically less congruent with observable activity sequences. In the writing task of this unit, in which he was asked to explain how the material of inheritance can be changed, Rodney, one of the students, wrote:

**Science text 5**

> What follows is an explanation of how the material of inheritance can be changed through two natural and one physical method. These are chromosome mutations, gene mutations (natural) and genetic engineering by scientists.
>
> In the event of a chromosome mutation, the chromosome makeup in the nucleus of cells changes. A well known effect of chromosome mutation, Down's Syndrome, is caused when the nucleus gains or loses chromosomes. Gene mutations, on the other hand, occur during cell division. A mistake occurs as the chromosomes are doubled. The best known cause of gene mutation is sickle cell anaemia.
>
> Recently scientists have entered the world of genetic engineering. This involves removing parts of a gene and replacing it with some other gene particle.

> [Rodney]

The activity sequences referred to in this text are not observable without the aid of specialized technology and are not rendered in such a way that a layperson could reconstruct them. How does a cell nucleus gain or lose chromosomes? How are they doubled during cell division? The text is semiotically distant from the experience to which it refers and is typical of those which these students will encounter more and more as they build on their foundational understandings of the topic. At this point on the mode continuum, language is the reality and learners are dependent on it as the instrument for learning other things. And these are not the things of immediate experience but the abstract and technical things of discipline knowledge.

How did Margaret help her students to use this knowledge base to dialogue with other discourses and to view knowledge construction as open to question? Students 'read around' the field intensively over the whole unit of work. Margaret provided them with text book material, newspaper articles on issues surrounding IVF, gene splicing and genetic engineering more generally. The class noticeboard was given over to newspaper articles collected by students and sometimes the early part of the lesson was spent on the latest of the acquisitions and some of the issues they raised. The class also watched and 'wrote up' a number of videos on sex determination, on IVF and on the issue of surrogacy and motherhood. At these times, specialized knowledge was treated as 'problematic' in a number of ways.

Margaret did not wait until the end of the unit to move into more reflexive work on the issues surrounding the field, but there was a rhythm to her interventions in this domain. She only asked her students to consider these issues when they knew enough about the 'science' behind them. For example, students talked about who owned the child in the Donor Gamete Program: the donor of the gamete or the woman whose uterus grows the baby? But their ability to participate effectively in these discussions was dependent on their understanding of how the program worked and the roles different people played in it. Nevertheless, there were some students for whom the issues had a burning personal significance. One student, who was an adopted child and had recently made contact with her birth mother, had discovered that she was a carrier for an inherited disease. As the class began to apply their understandings of inheritance to study of sex-linked diseases, exercises like the following took on a frightening personal relevance for her:

> Thalassemia is an inherited blood disease common among people of Mediterranean origin. It is caused by a single recessive gene. People with Thalassemia Minor are heterozygous. People with Thalassemia Major are homozygous recessive. What advice would you give a couple who are heterozygous and want to have children?

In responding to this question, students first had to apply their knowledge of Mendelian inheritance to work out that the couple had a 50 per cent chance of having children with Thalassemia Minor. The science provided them with an empirical base for the advice they would give the couple, but in applying their knowledge of inheritance to human situations, they were forced to confront the values underpinning their own views and those held by others with a stake in the issue.

As well as using science to help them think through the issues, students also problematized science in social terms. They talked and wrote about the advantages and disadvantages of genetic engineering, taking up such questions as the dangers to future generations of errors in genetic experiments or the possibility of new forms of 'germ warfare' falling into the wrong hands. Students did not leave the media out of the picture. One of the final tasks they completed asked them to consider three newspaper reports about new genetic technology for checking birth defects in human embryos, more specifically, techniques which allow probing for cystic fibrosis in the very early stages of pregnancy. At least one of the reports hailed this development as a cure. The students were asked to answer the following questions: Are these (techniques) cures? If not, what are these describing? In answering such questions, students were learning to be more critical of media representations of the so called 'cures' found by science but from an informed base. Rodney draws on his scientific knowledge of reproduction and his capacity for critique of media hype in answering these questions.

### Science text 6

> The so called cures that doctors have come up with for cystic fibrosis are nothing more than prevention of the inherited disease being developed in an embryo.
>
> [Rodney]

Notice his use of 'so called' to modify the nominal 'cures'. This device is an index of his ability to semioticize his distance from the verbal representations of others. An important step on the way to becoming critically literate is to see others' texts as constructs which can be resisted and, in this case, directly challenged.

In these exercises Rodney and the others in his class are being asked to engage in critique – to question the underlying messages of the discourse of 'the scientific discovery' promoted by popular news media, in which men in white coats work alone in their labs and come up with revolutionary discoveries and cures for the ills of common humanity. And at this end of the contextual continuum, students saw more and more clearly how 'fraught' the field had become, and it is no accident that they were forced to make greater use of discussion, critique and evaluation in both their spoken interaction and, less frequently in this case, in their writing.

At this stage, when she judged that the learners were ready to take a more reflexive and critical perspective on the field, Margaret, like Bill, stepped out of her instructional role and gave students more control over their own learning, both the content and the pacing of the lessons.

## 4    Commonalities in Bill and Margaret's pedagogic practice

I would now like to consider some important commonalities in the pedagogic practices of these two teachers and to reflect on these from the point of view of the contextual model.

- For each subject they study in the process of educational learning, students have to build up the meaning potential (the registers) it privileges as a discipline. Both Bill and Margaret *work to expand their students' awareness of what the subject demands* of them. And these registers are not a 'static potential' (if, indeed, that were possible). They are not exhaustively determined by a set of prescribed texts or syllabus documents. In their pedagogic practices, Bill and Margaret take up multiple perspectives on their discipline. They view their subject as a specialized domain of educational knowledge which has an interface with the world their learners inhabit before they come to school and with the broader society which will claim their attention when they leave it. So their students are actively apprenticed into the fields of human reproduction in Biology or that of the situation comedy genre in English but are encouraged to see these from the point of view of the ordinary consumer, the expert and the critic. Thus the meaning potential of the subject may privilege discipline knowledge but it also encompasses commonsense, and reflexive knowledge.

  In line with this, in day-to-day teaching, Bill and Margaret both work actively to build up the context for the written texts their students encounter or which they are asked to produce.
- Both teachers are *goal-oriented* in their pedagogic practices: they

have a strong sense of what they want their learners to achieve in each unit of work. There is nothing unusual about this in itself. What is distinctive about their planning, however, is that they are able to semioticize learning – to view the territory they want the students to cover in terms of the meanings they will need to make. Margaret and Bill plan for learning using categories like 'genre', 'field', 'tenor' (or 'audience') and 'mode' (among others). Taken together, these contextual parameters provide them with a 'look forward' framework – with implications for their classroom practice. Choosing to investigate a field as it is constituted by a particular discipline, for example, has implications for the roles students will play and the kinds of meanings they will encounter and make as they do so. And for the genres they need to engage with in the process.

- Margaret and Bill are able to make principled choices about what is to be learned and to view this territory from the point of view of the texts students will need to read and write as they move through this semantic space. In English, the field is already semiotic in the sense that language is the object of study. But Margaret, who works in a discipline where students use language primarily as an instrument of learning, has to choose genres which serve to 'get them into the field'. Both teachers *work explicitly on the structure of written genres with their students*. Bill tends to background his own role as an instructor, preferring to let the activity teach students what is required. Margaret, however, for whom language is an object just like any other scientific technology, takes an assertively informative role. I will use her own words, to describe what she does:

> [I] explicitly model the language demands of the genre. I show them and tell them how to do it; step one, two, three, etcetera. I show the connectors, the processes. I am really down at language level. And then they have the means for dealing with language on their own. They can deconstruct texts even in exams. The language functions are there even in short-answer questions.

- Having a metalanguage for relating literacy to learning enables them to communicate their goals for students' learning with students themselves. Bill talks freely of genre, field and mode with his students, although he prefers the term audience to that of tenor in keeping with the junior secondary syllabus. His students are familiar with grammatical terms like *modality*, *process type*, or *connectives* and use them to probe the texts they encounter. As both Margaret and Bill's pedagogic practice makes clear, the learners are *'in on the act' from the beginning*. Because this is a contextually sensitive metalanguage, students can increasingly take it over and utilize it to analyse any learning task independently.

The same principle makes a genuine dialogue with other teachers possible. The two schools in which Margaret and Bill first developed their 'language across the curriculum' literacy programs were committed to whole-school change. Teachers across different faculties could talk about what they were doing with genres like report, exposition, discussion and explanation – all useful for building up field knowledge in Geography, History, Science and English. Teachers often shared information and experiences about the genres they were teaching during staffroom discussions.

- For students who come from backgrounds in which reading is not a priority, the teacher has a crucial role to play in initiating them into the written mode. *Strategies like modelling, deconstruction, and joint negotiation are essential* if these students are to be initiated into educational learning. They are essential if students are to construct for themselves an adequate picture of the secondary school learning context and the kinds of demands it will make on their meaning resources.

- There is a high degree of *redundancy* in their oral language work. Both Bill and Margaret use classroom talk to help the students bridge from oral to written discourse. Bill, especially, spends a lot of class time amplifying the requirements of different learning contexts through talk. Activities in which he and the class jointly deconstruct his essays, in which they apply features of the genre to instances of it, or discuss issues like ageism or sexism in individual programs, provide the students with oral models on which they draw when it comes to writing. Margaret also uses strategies like modelling and joint-construction as a means to moving students into the written mode.

- Both teachers *take a structured approach to their subject.* They can deconstruct it from the point of view of the modes of discourse through which it is mediated, the roles students need to take up in classroom interaction, the prerequisite knowledge they need to understand certain concepts, or the genres through which this knowledge is communicated. They can analyse students' learning from these points of view, making decisions about what needs to happen at different stages of the learning process. Sometimes they may need to work along the content dimension, building up the field through a range of classroom activities. Another time, they will think about which roles and groupings will facilitate a particular kind of learning. Or, they will consider the extent to which their students can handle highly metaphorical or technical language and whether they need to unpack the written mode more carefully. Or, they may decide to work explicitly on the generic structure of the texts they want students to write.

- Finally, both teachers use the metalanguage as a 'look back' framework which not only *helps them to assess* what students have achieved over a unit of work, but to examine their own teaching practices in the light of this information. For instance, if their students' written texts are weak for content, they can ask themselves: *How well did I enable the students to build up the field?* or, if the students have had trouble structuring their written texts properly, Bill and Margaret can fruitfully ask: *Did I spend enough time on the genre and its schematic structure?* and so on.

## 5   Concluding remarks: some implications of the model

This model offers teachers a common perspective on literacy and learning across the curriculum because it is a framework for semioticizing learning. Goals for learning can be characterized in such a way as to foreground the meanings which are privileged in a given learning context. The contextual dimensions act as constraints on these meanings, helping both teacher and students to set 'the semiotic probabilities' of the context. For example, once the teacher has made decisions about the nature of the content to be explored and the activities by which it will be investigated (its field), the roles students will play in this classroom work (its tenor) and the semiotic dimension of this task (its media and modes), there are certain register probabilities already 'in the air' so to speak.

Becoming conscious of the contextual pressures of the learning environment, the teacher is better able to situate and motivate the kinds of reading and writing he or she asks students to do. And the text types chosen for reading and writing will, in turn, also facilitate a particular kind of learning in the classroom. Each subject can be represented as a meaning potential (a construction of agnate registers ) which students need to build up for themselves and to enact through texts of various kinds (genres).

Register values can be assigned to any school learning situation on the basis of perceived (and analysed) commonalities across curriculum contents, pedagogical relationships and uses of language. At a primary level of delicacy, these commonalities can be characterized as: instruction in an area of discipline knowledge; allocation of an expert role to incumbent members of the discipline, and, increasing engagement with written text as a primary medium of learning.

Educational learning privileges specialized registers and genres but encompasses those of everyday and reflexive domains because it has an interface with the worlds which learners inhabit before they come to school and after they leave it. This implies that the same situation can evoke a different register for different participants. The setting could be the classroom but its meaning potential could be amplified in any of three ways: along everyday, specialized or reflexive lines. This model is admittedly 'pedago-centric': it privileges the registers of the second domain as a means for setting learning goals. However, for analytical purposes in educational linguistics, it is useful to develop categories which allow for more than one contextual reading of learning situations, especially those which are dialogic and involve more than one participant. This is important if teachers are to assist students whose interpretation of the classroom language diverges in significant ways from their own. They need a model of context which not only enables them to sense when the students are assigning an unproductive register to the classroom context, but also to imagine what effect this is having on their ability to participate in learning.

At the same time, it is important not to proliferate possible readings of (registers for) learning contexts. Because teachers tend to privilege one reading of the learning contexts they establish in their classrooms, the learners will typically negotiate this, adjusting the meaning potential they have built up over time to the current demands of the classroom context. The environments in which they have already established this resource, however, are not unlimited: the contexts of the everyday domain, and even those in which learners can begin to be reflexive in understanding both self and other, are typically those bounded by home and the local environment. The situation types encountered by the learner in these domains are, as yet, ones which are deictically close to the 'here and now and you and me' of immediate experience and the registers by which such meanings are explored are constrained along similar lines.

We need, in short, to consider a learning context from more than one point of view and to build into it not just the pedagocentric view of the teacher and what is to be taught, but also that of the learner and how this relates to what is already learnt. But we also need to see the possibilities of the context, the 'yet to be voiced' (Bernstein 1986) readings which are made at the margins of society and which challenge the hegemonic views of both 'required knowledge' and the commonplace views of 'tacit understandings'.

## Notes

1 For certain differences in the everyday domain of learning which become criterial to the pedagogic processes in school, see Hasan, this volume.
2 For a succinct description of the relations between context of culture, context of situation, language system and text, see Halliday (1991).
3 See Rothery, this volume, for more detail on the structure of the narrative.
4 For further discussion of these points, see Veel (1993).

## References

Bernstein, Basil (1973) *Class Codes and Control. Vol. 1 Theoretical Studies Towards a Sociology of Language* (Rev. Edn). Routledge and Kegan Paul, London.

Bernstein, Basil (1975) *Class Codes and Control.* Vol. 3 *Towards a Theory of Educational Transmissions.* Routledge and Kegan Paul, London.

Bernstein, Basil (1986) 'On pedagogic discourse', in J.G. Richardson (ed.) *Handbook of Theory and Research in the Sociology of Education.* Greenwood Press, London, pp. 205–39.

Board of Secondary Education (1987) English Syllabus Years 7–10. NSW Australia.

Halliday, M.A.K. (1988) 'Language and socialisation: home and school', in L. Gerot, J. Oldenburg and T. Leeuwen (eds) *Language and Socialisation: Home and School. Proceedings from the Working Conference on Language in Education, held at Macquarie University, November 1986.* Macquarie University, Sydney.

Halliday, M.A.K. (1991) 'The notion of "Context" in language education', in Thao Le and Mike McCausland (eds) *Language Education: Interaction and Development. Proceedings of the International Conference held in Ho Chi Minh, Vietnam, 30 March–1 April 1991.* University of Tasmania, Launceston.

Halliday M.A.K. & Ruqaiya Hasan (1985) *Language, Context and Text: Aspects of Language in a Social-Semiotic Perspective.* Deakin University Press, Geelong, Vic. (Republished by Oxford University Press, Oxford, 1989.)

Hasan, Ruqaiya (1986) 'The implications of semiotic distance for language in education', in Anvita Abbi (ed.) *Studies in Bilingualism.* Bahri Publications, New Delhi, pp. 1–22.

Hasan, Ruqaiya (1988) 'Language in the processes of socialisation: home and school', in L. Gerot, J. Oldenburg and T. van Leeuwen (eds) *Language and Socialisation: Home and School. Proceedings from the Working Conference on Language in Education, held at Macquarie University, November 1986.* Macquarie University, Sydney.

Hasan, Ruqaiya (1989) 'Semantic variation and sociolinguistics', *Australian Journal of Linguistics,* 9: 221–75.

Macken, M. and J. Rothery (1991) *Developing Critical Literacy: A Model for Literacy in Subject Learning.* Monograph produced by Metropolitan East Disadvantaged Schools Program, Erskineville, NSW.

Martin, J.R. and J. Rothery (1991) 'Literacy for a lifetime. Notes for Teachers'. Film Australia, Sydney, NSW.

Matthiesen, Christian (1992) 'Register in the round: diversity in a unified theory of register analysis', in Mohsen Ghadessy (ed.) *Register Analysis: Theory into Practice.* Pinter, London.

Rothery, J. and M. Macken (1991) *Developing Critical Literacy Through Systemic Functional Linguistics: Unpacking the 'Hidden Curriculum' for Writing in Junior Secondary English in New South Wales.* Monograph produced by Metropolitan East Disadvantaged Schools Program, Erskineville, NSW.

Veel, Robert (1993) *Literacy in Science 7–10.* Write it Right Project, Metropolitan East Disadvantaged Schools Program, Erskineville, NSW.

# 9

## Plain English: from a perspective of language in society

NICKY SOLOMON

## 1  Introduction

The aim of this chapter is to take a close look at the Plain English movement in an attempt to deconstruct some of the assumptions implicit in its approach. In the following section, I will attempt to put Plain English in its historical perspective by briefly discussing the consumer needs which the movement addresses. This will provide the background against which the following questions can be considered:

1. What exactly does Plain English hope to achieve? In other words: what goal does it set for itself?
2. How does it attempt to achieve these goals?
3. What are the assumptions implicit in its recommended practice?
4. What success has it achieved so far?

Section 3 of this chapter addresses the first two questions, using extracts from Plain English practitioner documents. These document extracts will be analysed in order to classify the instructions as they pertain to paralanguage, to language and to the context of language use.

Section 4 examines the significance of the various classes of instruction: the view of language that is implicit in these instructions and the view of the relationship between the reader, the text and the occasion for the creation of the text. I will argue that the Plain English approach suffers from a certain degree of linguistic naivety, it fails to make use of linguistic insights provided by such scholars as Hymes, Halliday, Labov, Martin and others, and that its own instructions are at variance with its actual practices, thus throwing doubt on its theoretical grounding.

Section 5 will report on research carried out to assess the effectiveness of Plain English. The chapter closes by posing some of the questions that Plain English practitioners need to answer. It seems reasonable to suggest that in the absence of these answers, the very direction of the enterprise is likely to remain hidden from those who are being taught to produce Plain English documents: what it is they are trying to achieve and whether, and to what extent, it is in fact achievable.

## 2    The context of Plain English

The problems that Plain English addresses are real enough. Not very long ago, and in some cases even today, if one had the occasion to enter into a legal contract concerning a property, one would have to come to grips with a passage like the one below – only the reality would be much worse, because the real document would be several pages long!

**The Schedule**

> The goodwill of the Mortgagor's said business and also the goodwill of any other business or share in any other business which may now or at any future date be carried on by the Mortgagor on his own account or in partnership with any other person at the same address or elsewhere and also the interest of the Mortgagor in the book and business debts which may now or at any future date be due and owing to the Mortgagor from any business now or subsequently to be carried on by the Mortgagor on his own account or in partnership also all books of account records of customers clients or patients promissory notes cheques bills accounts bills of exchange and all other documents and instruments which may evidence or represent all or any of such book business debts due to the Mortgagor or in which he may have an interest AND ALSO (in addition to the chattels effects property matters and things specified in this Schedule) all other chattels effects property matters and things including but without restricting of the generality hereof stock-in-trade which at any time during the continuance of this security may be brought by the Mortgagor in or upon the said premises and which may be capable of being used in or in connection with business carried on by him whether of a like or a different nature or in addition or in substitution for all or any of the chattels so specified.
>
> (Form 138, Trader's Ordinary Bill of Sale)

It is documents such as these which give rise to the observation that legal documents are written by the lawyer for the lawyer for the management of others' property. In today's world, these others tend to be speakers of varied languages, coming from different cultures, and possessing different degrees of maturity and knowledge. From one point of view, these differences might be immaterial: people are alike in not being able to fathom the meaning of the type of language just quoted. Little wonder then that the signatories to a contract could often remain unaware of their rights and obligations, and worse still that they could find themselves embroiled in legal entanglements following commitments which they have undertaken by signing, but which they have failed to understand. Given the number of impenetrable documents in existence, it is not surprising that many businesses are inundated with requests for spoken explanations from customers and that employees unwittingly fail to comply with workplace regulations or are unable to understand the appropriate procedures for operating or repairing machinery.

Plain English recommends changes to document design and language so that the information in documents of the above type becomes accessible to readers. The changes so introduced in the documents are pragmatic responses to concerns that relate to:

- access and equity issues (i.e., people have the right to access relevant information);
- safety issues (i.e., accidents are avoided if notices and regulations are understood);
- economic issues (i.e., lack of understanding of written documents costs time and money).

As a movement, Plain English is not a recent initiative. It became popular in the United States in the early 1970s. The initial targets were insurance documents. These were redesigned in response to consumer demand to be able to access information about con-sumer rights. The new documents were not only welcomed by the consumers, but they also proved cost-effective for the companies. Similar initiatives soon followed in the United Kingdom, Canada, Europe and Australia targeting mainly government documents that were written to inform consumers about their rights and privileges. Since then it has influenced the writing of bureaucratic and legal documents. The movement has been supported by both government policy and the establishment of expert units and centres whose main purpose is the promotion of Plain English.

In Australia, the early influence of the overseas Plain English movement can be seen in the Australian consumer context, for example in the NRMA Plain English car policy document prepared in 1976 and the New South Wales Real Estate Institute residential tenancy agreement of 1977. However, it was only in the 1980s and 1990s that the Federal and State governments responded to the need to give all members of the community access to information. Some government initiatives include:

- 1984: The Australian Federal Government declared a policy of Plain English in official documents.
- 1984: a report on a National Language Policy recommended that 'a National Task Force be established to recommend on the reform of the language of the law'.
- 1985: The Law Reform Commission of Victoria began a review of the language of legislation.
- 1990: A reader friendly kit was launched as part of the International Literacy Year campaign.
- 1991: The Centre for Plain Legal Language at the University of Sydney was established.
- 1991: Australian Language and Literacy Policy recommended the promotion of Plain English.

The general policy to implement Plain English across a range of important Australian institutional contexts has been further accelerated by two related factors which together highlight the need for well-written documents. The first factor is a large migrant population influx, which resulted in an increased diversity in the cultural, educational and linguistic backgrounds of the readers. The effect of such diversity cannot be ignored given the different knowledge, resources and experiences that migrants bring to the range of reading tasks they encounter when involved in the migration and settlement process and when they enter the workplace. Secondly, there has been a significant change in work practices, resulting in an increase in the role of written communication. Changes in workplace practices have been in part due to the restructuring of Australian industries. This restructuring has radically changed the nature of work, which in turn has changed the purposes and kinds of both spoken and written communication. Multi-skilling, improved client relations, improved marketing techniques and effective communication in work teams and organisational teams all rely on effective training and are dependent on the effective written documentation such as memos, training manuals, policy documents, written records and reports.

Plain English has appeared to hold the key to some of the problems aggravated by these developments. Private and public sector workplaces are responding to the increased role of written communication with Plain English policies and Plain English training courses for workplace writers. There has been an interesting twist in the form of argument: previously, major responsibility for '-correct' interpretation had been placed on the readers of a document; poor comprehension and/or ignorance of workplace matters was considered to be the fault of the consumer or the employee and the solution to the problem was to learn 'to read'. Today, however, the onus for ensuring comprehensibility has shifted to the writers of the document – in the workplace these are often managers and trainers, and in vocational educational institutions they are mostly trade teachers. The upshot is that writers are now having to learn to write so that what they produce can be understood more readily by the readers. Faced with this situation, Plain English has been viewed as the technique for ensuring comprehensibility. Its scope has extended beyond legal and bureaucratic documents to include all kinds of documents that are to be read by a large and diverse audience. It is therefore timely to reflect on what Plain English is, what it professes to achieve and how it goes about achieving its goals.

## 3   The goals and strategies of Plain English

This section outlines the definitions of Plain English presented by those who practise the techniques. A problem encountered in stating what exactly Plain English hopes to achieve is the absence of scholarly papers. My sources are various articles originating in the Australian Plain English movement. Most of these are given as introductory material preceding the pages of instructions on how to write Plain English, and most neither acknowledge authorship nor give a date of publication. In these cases, I am obliged to simply cite the title of the paper and the publishing agency. However, the majority of the extracts are by Eagleson,[1] whose contribution to the Plain English movement has been enormously influential in Australia.

A definition that has become the hallmark of Plain English is:

> Plain English is the opposite of gobbledegook and of confusing and incomprehensible language. Plain English is clear, straightforward expression, using only as many words as are necessary. It is language that avoids obscurity, inflated vocabulary and convoluted sentence construction. (Eagleson 1990a)

The essence of this definition is reflected in most other definitions, although others offer additional understandings about what is meant by Plain English. Some definitions provide more information on the kind of language that Plain English is promoting, while at the same time challenging the assumption that Plain English is 'simple' English. One example of this is:

> Plain English is a matter of using the patterns and words of normal, everyday adult English. ... It is not a special or reduced version of the language. (Eagleson, unpublished papers)

Another description is as follows:

> Plain English is not a simplified form of English or a type of basic English. On the contrary, it is a full version of the language, including all features of normal adult English.
> (*Law Reform Commission of Australia*, Appendix 1, Drafting Manual 1987)

Other definitions, on the other hand, focus more on the purpose of Plain English. Let me give some examples:

> .... it is a question of our knowing how to use our precious language skilfully to communicate our message precisely so that our audience can understand it clearly. (Eagleson 1990b)

> Plain English is getting a clear message across to your audience in an appropriate way. This means being clear about what you want to say, who you're saying it to and how you're going to say it. Plain English is effective communication.
> (*Plain English Is Not a Simple Matter* 1990)

In terms of reaching an understanding of what it is that Plain English hopes to achieve, all the definitions, either implicitly or explicitly, express the view that the purpose of Plain English is about 'getting a clear message across to your audience in an appropriate way'. Their goal is therefore to encourage the writing of documents in such a way that information is understood by readers. However, in spite of the repeated assertions about what Plain English is and what Plain English isn't, curiously the nature of 'plain' English still remains unclear. This comes about because, in the majority of these assertions, the language that is used to characterise Plain English is itself problematic. How, for instance, should we interpret the words *clear, straightforward, normal, everyday, adult English*?

The words *clear* and *straightforward*, as attributive terms, do not have a clear reference: exactly what patterning in language would count as clear and straightforward? Who should the message be clear to – everyone, the 'average' reader or a selected audience? The word straightforward is another vague term. Among other things it can mean 'simple' or 'straight to the point'. But again, is such a term helpful? The words *normal* and *everyday* suggest that the Plain English writer should use the language appropriate to informal, familiar, everyday situations. Yet an examination of the range of domains in which Plain English is expected to perform sucessfully reveals a variety of contexts for language use, for example contexts of home, workplace and educational institutions. And within these, the range of situations in each domain is again varied, for example at work: giving opinions at meetings, chatting with friends at lunch, writing a submission for a grant, taking a telephone message for a colleague, writing a report on research findings, and so on. Could all of these be classified as *normal* or *everyday* language?

The terms *clear, straightforward, normal, everyday, adult English* seem to have meaning only in relation to what Plain English is attempting to avoid, that is, *gobbledegook, confusing and incomprehensible language, obscurity, inflated vocabulary/terms, convoluted sentence construction, extravagant structures.* However, an impression that the reader of these Plain English documents may gain is that clear, straightforward, normal, everyday, adult English is a single, homogeneous variety of English. The problem with such an interpretation is that it fails to accommodate the idea of linguistic variation, that is, the well-recognised fact that language differs according to context of use. It is also important to stress that clarity is determined by the reader's ability to understand as well as the writer's ability to write appropriately to the purpose of the document. No matter how clear the writing is, if the reader does not have the required knowledge, then understanding will not occur. Obviously, the same document may be clear and straight-forward to some readers but be unclear to others. The need for writers to consider their readers' meaning frameworks is elaborated below.

A significant source of information about the goals of Plain English and how these goals can be achieved is found in the various Plain English guidelines. I will now examine some extracts from such guidelines in order to review the different kinds of instructions given to Plain English writers. In what follows, I provide the gist of the goals enumerated in three important documents.

## Document A

The first document to be considered is called *Reader Friendly Documents Kit: Profit and Popularity with Plain English* (1990, Social Change Media, Department of Employment, Education and Training). It promotes Plain English by describing its many advantages and by offering hints on how to make documents reader friendly. In the first instance writers are encouraged to consider the reader. Then suggestions about the language and design of Plain English documents are provided. For example:

- Get straight to the point.
- Write directly to the reader. Imagine you are explaining the facts in person. Use 'we' and 'you'.
- Write short sentences, i.e., aim for less than 15 words in a sentence.
- Use active rather than passive voice and use verbs – not nouns made from verbs.
- Choose words your reader will know, eg. use 'inform' rather than 'advise'.
- Be consistent.
- Use clear layout and design.
- Tell the facts in your reader's logical order.
- Make information easy to find, e.g. use headings and other ways of signposting important facts.
- Put detail at the end. Don't let minor points confuse your main message.
- Use good visual design, e.g., white space around texts.

## Document B

*Beyond Readability: How To Write and Design Understandable Life Insurance Policies* (United States) describes a range of features that increase understandability of insurance policies. Such features include short sentences and short words, minimum of 10 point type, no undue prominence to any portion of the text, a table of contents if the policy is longer than three pages or 3,000 words. It goes on to offer advice on how to:

- make information easy to find, for example:
  - set a context at the beginning of the document – tell the readers what the policy is and what they will find in it;
  - put a heading on almost every paragraph instead of just a few headings for general sections, and include all of these headings in the table of contents;
  - make sure that the headings match the content and wording of the paragraph;
  - use questions or statements instead of one or two nouns as headings.
- write with clear, concise words and sentences:
  - write in the active voice;
  - write with verbs, not with nouns made out of verbs;
  - use personal pronouns or name the actors;
  - make parallel thoughts into parallel sentences;
  - drop or change difficult words that are not legally necessary;
  - define technical terms as you use them;
  - be consistent in style and in choice of words;
  - do not use shall.
- use graphic design to make the information visually attractive and functional:
  - keep lines of type 50–70 characters and leave lots of white space on the page;
  - consider setting test type with a ragged right margin;
  - use upper and lower case letters;
  - make the headings stand out;
  - consider colour for headings but use black ink for the text;
  - consider bold or italic for special words, rather than initial capitals.

## Document C

The third text, an article called 'Plain Language: Is It Legal?' (E. Kerr, *Law Society of New South Wales Journal*, June 1991), offers advice to legal drafters about the kinds of language features that help make legal language more accessible to readers. Some of these language features are said to be:

- organisation;
- short sentences;
- get rid of unnecessary words;
- draft in the present not the future tense;
- keep sentences clear;
- order ideas within sentences;
- use active voice, rather than passive;
- write positively;
- use verbs not nouns;
- use *shall* not *must*.

It is clear at a glance that the different kinds of advice offered by these guidelines fall into three categories:

1. Paralinguistic features affecting a document's appearance.
2. Linguistic features related to vocabulary and grammar.
3. Contextual features relevant to the addressee.

Instructions regarding paralinguistic features are a valuable contribution to the appearance of documents. Recommended features that might assist the reader include those related to the visual design of the document, such as the use of white space, use of colour and size of font, and features that guide the reading process by providing signals to readers to help them through lengthy documents, perhaps by highlighting key sections or by the use of headings, sub-headings, and font size and appearance variation. The advice to write short sentences is a recognition of the difficulty of reading lengthy sentences, which occur commonly in legal documents such as the one quoted in section 2 from the Bill of Sale.

Instructions regarding linguistic features are concerned with lexical choices, sentence construction and the global structure of the document. Some instructions focus on general advice while others are quite specific to the point of being close to prescriptive. Using these criteria we can organise the kinds of instructions from Documents A–C into the following categories:

- word choices, e.g., use *shall* not *must*, choose words your reader will know, write positively, use personal pronouns or name the actors, get rid of unnecessary words, draft in the present tense, not the future;

- clause structure, e.g., use verbs and not nouns, use active rather than passive voice, keep sentences clear, define technical terms as you use them, make parallel thoughts into parallel sentences;
- global structure, e.g., get straight to the point, set a context at the beginning of the document, put the reader first, tell the facts in the order that would be logical to your reader, put detail at the end and don't let minor points confuse your main message.

The appropriateness and adequacy of these linguistic instructions as a means of getting writers to produce *clear, straightforward, normal, everyday, adult English* will be considered in the next section where Plain English documents are critically reviewed for their linguistic features.

It may have been noted in the extracts from Plain English guidelines presented above that there are very few instructions regarding contextual features. Those that are mentioned pertain to the reader. Writers are asked to consider who will read the document. This is clearly a desirable attitude in the writer or speaker. However, awareness of the reader/listener does not automatically translate itself into an awareness of what linguistic strategies should be adopted, especially where the contexts are not everyday contexts. Plain English guidelines seldom provide such details. Further, writers are also encouraged to write directly to the reader, to *be friendly* by using words such as *we* and *you*, as if this kind of writer-reader relationship can be assumed non-problematically even in official documents. The soundness of this advice is very much open to doubt.

Be that as it may, the minimal attention given to contextual features in all but a few of these instructions seems to diminish the significance of the social context in which the written documents are written or read. The dominance of paralinguistic and generic linguistic features in these instructions places the focus on the document itself, without adequate attention being given to its social context and purpose. It is as if the document exists in a social vacuum, almost without any variation in context.

Nevertheless, while it is easy to critique the guidelines, it is also important to understand their context. They are written for people without linguistic knowledge. They are written for authors writing many different kinds of documents. It could therefore be argued that generic advice does have a place in that it can help writers to become more conscious of the language they use and the comprehensibility of what has been written.

# 4    Conception of language

Documents written in Plain English are useful for providing an insight into the conception of language implicit in the Plain English goals and in the various classes of instructions in the guidelines. In this section I will first present extracts from three Plain English documents and examine their relationship to the Plain English guidelines. I will then consider some questions that these guidelines and documents raise in relation to their underlying view of language.

## Extract A: From an NRMA insurance document

1. This policy
   Your 'Plain English' Third Party Property Damage Car Policy consists of:
   - this booklet which contains our standard third party property damage car policy wording
     and
   - a schedule which this booklet describes as 'the current schedule'.
     The current schedule is:
   - the schedule which we gave you with this booklet
     or
   - the schedule shown on your current renewal certificate if you have renewed this policy.

## Extract B: From Telecom Easycall booklet

STORE EASYCALL STEPS
IN YOUR TELEPHONE'S MEMORY
   To make Easycall easier still, your Telecom Touchphone 200 or other late model push button phone has memory buttons which can be used to store step-by-step Easycall instructions. Here's how easy it is to operate:
   Simply pick up the receiver of your Touchphone 200 and press the 'Store' button. Next, dial in the facility steps you wish to store. Then press the applicable memory button. And don't forget to write the name of each facility on the card provided under the plastic panel beside the memory buttons. Then you'll remember where they are and others can use them as well.

**Extract C: From a Commonwealth Bank booklet**

Electronic Banking Conditions of Use In Plain English
11. Can we change these Conditions?
i) We reserve the right to vary these
ii) We will give you at least 30 days' written notice if any variation would –

a) impose or increase charges relating solely to the use of your card and PIN, or the issue of any additional or replacement Card and PIN;
b) increase your liability for losses relating to transactions through Terminals;
c) adjust the daily transaction limits applying to the use of your Card.
iii) We will tell you of all other variations in advance through press advertisements or notices on Terminals or in branches. We will also give you notice of the variation with your account statement.
iv) The obligation to give you advance notice does not apply if variations are required in an emergency to restore or maintain the security of our electronic banking systems or individual accounts.
v) If there have been a lot of changes in a twelve month period we will send you a new brochure setting out all the current Conditions.
vi) We fulfil our obligations to give you notice under these Conditions if we post the notice by ordinary mail to the last address you gave us.

Do these documents follow the recommendations of Plain English guidelines?

An examination of these documents reveals a considerable amount of variation in the way some of the Plain English instructions have been applied. While the instructions pertaining to the paralinguistic features, such as the use of white space, bold print have been effectively and consistently used, this is not the case with the instructions pertaining to the linguistic and contextual features. Perhaps this indicates an inherent ambiguity in the rules.

Let us see more specifically the ways in which there is inconsistency between the Plain English instruction and its application:

- The instruction to 'be personal' has been followed in the language of the three documents. In the Insurance and Telecom documents this is reflected in the use of the personal pronouns *your, our* and *you.* In the Bank document the personal pronoun *we* is the subject of many of the sentences. However, this pattern is broken several times where a complex nominal group has been used. For instance in Extract A, we have *Your 'Plain English' Third Party Property Damage Car Policy, our standard third party damage car policy wording, the schedule which we gave you with this booklet*; in Extract B, we find *other late model push button phone, step-by-step Easycall instructions*; and in Extract C, note the very title *Electronic Banking Conditions of Use*, and other nominal expressions, e.g., *the daily transaction limits applying to the use of your Card, the obligation to give you advance notice*, etc.

- The instruction to use verbs and not nouns has been followed quite unevenly – even within the one document. For example, the instructions are followed in the Insurance document: *the schedule which we gave you with this booklet* is used rather than its nominalised version, *the accompanying schedule.* However, nominalisation is not consistently avoided, so we have such evidence of nominalisation present in groups such as *our standard third party property damage car policy wording*, not to speak of the non-finite clauses, e.g., *applying to the use of your Card* which function as Qualifier to *the daily transaction limits.*

- The instructions to use familiar words and to define technical terms as they are being used is also unevenly adhered to. For example, in the Insurance document the meaning of *schedule* is unclear, as is the meaning of *facility* in the Telecom document.

- The instructions *get straight to the point* and *don't let minor points confuse your message* are followed effectively in the Insurance and Bank documents. However, in the Telecom document the instructions are lost in an interpersonal spoken language overload, e.g., *Here's how easy it is to operate* and *Don't forget to ....* It is very much open to question whether the instructions would not have been more effective as instructions if the same information had been conveyed in a less conversational mode, perhaps by using imperatives sequenced and formatted in the following way:
  1. Pick up the receiver.
  2. Press the 'Store' button.
  3. Dial in the relevant facility steps.
  4. Press the applicable memory button.
  5. Write the name of each facility on the card provided.

Clearly, it is possible to go on with this examination of the consistency between the principles in the guidelines and the practice of writing the documents, but from the point of view of understanding how Plain English is being applied, and what it might manage to achieve in facilitating the writer's task, the following questions are of greater interest:

- Why are the linguistic instructions inconsistently applied?
- Why, despite their own intentions, do writers fail to keep nominalisation out of the documents?
- Do the instructions take into account contexts relevant to the various documents?
- What does Plain English have to say about the structure of the text?

In the following sub-sections, I will offer my response to these questions.

## 4.1   Why are the linguistic instructions inconsistently applied?

The uneven application of the instructions is, in a sense, inevitable. A consistent application would only be possible if language did not vary according to context. This therefore raises the question of the motive behind the provision of a single set of linguistic instructions relevant to all written documents. Does it reveal a desire to encourage a single, neutral form of language? Or is it a strategic move deliberately to focus on those aspects of language that are considered to be more familiar or simple and consequently easy to read? Both of these motives underestimate the variable nature of language.

The invariant nature of language, as presented in the linguistic features in the instructions, suggest there is a preferred language that is well suited to every type of document. Such a view is not informed by the work of sociolinguists and linguists such as Firth, Halliday, Hymes and Gumperz, to mention the outstanding names. The work of these scholars shares the understanding that discourses vary in correlation with the occasion of discourse – that every language has speech varieties. As early as 1967, Dell Hymes identified a set of concepts for describing the context of situation, each concept influencing the language in the speech activity. The concepts, by now common knowledge, are:

- the form and content of the message;
- the setting;
- the participants;
- the intent and effect of the communication;
- the key;
- the medium;
- the genre;
- the norms of interaction.

The tradition of scholarship introduced in this domain has been vigourously followed – even during the ascendency of formal grammars – not only in Europe and the United States, but also in Australia. The ethnographic focus has led to a renewal of interest in the different ways of using language to achieve the same/ similar purposes in different cultures and the way texts differ with differing social activities within the same culture. From a social-semiotic perspective, the work of Halliday, McIntosh and Strevens (1964), Halliday (1976) and Halliday and Hasan (1976, 1985) provides a theoretical framework for describing context of situation. Their notion of register provides an understanding of linguistic variety according to use. It extends Hymes' concepts by describing more specifically the kind of variation in language that corresponds to the variation in the context of situation. Registers are diatypic varieties in which the semantic configurations are typically associated with particular social contexts, defined in terms of field, tenor and mode, as follows:

*Field of discourse*: what is happening, what is it that the participants are engaged in.
*Tenor of discourse*: who is taking part, the status and roles of the participants.
*Mode of discourse*: what part the language is playing, including the nature of channel, spoken or written.

Each of these, together and separately, is reflected in the variety of language use. More recently, Martin has introduced a connotative semiotic modelling of the systemic functional framework to develop a genre-based approach to teaching writing (Martin 1992; Cope & Kalantzis 1993). This approach provides very much more specific insight into the relationship between context, genre and language.[2] This work centres on the identification of key genres and the way the purpose of the genre is achieved through a particular staging of information and the use of particular linguistic features, that realise the experiential, interpersonal and textual meanings of a text type (see the contributions by Veel and Coffin, and Macken-Horarik, in this volume). There is no evidence that Plain English has taken any of this scholarship concerning diatypic variation into account. Yet, there can be little doubt that from the perspective of language in society linguistic variation is inevitable. So attempts to provide globally applicable linguistic instructions for 'good writing' must ultimately fail to produce good writing.

## 4.2   Why despite their best intentions, do writers fail to keep nominalisation out of the documents?

A common instruction in Plain English guidelines is not to use nouns made from verbs. However, as pointed out earlier, such advice is not always followed. For example, both the NRMA Insurance policy (Extract A) and the Electronic Banking Conditions (Extract C) contain nominalisations. In Extract C alone, we find nominalisations such as *any variation, the use of your card, the issue of any additional or replacement Card and PIN, your liability, for losses relating to transactions through Terminals, the obligation to give you advance notice.*

Since nominalisations continue to be used with such frequency, it might be worth asking why they do so? Could they in some sense be functional to the discourse? An answer is suggested by Halliday (1989) and Halliday and Martin (1993) with particular reference to scientific writing. There Halliday's suggestion is that nominalisation is a means of condensing information that has typically already been provided earlier in the text. One way of illustrating the grammatical reasons for the use of nominalisations is to unpack some of the nominalisations by making the lexical selections grammatically congruent. This exercise, presented in Table 9.1, will hopefully make it clear that the non-nominalised form – i.e., not using verbs as nouns – would be rather problematic in the given textual contexts. Numbers and letters in Table 9.1 correspond to those in Extract C.

An important feature of (i)–(vi) is that the unpacked versions usually involve the use of many more words. It is a grammatical device that distils meaning. This can be seen in the use of *variation* in (ii). The nominalised verb *variation* summarises information

**Table 9.1**   Unpacking nominalisations

| Nominalisation | Unpacked version |
|---|---|
| (ii)  if any variation would ... | = we vary the policy in such a way that we ... |
|     (a)  the use of your card and PIN ... | = the way you use your card or PIN |
|     (b)  your liability for losses ... | = you are liable for losses |
| (iv)  The obligation to give you advance notice does not apply ... | = we are not obliged to notify you in advance ... |
| (vi)  our obligations to give you ... | = we are obliged to give you ... |

given early in the document, such as *Can we change these Conditions?* and *We reserve the right to vary these Conditions.* Effective use of nominalisation is usually justified by the progression of the discourse – the history of the text furnishes the basis for it. We may argue then that nominalisation is a device that allows the writer to package a lot of information into a nominal group, as pointed out by Halliday and Martin (1993). One other noteworthy feature of nominalisation is that it permits the writer to avoid saying who the doer of the action is, as for example in (iv). In this particular case, the change in the grammar also acts as a signal that this point is different from the others. It is about what the Bank does not wish to do, while all the other points concern what the Bank will do.

We may conclude that nominalisations encourage writers to abstract their meanings as things or objects. They are used to organise information for the purpose of making predictions about what will follow and for summing up what has already been presented. In these ways the use of nominalisations does something in the organisation of the meanings of a text that can probably not be achieved by the use of other grammatical devices.

The linguistic instruction to use verbs rather than nouns does not take account of these understandings about the use of nominalisation. It fails to treat nominalisation as a linguistic resource for making specific types of meaning in written documents. Since conciseness is a virtue that Plain English seeks, and since the use of nominalisation is one effective means of achieving conciseness, it is not surprising that Plain English writers use nominalisations in their documents. As with all generic instructions, the injunction never to use it must be taken with a pinch of salt! What we need is to consider the conditions in which it might be useful, as well as the problems that inappropriate over-use of nominalisations may cause, as in bureaucratic English.

## 4.3   Do the instructions take into account contexts relevant to the various documents?

As discussed above, at the end of section 4.1, Plain English instructions give minimal attention to contextual features. The main contextual feature that is considered relates to the reader through advice such as *engage with the reader* and *be personal*. Why is there this emphasis on establishing a personal relationship with the reader?

The instructions to engage the reader and to be personal need to be considered in the broader social context where issues of access and equity, improved client relations, negotiation and equality are the proclaimed ideals. The use of personal language is a linguistic resource, suggested in the Plain English instructions, for minimising the distance between the reader and the writer by setting up a dialogue so that successful negotiation can take place. Instructions to use personal language might also be motivated by the belief that the linguistic resources that set up more equal relationships are easy to understand.

Are such instructions always appropriate? In order to answer the question we may again appeal to the insights of systemic functional linguistics regarding interpersonal meaning, that is the kind of reader response that 'personal' documents invoke, and textual meanings, that is the structuring of information in the document. When documents are personalised they set up a dialogic exchange. This is achieved through, for example, the removal of status markers, the use of names, the use of questions and the use of appropriate levels of modality. All of these help to establish equal role relations between the reader and the writer. This might be what is required and appropriate in particular contexts, but there will be times when it reflects the existing conditions less than faithfully. For example, in official policy documents, a minimisation of social distance through the use of personal language can mislead the reader. When authority is made invisible readers may not appreciate the non-negotiability of the information, as for example between a client and a powerful corporate body (e.g., NRMA) or between a client and the State (cf. intervention in legal language). Seen from this point of view, the bland friendliness of some official documents could be interpreted as a sinister design against the unwary reader, who may need protection. They may need clues in the text to help them see that, in fact, the policy information is not negotiable. To see the force of this argument, consider Extract C: behind its 'friendly, casual' way of giving information, note how well the interests of the Bank are protected, how little is granted to the reader by this 'friendly' agency!

The choice of active or passive voice in a clause makes subtle meaning distinctions mainly because this choice organises the clause as a message (Halliday 1985). This means that the implications of choosing active, as opposed to passive, are not limited only to the verbal group: they flow into larger portions of the text, modifying its meanings. Table 9.2, the sentences of which are taken from Extract C, illustrates differences in both interpersonal and textual meanings, construed by the use of active/passive voice.

In both examples there is a significant difference in the Themes (the underlined words) of the active and passive voice clauses. In clauses with an active voice, Theme conflates with the Agent of the Process: the clauses are concerned with *We* i.e., the Bank. In clauses with a passive voice, the Theme of the clauses is *you* and

**Table 9.2**   Meaning and active/passive voice

| Active voice | Passive voice |
| --- | --- |
| (iii)  We will tell you of all other variations in advance through press advertisements or notices on Terminals or in branches. We will also give you notice of the variation with your account statement. | (iii)  You will be told of all other variations through press advertisements or notices on Terminals or in branches. Also you will be given notices of the variation with your account statements. |
| (vi)  We fulfil our obligations to give you notice under these Conditions if we post the notice by ordinary mail to the last address you gave us. | (vi)  Our obligations to give you notice under these Conditions are fulfilled if the notice is posted by ordinary mail to the customer's last known address. |

*our obligations to give you notice under these conditions,* respectively. In both cases the Theme conflates with Medium (see Halliday (1985) for the terms Agent and Medium). Note also how in (vi) the passive version 'impersonalises' the information. The messages in the right column are about you and the bank's procedures to handle certain situations. A consistent use of the active voice throughout the document, along the design of the left column, would construct an interpersonal prominence through an interpersonal structuring of the information. On the other hand, a consistent use of the passive voice would construct a different thematic progression (Fries 1981), one in which other meanings would be foregrounded. Whether the writer should use active voice or passive voice is not a matter of a prior decision. The relevant issue is: what is it that the writer wishes to achieve and why? It is only in the light of this consideration that the decision about the use of one voice or the other has any meaning.

While the importance of engaging the reader cannot be questioned, writers do need to be aware that the grammatical devices for doing so significantly impact on other kinds of meaning in the document. It is also important for writers to realise that even a high degree of personal language may not help readers understand concepts about which they have little knowledge. As pointed out in section 1, the reader's understanding of information in a document is only in part due to the way it has been written; the readers' knowledge and experiences are also critical in the achievement of this understanding. Plain English addresses the issue of comprehensibility, among other things, by an advice *to choose words your reader will know* and *avoid unfamiliar words and unfamiliar language.* But the use of familiar words is surely only part of the story: the introduction of words referring to unfamiliar concepts, especially in unfamiliar discourse types, is often unavoidable, and languages of the world have ways of coping with this situation. In some instances, writers can draw on the linguistic resources for explaining and defining terms and concepts, such as the use of apposition, identifying relational clauses, defining relative clauses and elaborating clause complexes (Martin 1986). They can also support the written language with the use of other modalities of semiosis, such as diagrams. And while using these various devices, writers need to be conscious of the problems of, and difficulties with, 'simplifying' complex information. Plain English injunctions in this respect appear to give scant information, referring simply to words, as if grammatical patterns played little or no part in the process. And when a quasi grammatical comment is made, for example *write short sentences, use active voice, do not use a verb as noun,* the 'timelessness' of this injunction appears quite misplaced in the light of considerations to which attention has already been drawn in this discussion.

### 4.4   *What does Plain English have to say about the structure of the text?*

There are few instructions about the structure of the text in the Plain English guidelines. There is some reference in a general sense, for example, Document A (see section 3) asks the writer to *get straight to the point, tell the facts in your reader's logical order, put detail at the end,* or Document B advises the writer to *set a context at the beginning of the document – tell the readers what the policy is and what they will find in it.* Such advice fails to take into account the fact that information in a document is organised according to its context and purpose. Recent work in text linguistics (Halliday & Hasan 1985; Halliday & Martin 1993; Ventola 1987; Christie 1990) shows that there exists a systematic relationship between the social environment and the functional organisation of language. For instance, Martin (1986) has suggested that as the mode of a text becomes more abstract, that is as it becomes more distant from the immediate experience of the actual events, the grammar of a text becomes less iconic. In other words, the language and structure of an abstract text mirrors less closely the structure of the activity sequences to which it refers. An abstract text is therefore less constrained by the immediate situation. Rather, its shape and structure are determined more by the goal of the text itself.

According to Martin (1986) the structuring of information in documents is not random but occurs in a particular sequence appropriate to the purpose of the document and the document's distance from what it is describing. Sometimes the sequencing changes, but this usually occurs for a particular reason. This non-random organisation of information is particularly helpful to readers. When confronted with particular documents, readers are able to predict what kind of information is in the document and where information can be found in the document. This predictability is based on their expectations, through their experiences with similar documents, picking up how the information unfolds.

Plain English has proceeded to 'facilitate' writing skills without paying any attention to these arguably significant developments in text linguistics.

I have discussed these questions in some detail in order to bring into focus the conception of language on which the Plain English instructions for handling written language are based. The foregoing discussion probably shows that Plain English does not appear to have come to terms with the complex relation between language system and language use. While the Plain English linguistic instructions might have a certain appeal in that they offer a simple tool, they work only if they are ignored. The claim is not that the documents written in Plain English are inferior – they are infinitely better than those they replace – rather my concern is that if, abandoning the internalised native speaker expertise, someone attempted to follow literally the 'simple' 'easy to follow' instructions in the guidelines provided by Plain English, two curious outcomes might result: one might find that one does not really know what one is expected to do (cf. *write short sentences*: how short is short?) and/or one might produce documents that are quite inferior to what Plain English practitioners actually do produce. For example, imagine a document on Bill of Sales, which uses no unfamiliar words, uses only active voice and never uses verbs as nouns! Potentially then, Plain English advice may lead writers to a kind of language use that inhibits the range of meanings needed for effective communication. The formulation of these instructions strongly suggests the idea of language as simply a conduit for passing a message from the speaker/writer to the addressee/reader; language in Plain English is not a resource for making meanings – it is simply a clothing for pre-existing meanings.

## 5   Research on the effectiveness of Plain English

The linguistic problems that have been mentioned above may be regarded simply as academic points of criticism. If Plain English is successful in achieving its goal of increasing the comprehensibility of written documents, then does the naivety of the linguistic instructions matter? Anecdotes from those who promote Plain English suggest that they would answer this question in the negative. Assertions supporting Plain English often draw attention to the cost-saving benefits for companies that use Plain English documents. However, the basis for these assertions is not immediately obvious. The little formal research that has been carried out questions the claims of successes. Below I provide a brief description of two pieces of research.

The first research was conducted by the Communication Research Institute of Australia (CRIA); it was duly reported in an Occasional Paper (Penman 1990). The paper describes two studies that address the issue of whether or not documents that have been written in Plain English increase understanding. The second source is Nevile (1990), whose focus is on the changes of meaning through translating existing documents into Plain English.

Turning first to the CRIA report, the motivation for Penman's research was to demonstrate the merits of Plain English which, according to the Institute, had not been properly substantiated, particularly regarding the access and equity principles. The focus of Penman's enquiry was: Do insurance contracts written in Plain English ensure better understanding? Two studies were conducted.

The first of these studies examined the comprehensibility of an insurance investment document. Four different versions of the document were used. Version 1 was the document in public use, while Versions 2, 3 and 4 were three different Plain English versions of the same policy as Version 1. The design features were standardised in all four. The study was conducted on eighteen participants with a range of educational and occupational backgrounds. All participants were over twenty-five years old and came from an English speaking background. The reading protocol method was modified during a pilot test so that it was appropriate for Australian culture and the document being tested. Participants, tested individually, were asked to read one of the versions of the document aloud and to make sense of it as they were reading. They were asked to say whenever they had problems throughout the test and their reading and comments were recorded. The study discovered that all readers found all four versions of the policy document difficult to understand; in fact, they failed to understand whole sections of the document in each of the four different versions.

The second study tested the comprehensibility of car insurance documents, using a Plain English policy that was in use at the time and a prototype version of a new one. The prototype version was not based on the principles of Plain English. The focus of the study was to find out how easy it was for readers to find and understand policy information. Seventeen respondents were involved – eight were tested with the current Plain English policy and nine on the new prototype version. Eighteen scenario questions that could be answered using either policy were developed. These questions were based on the kind of information that people look for in such booklets. An example is: *How much would the NRMA pay if your caravan or trailer was stolen?* The study found that more people could find the right answers in the new version than in the Plain English version of the policy booklet.

The results of these two studies led Penman to conclude that 'Documents written in Plain English are not good enough to ensure understanding' (1990: 8); although the complexities of language in legal documents were removed, the document remained incomprehensible. According to Penman, this is due to the inadequacy of the Plain English translation method, which she believes does not take into account the meaning frameworks used by readers to understand the documents. Another explanation relates to the transmission – or conduit – model of communication that underlies Plain English principles. In such a model, communication is a process in which one person encodes a message based on his/her ideas and thoughts, then sends the message to a receiver who then decodes the ideas. The writer simply needs to package his/her words appropriately (according to Plain English principles that means using clear and simple words) and the readers will find the meaning. This understanding ignores the complex and context-dependent relationship between text and reader (Nevile 1990: 11).

Penman's research, in highlighting the inadequacy of the translation method in terms of increasing comprehension, also brings to attention changes in meaning made by translating documents. Nevile (1990), in his discussion, considers whether or not Plain English examples can preserve the content of the original version. Nevile's research focuses on the Plain English advice to avoid language known only to people with specific knowledge or interests and look for positive/negative sections from which you can cut the negative and save words. Using examples offered by those espousing Plain English principles, Nevile argues that such advice ignores the role of linguistic context. He argues that the experiential meaning of sentences using technical terms is different from sentences using non-technical ones and that the changes to the structure of the clause that occur when following Plain English advice, significantly alters the meaning. Nevile concludes that while readability may be increased in Plain English terms, it 'may often be bought at significant cost to content' (Nevile 1990: 35).

What do these results suggest? The two research efforts focus on different aspects of Plain English and consequently their results inform a review of Plain English in quite different ways. The outcomes of the CRIA research, that focused on comprehensibility, challenge the idea that changing the language in a document will necessarily allow readers to understand the information. According to Penman, such a finding means that writers have to move away from the idea that meaning lies in the language. Because different language characteristics are necessary for different users in different contexts, writers need to develop strategies that allow the reader to generate the meaning necessary for action.

The outcomes of Nevile's research, which focused on linguistic meanings, challenge the idea that documents which have been re-written using Plain English principles replicate the meanings of the original. Inevitably, a change of meaning is involved. However, if we take Penman's research into account, the significance of the meaning changes needs to be tested with the readers, given the fact that reader comprehension is the goal. Nevertheless, Nevile's research makes some important points about changes in meaning that cannot be ignored. It reminds writers about the role of linguistic understanding in the rewriting of documents.

## 6  Conclusion

The research described above is only indicative. More research is needed to appreciate fully what it is that the use of Plain English achieves. At the least it seems desirable for writers to test their Plain English products with sample readers. And these sample readers need to be representative of the culturally and linguistically diverse targeted readership. It is only then that writers will know whether or not their goal of increasing comprehension has been achieved.

At the same time, the positive impact that Plain English has already made cannot be ignored. It has highlighted the need to bring about change in the kinds of English language used in written documents. This is beyond question. It has encouraged writers to think about their reader, the document design and the language features. The paralinguistic instructions have been effectively applied and it would appear that the information in many documents is more accessible. Nevertheless, as the Plain English movement gains momentum, it will need to refine its methods for addressing problems of information access encountered by readers. The current linguistic instructions, as illustrated earlier, are inadequate: first, because they have a perspective on language that suggests that there is an arbitrary association between words and their meaning; and secondly, because the instructions do not appear to inform actual practice in any case. A model of this kind for teaching writing skills can hardly be expected to educate precisely where such education may be needed – that is in those cases where the writers may not have an 'intuitive' understanding of what counts as clear, straightforward language. Increasingly, practitioners will need guidance that they can follow. They need to understand more fully the processes through which meanings are made in written language. They need to be conscious of the available range of linguistic resources available. They need to be able to use language in such a way that it is appropriate to the purpose of the document and the 'meaning framework' of their readers. Even when both readers and writers collaborate in the construction of documents, with the writers taking on the role of the scribe, the readers will look to the writers for the linguistic realisations of what they are attempting to articulate.

The Plain English movement can gain from the insights of other related work. The genre-based approach to the teaching of writing is one such body of work. Its theoretical base is systemic functional linguistics, a theory which focuses on language in society and therefore provides an understanding of the relationship between language, genre and context. Plain English linguistic instructions can take advantage of the findings of the genre approach – findings about context, its relation to language and text characteristics – as well as genre pedagogy that makes explicit these linguistic features and their relationship to the function of the text. This work can complement the other aspects of text design that are the concern of the Plain English movement. The two can be brought together to the advantage of those involved in the various social processes.

# Notes

1  Robert D. Eagleson, recently retired Associate Professor of English at the University of Sydney, is a consultant in the redrafting of legal and business documents. He has been a key player in the promotion of Plain English and has made a significant contribution to reforms in plain language legal documents. He was co-founder of the Centre for Plain Legal Language at the University of Sydney.

2  [See both Luke and Hasan in this volume; also Hasan (1995) for a critique of Martin's framework. Editors.]

# References

Brown, K. & N. Solomon. 1992. *What is Plain English and Writing Plain English Workplace Documents: Training Manuals.* Centre for Workplace Communication and Culture: University of Technology, Sydney.

Christie, F. (ed.). 1990. *Literacy for a Changing World.* Hawthorn, Vic.: Australian Council for Educational Research.

Cope, B. & M. Kalantzis. 1993. *The Powers of Literacy: A Genre Approach to Teaching Writing.* London: Falmer Press.

Eagleson, R.D. 1990a. *Writing in Plain English.* Canberra: AGPS.

Eagleson, R.D. 1990b. Plain English: Simple or Simplistic. *Vox* No. 4.

Fries, P.H. 1981. On the Status of Theme in English: Arguments from Discourse. *Forum Linguisticum* 6(1): 1–38.

Halliday, M.A.K. 1976. *System and Function in Language: Selected Papers* (ed. G.R. Kress). London: Oxford University Press.

Halliday M.A.K. 1985. *Introduction to Functional Grammar.* London: Edward Arnold.

Halliday M.A.K. 1989. *Spoken and Written Language.* London: Oxford University Press.

Halliday, M.A.K., A. McIntosh & P. Strevens. 1964. *The Linguistic Science and Language Teaching.* London: Longman.

Halliday, M.A.K. & Ruqaiya Hasan. 1976. *Cohesion in English.* London: Longman.

Halliday, M.A.K. & Ruqaiya Hasan. 1985. *Language, Context and Text: Aspects of Language in a Social-Semiotic Perspective.* Geelong, Vic: Deakin University Press.

Halliday, M.A.K. & J.R. Martin. 1993. *Writing Science: Literacy and Discursive Power.* London: Falmer Press.

Hasan, Ruqaiya 1995. The Conception of Context in Text. In P.H. Fries & M. Gregory (eds) *Discourse and Meaning in Society: Functional Perspectives – Meaning and Choice in Language: Studies for Michael Halliday, Vol. Two.* Norwood, NJ: Ablex.

Hatherly, S. & J. McLeod. 1991. *Writing and Teaching to Improve Literacy: Plain English in Practice.* Sydney, NSW: New South Wales Department of Technical and Further Education.

Hymes, D. 1967. Models of the Interaction of Language and Social Setting. *Journal of Social Issues* 23.

Kerr, Edward. 1991. Plain Language: Is It legal? *Law Society of New South Wales Journal,* June.

Kress, G. 1993. Participation and Difference: The Role of Language in Producing a Culture of Innovation. In Allan Luke & Pam Gilbert (eds) *Literacy in Contexts: Australian Perspectives and Issues.* St Leonards, NSW: Allen & Unwin.

Martin, J.R. 1986. Intervening in the Process of Writing Development. In C. Painter & J.R. Martin (eds) *Writing to Mean: Teaching Genres Across the Curriculum.* Budoora, Vic.: Applied Linguistics Association of Australia Occasional Papers No. 9.

Martin, J.R. 1992. *English Text: System and Structure.* Amsterdam: John Benjamins.

Nevile, M. 1990. Translating Texts into Plain English: The Cost of Increased Readability. Open Letter. *Australian Journal of Adult Literacy: Research & Practice* 1 (2): 27–38.

Norrish, D. 1989. Your Guide to Writing Trade Materials in Plain English. *Literacy Exchange* (NSW) April.

Penman, R. 1990. Comprehensible Insurance Documents: Plain English Isn't Good Enough. *Occasional Paper No. 14,* August. Canberra, ACT: Communication Research Institute of Australia.

Salter, K. 1991. Plain English in TAFE: The Whole Process. Open Letter. *Australian Journal of Adult Literacy: Research & Practice* 2 (1): 59–69.

Ventola, E. 1987. *The Structure of Social Interaction: A Systemic Approach to the Semiotics of Service Encounters.* London: Pinter.

## Documents referred to

Social Change Media. 1990. *Reader Friendly Documents Kit: Profit and Popularity with Plain English.* Department of Employment, Education and Training.

*Plain English Is Not a Simple Matter.* 1990. Video NSW Adult Literacy Council and Summer Hill Films.

*Beyond Readability: How To Write and Design Understandable Life Insurance Policies.* United States.

*Law Reform Commission of Victoria,* 1987. Plain English and the Law. Victorian Government Printer, Melbourne.

# 10

## Genres of power? Literacy education and the production of capital

### ALLAN LUKE

The laws of the generative process of language are not at all the laws of individual psychology, but neither can they be divorced from the activity of speakers. The laws of language generation are sociological laws. (Voloshinov 1986, p. 98)

## 1  Introduction: a sociological frame[1]

Voloshinov's descriptions of the material and political bases of speech genres have been central to attempts by literary theorists and linguists to develop a political sociology of language. This chapter extends that analysis to argue that not only are the 'laws of language generation sociological laws', but as well that models of language and literacy education are in the first instance sociological, and that their sociological assumptions and consequences should be the subject of examination and debate.

The history of literacy instruction is a history littered with pedagogical theories and instructional schemes, with social and cultural panaceas and promises. Approaches to curriculum, instruction and evaluation have been built on a range of doctrinal and disciplinary 'truths' about literacy: from Christian, Muslim, Jewish and other religious models of reading and hermeneutics, copying and scribing to secular models of training drawn from moral philosophy and rhetoric, classical and literary studies, and, in the last century, from the human sciences of psychology and linguistics. As participants in the twentieth-century movement of secular schooling and educational research to find the definitive formula for teaching literacy, many contemporary educators, psychologists and linguists have tended to view this history non-dialectically and non-materially, as a positivist replacement of untruths by 'truths', of wrong theories by right ones, of archaic practices and folk wisdoms by 'state of the art' pedagogic sciences.

With the increasing significance of linguistics in the curriculum, one of the principal claims made by applied linguists and educators is that a 'true' social theory of language is adequate grounds for decisions about pedagogy. My argument here is that current socially based models of literacy pedagogy – among them 'genre-based' and Freirean 'critical pedagogy' approaches – stop short of coming to grips with their assumptions about the relationship between literacy and social power. Without a rigorous sociological analysis, teachers and teacher educators are forced to rely on common sense, anecdotal and personal accounts of what kinds of textual performances and knowledges are 'empowering' for particular clientele, and, more significantly, of how the transmission of these performances and knowledges fits a larger educational project of political and economic change.

Viewed sociologically, literacy training is not a matter of who has the 'right' or 'truthful' theory of mind, language, morality or pedagogy. It is a matter of how various theories and practices shape what people do with the technology of writing – and of how, once institutionalised, these selections and constructions serve particular class, cultural and gendered formations. In this way, literacy education has been and remains a battleground for a politics of representation: in community and school pedagogies, a textual canon and archive, a corpus of practices and differing literate subjectivities are shaped and transmitted, acquired and contested. Divergent approaches to literacy have been used by particular groups to make claims to shape what will count as literacy, who will be given access to particular texts, practices and indeed 'literacies'.

The history of literacy education thus is about power and knowledge. But it is about power not solely in terms of which texts and practices will 'count' and which groups will have or not have access to which texts and practices. It is also about who in the modern state will have a privileged position in specifying what will count as literacy. This is, in part, because literacy has been tied up so directly with the distribution and consecration of capital and knowledge in Western cultures – as a way of regulating and monopolising access to principal means of production and modes of representation. Schooling and literacy are used to regulate and broker not just access to material wealth and the means for producing that wealth, but as well access to legally constituted 'rights', to cultural and sub-cultural histories and archives, to religious virtue and spiritual rewards, and to actual social networks, gendered desires and identities.

The sociological lesson of the history of literacy is not a celebration of the evolution of language functions or semiotic structures. In critical sociological terms, it is impossible to theorise or study empirically the social or intellectual 'function' of texts independent of the complex ideological forces, powers and struggles implicated in the social formation and organisation of technology and knowledge. Marxian, Frankfurtian, poststructuralist, feminist and other social theoretic positions are sceptical of evolutionary approaches to social function (e.g., Durkheim, Parsons) that fail to theorise struggle, conflict and, indeed, difference as intrinsic (and not incidental) elements of the emergence and change of forms and modes of representation. Accordingly, to understand and influence how literacy is tied up with social and cultural difference and conflict requires that we build a sociological model of how literacy education figures in (1) the differential organisation and distribution of power and capital; and (2) the normalisation and regulation of difference in literate populaces.

It is the former task that is the focus of this chapter. My aim is to address sociological issues in what have been called 'genre-based' models of literacy instruction, and to identify key areas for theoretical and practical remodelling. In so doing, I use recent work in social theory and sociological theory, drawing from Pierre Bourdieu's (1977, 1984, 1986, 1990a, 1990b, 1991a) discussions of power and capital.

## 2    The social and political consequences of pedagogy

Much has been made of the linguistic turn in the social sciences and its resultant effects in education. Certainly, the 1960s and 1970s move from behaviourist and, later, cognitivist theories towards theories of pedagogy which place language, semiosis and the speaking subject at the heart of education has been significant, however erratically this has filtered down to classroom practice. But accompanying it has been a larger, more subtle shift from psychological explanations to social explanations. In *Language as Social Semiotic* (1978), Halliday argued that much theorising about language has been predicated on intra-organistic models. This would certainly seem to be the case in language in education, where psychological and psycholinguistic models of language development, personal response and growth models of literary study continue to have significant influence. There language and literacy are theorised by reference to the internal states of human subjects – for example, in psycholinguistic models of language acquisition, developmental stage theories, schema theory, and humanist models of personal response and expression.

The early work of the Bakhtin Circle and the Prague School notwithstanding, a major shift to social models of language began with the postwar emergence of American sociolinguistics, and its hybrid fields of application including ethnography of communication, language planning, and so forth (Williams, 1992). But these models have tended to rely on concepts of free will and individual difference, explaining difference in terms of 'aims', 'intents' and 'choice'; power in terms of concepts of 'status' and 'role'; cultural and sociopolitical constraints in terms of 'rule', 'norm' and 'convention'.[2] In so doing, they have theorised a social self in ways that view agency first as an individual property: neither collective or intersubjective, nor necessarily connected with political ideology or cultural hegemony.

Mid-twentieth-century attempts to make 'sociological' linguistics and psychology thus have tended to import liberal and neo-liberal sociologies (e.g., symbolic interactionism, structural functionalism, ethnomethodology) which stop short of theorising conflict, power and difference. While prestructuralist and psychological models tend to explain social action and practice by reference to the internal intents and goals of individual human actors (Bourdieu, 1991b), functionalist and interactionist models tend to nominalise and reify Society or Social Structure or Culture as non-problematic 'factors' or 'variables' for explaining away power, conflict and difference. The common educational manifestations of these models are those curricular and instructional models which identify 'social context' as a key 'factor' or 'variable' for language and literacy education, but tend to represent it as a neutral backdrop or location where androgynous bourgeois agents assert individual choice and personal difference.

A range of historical factors influencing the political economy of schooling could account for the recent popularity of 'social' explanations of language, literacy and pedagogy. The latest responses to state legitimation crises – the 1990s re-emergence of political liberalism in the United States, increased academic and governmental recognition of cultural difference in school clienteles, the revival of the human capital model – are signs of a general movement away from monocultural or acultural state policy. However, there is disturbing evidence that this most recent 'social turn' in pedagogy could become an excuse for educational business as usual. Principal cases in point are 'social constructivist' models deployed in literacy, mathematics and science and other curricular subjects. Drawing from the symbolic interactionism and the strong revival of reflexive phenomenology in educational research, they stress how knowledge and text are constructed by human subjects in sites like classrooms and communities. There the emphasis is on intersubjective negotiation of texts and contexts, procedures and processes. However, without a sociological theory of power, conflict and difference, such models fail to provide an account for why and how some discourses, knowledges and texts 'count' more than others. While appearing to 'empower' students by reconceptualising them as social agents and speaking/writing subjects in the production of knowledge, these approaches stop short of providing empirical or normative grounds for deciding which knowledges, which texts and which discourses should and will 'count' for which consequences in larger social and institutional settings. In this way, depoliticised approaches to 'social construction' can readily become instructional means for more of the same: personal growth, 'empowerment', 'self-esteem' and so forth.

At the same time, psychological views of the acquisition and consequences of literacy remain dominant in educational practice. The assumption that literacy naturally makes one a better person by changing one's internal cognitive capacities and moral fibre retains a great deal of currency. There is now considerable cross-cultural evidence that the cognitive and moral effects of literacy are themselves artefacts of the social and institutional practices of literacy instruction – the secondary 'pedagogic work' (Bourdieu & Passeron, 1990) where literacy is selected, shaped and constructed for students. But if literacy education entails the construction, naturalisation, and transmission of particular 'cultural arbitraries' (Bourdieu & Passeron, 1990) as 'valued' and 'useful' knowledge, how we can remake pedagogy as part of a broader political and social agenda for redistributing knowledge and reshaping power relations is far from self-evident. With the move away from psychological, individualist models which conceal their class and patriarchal origins, the need now is for a broader debate over how to theorise and practice literacy education as a social and political intervention.

In English-speaking countries over the 1980s, two approaches to literacy education have been influential in refocusing teachers and teacher educators on social consequences (Green, 1992). Despite their differences, Freirean and 'genre' approaches to literacy share the aim of increasing student 'power', power conceived broadly in terms of the enhanced action with influence and effect in the economy and polity.

The emergence in the 1970s and 1980s of Freire's 'critical pedagogy' in such varied fields as adult basic education, language arts, English as a Second Language, and college composition, focused many educators on the ways in which particular pedagogies – such as psychological skill-centred or neoclassicist transmission models – yield class and culturally stratified outcomes. The work of Freire – elaborated by Giroux, Shor, McLaren, Lankshear and others (e.g., Lankshear & McLaren, 1993) – theorises the effects of literacy in terms of the institutional disenfranchisement of particular groups of students. They argue that conventional schooling and literacy education have ordained 'cultures of silence' among those socioeconomic underclasses in developed, newly industrialised and late capitalist nations.

The Freirean model sets out to open and build textual and institutional spaces for (oppressed and marginalised) subjects to speak and write. What Lankshear and Lawler (1987) term 'proper literacy', then, is a means for a critical analysis of social systems and institutions, for the development of action plans and political projects geared towards cultural and economic transformation. Freire's (1971) initial synthesis of existential and marxian models of the subject, augmented by the Frankfurtian emphasis on psychotherapy, stresses the possibility of dialectically remaking self/other, dominator/dominated, teacher/student binary oppositions. 'Critical pedagogy' has as its aim 'social transformation', particularly as it is drawn into closer alignment with the traditions and practices of American educational progressivism. Teachers and learners are recast as Gramscian 'transformative intellectuals' working from articulated and textually realised visions of social and economic change. A salient criticism of the Freirean model is that it tends to overestimate and romanticise the institutional consequences of 'voice' and particular forms of narrative writing. In its pedagogical approach, it tends to be based on less visible pedagogies (Bernstein, 1990, p. 72), which run the risk of hiding their own intersubjective and political sources of authority.

In Australia, the application of systemic functional linguistics and the family of instructional approaches which have come to be known as 'genre approaches', have had a similar influence in shifting debates over literacy from personal growth, individualist accounts of development, to larger issues of how textual access is part of a systematic effort at 'gatekeeping' (Martin, 1993) knowledge, educational credentials, material goods and social resources. This model stresses instruction that gives explicit mastery and awareness of those linguistic structures and forms seen to be necessary for increased access to dominant polities, economies and cultures (Cope & Kalantzis, 1993). Following Bernstein, the genre model stresses an 'explicit' pedagogy which 'brings to consciousness' language structures for teachers and students (Martin, 1993).

The resultant literate subject is not the revolutionary, transformative agent conceptualised by Freire, but rather one with enhanced individual agency in mainstream institutions, asserted through expanded lexicogrammatical 'choice' and 'control' of the discourse technologies of disciplinary knowledge (Halliday & Martin, 1993). So the model's tactical emphasis is on social mobility for those groups marginalised by literacy education, rather than the imperative for pedagogy as a site for the articulation of large-scale social projects and change. Accordingly, genre approaches have tended to place considerably less emphasis on the development of a 'reading' or analysis of structures of institutional oppression and domination, and more on the development of control over the text forms of dominant institutions, disciplines and other organised sites of knowledge. A salient criticism of the genre model is that its emphasis on the direct transmission of text types does not necessarily lead on to a critical reappraisal of that disciplinary corpus, its field or its related institutions, but rather may lend itself to an uncritical reproduction of discipline (Lee, 1993).

In Australia at least, the combined effect of these two approaches to literacy has been to push advocates of other pedagogical models – including whole language and process approaches, technocratic skills models of reading, the neoclassical 'cultural literacy' movement, and literary deconstructionism – to enter into a vigorous, at times acrimonious, debate over the social consequences of pedagogy. Unlike in many other countries, where debate remains focused on 'the basics' and 'declining standards', in Australian education the matter of which social class and cultural constituencies benefit from literacy training retains centre stage. This is part of continued national debate over 'equity' and 'social justice' as areas of educational intervention (Lingard, Knight & Porter, 1993), and the Labor government's major investment in language and literacy education as a linchpin of economic reform. But equity-oriented policy has to contend with two divergent models of literacy education, two competitive narratives about the literate subject in the world. Not surprisingly, on the table are two alternative visions of the necessity, possibility and strategies for social change and agency in postmodern, advanced industrial economies. These are nothing less than two distinct political agendas, both of which present themselves as projects for social justice.

Each model is based on broad assumptions about the sociological effects and consequences of literacy. The Freirean model theorises 'empowerment' as the opening of pedagogical spaces for marginalised peoples to articulate their interests and develop an analysis of the world; there power is vested phonocentrically in the 'dangerous memories' of individual and collective voice. By contrast, genre-based pedagogies tend to begin from the logocentric assumption that mastery of powerful texts types can lead to intellectual and cognitive development, educational achievement and credentials, and enhanced social access and mobility. However, both models tend to presuppose what we might call a 'hypodermic effect' of literacy: that their preferred literate practices directly inculcate 'power'.

## 3 Genre/power/pedagogy

Part of the problem in the debate over genre has been the tendency to switch between different kinds of logical and analytical claims, often without marking the differing epistemological grounds and ontological assumptions upon which the claims have been made. Indeed, justifications for genre interventions tend to chain together linguistic claims with sociological claims, cognitive/intellectual claims, normative pedagogical claims, and normative political claims. That is, the justification for genre approaches is based on a movement from those linguistic 'truths' yielded by systemic text analyses; to sociological 'truths' about how schools and social structures work to structure and produce unequal outcomes; to psychological and developmental 'descriptions' of the cognitive and intellectual effects of writing, literacy and particular genres; to pedagogical 'truths' about how pedagogies and classrooms work; to political imperatives about what should be done.

This has made it difficult to generate a sustained and coherent debate over genre-based pedagogies. Teachers, teacher educators and researchers frequently find themselves arguing on shifting and incommensurate epistemological and disciplinary grounds. As noted, my aim here is to take up the sociological claims of the model, and on that basis critique and remodel its normative political claims about what should be done. To do so requires an overview of the genre/pedagogy/power equation, to which I now turn.

## 3.1   The genre/pedagogy/power equation

The argument in favour of direct teaching of genre has been based on several key assumptions. First, lack of access is seen to lead to inequality and unequal educational outcomes. This lack of access, in turn, is attributed to implicit, unstated and elitist criteria for performance and achievement which have the effect of excluding marginal socioeconomic, cultural and gender groups from the development of knowledge and practice in high-status educational and cultural fields. Secondly, the problem of unequal access is to be dealt with by making explicit and attainable the criteria through direct instruction that transmits mastery of 'genres of power' from the dominant culture. Such pedagogies are seen to lead to identifiable changes in student achievement and, hence, access to further education, social institutions, higher economic capital, better paying jobs, tertiary education and so forth among those groups currently marginalised by invisible, discriminatory pedagogies.

There are several key propositions here. A principal debate has been over the *linguistic claim* that 'genres of power' or 'highly valued genres' exist as they are synchronically described by genre-based linguists. This has been, and will continue to be, the source of ongoing theoretical and empirical dispute, both over the metalanguage of description, over the accuracy, exhaustiveness and comprehensiveness of that description, over the structuralist privileging of particular categories of description or of scientific description *per se*, and, most recently, over whether such text types have a diachronic and ontologically valid basis in the social world (cf. Threadgold, 1989, 1994). Here I briefly take up the most immediate sociological aspect of the linguistic claim: genre and the theorisation of difference and conflict.

Voloshinov's seminal definition of 'speech genres' is in many ways convergent with the sociological assumptions of systemic linguistics (Threadgold, 1986). Specifically, he pointed to the co-constitutive relationship of social structure and semiosis, critiquing mentalist and psychological concepts of ideology. The dialectical materialist critique of romanticism and formalism thus is at the heart of the notion of a 'speech genre', which recognises the intersubjective and culturally situated genesis of texts. When Voloshinov (1986, p. 86) argues, contra Vossler, that the 'immediate social situation and the broader social milieu wholly determine – and determine from within so to speak – the structure of an utterance', he lays the groundwork for a description of the context of situation. However, that description differs considerably from the benign, consensual description of the social order which typifies most descriptions of 'genre' presented to educators. Voloshinov's position is that 'differently oriented accents intersect in every ideological sign. Sign becomes an arena for class struggle' (1986, p. 23).

This is nothing less than an emergent definition of heteroglossia: a recognition of the polyvocality of any sign, where a range of 'themes', ideologies, discourses, speaking positions come into play and exchange in a given text or utterance. For Voloshinov, then, speech genres never have singular cognate functions, nor are they simply moments of the choice, assembly and reproduction of forms and techniques: rather they are the sites where 'differently oriented social interests within one and the same sign community' intersect, contest and struggle. Any genre, 'form' or 'ideological sign' is in the first instance a nexus for struggles over difference, identity, and politics. In this light, to teach genre while effacing its genesis in 'class struggle', which we should update into a broader classification of 'struggles over difference', would be to freeze and dehistoricise the cultural and political dimensions of any given 'context of situation'. Yet many educational descriptions of 'how texts work' tend to separate analytically ideology from function (where they mention ideology at all), and thereby to represent particular genres as principally geared for doing intellectual work, rather than as *always* sites for the contestation of difference.

Yet even if we qualify and bracket the validity of the linguistic claim, we need to contend with the *sociological claim about the causes of educational failure*. Drawing strongly from marxian theories of ideology as distortion and concealment of class interests, Bernstein (1990) and Bourdieu and Passeron (1990) argue that one of the principal means by which this disenfranchisement occurs in traditionalist and progressivist pedagogies alike is by the invisibility of classroom rules and criteria governing worth and value of specific texts, procedures and moral identities. Curriculum hides its class, patriarchal and cultural bases by representing its selections and claims as natural, truthful and scientific, as, quite simply, the way things are and should be. In this way, that which is inaccessible to marginalised students – for example, the selective tradition of texts, practices, procedures and bodily dispositions – is lent authority as 'Culture' and 'Knowledge' and thereby is placed beyond criticism and dispute. By naturalising itself, curriculum thus can effectively normalise and discipline children into particular literate practices and procedures with little recourse to overt physical coercion and cultural imposition.

This is a theoretically plausible and empirically accurate description of how schools systematically exclude particular groups of children (e.g., Walkerdine, 1990). Invisible, progressivist pedagogies, and visible, skill-based and cultural heritage pedagogies share a drive towards 'naturalisation' of a textual canon, particular text types and practices – when in fact they are the politically interested artefacts of school culture. Neomarxian curriculum theory has developed several templates for analysing the politics of knowledge selections. Bourdieu and Passeron (1990) and Williams (1976) would argue that schooling makes selections of arbitrary knowledges and a textual corpus on the basis of dominant class, patriarchal and cultural interests.

Alternately, Habermas's (1971) theory of 'knowledge and human interests' has been used to differentiate between forms of knowledge on the basis of their teleological principles and affiliated sociocultural uses. 'Technical/scientific', 'symbolic' and 'emancipatory' knowledges can be described on the basis of their potential for differing kinds of action. This model precludes simple binary hierarchies from the simple to the complex, from the commonsense to the technical, from the concrete to the abstract. Habermas's view is that knowledge cannot be viewed in singular or autonomous terms, but always in terms of material interests, consequences and possibilities: that purely intellectual or ideational function cannot be analytically or practically separated from ideological interests and actions. Importantly, it provides a typology for viewing the ideological interests at work in the selection of school texts and knowledges.

However, genre approaches do not assume that genres are cultural arbitraries, nor ruling-class selections, nor random forms of work which have developed to maintain the discipline, authority and procedures of secular schooling. Rather, systemic linguists have tended to view genres as ways of doing the intellectual and cognitive work of knowledge acquisition, reproduction and transmission, and for the emergence of the systematic study of the natural and social world, that is, for doing work in the disciplinary/discursive fields of science. This valorisation of scientific knowledge, practice and discourse here tends to position science as if it can be viewed as a discourse and intellectual technology whose structures and effects can be learned and used prior to or independently of an analysis of their ideological location and consequences.[3] Furthermore, following reformulations of Bernstein's code theory and the development of hierarchies of genres and intellectual/social functions, a set of implied cognitive claims emerge: for example, that mastery over particular linguistic forms is evidence of cognitive mastery of 'technicality', 'abstraction' and so forth (Halliday & Martin, 1993). In this way there are *psychological **and** developmental claims* at work in genre-based models as well: that language and cognitive development follows identifiable onto/phylogenic routes from the common sense and cognitive practices of everyday life to the 'uncommon sense', 'specialisation' and levels of 'technicality' of scientific knowledge, across a typology of genres leading from personal, concrete, everyday to more technical, specialised and critical. Scientific mastery and knowledge – the ethos of *technical control* which is aspired to in systemic linguistics qua science – becomes the teleological principle of genre-based pedagogy, and indeed, its principle of power.

If we follow the argument further, the hypodermic effect between pedagogy and power can be established. The tendency among genre-based approaches to literacy is to deal with the question of explicit pedagogy through the generation of explicit linguistic descriptions of texts which describe those 'functional', powerful and 'highly valued' texts required for academic achievement, scientific endeavour and social participation.[4] These linguistic descriptions then can be transmitted to children directly and explicitly, in ways that increase their awareness of how texts work. In other words, the 'explicitness' of the linguistic description (i.e., the linguistic claim) is used to justify the 'explicitness' in pedagogy (i.e., the pedagogical claim), with Bernstein's critique of visible/invisible pedgogies providing a mediating justification (i.e., the sociological claim). The assumption is that this transmission will lead to increased language awareness and therefore 'choice' and 'control' in the construction of texts, linguistic and intellectual achievements that will result in improved school achievement. Taken together, these steps are seen as part of a political approach to the problem of unequal outcomes (a further sociological and political claim).

Thus far I have taken up sociological aspects of the linguistic claim, noting the tendency in many educational descriptions of genre to downplay difference and conflict. I have also suggested that there is ample evidence for a key aspect of the sociological claim: that the invisibility of criteria and practices make school knowledge inaccessible and non-criticisable. However, my outline of the logic of genre teaching suggests a much more fundamental and unresolved issue: the tendency to move from the linguistic claim and its affiliated developmental psychological claims, to normative sociological and political claims about what *should* be taught. Does the technical description of the text – itself the product of a particular disciplinary metalanguage – necessarily lead to the conclusion that text and that metalanguage are ethically, politically and culturally worthy of transmission? The validity of this jump from the descriptive to the prescriptive, from scientific/technical claims to culturally and morally regulative claims, depends on how we conceptualise the relationships between text types, power and social organisation. Literacy instruction in stratified social organisations is linked to the reproduction of unequal cultural capital. But exactly how the cultural capital generated in literacy training leads to differing kinds and levels of access to social and materials goods and resources is a more complex matter. To unknot this requires that we reconsider the relationships between pedagogy and power, power and capital.

## 3.2 The cliché of power

While the positions of Freirean, genre-based, and even personal growth pedagogies may appear to be different in where they ultimately source power, all have tended to totalise power. Whether viewed in terms of mastery of genres, mastery of reason, mastery of the self, or mastery of skills, power is treated as something which can be identified, transmitted and possessed. By investing power in particular genres, texts, skills, abilities, competences, the range of educational interventions tend to reify power: that is, to turn it into an object which can be (semiotically, pedagogically, institutionally, psychologically) deconstructed and pedagogically reassembled and transmitted. Accordingly, much of the debate in Australia over genre could be reframed in terms of differing understandings of where and how power resides: In texts? In writer/speaker agents? In ideology? In institutions? In the economy and polity?

The cliché of power is not a problem distinct to systemic approaches to literacy. It typifies many other current interventions in curriculum and instruction. Across the 1980s, popular notions of empowerment have had a great deal of valency in public, political and popular culture – replacing such terms as success, efficiency and excellence as normative benchmarks of value and worth. Within twentieth-century secular, state educational systems, the normative order has been replaced by an instrumental order. That is, the supplanting of Protestant, overtly morally regulative goals and benchmarks in literacy education by industrial, technocratic discourses shifted the goal and outcome statements of schooling from stress on a particular kind of person (e.g., the cultured person, the cultivated or moral or obedient colonial) to those purely instrumental statements about abilities, skills, competences and, indeed, mastery of genre. In state educational systems with a variety of political, religious and cultural constituencies, then, normative goals have had to be cloaked in value-neutral terms sufficiently to be 'read off' as representative of the political interests of competing interpretative communities and local sites. Within a secular educational system, the most effective way of achieving this is to move towards formulating the goals of the system in purely instrumental and technical (and hence economically beneficial) terminology – that is, to strip culture, politics and morality out of curriculum debates.

Without its 1960s revolutionary connotations (e.g, 'power to the people', 'power comes out of the barrel of a gun'), the term 'power' has been readily appropriated into mainstream institutional discourses: ranging from 'new age' discourses on self-development, born-again religious discourse, entrepreneurial and corporate discourses used to justify predatory economic and geopolitical practices. These are paradigm cases of repressive tolerance. It should not be surprising that 'power' and 'empowerment' are sufficiently polysemous terms to be readily assimilated as normative goals of an educational system: particularly as the shelf-life of such modernist, industrial-era terms for educational success and achievement has been shortened by successive economic and cultural legitimation crises, crises of narcissism, crises of multiculturalism, and so forth. But in the recycling of the term 'empowerment', power has become a possession: something that can be transmitted (and therefore, bought, owned, rented, leased, and yes, foreclosed), something that is apparently culture-neutral and politically neutral, and something that has economic exchange value.

In this context of the politics of schooling and curriculum, a model of power as technical control over 'valued' text types, with no regulative moral or political framing (valued by whom?), fits well with instrumental approaches to schooling and training. Indeed, in the current educational economy most contemporary pedagogies tend to reify power, to turn power into an object in the world which can be commoditised, containerised and, quite literally, bought and sold on an educational marketplace. As Gore (1992) points out in her analysis of American 'critical pedagogy', the term 'em-powerment' suggests that power is a property which can be possessed and transferred between 'agents', from teachers to students, from pedagogies to students. She goes on to argue that the resultant pedagogies suggest that people can 'give up' and 'share' power. The danger here is that the 'pedagogy equals power equation' tends to have a one-dimensional, singular ontology of power. That is, it tends to psychologise or textualise power, because all power is seen to be of the same logical type and empirical status.

## 3.3  Power and capital

The determinants and consequences of power have been central concerns of sociological theory since the nineteenth century and they remain a focus of the full range of social theoretic positions – including Frankfurt School critical theory, neomarxism, and variants of poststructuralist feminism. Classical and contemporary sociological explanations have tended to see power as an investment both of social systems and structures and of human agency. The former is apparent in both economic determinist explanations (e.g., Althusser) which invest power in economic structures and the control over the means of production, and in those versions of structural functionalism (e.g., Parsons) which invest power in the self-stabilising and self-preserving characteristics of the social system itself. The latter we find manifest in neo-liberal social theory, which posits individual choice as the source of sovereign power, and in latter-day variations, like rational action theory. These versions tend to invest power in the individual, and explain away social action by reference to individual choice, rational decision-making and action, personal constructs, and so forth. Hence, a host of explanations of power vacillate between the classical sociological polarities of structure/agency. In contemporary cultural studies, this polarity is found in ongoing debate over the authority/power of texts and the relative autonomy of readers, audiences and fans.

Foucault's position is that power is relational and multi-circuited; it is not centralised, top down, or the possession of any individual. By this model, it is difficult to assume that any text type *per se* can have power. As McCormack (1993) has argued, local sites where texts are deployed have power relations which are multimodal, fluid, dynamic and informed by cultural dynamics. Using the example of the shop and factory floor, McCormack goes on to comment that whether and how the production or reproduction of a text has power will be largely dependent on whether and how its deployment is strategically timed, the cultural dynamics of the workplace, the extant relations between workers and so forth, as much as it might depend on any worker's 'control' over a text type.

In many local sites, writing may function primarily as an institutional means of surveillance, rather than for doing cognate work. Foucault's (1977) description of the emergence of schooling and examination as forms of discipline is based on a theorisation of the relationship of discourse, discipline and power. For Foucault, institutions like prisons, armies, workplaces and schools are built around the rituals and practices of legal and discursive knowledge and power. That is, institutions build up regimes of 'truths' for the categorisation of human subjects, and they deploy regimes of practices for the monitoring and surveillance of subjects. These micro-techniques for the construction of the human subject include physical training and punishment and, in its incorporeal forms, the gaze of the confessional, the panopticon and the examination. The political and conceptual terminus of these regimes of power, knowledge and truth is self-discipline.

The technology of writing plays a significant part in the development of institutional control. For Foucault (1977, p. 189)

> a 'power of writing' was constituted as an essential part of the mechanisms of discipline. On many points it was modelled on the traditional methods of administrative documentation, though with particular techniques and important innovations. Some concerned methods of identification, signalling and description.

The examination is a focal technology in the means of correct training. In the case of institutions, writing enables the mapping of the aptitude, level and abilities of individuals – the placement of individuals on cellular grids of specification, which further enables the construction and internalisation of particular social subjectivities. So Foucault argues that one of the principal institutional uses of writing is the surveillance of the population, the monitoring, control and administration of bodies into measures of merit, value and moral worth. Matriculation examinations and reading achievement tests are exemplary instances.

For both Foucault and Bourdieu, the body is the target and locus of pedagogical power. Discipline and the pedagogical work of institutions targets and trains the body, generating docility, whether through direct physical coercion, training or, preferably, discourse and self-monitoring. Language, literacy and other educationally acquired competence thus become 'embodied competence' (Bourdieu, 1986; cf. 1991a, pp. 81–89), a set of bodily practices and inscriptions which are internalised by the habitus and durably represented across a range of social fields.

At the same time, Foucault's analysis carefully avoids a 'top down', binary model of power/powerlessness. For Foucault (1978, p. 94), power is neither a singular nor an individual possession: 'Power is not something that is acquired, seized, or shared, something that one holds on to or allows to slip away; power is exercised from innumerable points.' He goes on to argue that power is tied up with a 'multiplicity of force relations ... through ceaseless struggles and confrontations' (p. 93). While he recognises that it is embodied in laws, in 'legal-juridico discourse', and 'in various social hegemonies' (p. 93), he is careful to insist that its conditions for possibility are reflexive and local. His point is that there is no central or singular heart of power, that power always unfolds in relation to local sites and subjects, and that participants in local sites are complicit and necessary for the playing out of power/knowledge relations.

Foucault's emphasis on surveillance and techniques of power has helped move critical educational work away from dominant ideology theses, to studies more sensitive to how power is reflexively constituted and contested in local sites. His writing suggests that the question of which written texts may be invested with power how, where and when is totally contingent on the local variables and reflexive power relations at work in, to recall McCormack's example, the factory floor or office. In fact, notes McCormack (1993), when not to write, when writing can commit a breach of strategic power relations, when committing something to written record can make you the object of surveillance or coercion, when silence has more efficacy than speech or writing – these instances are rarely considered in genre pedagogies. This reflexive concept of power can profitably move us beyond the supposition of transferable effects of particular genres towards closer attention to the contestation, the workings of difference and competing interests and positions at work in any given text in its local context. It also stresses the need to rethink and reteach genres as political sites of contest.

But at the same time there is a danger that such a broad framing defines power in metaphysical terms, akin to Nietzschian concepts of 'will'. We can claim that power is global and diffuse and at the same time site or field-specific. But investigation of social phenomena requires analytical and empirical differentiation between sites and kinds of power. Unless it enables the description of local practices and technologies of power in terms of family resemblances (McHoul, 1991), the model may lack heuristic value in the critique and building of practices. Without classificatory categories of power, the danger is that the Foucauldian model falls into situational relativism (i.e., every site deploys power differently and there are no shared characteristics) or a globalisation of the principle that defies empirical analysis (i.e., that everything, everywhere is power, differentiated only by site).

The other principal issue which Foucault's description raises concerns the problem of normativity (Fraser, 1989). In spite of his insistence that power is not negative and can have constructive social and material effects, Foucault offers little documentation of what such effects or constructs might look like, almost exclusively focusing on instances of institutional regulation. And without an exemplary archaeology of the subject's constructive use of power (McNay, 1992), it is difficult to build a prescriptive model of what should and can count as productive power. This would be a prerequisite for remodelling literacy teaching and the curriculum.

There is some recognition of this problem in his later work, where Foucault (1988) describes a preliminary grid for examining disciplinary 'technologies': technologies of production; technologies of signification; technologies of domination; technologies of the self.[5] There he attempts to describe the kinds of institutional force and regulation operant in contemporary society. This model has been used to describe the shift from overtly coercive bodily disciplines of traditional pedagogies to an emphasis on self-monitoring and the confessional in progressive, child-centred literacy teaching (Luke, 1992). But for our present educational purposes what is needed is a multi-dimensional ontology of power: a typology of interrelated but distinct categories for the analysis of relations of power and knowledge.

As an alternative, Bourdieu describes power in terms of the kinds of 'capital' available and realised by human subjects as they engage in productive work in distinct cultural fields:

> The active properties that are chosen as principles of construction of the social space are the different kinds of power or capital that are current in the different forms. ... The kinds of capital, like trumps in a game of cards, are powers which define the chances of profit in a given field... . The position of a given agent in the social space can thus be defined by the position [s]he occupies in the different fields, that is, in the distribution of the powers that are active in each of them. (Bourdieu, 1990a, p. 230)

Although it emphasises the embodied character of cultural capital, this does not mark a return to a simple transmission/carrier model of power. One's capital is not defined solely in terms of embodied and officially sanctioned competence (e.g., literate competence acquired in the school and fully credentialled through grades or degrees). '*The conversion or transformation of capital is mediated by one's position within the relations of power and knowledge in a social field*' (p. 231). These fields, in turn, are the discursive and institutional domains where cultural and textual practice and action occur (e.g., the scientific field, the artistic field), not simply schemata or disciplinary corpuses, but actual 'spaces of conflict and competition' (Bourdieu & Wacquant, 1992, p. 17).

Following Marx, Bourdieu (1986, p. 241) defines capital as 'accumulated labor', in material, objective forms and embodied forms. Accordingly, the 'immanent structure of the social world' is to be found in the distribution of the different 'types and subtypes of capital at a given moment of time' (p. 242). The distribution, availability and relationality of capital influences the chances for successful participation in the social structure. That is, as s/he leaves the school, a student's differential access and participation across social fields is constrained by available and convertible capital. Bourdieu (1986) distinguishes four kinds of capital: economic, cultural and social, and an overarching element, symbolic capital, the availability of which constrains the realisation of the other three.

As against classical political economy, Bourdieu views economic capital as but one factor in the objective life chances of particular groups and individuals. That is, people have differential access to material goods and resources which are directly translatable into money. Here economic capital may be institutionalised in the form of property rights and, in instances, be readily transformed into cultural capital (e.g., access to training credentials, cultural artefacts and objects of value) and social capital (e.g. access to particular institutional facilities, social relations and cultures). In capitalist societies, one can literally buy his or her way into particular social networks and goods. However, whether one has the competence to use this access to convert it into further economic capital depends in part on her or his embodied competence, a key form of cultural capital.

The reproduction and transmission of cultural capital is the subject of Bourdieu and Passeron's (1990) study of the French educational system, where they document how individuals acquire embodied linguistic and literate competence through the primary 'pedagogic action' of families and communities, and the secondary 'pedagogic work' of schools, universities and other educational institutions. Cultural capital takes three forms: embodied, objectified and institutional. Embodied cultural capital is the sum total of active and tacit knowledges, skills, and dispositions, internalised by the bodily habitus in the processes of socialisation and education (cf. MacLennan, 1981). Language and literacy learning thus entail far more than cognate learnings and skills, but is principally bodily training and practice. The earliest language training and the institutional writing of a text alike require the fluid coordination of appropriate bodily postures, gestures, and dispositions, particularly if the performance is to mark the possession of cultural and symbolic capital.

Cultural capital is also 'objectified' in cultural goods, specific 'material objects and media' (e.g., 'writings, paintings, monuments, instruments') that are physically transmissible to others. Finally, cultural capital can take the form of 'institutionalised capital', for example, in the form of academic qualifications, professional certification, and other credentials. An autodidact may have embodied capital, but without 'officially recognised, guaranteed competence' (Bourdieu, 1986, p. 248) the exchange value of such capital is limited. Through educational and employing institutions, the 'meta-field' of the state is able to delimit and regulate official investment and exchange rates for the conversion of cultural capital into economic capital, a matter constantly in flux through the inflation and devaluation of qualifications (Bourdieu & Wacquant, 1992). This is particularly the case in times of high unemployment, when educational expansion leads to a total increase in available 'institutional capital', a surplus of qualified workers in a particular cultural or social field. In these situations, the increased 'access' and 'inclusivity' aimed for in literacy education may be countered by spiralling credential inflation.

Yet any literate cultural capital is only of value in so far as it can be used in specific institutional contexts. Social capital refers to cultural and sub-cultural group membership, access to both those cultural and inherited group members (families, tribes, sub-cultures) and to those institutions (e.g., classes, schools, parties) through participation in ceremonies and rituals of symbolic and economic exchange. Social capital both relies on the possession of economic and cultural capital, but it asserts a 'multiplier effect' (Bourdieu, 1986, p. 249) on the capital possessed by an individual. In simple terms, this means that those practices acquired in schooling and community life can only be realised and 'multiplied' by access to institutional sites. And while credentialled mastery of a particular textual practice itself may be a necessary condition for admission to a corporation, bureaucracy or tertiary institution, it is rarely, in and of itself, sufficient for entry. Other factors, particularly gender and race, may significantly preclude or enable social access.

Yet ultimately, capital is only capital if it is recognised as such; that is, if it is granted legitimacy, symbolic capital, within a larger social and cultural field (Bourdieu, 1991a, pp. 72–3). What this suggests is that realisation of one's economic, cultural and social capital is contingent on institutional pre-conditions which delimit and authorise what one is 'entitled' to do, and whether one has 'recognised authority' (e.g., fame, reputation, bearing). Following Austin, Bourdieu describes symbolic power in terms of one's capacity to satisfy sanctions authorising as 'legitimate identity'. (1991a, p. 75). This he argues is embodied, evidenced in proper posture, garments, gesture and so forth. But as well it is manifest in discourse:

> There is a whole dimension of authorised language, its rhetoric, syntax, vocabulary, and even pronunciation, which exists purely to underline the authority of the author and the trust he demands. In this respect, style is an element of the *mechanism*, in the Pascalian sense, through which language aims to produce and impose the representation of its own importance. (Bourdieu, 1991a, p. 76)

In overview, while power and capital 'appear to be based on the qualities of the person alone', 'the source of the profit of distinction, procured by any use of the legitimate language, derives from the totality of the social universe and the relations of domination that give structure to it' (1991a, p. 73). In this regard, the value of embodied cultural capital gained in literacy training depends on the relative distribution, weight and scarcity of that capital on the market, rather than to any intrinsic power of the skill, text, competency or genre acquired. Consequently, the increased success of the educational system in producing particular competences (i.e., embodied capital), which lead to the production of textual artefacts (i.e., objectified capital), and formally credentialled 'distinction' and 'achievement' (i.e., institutionalised capital) in a capitalist state will necessarily lead to the decreasing value of these kinds of capital on a linguistic market.

Bourdieu's model of power/capital thus suggests:

(i) that it is misleading to assume that any genre, skill, text has generalisable power, tied up with a singular kind of capital in social structures;

(ii) that capital and power only exist in relation to cultural fields, which constitute distinct but related 'linguistic markets';

(iii) that the individual's capacity to convert and combine different kinds of capital is contingent on the particular laws of conversion at work within and between fields;

(iv) and that the state operates as a 'meta-field' regulating and constraining the availability, value and use of capital, and its conversion across fields.

In this way, possession of cultural and symbolic capital is neither necessary nor sufficient for economic and social power. The cultural capital generated in literacy training can only be realised and articulated through a series of contingencies which arise in the cultural and social field. For example, textual practice might not be recognised as institutionally legitimate and might not lead directly to credentials; or it may translate into objectified capital (textual artefacts) which has little value within specific fields. Even given the realisation of embodied, objectified and institutionalised cultural capital, its conversion into economic capital might depend on, for instance, actual physical and social access to particular institutions, social networks and acquaintances (e.g., 'mateship', 'old boy', 'ivy league' and other patriarchal cultural networks): 'the economic and social yield of educational qualification depends on the social capital, again inherited, which can be used to back it up' (Bourdieu, 1986, p. 244). Or, to take another example, while one might be able to translate social capital into cultural capital by gaining access to the 'right school', one's lack of economic capital may prevent one from using the acquired cultural capital. In turn, all of these conversions are influenced by larger forces and movements in the conversion of capital, that is, within the 'meta-field' of the state and economy (Bourdieu, 1986).

To consider a final, contrastive case, the fact that I and many readers of this chapter were able to achieve mobility in the 1950s from migrant, working-class backgrounds to the class and cultural positions of university teachers cannot be accounted for simply in terms of my mastery of 'genres of power', any more than it can be explained by possession of particular skills or IQ. That mastery of particular literate texts and practices, my embodied cultural capital, was a necessary but not sufficient condition for social access. Several other contingencies would be at play in such a case. It required available economic capital to attend high school and university. To convert the resultant cultural capital into economic capital required access to particular social institutions. All of this would have to be set against the larger sociological backdrop of the economic conditions of the 1950s, when youth in Western countries were gaining further employment, higher wages and more extended access to material goods than our parents because of a range of macroeconomic forces, not the least of which was the expansion of the Western economy and the globalisation of production and markets in the third world. Finally, my capacity to convert cultural capital into social and economic capital was utterly dependent on the postwar opening of US institutions to people of colour.

For Asian-Americans of my parents' generation, there were strict limits on the degree to which embodied, objectified and institutionalised cultural capital could be translated into economic capital. Few Asian-American women were encouraged or accepted in American tertiary education (although, quite ironically, highly selected cohorts of ruling-class, Chinese women were admitted to ranking US universities in the interwar period). The first generation of Chinese-American and Japanese-American men who had sufficient economic and cultural capital to attend university and gain credentials were disbarred from rudimentary social capital on the basis of colour and culture. Their mastery of genre notwithstanding, institutional racism prevented many of them from converting their institutionalised cultural capital into economic capital. In other instances, Asian men were able effectively to bypass mainstream Anglo-American credentialling institutions, and translate their sub-cultural social and embodied capital in the Chinese-American or Japanese-American communities into economic capital.

The simple lesson here is that textual 'power' and 'function' are never independent of ideology, culture and economics. Genre instruction is not a simple matter of the transmission of cultural capital. Its claims are based on presuppositions about the ways economic, social and cultural capital are converted into each other. To stress one type of capital and to 'ignore ... what makes the specific efficacy of the other types of capital' would be a significant mistake. It could move us towards what Bourdieu (1986, p. 253) describes as 'semiologism (nowadays represented by structuralism, symbolic interactionism, or ethnomethodology) which reduces social exchanges to phenomena of communication and ignores the brutal fact of universal reducibility to economics'. What is needed is a pedagogy which goes far beyond the transmission of genres, and offers social and cultural strategies for analysing and engaging with the conversion of capital in various cultural fields. An effective literacy pedagogy would have to build for students a critical social theory of practice.

## 4   What is to be done: learning to read power

Historically, the move towards genre has been valuable. It has tabled the issue of explicit access. Further, as Hunter (in press/1995) recently observed, it has marked a normative shift from the literary to the expository, from literature-based to rhetoric-based curriculum, a tradition that can be traced back to Bain and, ultimately, the Sophists. However, in so doing it has made some crucial omissions of elements which were central to Halliday and colleagues' initial project: to build a sociologically theorised and politically responsible linguistics with attendant domains of application. To do so, I would argue that we need to move from genre and refocus the critical literacy curriculum on the analysis and critique of cultural fields and discourses, on strategies and social relations. This would move towards a pedagogical *rapprochement* with the strengths of both critical and feminist pedagogies, an emphasis on the relationship between knowledge, texts and difference, and the continual interrogation of power.

Bourdieu (1991a) warns specifically of the historical role of education in the production of a 'standardised' and 'normalised' linguistic product for a linguistic and symbolic market, where, for instance, particular gendered relationships and forms of capital are produced and reproduced intergenerationally. I have here also noted the danger that genre has already become a reified, static category, for freezing and representing the historical products of ideologies, struggles and cultures as *the* canonical and reproducible rules of the culture: to paraphrase Jakobson (1956, p. 58), a 'filing cabinet of prefabricated representations' that agents 'select' appropriate to each situation.

As Voloshinov remarks, the development of a typology of 'ideological signs' would be necessary, not just for Marxism, but for a sociological analysis of the 'linguistic markets' where textual competence is brought for contestation, conflict and exchange (Mey, 1985; Bourdieu, 1991a). The question here is whether particular genres and texts can be said simply to 'have power' and whether control or mastery of particular texts can be seen to yield the determinant sociological effects claimed. The answer is that whether and how school-acquired textual practices yield social power is contingent. It depends on the institutional sites in question: places, Voloshinov and Foucault remind us, of dynamic struggle over difference. It depends on the linguistic markets in question: the dynamic social and cultural fields where linguistic capital yielded by genre-based teaching, or any other model, is brought to bear. There are no guarantees of power, no genres of power. Power is utterly sociologically contingent.

But the move within genre pedagogy at present seems to be towards an emphasis on increasingly fine-grained synchronic analysis of texts. My proposal here would be to move text analyses and ways of teaching texts outward towards diachronic social analyses of education, text-based economies and cultures. Without such an analysis, the emphasis on lexicogrammatical features may lead teachers towards a descriptivism that 'reads off' and takes for granted individual cognitive effects and social functions. As an alternative, I would argue for an approach to literacy which reframes the text not as a genre but as a *social strategy* historically located in a network of power relations in particular *institutional sites* and *cultural fields* (e.g., Fairclough, 1992). Such a pedagogy would focus on discourses, registers and knowledges requisite for these sites. The social identities and power relations in these sites and fields would become primary objects of analysis, critique and study (e.g., Freebody, Luke & Gilbert, 1991). In short, a sociologically grounded literacy pedagogy would need to reinvent and repoliticise the systemic concepts of 'field' and 'tenor', and make them focal points of classroom practice.

To conclude, genre pedagogy urgently requires careful consideration of the determinate conditions of existence of power and capital. Indeed, the making invisible and naturalising of particular textual strategies and bodily practices is part and parcel of exclusionary and discriminatory education. Yet the danger here is we will 'denaturalise' and demystify cultural texts by making explicit their codes, patterns and conventions, but fail to situate, critique, interrogate, and transform these texts, their discourses and their institutional sites. Where this is the case, we risk 'renaturalising' these texts – coming full circle back to enshrining, reproducing and making invisible their bases in conflict, power and difference. To do so is to place these 'genres', their teaching and reproduction in classrooms, workplaces and bureaucracies beyond criticism – to represent them as essential and compellingly functional, but not political or ideological.

Without reconsidering its own social and cultural consequences, genre teaching runs the risk of becoming an institutional technology principally engaged in self-reproduction of the status and privilege of a particular field of disciplinary knowledge, rather than part of a broadly based political project for remaking the institutional distribution of literacy and its affiliated forms of capital. The risk is described by Voloshinov (in Gardiner, 1992, p. 91):

> The ruling class strives to lend the ideological sign a supraclass, external character, to extinguish or exhaust the struggle of class relations that occurs within it, to make it the expression of only one, solid and immutable view. ... In the normal conditions of social life the contradiction with which every ideological sign is invested cannot completely unfold because the ideological sign in the prevalent ruling ideology is somewhat reactionary and, as it were, attempts to arrest, to render immobile the *preceding moment* in the dialectical flow of social coming-to-be, to mark and fix *yesterday's* as *today's* truth.

Criticism, contestation and difference is not a genre, not a skill, not a later developmental moment, not a reading position. It is, according to Voloshinov, a constitutive and available element of every sign, utterance and text. It can be, following Bourdieu, a principal strategy in realising, converting and contesting economic, cultural and social capital. That is, unless dominant cultures and pedagogical practices, however intentionally or unintentionally, silence it.

# Notes

1 The author thanks James Ladwig, John Hodgens and Carmen Luke for theoretical advice and resources; Peter Freebody, Jay Lemke, Ruqaiya Hasan and Geoff Williams for editorial debate and critique.

2 Persistent attempts in the fields of interactional sociolinguistics and ethnography of communication to theorise context continue (e.g., Duranti & Goodwin, 1992). Yet even when notions of 'power' are grafted on to such models there is a tendency to rationalise conflict as a product of individual, group or cultural difference.

3 Halliday and Martin (1993) argue that the democratisation of access to scientific knowledge, its technical procedures and discourse technologies requires linguistic analysis; indeed, that systemic functional analyses are capable of demystifying what are, particularly for marginal groups, texts as powerful as they are inaccessible. However, they do not sustain a political critique of the efficacy and value of science in post-industrial culture. Taken together, recent postmodern and post-structuralist, neomarxian and feminist work shows that it is difficult, if not impossible, to isolate analytically the procedures and practices of science from a social analysis of its ideological interests and political and material consequences.

4 Note here that academic achievement and scientific endeavour are not necessarily mutually inclusive nor exclusive. That is, Bourdieu and Passeron's (1990) point is that many texts requisite for academic achievement have little direct link with anything of intellectual or educational value, and may have little consequence in other cultural fields. Such texts typically are instruments of examination, disciplinary and 'magisterial' power (e.g., standardised achievement tests, work-sheets, short essay answers, show-and-tell sessions, oral examination, etc.). Yet the tendency of many working in the field has been to assume that if a text has been made to 'count' for academic achievement in schooling, it must have evolved to serve some valuable intellectual and/or scientific function, and hence is worthy of deconstruction and explicit teaching. A curriculum based on the principle of 'survival of the most functional' that fails to ask: 'Functional for what?' 'For whom?' and 'In whose interests?' may lead to the reproduction of text types and practices whose selection and valorisation serves ideological or disciplinary functions within school culture, rather than any rational purpose within a scientific or cultural field.

5 Foucault's later technologies, as McCarthy (1992) observes, are similar to Habermas's categories of relations to the objective world (e.g., production), to the social world (e.g., signification) and the self.

# References

Bernstein, B. 1990. *The Structuring of Pedagogic Discourse: Class, Codes and Control*, Vol. 4. London: Routledge and Kegan Paul.

Bourdieu, P. 1977. *Outline of a Theory of Practice*. Trans R. Nice. Cambridge: Cambridge University Press.

Bourdieu, P. 1984. *Distinction: A Social Critique of the Judgement of Taste*. Trans R. Nice. London: Routledge and Kegan Paul.

Bourdieu, P. 1986. 'The Forms of Capital'. In J.G. Richardson, ed., *Handbook of Theory and Research for the Sociology of Education*. New York: Greenwood Press (pp. 241–58).

Bourdieu, P. 1990a. *In Other Words: Essays Towards a Reflexive Sociology*. Trans M. Adamson. Stanford, CA: Stanford University Press.

Bourdieu, P. 1990b *The Logic of Practice*. Trans R. Nice. Cambridge: Polity Press.

Bourdieu, P. 1991a *Language and Symbolic Power*. Ed. J.B. Thompson. Trans G. Raymond & M. Adamson. Cambridge: Polity Press.

Bourdieu, P. 1991b. 'On the Possibility of a Field of World Sociology'. In P. Bourdieu & J.S. Coleman eds, *Social Theory for a Changing Society*. Boulder, CO & New York: Westview Press & The Russell Sage Foundation (pp. 373–88).

Bourdieu, P. & Passeron, J.C. 1990. *Reproduction in Education, Society and Culture*. 2nd Edition. Trans R. Nice. London: Sage.

Bourdieu, P. & Wacquant, L.J.D. 1992. *An Invitation to Reflexive Sociology*. Chicago, IL: University of Chicago Press.

Cope, W. & Kalantzis, M. eds 1993. *The Literacies of Power and the Powers of Literacy*. London: Falmer Press.

Duranti, A. & Goodwin, C. eds 1992. *Rethinking Context: Language as an Interactive Phenomenon*. Cambridge: Cambridge University Press.

Fairclough, N. ed. 1992. *Critical Language Awareness*. London: Longman.

Foucault, M. 1977. *Discipline and Punish: The Birth of the Prison*. Trans A. Sheridan. London: Allen Lane.

Foucault, M. 1978. *The History of Sexuality. Vol. I: An Introduction*. Trans R. Hurley. New York: Random House.

Foucault, M. 1988. *Technologies of the Self*. Eds L.H. Martin, H. Gutman & P.H. Hutton. London: Tavistock.

Fraser, N. 1989. *Unruly Practices: Power, Discourse and Gender in Contemporary Social Theory*. Chicago, IL: University of Chicago Press.

Freebody, P., Luke, A. & Gilbert, P. 1991. 'Reading Positions and Practices in the Classroom', *Curriculum Inquiry* 21(4), 435–57.

Freire, P. 1971. *Pedagogy of the Oppressed*. Ed. R. Schall. New York: Herder & Herder.

Gardiner, M. 1992. *The Dialogics of Critique: M.M. Bakhtin and the Theory of Ideology*. London: Routledge and Kegan Paul.

Gore, J. 1992. 'What We Can Do for You! What *Can* "We" Do for "You"? Struggling over Empowerment in Critical and Feminist Pedagogy.' In C. Luke & J. Gore eds, *Feminisms and Critical Pedagogy*. London: Routledge (pp. 54–73).

Green, W. 1992. 'After the New English: Cultural Politics and English Curriculum Change'. Unpublished PhD thesis, Murdoch University, Perth, WA.

Habermas, J. 1971. *Knowledge and Human Interests*. Trans T. McCarthy. Boston, MA: Beacon Press.

Halliday, M.A.K. 1978. *Language as Social Semiotic*. London: Edward Arnold.

Halliday, M.A.K. & Martin, J.R. 1993. *Writing Science*. London: Falmer Press.

Hunter, I. in press/1995. 'After English: Towards a Less Critical Literacy'. In S. Muspratt, A. Luke & P. Freebody eds, *Constructing Critical Literacies*. Cresskill, NJ & Sydney: Hampton Press & Allen & Unwin.

Jakobson, R. 1956. *The Fundamentals of Language*. The Hague: Mouton.

Lankshear, C. & Lawler, M. 1987. *Literacy, Schooling and Revolution*. London: Falmer Press.

Lankshear, C. & McLaren, P.L. eds 1993. *Critical Literacy: Politics, Praxis, and the Postmodern*. Albany, NY: State University of New York Press.

Lee, A. 1993. 'Gender and Geography: Literacy Pedagogy and Curriculum Politics'. Unpublished PhD thesis, Murdoch University, Perth, WA.

Lingard, R., Knight, J., & Porter, P. eds 1993. *Schooling Reform in Hard Times*. London: Falmer Press.

Luke, A. 1992. 'The Body Literate: Discourse and Inscription in Early Childhood'. *Linguistics and Education* 4(1), 107–29.

Martin, J.R. 1993. 'Genre and Literacy: Modelling Context in Educational Linguistics', *Annual Review of Applied Linguistics* 13, 141–72.

MacLennan, D. 1981. 'Embodiment and Social Context: Pierre Bourdieu's Concept of the Habitus'. Paper presented at the meetings of the Canadian Anthropology and Sociology Association, Halifax, Nova Scotia.

McCarthy, T. 1992. 'The Critique of Impure Reason: Foucault and the Frankfurt School'. In T.E. Wartenberg ed., *Rethinking Power*. Albany, NY: State University of New York Press (pp. 121–48).

McCormack, R. 1993. 'Review of Joyce, "Workplace Texts"', *Education Australia* 16, 18.

McHoul, A.W. 1991. 'readingS'. In C.D. Baker & A. Luke eds, *Towards a Critical Sociology of Reading Pedagogy*. Amsterdam & Philadelphia, PA: John Benjamins (pp. 191–210).

McNay, L. 1992. *Foucault and Feminism: Power, Gender and the Self*. Cambridge: Polity Press.

Mey, J. 1985. *Whose Language? A Study in Linguistic Pragmatics*. Amsterdam: John Benjamins.

Threadgold, T. 1986. 'The Semiotics of Volosinov, Halliday, and Eco', *American Journal of Semiotics* 4(3–4), 107–42.

Threadgold, T. 1989. 'Talkin' About Genre: Ideologies and Incompatible Discourses', *Cultural Studies* 3(1), 101–27.

Threadgold, T. 1994. 'Genre'. In R.E. Asher ed., *The Encyclopedia of Linguistics and Language*. Oxford: Pergamon Press (pp. 1408–11).

Voloshinov, V.N. 1986. *Marxism and the Philosophy of Language*. Trans L. Matejka & I.R. Titunik. Cambridge, MA: Harvard University Press.

Walkerdine, V. 1990. *Schoolgirl Fictions*. London: Verso.

Williams, G. 1992. *Sociolinguistics: A Sociological Critique*. London: Routledge.

Williams, R. 1976. *Marxism and Literature*. Oxford: Oxford University Press.

# 11

## Literacy and linguistics: a functional perspective*

### M.A.K. HALLIDAY

## 0  A linguistic view of literacy

In this chapter I shall try to explore the concept of literacy from a linguistic point of view. By 'linguistic' here I mean two things: (1) treating literacy as something that has to do with language; and (2) using the conceptual framework of linguistics – the theoretical study of language – as a way of understanding it. More specifically, the framework is that of functional linguistics, since I think that literacy needs to be understood in functional terms. The chapter is thus intended to complement Hasan's chapter in this volume, in which she presents a model of literacy as a fundamental process of social evolution: as the driving force of the educational practices by which our society is kept going – and by which it may also be modified and changed.

The term 'literacy' has come to be used in recent years in ways that are very different from its traditional sense of learning and knowing how to read and write. It no longer has a single accepted definition. One leading writer on literacy, Harvey Graff, has attempted to define it in a unified way – although his own practice shows that he feels the need either to narrow the definition or to extend it.[1] It is now almost twenty-five years since we launched our 'initial literacy' programme *Breakthrough to Literacy* (Mackay, Thompson & Schaub 1970) from the Programme in Linguistics and English Teaching at University College London.[2] When we used that title, people assumed we were boasting; they thought we were saying that here at last was a programme that broke through, that for the first time enabled children to succeed in becoming literate. What we actually had in mind was that becoming literate was itself a breakthrough. The only double meaning we had intended was the obvious one, in the grammar, whereby *break-through* could be read either as a process (a verb, perhaps in the imperative) or, by grammatical metaphor, as the result of such a process (as in *you've made a breakthrough*). No doubt by using the learned term *literacy*, instead of just *reading and writing*, we were signalling that this was a breakthrough to a higher mode of meaning: that, in becoming literate, you take over the more elaborated forms of language that are used in writing – and the system of social values that goes with them. (We might even feel that the tension set up between the Anglo-Saxon word *breakthrough* and the Latin word *literacy* represents what today would be seen as 'impacting of the material and the discursive', so helping us to locate literacy in the overall context of the social semiotic.)

In the generation or so since *Breakthrough* first appeared, literacy has come to mean many different things. The concept of literacy is incorporated into the framework of various disciplines: psychology, sociology, history, politics, economics – and these new senses of literacy are sometimes contrasted with a 'traditional, purely linguistic' conception. But I would argue that in fact literacy seldom has been seriously investigated as a linguistic phenomenon. It has not typically been interpreted, in the terms of a theory of language, as a process that needs to be contextualized on various linguistic levels, in ways which bring out something of the complex dialectic relations within and between them. To cite one piece of evidence for this, it is my impression that in university linguistics courses, if literacy is dealt with at all then the level of *conscious* understanding that is brought to the discussion of it is below even the level of *unconscious* understanding which must have been reached when language was first written down, some two hundred generations ago. And while the 'literacy debate' has moved on to higher, more rarefied levels, it tends to be forgotten that reading and writing are activities constructed in language. Yet it is impossible to explain these activities, no matter how we relate them to other theoretical concerns, without reference to language as the source from which they derive their meaning and their significance.

In many instances the term *literacy* has come to be dissociated from reading and writing, and written language, altogether, and generalized so as to cover all forms of discourse, spoken as well as written. In this way it comes to refer to effective participation of any kind in social processes.[3]

Having argued for much of my working life that we still do not properly value spoken language, or even properly describe it, I naturally sympathize with those who use the term in this way, to the extent that they are by implication raising the status of speaking, of the spoken language, and of the discourse of so-called 'oral cultures'. The problem is that if we call all these things literacy, then we shall have to find another term for what we called literacy before; because it is still necessary to distinguish reading and writing practices from listening and speaking practices. Neither is superior to the other, but they are different; and, more importantly, the interaction between them is one of the friction points at which new meanings are created.[4] So here I shall use literacy throughout to refer specifically to writing as distinct from speech: to reading and writing practices, and to the forms of language, and ways of meaning, that are typically associated with them.

## 1   The written medium

At this first level, then, literacy means writing language down; and to be literate means to write it and to read it. We tend to use expressions like 'to know how to' read and write; but I think it is more helpful to conceive of literacy as activity rather than as knowledge.[5]

When you write, your body engages with the material environment. You make marks in sand, or arrange wooden shapes, or move a pointed stick across a surface so that it leaves a mark. (As a small child, I had a magnificent set of large wooden letters; but since they were letters, I posted them. After that I made letter shapes out of any suitably inert sinuous material, like wet string, or my father's watch chain.) Or, if you use *Breakthrough to Literacy*, you arrange printed cards on a stand; in this way you can be engaging with the written symbols without being required first to master the material processes of constructing them.

The nature of the material environment, and the way our bodies were able to create patterns in it, opened up the possibility of writing, and also circumscribed the forms which writing took.[6] (I will come back in the next section to the question of how this actually came to happen.) In the process, a whole variety of new **things** came into being. The patterns of writing create systemic properties which are then named as abstract objects, like the **beginning** and **end** of a page or a line, **spaces** between **words**, and **letters**, **capital** (or **big**) and **small**. The different kinds of letter have their own names: they are called **ey**, **bee**, **sea** and so on; and there are other symbols called **comma**, **question mark**, **full stop** (or **period**). Children learn that **writing** is different from **drawing**; and that whereas 'what I have drawn' is named with reference to my world of experience, such as a cat or a house, 'what I have written' is of a different order of reality: either it has its own name, as an object created in the act of writing ('you've written a "c"'), or it is named with reference to another symbol – to an element of the language, usually a phoneme or a word ('you've written /**k**/'; 'you've written **cat**'). This last is of course very complex, since it is a symbol standing for a symbol.

Names, however, do not occur as lexical items in isolation; they function as elements in lexicogrammatical formations, like *What shall I do? – Go and read your book*. These clause, phrase and group structures construe the relationships among writer, reader and text, with wordings such as

> The capital letter goes at the beginning of the sentence.
> You must put two ells in *silly*.
> I've written a letter [where *letter* is ambiguous; contrast *I've written you a letter*, where it is not].
> *Hippopotamus* – that's a very long word.
> You say it, and I'll write it down.

If we analyse expressions like these grammatically, in terms of the processes and participant roles in the clauses, and the experiential structures of the nominal groups and prepositional phrases, we gain interesting insights into the nature of writing, at this level of the written medium.

At this level, then, to talk about literacy in social processes means that these are being enacted, at least in part, by language in the written medium; and being literate means engaging with language in its written form: distinguishing what is writing from what is not writing, and producing and recognizing graphic patterns. These patterns include the symbols themselves, and their arrangements relative to each other and to the frame. They also take into account the many variants of these forms and arrangements, such as type face, printing style, and layout; including, today, all the innovations coming in the wake of the new technology – but those will take us up to another level. Meanwhile the next link in our chain of linguistic interpretation will be to consider the nature of writing systems.

## 2   Writing systems

It would be wrong to suggest that, historically, writing began as language written down: that writing simply grew out of speaking when certain people began devising a new means of expression. That is not likely to be how it happened. People came to write not by constructing a new medium of expression for language, but by mapping on to language another semiotic they already had. Writing arose out of the impact between talking and drawing (i.e., forms of visual representation).

If you create a certain outline, and say it represents a horse (the object), you have 'drawn a horse'. If you say it represents *horse* (the word), you have 'written *horse*'. It may be exactly the same outline, in both cases. But in the first case it cannot be 'read', whereas in the second it can. When you can read the outline, and match it to a **typically unambiguous** wording, it is writing. This process seems to have been initiated successfully only three or perhaps four times in human history, and then to have spread around – although the line between doing something yourself and copying someone else is not as clearly marked as that formulation suggests. In the course of this process, however, there evolved various different kinds of writing system: that is, different ways in which the visual, non-linguistic semiotic came to be mapped on to the (hitherto only spoken) linguistic one.

The significant variable here is: at what point do the written symbols interface with the language? – at the level of lexicogrammar, or at the level of phonology? In other words, do the symbols stand for elements of **wording**, or for elements of **sound**? If the written symbols interface with the wording (a writing system of this kind is called a 'charactery'), then they will stand for **morphemes**, which are the smallest units at the lexicogrammatical level. In principle they might also stand for **words**; but in practice that would not work, because there are too many words in a language. The number of morphemes in a language is typically of the order of magnitude of 10,000; the number of words will always be considerably higher.[7] If the written symbols interface with the sound, on the other hand, then they may stand either for syllables (a 'syllabary') or for phonemes (an 'alphabet'), or for something in between the two – depending on the phonological system of the language in question.

A writing system may be relatively homogeneous, belonging clearly to one type, like Chinese (morphemic) or Italian (phonemic); or it may be much more mixed, like Japanese or English. In Japanese, two systems interact – one purely syllabic, the other in principle morphemic – while English is in principle phonemic but contains various sub-systems and is modified in the direction of the morphemic.[8] The differences among different writing systems lie not in the **form** of the symbols but in their **function** relative to the language concerned; specifically, what linguistic elements, identified at what level, the symbols represent.

Like sound systems (phonologies), writing systems (or 'graphologies') usually contain prosodic and paralinguistic features over and above their inventories of elementary symbols. These are patterns extending over longer stretches, affecting more minimal segments; some of them construct systems (these are the 'prosodic' features), while others (the 'paralinguistic') do not. In phonology, intonation and rhythm are typically prosodic features, while voice quality is typically paralinguistic; but again it is the function rather than the form that determines their significance. In writing, some of the features referred to briefly in the previous section are of this kind: punctuation symbols function prosodically, while typeface (roman, italic, bold, etc.) and graphic design (indentation, line spacing and so on) function paralinguistically – although all paralinguistic features are available as potential resources for constructing further systems.

If we talk about literacy in the context of this level of the interpretation, we would mean operating with a writing system of a particular kind. Literacy in this sense has a great deal of effect on cross-linguistic movements of one kind or another: for example, patterns of borrowing between languages, and the maintenance of personal identity under the transformation of proper names. It also affects internal processes such as the creation of technical vocabulary, as well as the intersection of written text with other, non-linguistic semiotic systems.[9] For a person to be literate, in this sense, means to use the writing system with facility; and also to have some understanding of how it works, so as to be able to extend it when the need arises (e.g. in inventing brand names for products, or new personal names for one's unfortunate children).

Some people achieve this understanding of a writing system at an unconscious level, without going through the process of knowing it consciously; but others don't, and for certain purposes one may need to have access to it as conscious knowledge, for example as a teacher coping with children's – or adults' – problems in learning. To be literate is also to reflect on what writing is **not**: it is not pictures of things, or representations of ideas (the terms 'pictograph', 'ideograph' refer to the origins of symbolic **forms**; as functional terms they are simply self-contradictory). It is also to reflect on the limits of a writing system – can everything that is said also be written down? in what ways is it transformed, or deformed, in the process? – and on how writing systems interact with other visual semiotics such as maps, plans, figures and charts (which will take us up to another level).[10] Meanwhile to investigate questions that are raised by our exploration of writing systems, we need to look into the nature of written language.

# 3  Written language

As a writing system evolves, people use it; and they use it in constructing new forms of social action, new contexts which are different from those of speech. These contexts in turn both engender and are engendered by new lexicogrammatical patterns that evolve in the language itself. If we reflect on the lexicogrammar of written English, for example, we soon recognize features that are particularly associated with language in its written mode.

A great deal has been written, since the early 1970s, on spoken and written language; much of it purports to show that written language is more logical, more highly structured and more systematically organized than speech. This is the popular image of it; and it is very largely untrue – although you can readily see how such a picture came to be constructed. If you compare tape-recorded speech, with all its backtracking, rewording and periods of intermittent silence, with the highly edited, final form of a written text from which all such side-effects of the drafting have been eliminated; if you regard the overt intrusion of 'I' and 'you' into the text as making it less logical and less systematic; and if you then analyse both varieties in the terms of a logic and a grammar that were constructed out of, and for the purposes of, written language in the first place – you will have guaranteed in advance that written language will appear more orderly and more elaborately structured than spoken. And you will also have obscured the very real and significant differences between the two.

It is true, of course, that first and second person are much less used in written than in spoken texts. The system of person in the grammar construes a context which is typically dialogic, with constant exchange of roles between speaker and listener; this is not the pattern of written language, which is typically monologic and, except in a genre such as informal correspondence, does not accommodate a personalized reader as co-author of the text. (This is not to deny the role of the reader as an active participant in discourse, but the reader reconstitutes the text rather than sharing in its construction.) Hence there is less of a place for personal forms when making meaning in writing. And interpersonal meaning is made less salient in other ways besides; for example, there is much less variation from the unmarked choice of mood – most writing is declarative, except for compendia of instructions where the unmarked mood is imperative. The discursive relationship between writer and readers tends to be preset for the text as a whole. But it would be wrong to conclude from the absence of 'I' and 'you', and of interrogative clauses, that the writer is not present in the lexicogrammar of the written text. The writer is present in the attitudinal features of the lexis, in words which signal 'what I approve/disapprove of'; and, most conspicuously, in the network of interpersonal systems that make up modality. Modalities in language – expressions of probability, obligation and the like – are the grammar's way of expressing the speaker's or writer's judgment, without making the first person 'I' explicit; for example, *that practice must be stopped* means 'I insist that that practice is stopped', *it couldn't possibly make any difference* means 'I am certain that it doesn't make any difference'. Modalities never express the judgment of some third party. They may be presented as depersonalized, or objectified, especially in written language (e.g., *it seems that, there is a necessity that*); but all are ultimately manifestations of what 'I think'. The account given so far assumes that the clause is declarative. If, however, it is interrogative, the onus of judgment is simply shifted on to the listener: *could it possibly make any difference?* means 'do you think it possible that it makes some difference?'.

However, a more significant feature of written language is the way its ideational meanings are organized. If we compare written with spoken English we find that written English typically shows a much denser pattern of lexicalized content. Lexical density has sometimes been measured as the ratio of content words to function words: higher in writing, lower in speech (Taylor 1979). But if we put it this way, we tie it too closely to English. In a language such as Russian, where the 'function' elements more typically combine with the 'content' lexeme to form a single inflected word, such a measure would not easily apply. We can, however, formulate the content of lexical density in a more general way, so that it can be applied to (probably) all languages. In this formulation, lexical density is the number of lexicalized elements (lexemes) in the clause. Here is a sentence taken from a newspaper article, with the lexical elements in bold:

> Obviously the **government** is **frightened** of **union reaction** to its **move** to **impose proper behaviour** on **unions**.

There are nine lexemes, all in the one clause – lexical density 9. If we reword this in a rather more spoken form we might get the following:

> ||| Obviously the **government** is **frightened** || how the **unions** will **react** || if it tries to make them **behave properly** |||

There are now three clauses, and the number of lexemes has gone down to six – lexical density 6/3 = 2.[11]

Needless to say, we will find passages of varying lexical density both in speech and in writing, with particular instances showing a range of values from zero to something over twenty. To say that written texts have a higher lexical density than spoken texts is like saying that men are taller than women: the pattern appears over a large population, so that given any text, the denser it is the more likely it is to be in writing rather than in speech. This explains the clear sense we have that a passage in one medium may be in the language of the other: someone is 'talking like a book', or 'writing in a colloquial style'.

How does the difference come about? It is not so much that when we reword something from a written into a spoken form the number of lexemes goes down; rather, the number of clauses goes up. Looking at this from the other end we can say that spoken language tends to have more clauses. But if one lexically dense clause in writing corresponds to two or more less dense clauses in speech, the latter are not simply unrelated to each other; they form hypotactic and/or paratactic clause complexes. Thus the spoken language tends to accommodate more clauses in its 'sentences'; in other words, to be less lexically dense, but more grammatically intricate. This may not emerge from averaging over large samples, because spoken dialogue also tends to contain some very short turns, and these consist mainly of one clause each. But given any instance of a clause complex, the more clauses it has in it the more likely it is to be found occurring in speech.

Most of the lexical material in any clause is located within nominal constructions: nominal groups or nominalized clauses. Thus in the example

> The **separable** or **external soul** is a **magical stratagem** generally **employed** by **supernatural wizards** or **giants**.

there are two nominal groups, *the separable or external soul* and *a magical stratagem generally employed by supernatural wizards or giants*; and all nine lexemes fall within one or the other. But what makes this possible is the phenomenon of grammatical metaphor, whereby some semantic component is construed in the grammar in a form **other than** that which is prototypical; there are many types of grammatical metaphor, but the most productive types all contribute towards this pattern of nominalization. What happens is this. Some process or property, which in spoken language would typically appear as a verb or an adjective, is construed instead as a noun, functioning as Head/Thing in a nominal group; and other elements then accrue to it, often also by grammatical metaphor, as Classifier or Epithet or inside an embedded clause or phrase. In the following example the two Head nouns, *variations* and *upheaval*, are both metaphorical in this way:

> These small variations of age-old formulas heralded a short but violent upheaval in Egyptian art.

How do we decide that one of the two variants is metaphorical? If they are viewed synoptically, each of the two is metaphorical from the standpoint of the other; given an agnate pair such as *her acceptance was followed by applause* and *when she accepted, people applauded*, we can say only that there is a relationship of grammatical metaphor between *her acceptance* and *she accepted*, but not – at least in any obvious respect – that one is metaphorical and the other not, or less so. If they are viewed dynamically, however, one form does turn out to be the unmarked one. Thus, in instances of this type, there are three distinct histories in which 'accept' is construed as a verb **before** it is construed as a noun:

1. diachronically, in the history of the language;
2. developmentally, in the history of the individual;
3. instantially, in the history of the text.

Thus (1) the noun is usually derived from the verb, rather than the other way round (the derivation may have taken place in ancient Latin or Greek, but that does not affect the point); (2) children usually learn the verbal form significantly earlier than the nominal one; (3) in a text, the writer usually proceeds from verb to noun rather than the other way round, e.g.,

> She accepted the commission. Her acceptance was followed by applause.

In all these histories, the process starts life as a verb and is then metaphorized into a noun.[12]

One of the reasons why these nominalizing metaphors appeared in written language may be that writing was associated from the start with non-propositional (and hence non-clausal) registers: for example, tabulation of goods for trading purposes, lists of names (kings, heroes, genealogies), inventories of property and the like. But another impetus came from the development of science and mathematics, originating in ancient Greece, as far as the European tradition is concerned. To pursue these further we shall have to move 'up' one level, so as to take account of the contexts in which writing and written language evolve (see section 7 below). Meanwhile, we have now reached a third step in our linguistic interpretation of literacy: literacy as 'having mastery of a written language'. In this sense, if we say that someone is literate it means that they are effectively using the lexicogrammatical patterns that are associated with written text. As I said earlier, this does not imply that they are consciously aware of doing so, or that they could analyse these patterns in grammatical terms. But it does imply that they can understand and use the written wordings, differentiate them from the typical patterns of spoken language, and recognize their functions and their value in the culture.

I am not suggesting that written language is some kind of uniform, homogeneous 'style'. On the contrary, writing covers a wide range of different discursive practices, in which the patterns of language use are remarkably varied. But the fact that such practices are effective, and that such variation is meaningful, is precisely because certain 'syndromes' of lexicogrammatical features regularly appear as a typical characteristic of text that is produced in writing. This means, of course, that there are other combinations of features which do not appear, or appear only seldom, even though they would not be devoid of meaning: for example, we do not usually combine technical or commercial reports with expressions of personal feeling. But we could do; such gaps, or 'disjunctions', are not forced on us by the language, and with new developments in language technology there are already signs of change (cf. section 5 below).[13] By thinking about what does not usually occur, we become more aware of the regularities, of what is common to the varied forms of written discourse.

The value of having some explicit knowledge of the grammar of written language is that you can use this knowledge, not only to analyse the texts, but as a critical resource for asking questions about them: why is the grammar organized as it is? why has written language evolved in this way? what is its place in the construction of knowledge, the maintenance of bureaucratic and technocratic power structures, the design and practice of education? You can explore disjunctions and exploit their potential for creating new combinations of meanings. The question then arises: are the spoken and written forms of a language simply variants, different ways of 'saying the same thing'? or are they saying rather different things? This takes us to the next link in our exploratory chain.

## 4    The written world

I referred in the last section to the way in which metaphorical patterns of nominalization are built up in the course of a text. The example referred to in note 12 was a paper entitled 'The fracturing of glass', in *Scientific American* (December 1987); it contains the following expressions, listed here in the order in which they occur (in different locations spaced throughout the text):

1. the question of how glass cracks
2. the stress needed to crack glass
3. the mechanism by which glass cracks
4. as a crack grows
5. the crack has advanced

6. will make slow cracks grow
7. speed up the rate at which cracks grow
8. the rate of crack growth
9. we can decrease the crack growth rate 1,000 times.

Note how the metaphorical object *crack growth rate* is built up step by step beginning from the most congruent (least metaphorical) form *how glass cracks*.

To see why this happens, let us focus more sharply on one particular step:

> ... we have found that both chemicals [ammonia and methanol] speed up the rate at which cracks grow in silica. ... The rate of crack growth depends not only on the chemical environment but also on the magnitude of the applied stress. (p. 81)

This shows that there are good reasons **in the discourse** (in the 'textual' metafunction, in systemic terms). In carrying the argument forward it is often necessary to refer to what has already been established – but to do so in a way which backgrounds it as the point of departure for what is coming next. This is achieved in the grammar by thematizing it: the relevant matter becomes the Theme of the clause. Here the Theme *the rate of crack growth* 'packages' a large part of the preceding argument so that it serves as the rhetorical foundation for what follows.

When we look into the grammar of scientific writings we find that this motif recurs all the time. The clause begins with a nominal group, typically embodying a number of instances of grammatical metaphor; this summarizes the stage that has now been reached in the argument and uses it as the taking-off point for the next step. Very often, this next step consists in relating the first nominal to a second one that is similarly packaged, in a logical-semantic relationship of identity, cause, proof and the like. Thus a typical instance of this clause pattern would be the following:

> The sequential appearance of index-minerals reflected steadily increasing temperature across the area.

Here is a condensed version of the context in which this is built up:

> [Barrow] recognized a definite and consistent order of appearance or disappearance of particular metamorphic minerals (**index minerals**), across the area. ... The differences in mineralogy observed by

Barrow could not be due to chemical differences because the rocks all have similar bulk chemical compositions. The most likely explanation ... is that the sequential appearance of index minerals reflected steadily increasing temperature across the area.

(Clark & Cook 1986: 239).

In a study of the evolution of the grammar of scientific English from Chaucer to the present day (reference in note 13 above), I found that this clause pattern is already operational in Newton's writing (the English text of the *Opticks*), becomes well established during the eighteenth century, and has become the favourite clause type by the early years of the nineteenth century. Since this kind of nominalization is frequently objected to by stylists, it is valid to point out that, however much it may become ritualized, and co-opted for use in contexts of prestige and power, it is clearly discourse-functional in origin.

However, while these nominalizing metaphors may have been motivated initially by textual considerations, their effect in the written language – perhaps because they arose first in the language of science – has been to construct an alternative model of human experience. Spoken language is organized around the clause, in the sense that most of the experiential content is laid down in the transitivity system, and in other systems having the clause as point of origin; and this – since the clause construes reality as processes (actions, events, mental processes, relations) – creates a world of movement and flux, or rather a world that is moving and flowing, continuous, elastic, and indeterminate. By the same token the written language is organized around the nominal group; and this – since the nominal group construes reality as entities (objects, including institutional and abstract objects, and their quantities, qualities and types) – creates a world of things and structures, discontinuous, rigid, and determinate. Here experience is being interpreted synoptically rather than dynamically (Martin 1991).

This is the same complementarity as we find between the two different media. Spoken language is language in flux: language realized as movement and continuous flow, of our bodily organs and of sound waves travelling through air. Written language is language in fix: language realized as an object that is stable and bounded – as text in material form on stone or wood or paper. Thus the complementarity appears at both the interfaces where the discursive connects with the material (both in the meaning and in the expression); and both are significant for the social-semiotic functioning of language. If we use David Olson's distinction between communicative and archival functions (Olson 1989), spoken discourse is typically communicative, and becomes archival only under special conditions (e.g., a priesthood transmitting sacred oral texts); whereas written discourse is typically archival, a form of record-keeping, and hence can accumulate knowledge by constant accretion, a necessary condition for advancing technology and science.[14] And on the other hand, those who are constructing scientific knowledge experimentally need to hold the world still – to stop it wriggling, so to speak – in order to observe and to study it; and this is what the grammar of written language does for them.

Thus the written world is a world of things. Its symbols are things, its texts are things, and its grammar constructs a discourse of things, with which readers and writers construe experience. Or rather, with which they **re**construe experience, because all have been speakers and listeners first, so that the written world is their secondary socialization. This is critical for our understanding of the educational experience. Despite our conviction that we as conscious subjects have one 'store of knowledge' rather than two, we also have the sense that educational knowledge is somehow different from 'mere' commonsense knowledge; not surprisingly, since it is construed in a different semiotic mode. The language of the school is written language.

But, of course, educational knowledge is **not** constructed solely out of written language. Whereas our primary, commonsense knowledge is – in this respect – homoglossic, in that it is construed solely out of the clausal grammar of the spoken language, our secondary, educational knowledge is heteroglossic: it is construed out of the dialectic between the spoken and the written, the clausal and the nominal modes. Even though the scientific textbook may be overwhelmingly in nominal style, provided we are reasonably lucky, our total educational experience will be multimodal, with input from teachers, parents and peers, from classroom, library, teachers' notes and handouts, all of which presents us with a mix of the spoken and the written worlds. At its worst, this is a chaos, but it does offer the potential for more effective participation in social-semiotic practices than either of the two modes can offer by itself.

Literacy, then, in this context, is the construction of an 'objectified' world through the grammar of the written language. This means that in at least some social practices where meanings are made in writing, including educational ones, the discourse will actively participate in an ideological construction which is in principle contradictory to that derived from everyday experience. To be literate is, of course, to engage in these practices, for example as a teacher, and to construe from them a working model to live with, one that does not deny the experience of common sense. Again, I would observe that, in order to turn the coin – to resist the mystique and the seductive appeal of a world consisting entirely of metaphorical objects – it is helpful to have a **grammatics**, a way of using the grammar consciously as a tool for thinking with. It seems to me that, as David Bohm (1980) suggested with his demand for a return to the 'rheomode',[15] the two worlds have been pushed about as far apart as they can go, and in the next period of our history they are bound to move together again. I think, in fact, they are already starting to do so, under the impact of the new forms of technology which are deconstructing the whole opposition of speech and writing. This is the topic we have to take up next, as the next link in the interpretative chain. But in doing so, we are back where we started, concerned once again with the nature of the written medium.

## 5   The technology of literacy

The critical step in the history of writing technology is usually taken to be the invention of printing with movable type. The significance of this from our present point of view is that it created maximum distance between written and spoken text. A written text now not only existed in material form, it could be cloned – it had become a book. Books existed in lots of copies; they were located in libraries, from which they could be borrowed for variable periods of time;[16] they could be possessed, and bought and sold, as property. Producing books was a form of labour, and created value: printing, publishing, bookbinding were ways of earning a living. The book became an institution (the book of words, book of rules), without thereby losing its material character; note the expression *they threw the book at me* 'quoted the authority of the written word'. With printing, language in its written form became maximally objectified; and this extreme dichotomy between speech and writing was a dominant feature of the five hundred years of 'modern Europe' from about 1450 to 1950.

We have seen how this object-like status of the written word is enacted metaphorically by the nominalizing grammar of the written language. Meanwhile, however, the technology has turned itself around. Within one lifetime our personal printing press, the typewriter, from being manual became first electric then electronic; and from its marriage with the computer was born the word processor. With this, in hardly any time, the gap between spoken and written text has been largely eliminated. On the one hand, whereas in the printing era the written text passed out of the writer's control in being transmitted, we now once again control our own written discourse; and since we have our own private means of transmission, the communicative function of writing has come to the fore, as people write to each other by electronic mail. And as the functional gap has lessened, so also the material gap has lessened, and from both ends. With a tape recorder, speech becomes an object: it is on the tape; can be 'played' over and over again (so listening becomes like reading); can be multiply copied; and can be stored (and so used for archiving functions). With a word processor, writing becomes a happening; it can be scrolled up the screen so that it unfolds in time, like speech. The tape recorder made speech more like writing; the word processor has made writing more like speech.

We have seen the effects of this in education. Teachers who favour 'process writing' are emphasizing the activity of writing as well as – and sometimes at the expense of – the object that results from it.[17] Children who learn to write using a word processor tend to compose their written discourse in a manner that is more like talking than like traditional writing exercises (Anderson 1985). What is happening here is that the consciousness barrier is disappearing. When the material conditions of speaking and writing are most distinct, the consciousness gap is greatest: speaking is unselfconscious, proceeding as it were from the gut, while writing is self-conscious, designed and produced in the head. (This is why the writing of a six-year-old typically regresses to resemble the spoken language of age three.) Although writing and reading will always be more readily accessible to conscious reflection than speaking and listening, **relatively** we now have more occasions for being self-conscious when we speak (international phone calls, talkback shows, interviews, committees and so on), and more chances of remaining unselfconscious when we write.

This suggests that the spoken and the written **language** will probably come closer together; and there are signs that this is already beginning to happen. Not only textbook writers but also public servants, bankers, lawyers, insurers and others are notably uneasy about the 'communication gap'; they are even turning to linguists to help them communicate – note the success of the Plain English movement towards greater reader friendliness in written documents.[18] I have referred already to the scientists wanting a discourse of continuity and flow, and suggested that the way to achieve this is to make their technical writing more like speech, so that they are not cut off from the commonsense construction of experience. But we need to think grammatically about this. To the extent that written discourse is **technical**, to that extent it probably has to objectify, since most technical constructs are metaphorical objects, organized in paradigms and taxonomies.[19] Even non-technical writing has numerous functions for which a nominal mode seems called for. So it is not, I think, a question of neutralizing the difference between written language and spoken. What the technology is doing is creating the material conditions for interaction between the two, from which some new forms of discourse will emerge. Again, the effects are likely to be felt at both the material interfaces of language: new forms of publication, on the one hand, with (say) print and figures on paper combining with moving text and graphics on the screen; and on the other hand new ways of meaning which construe experience in more complex, and hence more 'realistic', ways arising out of the complementarities of the spoken and the written modes. Such a construction of experience would seem to call once again for the poet-scientist, in the tradition of Lucretius; I think Butt (1988a, 1988b) would say that Wallace Stevens is the first such figure in our own times, at least among those writing in English, but there are also scientists with the semantic prosodies of poetry, like Stephen Hawking. And if science is to technology as poetry is to prose, then the marriage, or perhaps *de facto* relationship, has already been arranged: in the post-industrial, information society the real professional is the semiotician-technician, for whom the world is made of discourse/information and the same meta-grammar is needed to construe both the grammar of language on the one hand, and the 'grammar' of the teleport, on the other.[20]

At this fifth level, then, literacy is a technological construct; it means using the current technology of writing to participate in social processes, including the new social processes that the technology brings into being. A person who is literate is one who effectively engages in this activity (we already refer to people as 'computer-literate', a concept that is now much closer to literacy in its traditional sense than it was when coined). But – the other side of the coin again – I think that here, too, and perhaps especially in this context, we need the concept of literacy as informed defence. To be literate is not only to **participate** in the discourse of an information society, it is also to resist it, to defend oneself – and others – against the anti-semantic, anti-democratic 'technologizing' of that discourse. And here more than ever one needs to understand how language works, how the grammar (in its systemic sense of lexicogrammar) interacts with the technology to achieve these effects. If you hope to engage successfully in discursive contest, you have first to learn how to engage with discourse.

# 6   The frontiers of literacy

We were able to define writing, historically, as the mapping of non-linguistic visual communication practices on to language. This, as I have tried to suggest in the foregoing sections, was an important move in the history of 'semogenesis', the potential for producing meaning – comparable in many ways to the shift in the potential for material production that took place along with settlement.[21] We now need to take this one level up, and in doing so we shall perhaps reveal the counter-tendencies that always existed and are now coming to be foregrounded once again. What is happening today is not a loosening of the bond between the written symbol and the language (that could be achieved only by destroying the writing system altogether, and this has never happened)[22] but the creation of new systems of visual semiotic that are not themselves forms of writing – that have no (in principle) unique mapping on to lexicogrammatical or phonological elements – yet are used in conjunction with written text.

Take a mathematical expression as an example. Mathematics is not, of course, a form of visual semiotic, but it is expressed in symbols that look like, and in some cases are borrowings of, written symbols. The simplest of all such expressions would be something like 2 + 2 = 4. This is not writing; we cannot read it, because it has no exact representation in wording. We can, of course, **verbalize** it – that is, find semantically equivalent wordings, such as *two and two make four, two plus two equal(s) four, two added to two comes to four, four is the sum of two plus two* and so on. But each of these has its own written form (I have just written them here); and, of course, they are all different – although they are all equivalent mathematically, they are certainly not synonymous. Linguistically they mean different things, as the grammar can readily show.

I am not saying that the boundary between what is and what is not writing is absolute, clearcut and determinate. We saw above that readers are presented with a lot of visual symbols that are on the fringes of writing: the prosodic and paralinguistic features referred to in section 2. But they are also presented, nowadays, with a great deal of visual information that is clearly not writing, and yet has to be processed along with a written text: maps, charts, line graphs, bar graphs, system networks, diagrams and figures of all kinds. None of these can be read aloud; they have no unique implication of wording, even though again they can often be verbalized: for example, a feature on a weather map could be verbalized as *a cold front is moving in a northeasterly direction across the Tasman Sea.*

So although these are not made of language, they are semiotic systems whose texts can be translated into language, and that offer alternative resources for organizing and presenting information. Reporting on his research in Vancouver, Mohan (1986) explores this potential in an educational context in his work with English as a Second Language students in primary school. It is exploited in artificial intelligence in text generation systems, which use non-linguistic representations (e.g., maps) as the source of information to be presented in text form. These can also now be incorporated into the text itself, and obviously the graphics capabilities of personal computers will encourage writers more and more to integrate non-verbal material into their writing.

In the context of a discussion of literacy, the critical feature of these non-verbal texts is that referred to above: that they can be translated into natural language. This means that they can be interpreted semantically – they can be construed into meaningful wordings, even though always with a fair amount of semantic 'play'. We tend to assume that such semiotic systems are from a linguistic viewpoint metafunctionally incomplete: that they construct ideational meanings (experiential and logical) but not interpersonal ones. (What this means is that we assume all the interpersonal choices are unmarked: declarative or imperative mood, according to the semiotic function; non-modalized; attitudinally neutral, and so on.) But if we think about these texts grammatically, we find that the situation is more complex. There are interpersonal devices, some of them very subtle; the problem is that it is here that the distance from language is probably greatest, so these meanings are the hardest to 'read aloud'.[23] On the other hand, the ideational meanings may be very indeterminate and ambiguous, and the textual meanings are notoriously hard to retrieve: texts are usually presented in the context of other textual material which **is** in language, but this, while it may solve some problems, often creates another one – namely, that we do not know how the verbal and the non-verbal information is supposed to be related.[24]

Somewhere in this region lie the frontiers of literacy as traditionally understood. But it would be foolish to try to define these frontiers exactly. What is relevant is that, in social processes in which writing is implicated, we typically find it associated with a variety of non-linguistic visual semiotics, which accompany it or in some cases substitute for it (like the – often totally opaque – signs displayed for passengers on international airports). Being literate means being able to verbalize the texts generated by these systems: 'reading' the weather charts, stock exchange bulletins and share prices, street maps and timetables, pictorial instructions for kit assembly and the like. (Perhaps we should include here the filling in of forms; these are, in principle, made of language, but I suspect that in coming to terms with them we rely heavily on their non-verbal properties!) Being literate might also include, finally, knowing what meanings have been lost, and what new meanings imposed, when there is translation between the verbal and the non-verbal; and exploring the semiotic potential that lies at their intersection – the new meanings that can be opened up when writing impacts on other visual systems that lie outside (but not too far outside) the frontiers of language.

# 7   The contexts of literacy

These other systems of visual semiotic, referred to in the last section, could be thought of as the contexts for a **writing system**. The contexts of a **written language**, on the other hand, are the systems and processes of the culture – the various contexts of situation that engender written language and are engendered by it.

Writing does not simply duplicate the functions of speech. It did not originate, or develop, as a new way of doing old things. Writing has always been a way of using language to do something different from what is done by talking. This is what children expect, when they learn to read and write; as Hammond (1990) pointed out, in explaining why a class of children who had just been talking about a recent experience in very complex terms regressed to more or less infantile language when asked to write about it, it made no sense to them to go over the same task again in writing. They expect what we can call a 'functional complementarity' between speech and writing.

Historically, as already implied, writing evolved with settlement; and if we think about it historically, we can construct the metaphor linking writing with its contexts in other social processes. Under certain conditions, people settle down: they take to producing their food, rather than gathering it wherever it grows or hunting it wherever it roams. Instead of moving continuously through space-time, these people locate themselves in a defined space, marked out into smaller spaces with boundaries in between. (We can notice how this unity of people and place becomes lexicalized, in terms like *village, homestead, quarter.*)

These people create surplus value: they produce and exchange durable objects – goods, and property. The language that accompanies these practices is similarly transformed: it becomes durable, spatially defined, and marked with boundaries – it settles down. This is writing. In the process it also becomes an object, capable of being owned and exchanged like other objects (written text and books).

The meanings construed by this language-as-object are themselves typically 'objects' (inventories, bills of lading, etc.) rather than processes. Meanings as things split off from meanings as events; the nominal group replaces the clause as the primary meaning-producing, or 'semogenic', agent in the grammar. This is written language. The nominal group then functions to construe other phenomena into objects (nominalization), thus 'objectifying' more complex forms of social organization (noun as institution) and their ideological formations (noun as abstraction).

Production processes are technologized; objects are created by transformation out of events (e.g., heating). The nominalizing power of the grammar transforms events into objects, and their participants into properties of those objects (grammatical metaphor). These transformed 'objects' become the technical concepts of mathematics and science.

All experience can now be objectified, as the written language construes the world synoptically – in its own image (writing is language synoptically construed). Writing is itself technologized (printing). The flux of the commonsense environment, reduced to order, is experimented with and theorized. Writing and speech are maximally differentiated; written knowledge is a form of commodity (education), spoken knowledge is denied even to exist.

What I am trying to show, in this highly idealized account (of processes that are in fact messy, sporadic and evolving, not tidy, continuous and designed), is that our material practices and our linguistic practices – not forgetting the material interfaces of the linguistic practices – collectively and interactively constitute the human condition. They therefore also change it. In our present era, when information is replacing goods and services as the primary form of productive activity, it seems certain that the split between speech and writing will become severely dysfunctional. But it is still with us, and throughout this long period of history writing has had contexts different from those of speech. In some ways these are complementary; in other ways they are contradictory and conflicting.

Malinowski gave us the concepts of 'context of situation' and 'context of culture'; we can interpret the context of situation as the environment of the text and the context of culture as the environment of the linguistic system. The various types of social process can be described in linguistic terms as contexts of language use. The principle of functional complementarity means that we can talk of the contexts of written discourse.

Certain contexts of writing are largely transparent: if we represent them in terms of field, tenor and mode then there is a fairly direct link from these to the grammar of the text. Such relatively homogeneous forms of discourse, like weather reports, sets of instructions (e.g., recipes), shopping lists and other written agendas, and some institutional discourses, can be specified so that we can construe them in either direction: given the context, we can construe the features of the text, and given the text we can construe the features of the context. To be literate implies construing in both directions, hence constructing a relationship between text and context which is systematic and not random.

Other written texts are not like this; they present a more or less discordant mix of multiple voices. These are texts whose context embodies internal contradictions and conflicts. As an example, one large class of such texts consists of those designed to persuade people to part with their money. The goods and services offered have to display all desirable qualities, even where these conflict with one another, as they often do; and to combine these with a price-figure that is in fact in conflict with their claimed value, and has to be presented as such but with the inconsistency explained away ('you'd never believe that we could offer ... but our lease has expired and we must dispose of all stock', etc.). In the following example the text has to reconcile the 'desirable building land' with the fact that it is on a site that should never have been built on; the linguistic unease is obvious:

> ... is a high quality, bushland, residential estate which retains environmental integrity similar to a wildlife reserve.

Such features need, of course, to be demonstrated with full length texts.[25]

Another example is technocratic discourse, which, as Lemke (1990) and Thibault (1991b) have shown, intersects the technical-scientific with the bureaucratic – the authority of knowledge with the authority of power – to create a contradictory motif of 'we live in an informed society, so here is explicit evidence; but the issues are too complex for you to understand, so leave the decision-making to us'; they go on to 'prove' that children who are failing in school do not benefit from having more money spent on them, or that the environment is not under serious threat. Reproduced below, however, is an example of a different kind (though not unrelated to these last). It is a party invitation addressed to tenants in a prestigious 'executive residence' (name withheld).

Dear tenant
IF YOU JUST WANNA HAVE FUN …
Come to <u>your</u> MOONCAKE NITE THEME PARTY next Saturday.
That's September 20 – from 7.30 p.m. until the wee hours!!
A sneak preview of the exciting line-up of activities includes:

* Mr/Ms                        Tenant Contest
* Find <u>Your</u> Mooncake Partner
* Pass the Lantern Game
* Bottoms Up Contest
* Blow the Lantern Game
* Moonwalking Contest
* DANCING
* PLUS MORE! MORE! MORE!

For even greater fun, design and wear your original Mooncake
creation, and bring your self-made lantern passport!
But don't despair if you can't because this party is <u>**FOR**</u> you!
Lantern passports can be bought at the door.
Just c'mon and grab this opportunity to chat up your neighbour.
Call yours truly on <u>ext.</u> <u>137</u> NOW! Confirm you really wanna have
fun!! Why – September 20's next Saturday.
See you!

Public Relations Officer
P.S. Bring your camera to 'capture' the fun!

In the cacophony of voices that constitute this text, we can
recognize a number of oppositions: child and adult, work and
leisure, 'naughty' and 'nice', professional and commercial – constructed by the lexicogrammar in cahoots with the prosody and
paralanguage. But this mixture of bureaucratic routine, comics-
style graphic effects, masculine aggression, childism and
condescension, straight commercialism, conspiratorialism and
hype adds up to something that we recognize: late capitalist
English in the Disneyland register. Presumably there are institutions in southern California where people who are being trained
to 'service' business executives learn to construct this kind of discourse. The context is the disneyfication of western man (I say
'man' advisedly), whereby the off-duty executive reverts semiotically to childhood while retaining the material make-up of an
adult.

Literacy today includes many contexts of this contorted kind,
where the functions of the written text have to be sorted out at various levels. To be literate is to operate in such complex, multiple

contexts: to write with many voices, still ending up with a text, and to read such texts with kaleidoscopic eyes. Once again, the grammatics will help: it is the point about conscious knowledge again. And once again there is the other side of the coin, literacy as active defence: resisting the disneyfication, as well as more ominous pressures; probing the disjunctions, and extending the semogenic potential of the culture. This leads into the final heading, section 8 below.

# 8   The ideology of literacy

There is of course no final step; but this is as far as I shall try to go. In using the term 'ideology' here I do not mean it in the classical marxist sense where it is by definition false consciousness; nor am I implying that it is a coherent, ordered system of hidden beliefs that are taken over by the oppressed from the dominant group that is oppressing them. I use it as Martin (1986), Hasan (1986) and others have used it – though not as an explicitly stratal construct.[26] If we conceive ideology in this way, I think we have to take seriously Gramsci's point that it is not so much a coherent system of beliefs as a chaos of meaning-making practices, within and among which there is incoherence, disjunction and conflict – which is why it always contains within itself the conditions for its own transformation into something else (Thibault 1991a). But in agreeing that ideological constructions are typically anything but consistent, I would add that there is a certain mystique at present about the opposition between order and chaos. In foregrounding chaos – as end-of-millennium postmodernist thinkers do, whether in physics or in semiotics – people have tended to reify the dichotomy, that is, to treat it as a property of the phenomena under study, whereas I see it more as the standpoint of the observer. Anything we can contemplate is bound to be a mixture of order and chaos, and either can be made to figure against the grounding of the other. Rather than arguing that one or other is correct – at least in relation to semiotic practices – I would ask what we can learn about them by interpreting them one way and then the other.

The dominant ideological aspect of literacy is obviously the authority of the written word. Consider this in relation to school textbooks. If they are to function effectively, the readers they are addressed to must believe in what they say. Luke, Castell and Luke (1989: 245ff), as also Olson (1989: 233ff), raise the question of how textbooks derive and maintain their authority. They show that textbooks sanctify 'authorized (educational) knowledge' simply by authorizing it – what is in the text book is thereby defined as knowledge – and text books maintain this authority by various means such as claiming objectivity and creating distance between performer and reader, and so come to be accepted as 'beyond criticism'. They then go on to point out that textbooks strive for clarity, explicitness and an unambiguous presentation of the facts; they seek to 'delimit possible interpretations'. I think they do strive for these things; but I also think they often fail to achieve them. Consider these examples:

1. In many algebra books you will see numerals like '– –6'. This means, of course, the <u>opposite of</u> 6, that is, the opposite of positive 6. Thus – –6 is exactly the same number as negative six or $-6$.
2. Your completed table should help you to see what happens to the risk of getting lung cancer as smoking increases. Lung cancer death rates are clearly associated with increased smoking.
3. In the years since 1850, more and more factories were built in northern England. The soot from the factory smoke-stacks gradually blackened the light-coloured stones and tree trunks. Scientists continued to study the pepper moth during this time. They noticed the dark-coloured moth was becoming more common. By 1950, the dark moths were much more common than the light-coloured ones. However, strong anti-pollution laws over the last twenty years have resulted in cleaner factories, cleaner countryside and an increase in the number of light-coloured pepper moths.

I have commented on texts such as these elsewhere;[27] they can be obscure, ambiguous, or even misleading to someone who does not already know what it is they are trying to say.

Looked at from the point of view of order, such 'failures' are highly dysfunctional: the passages in question fail to give an unambiguous message. But from the point of view of chaos, they are positively functional, because not only do they admit of multiple interpretations, but they can also be used to explore such multiple interpretations – to consider alternative readings and argue about which to accept. For example, in *lung cancer death rates are clearly associated with increased smoking* it is the grammar that reveals that there are other ways of interpreting the statistics on smoking; it also shows what the alternatives are: does *are associated with* mean 'are caused by' or 'cause' (cf. *means* in *higher productivity means more supporting services*)? are *lung cancer death rates* 'how many people die of lung cancer' or 'how fast people with lung cancer die'? Looking at them in this light we might conclude that literacy is the ability **not** to retrieve a single, fixed and correct meaning from the text. Similarly, with the pepper moths, the grammar offers interesting alternatives to a Darwinian explanation!

To say that a textbook authorizes and sanctifies knowledge means that it derives its authority from its function in the educational context. But what is it that sanctifies the written text? It is not simply the high status that is accorded to the social contexts of writing; it is equally the written words themselves, and most of all, perhaps, the interaction between the two. In other words, the authority of the text rests ultimately on the perceived resonance of form and function: the 'fit' between its linguistic properties (especially its lexicogrammar and discourse semantics) and the sociocultural processes by which its value and scope of action are defined.

From this point of view, to be literate is not just to have mastered the written registers (the generic structures and associated modes of meaning and wording, as described in section 7 above), but to be aware of their ideological force: to be aware, in other words, of how society is constructed out of discourse – or rather, out of the dialectic between the discursive and the material.[28] There is a vigorous debate on this issue among educators in Australia, between those who favour explicit teaching of the linguistic resources and those who consider that such teaching is unnecessary and can even be harmful. Essentially, this is an ideological debate about the nature of literacy itself: does literacy enable, or does it constrain? Is control over the linguistic resources with which educational knowledge is constructed a liberating or enslaving force? The former group sees it as enabling, admits the (often arbitrary) authority of the written genres, but insists that all members of society should have the right of access to them, as the gateway to becoming educated: children should be taught to master the structures of the genres the school requires and the grammatical resources by which these structures are put in place. The latter group sees it as constraining, considering that any acceptance of formal structure limits the freedom and creativity of the individual; ideologically, this is the motif of individual autonomy and salvation that derives from liberal protestant romanticism. In this view, children should **not** be taught these structures, but instead should be ideologically armed so they can defend themselves against them.[29] (As far as I am aware, these same principles have not been thought to apply to numeracy, the most highly structural activity of all.)

This motif of literacy as both 'access to' and 'defence against' has recurred several times throughout my chapter. My comment on this debate is that defence will be effective only if it is **informed** defence – a point made also by Hasan in this volume; to me it seems dangerously quixotic to say 'go out and fight against those who control the meanings; but you need not try to master their discourse yourselves'. What both sides agree on, however, is that literacy means being able to participate effectively in social processes by working with written language. They are concerned with literacy at this highest level – with what Hasan, in her accompanying chapter, calls 'reflection literacy'. Hasan embraces within this concept the ability to understand how systems of value, and patterns of power and prestige, are construed and maintained in language (typically, in varieties of written language); and to use that understanding in bringing about social change, or in resisting those changes that are socially divisive and corrupt.

But if we are adopting a linguistic perspective, we cannot isolate 'using written language' from 'using language' in general. It is true that written language has these special features of its own, its distinctive registers and genres. But everyone who writes, speaks; and our understanding of written language derives ultimately from our understanding of speech, and from written language in contexts that are defined by speaking. Our construction of experience comes from the interplay between the clausal and the nominal in the grammar – between reality as happening and reality as things. Our modes of discourse range from the clearly structured genres typical of conscious writing to the unbounded flow of casual conversation (still structured, but in a rather different way). So as well as separate concepts of literacy and oracy, we need a unified notion of **articulacy**, as the making of meaning in language, in whatever medium. If literacy is redefined so as to include all this and more besides, so be it; but then, as I said at the start, if we want to understand it fully, we shall still need some way of talking about it in its specific sense, of living in a world of writing.

# 9   Conclusion

I have tried to trace a course through what Graff called the labyrinth of literacy, while interpreting literacy in linguistic terms. The route has led through a number of stages, which could be summarized as follows:

1.  **The written medium**
    engaging with the material environment to produce abstract symbolic objects called 'writing'.
2.  **Writing systems**
    mapping these symbols on to elements of language and constructing them into written text.
3.  **Written language**
    construing meaning through lexicogrammar in written text: lexical density, nominalization, grammatical metaphor.
4.  **The written world**
    construing experience through semantics in written language: the world objectified as the basis of systematic knowledge.
5.  **The technology of literacy: (1) revisited**
    from books to computers: refining the medium, realigning writing and speech, technologizing discourse.
6.  **The frontiers of literacy: (2) revisited**
    from writing to other systems of visual semiotic: expanding the potential for meaning.
7.  **The contexts of literacy: (3) revisited**
    from text to context: locating written language in its sociocultural environment.
8.  **The ideology of literacy: (4) revisited**
    from the construction of experience to participation in the social-semiotic process.

This suggests a kind of helical progression, as set out in Figure 11.1.

This recalls Bruner's well-known helical model of learning. I should stress, however, that this is not to be taken as a linear sequence of learning steps. Although there is, broadly, a developmental progression in the ordering of these motifs, such that each

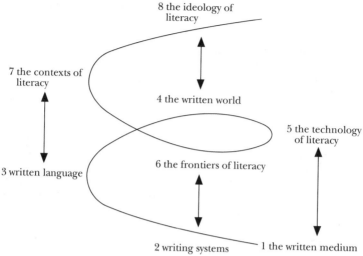

**Figure 11.1**

implies some engagement with the one before, they are analytic constructs and not pedagogic practices. Leaving aside considerations of maturity, an adult moving into the literate world could operate from the start with concepts from any stage. This principle is clearly enshrined in Hasan's discussion of 'levels' of literacy in the model she has presented here.

We are all familiar with the claim that linguistics has nothing useful to say on the subject of literacy. But it always seems to be a kind of linguistics very remote from life that is cited to justify the argument. It is a pity, because to reject linguistic insights seals off an important avenue of understanding. What I have tried to suggest here is that a functional linguistic perspective provides a valuable complementarity to the view from sociology and the philosophy of education.

## Notes

*   This is a revision of a paper presented at the Inaugural Australian Systemic Functional Conference, Deakin University, 1990 and appearing in Frances Christie (ed.), *Literacy in Social Processes*, Centre for Studies of Language in Education, Northern Territory University. I am grateful for the opportunity to revise it for inclusion in the present publication.

1   Graff (1987: 18–19) writes that 'literacy is above all *a technology or set of techniques for communications and for decoding and reproducing written or printed materials*: it cannot be taken as anything more or less' [his italics]. Compare this with his formulation 'the skills of literacy: *the basic abilities to read and write*' [his italics].

2   See especially the revised and illustrated edition of the *Teacher's Manual* (Mackay, Thompson and Schaub 1978). For an account of the Programme, see Pearce, Thornton & Mackay (1989).

3   The following is taken from Australia Post's description of International Literacy Year 1990: 'Literacy involves the integration of listening, speaking, reading, writing and critical thinking; it incorporates numeracy. Literacy also includes the cultural knowledge which enables a speaker, writer or reader to recognise and use language appropriate to different social situations' (Australian Stamp Bulletin No. 203, January–March 1990, p. 10).

4   The situation is similar to that which arises with the term *language*. If we want to extend it to mathematics, music and other semiotic systems, in order to emphasize their similarities of form or function or value in the culture, then we have to find another term for language. The expression 'natural language' arose in response to just this kind of pressure. I am not aware of any comparable term for literacy in its canonical sense. [For further discussion, see Hasan in this volume.]

5   Graff (1987: 23) quotes the following from Lewis (1953: 16): 'The only literacy that matters is the literacy that is in use. Potential literacy is empty, a void.'

6   See Thibault (1991a) on how these 'meaning making practices' are 'enabled and constrained' by the material (and other) conditions in which they take place.

7   I put it this way for simplicity; the actual situation is obviously much more complex. The number of words in a language is open-ended – new ones can always be constructed; whereas morphemes, unless borrowed, form a closed set. Moreover, in many languages it is hard to decide what a word is, or whether one word is the same as another (e.g., different inflectional variants of the same stem). But it is a reasonable approximation to say that a language has too many words to be able to afford a separate symbol for each. For an excellent account of writing systems, see Mountford (1990). See also Halliday (1989a).

8   For an excellent brief account of the English writing system see Albrow (1972/1981). Albrow's account reveals the various subsystems that coexist in the writing system of English, thus distinguishing clearly between what are simply irregularities and what are systematic variations.

9   For example: a language written in a strongly phonemic script will not only 'rephonologize' but also 'regraphologize' borrowed words;

hence Italian and Czech *filosofia* (not *ph-*). A language written morphemically will tend to calque (translate the component parts) rather than borrow; for example, Chinese *xiangguang* 'facing light' = phototropic (but this is part of an extended linguistic syndrome in Chinese, including other features such as syllable structure). Writing English personal names in Chinese, and Chinese personal names in English, creates real problems of identity (which deserve a paper to themselves!). Constructing new technical meanings might seem to be the same in all languages, but it is also shaped by the writing system, especially where the lexical resources are drawn from outside the language, as in English (Graeco-Romance) and Japanese (Chinese, English); at the same time the writing system in its turn is shaped by these semogenic processes. It would take too long to illustrate these points in detail; but consider the relationship of graphology to phonology in series such as *analyse, analysis, analytic, analyticity* in English (where each of the four words is accented on a different symbol); or the use of *kanji, hiragana* and *katakana* in creating new meanings in written Japanese.

10  [For a discussion of some of these issues with special reference to maps in geography texts, see van Leeuwen and Humphrey in this volume. Editors.]

11  There are of course many possible rewordings. We might for example keep the word *move* and end with *if it moves so as to make the unions behave properly*; this adds two lexemes, *move* and *unions*, but it also adds one clause, a hypotactic clause of purpose, giving a ratio of 8/4, still = 2. Other variants would alter the lexical density; but it would be difficult to find a convincing 'spoken' version in which it was not significantly lower than in the written one.

12  For an instance of how grammatical metaphor is built up in the course of a text, see Halliday (1988).

13  See Lemke (1984) who introduces the notion of 'disjunctions' in the context of a general theory of language as a dynamic open system which provides an essential component of the present interpretation.

14  Note the apparent paradox that, in the archival function, written language becomes the dynamic member of the pair. The spoken archive (canon of sacred texts, traditional narrative and song, etc.) can **change** in the course of transmission, but it cannot grow – it cannot become a library of knowledge.

15  See especially chapter 2. Bohm is expressing his dissatisfaction with the 'fragmentation' imposed by language on the world, and seeking 'a *new mode* of language' [his italics] which would represent continuity and flux. His suggestions are linguistically naive; but the interesting point is that he is trapped in the confines of written language – in particular the metalanguage of his own science, physics – and does not see (or rather hear) the 'rheomode' that is all around him.

16    According to *The Return of Heroic Failures*, by Stephen Pile (Penguin Books, 1988), the most overdue book in the history of the lending library was borrowed from Somerset County Records Office, in England, by the Bishop of Winchester in 1650, and returned to the library by the Church Commissioners 335 years later, in 1985. The book in question was, appropriately, the *Book of Fines*.

17    This issue has been foregrounded in the 'genre debate' in Australia; see for example, Painter & Martin (1987) and also Moore (1990).

18    See for example, *Plain English and the Law, Report and Appendices 1–8*, published by the Law Reform Commission of Victoria (for which Robert Eagleson was Commissioner-in-charge of the Plain English Division), 1987. [For a critical review of Plain English, see Solomon in this volume. Editors.]

19    Martin (1990) has argued convincingly that the technicalization of discourse must depend on nominalization and grammatical metaphor. On the other hand, Whorf pointed out that the technical terms of Hopi metaphysics were typically verbs. (But probably not taxonomized?)

20    For an overview of the development and present state of information technology see Jack Meadows (1989).

21    There are striking homologies, both phylogenetic and ontogenetic, between semiotic and material 'histories' (e.g., it seems that infants begin to use symbols along with reaching and grasping, to use proto-language along with crawling, and to use language along with walking). In human history, people began to write when they settled down (even here we might detect an ontogenetic parallel!); that is, when they moved from hunting and gathering to husbandry and agriculture. Whether these new practices improved the human condition is open to question (I happen to think they did); what is not open to question is that they changed it.

22    The nearest example I can think of is one where a writing system was replaced by another one, leading to the 'de-mapping' of the first which then remained in existence as an art form – Chinese characters as used by Vietnamese painters, for example.

23    Since I am addicted to maps, let me use the map as an example. Obviously, there is the matter of projection: on a world map, the projection defines the mapmaker's orientation towards the subject-matter (compare projection in the sense in which we use it in systemic grammar); but also towards the user, who is being treated more as an equal with conical projection, whereas Mercator is for outsiders (compare the projection of mood in report and in free indirect discourse). But there are many directly interpersonal signals: choice of colouring (there is one atlas where the colour is so strident it is difficult to read the print), size and variety of typeface, pictorial representations of various kinds, not to mention all the modern descendants of the old-fashioned ships and sea monsters. At the least,

such things indicate degrees of concern for the user; but some are more specific, for example using special symbols to indicate that the mapmaker is only guessing (probability), or that some feature is present only some of the time (like rivers in Australia – usuality). Note in this connection O'Toole's use of systemic metafunctions in interpreting the semiotics of visual art (O'Toole 1990, 1994).

24  There is a case to be made for defining 'writing' in such a way that it includes these other forms of visual semiotic. If the semantic system is part of language (as I think all functional linguists would agree, even if they would interpret its relationship to the lexicogrammar in different ways), then by that token visual systems which can be verbalized, and thus shown to represent language at the semantic level, could be considered to be writing systems. Against this are the following considerations: (1) they are all domain specific and therefore partial, whereas a writing system represents the whole of a language; (2) they are language-neutral, a 'universal character' rather than a writing system; (3) some, at least, cannot be decoded out of their context – that is, you cannot construe the context from the text.

25  For detailed treatment of a fund-raising text, approached by various linguists from different angles, see Mann and Thompson (1992).

26  Martin (e.g., 1992) stratifies the context into three levels, or 'strata', those of register, genre and ideology, and shows that these can be networked, as systems of paradigmatic relations, like the lexicogrammar and the discourse semantics.

27  See Halliday (1989b). It should be pointed out that almost any clause in English can be shown to be in many ways ambiguous in its grammar, but most interpretations are too farfetched to pose real problems to a reader. I am not talking about these. The examples I am talking about are those that are problematic for the readers for whom they are intended (e.g. because of the kinds of grammatical metaphor they are using). It is after one has recognized them as problematic that the 'grammatics' can be brought in to explain the problem – and also to suggest how it might be avoided.

28  See Hasan in this volume, and (1995).

29  See the original project reports by Martin and Rothery (1980–81); the critique by Sawyer and Watson (1987); the reply to this critique (Martin, Christie & Rothery 1985); see also Reid (1987), and Threadgold (1988; 1989).

# References:

Albrow, K.H. 1972. *The English Writing System: Notes towards a Description.* London: Longman (Schools Council Programme in Linguistics and

English Teaching, Papers Series II, vol. 2; reissued London: Schools Council, 1981).

Anderson, J. 1985. *C.O.M.P.U.T.E.R.S in the Language Classroom.* Perth: Australian Reading Association.

Bohm, D. 1980. *Wholeness and the Implicate Order.* London: Routledge & Kegan Paul.

Butt, D. 1988a. 'Randomness, order and the latent patterning of text', in David Birch & Michael O'Toole (eds), *Functions of Style.* London: Pinter.

Butt, D. 1988b. 'Ideational meaning and the "existential fabric" of a poem', in Robin P. Fawcett & David J. Young (eds), *New Developments in Systemic Linguistics, Vol. 2: Theory and Application.* London & New York: Pinter.

Clark, I.F. & Cook B.J. (eds) 1986. *Geological Science: Perspectives of the Earth.* Canberra: Australian Academy of Science.

Graff, Harvey J. 1987. *The Labyrinths of Literacy: Reflections on Literacy Past and Present.* London: Falmer Press.

Halliday, M.A.K. 1988. 'On the language of physical science', in Mohsen Ghadessy (ed.), *Registers of Written English.* London: Pinter.

Halliday, M.A.K. 1989a. *Spoken and Written Language.* Geelong, Vic.: Deakin University Press, 1985 (reissued Oxford: Oxford University Press, 1989).

Halliday, M.A.K. 1989b. 'Some grammatical problems in scientific English', *Australian Review of Applied Linguistics* Series S, no. 6, 13–37 (reprinted in M.A.K. Halliday & J.R. Martin, *Writing Science: Literacy and Discursive Power.* London & Washington, D.C.: Falmer Press, 1993).

Hammond, J. 1990. 'Oral and written language in the educational context', in M.A.K. Halliday, John Gibbons & Howard Nicholas (eds), *Learning, Keeping and Using Language: Selected Papers from the Eighth World Congress of Applied Linguistics, Sydney 1987.* Amsterdam: Benjamins.

Hasan, Ruqaiya 1986. 'The ontogenesis of ideology: an interpretation of mother-child talk', in T. Threadgold, E. Grosz, G. Kress & M.A.K. Halliday (eds), *Semiotics, Ideology, Language.* Sydney: Sydney Association for Studies in Society and Culture (Sydney Studies in Society & Culture No. 3).

Hasan, Ruqaiya 1995. 'The conception of context in text', in Peter H. Fries & Michael Gregory (eds), *Discourse and Meaning in Society: Functional Perspectives – Meaning and Choice in Language: Studies for Michael Halliday, Vol. Two.* Norwood, NJ: Ablex.

Lemke, J.L. 1984. *Semiotics and Education.* Toronto: Victoria University (Toronto Semiotic Circle, Monographs, Working Papers & Prepublications).

Lemke, J.L. 1990. 'Technocratic discourse and ideology', in M.A.K. Halliday, John Gibbons & Howard Nicholas (eds), *Learning, Keeping and Using Language: Selected Papers from the Eighth World Congress of Applied Linguistics, Sydney 1987.* Amsterdam: Benjamins.

Lewis, M.M. 1953. *The Importance of Illiteracy.* London: Harrap.

Luke, C., de Castell, S. & Luke, A. 1989. 'Beyond criticism: the authority of the school textbook', in Suzanne de Castell, Allan Luke & Carmen Luke (eds), *Language, Authority and Criticism: Readings on the School Textbook.* London: Falmer Press.

Mackay, D., Thompson, B. & Schaub, P. 1970. *Breakthrough to Literacy.* London: Longman (for the Schools Council).

Mackay, D., Thompson, B. & Schaub, P. 1978. *Breakthrough to Literacy: Teacher's Manual. Illustrated Edition: The Theory and Practice of Teaching Initial Reading and Writing.* Schools Council Programme in Linguistics and English Teaching. London: Longman (for the Schools Council).

Mann, W.C. & Thompson, S.A. (eds) 1992. *Discourse Description: Diverse Linguistic Analyses of a Fund-raising Text.* Amsterdam: Benjamins.

Martin, J.R. 1986. 'Grammaticalizing ecology: the politics of baby seals and kangaroos', in T. Threadgold, E. Grosz, G. Kress & M.A.K. Halliday (eds), *Semiotics, Ideology, Language.* Sydney: Sydney Association for Studies in Society and Culture (Sydney Studies in Society & Culture No. 3).

Martin, J.R. 1990. 'Literacy in science: learning to handle text as technology', in Frances Christie (ed.), *Literacy in a Changing World.* Melbourne: Australian Council for Educational Research (reprinted in M.A.K. Halliday & J.R. Martin, *Writing Science: Literacy and Discursive Power.* London & Washington DC: Falmer Press, 1993).

Martin, J.R. 1991. 'Nominalization in science and humanities: distilling knowledge and scaffolding text', in Eija Ventola (ed.), *Functional and Systemic Linguistics: Approaches and Uses.* Berlin & New York: Mouton de Gruyter.

Martin, J.R. 1992. *English Text: System and Structure.* Amsterdam: Benjamins.

Martin, J.R. & Rothery, J. 1980–81. 'Writing project report 1 & 2'. *Working Papers in Linguistics 1 & 2.* Sydney: University of Sydney Linguistics Department.

Martin, J.R., Christie, F. & Rothery, J. 1985. 'Social processes in education – a reply to Sawyer & Watson (and others)'. *Working Papers in Linguistics 5.* Sydney: University of Sydney Linguistics Department.

Meadows, J. 1989. *Info-technology: Changing the Way we Communicate.* London: Cassell.

Mohan, B. 1986. *Language and Content.* Reading, MA: Addison-Wesley.

Moore, H. 1990. 'Process vs product, or down with the opposition', in M.A..K. Halliday, John Gibbons & Howard Nicholas (eds), *Learning, Keeping and Using Language: Selected Papers from the Eighth World Congress of Applied Linguistics, Sydney 1987.* Amsterdam: Benjamins.

Mountford, J. 1990. 'Language and writing systems', in N.E. Collinge (ed.), *An Encyclopedia of Language.* London & New York: Routledge.

Olson, D.R. 1989. 'On the language and authority of textbooks', in

Suzanne de Castell, Allan Luke & Carmen Luke (eds), *Language, Authority and Criticism: Readings on the School Textbook*. London: Falmer Press.

O'Toole, L.M. 1990. 'A systemic-functional semiotics of art', *Semiotica* 82(3/4).

O'Toole, L.M. 1994. *The Language of Displayed Art*. London: Leicester University Press.

Painter, C. & Martin, J.R. (eds) 1987. *Writing to Mean: Developing Genres across the Curriculum*. Applied Linguistics Association of Australia, Occasional Paper No. 8.

Pearce, J., Thornton, G. & Mackay, D. 1989. 'The programme in linguistics and English teaching, University College London, 1964–1971', in Ruqaiya Hasan & J.R. Martin (eds), *Language Development: Learning Language, Learning Culture – Meaning and Choice in Language: Studies presented to Michael Halliday, Vol. One*. Norwood, NJ: Ablex (Advances in Discourse Processes XXVII).

Reid, I. (ed.) 1987. *The Place of Genre in Learning: Current Debates*. Geelong, Vic.: Deakin University Press.

Sawyer, W. & Watson, K. 1987. 'Questions of genre'. *The Teaching of English* 52.

Taylor, C. 1979. *The English of High School Textbooks*. Canberra: Australian Government Publishing Service (Education Research and Development Committee, Report No. 18).

Thibault, P.J. 1991a. *Social Semiotics as Praxis: Text, Social Meaning Making and Nabokov's "Ada"*. Minneapolis: University of Minnesota Press.

Thibault, P.J. 1991b. 'Grammar, technocracy, and the noun: technocratic values and cognitive linguistics', in Eija Ventola (ed.), *Recent Systemic and other Functional Views on Language*. Berlin: Mouton de Gruyter.

Threadgold, T. 1988. 'The genre debate', *Southern Review* 21(3), November.

Threadgold, T. 1989. 'Talking about genre: ideologies and incompatible discourses', *Cultural Studies* 3(1).

# 12

---

# Literacy, everyday talk
# and society[1]

## RUQAIYA HASAN

## 1 Introduction

One problem with the word *Literacy* is that it is semantically saturated: in the long history of education, it has not simply meant
different things to different generations, but also different things
to different persons in the same generation (Luke 1988). This
might be read as a sign that in the somewhat fading academic jargon of yesterday, the term is ripe for deconstruction. My chapter is
an attempt to do just that by enquiring into the many meanings of
literacy – but not simply as an exercise in empty semanticisation: I
believe the meanings assigned to *literacy* are significant for what
they imply. So for each interpretation it should be possible to ask:
if this interpretation of literacy is accepted, what would this imply
about the pupils and the teachers engaged in its processes? What
about the pedagogic practices relevant to the achievement of its
goals? And what conceptions of learning and knowledge would
this interpretation presuppose? Sociologists of education (cf.
Bernstein 1975, 1986, 1987, 1990; Bourdieu and Passeron 1977)
have argued that a close relationship exists between a society's
pedagogic institutions and the principles underlying its social
structure. Their theories highlight the logic following which
today's pedagogic institutions functioning as the powerful arm of
the state tend also to be the prime site for the reproduction and
(closely watched) production of knowledge. This chapter will
draw attention to similar concerns with specific reference to literacy pedagogy as perhaps the most crucial pedagogic action in
today's world. To approach literacy this way furnishes a much
wider context for the literacy debate which has often appeared
to be concerned only with formulating THE valid definition of

literacy, with rival definitions typically tending to be couched in terms of the goals of literacy. But if the definition of literacy necessarily implicates wider social processes, then the affirmation of some definition – some goal(s) – represents not a conclusion, but a beginning. The goals of literacy can hardly have a value in and of themselves: they need to be seen in the context of the wider social environment which is at once the enabling condition and the enabled product of literacy pedagogy. The multiplicity of meanings ascribed to literacy suggests that it is a multi-faceted process embracing phenomena of different kinds; the controversies raging today around *literacy* tend to assume that only some one facet is important; the others can be safely ignored. I will suggest that this view is open to question: to understand literacy is to understand how the various facets enter into the formation of that complex whole which we call *literacy*.

## 2 Literacy: an initial exploration

The referential range of *literacy* is well captured by *The Macquarie Dictionary* which glosses it as *the state of being literate; possession of education*, claiming also that being *literate* is being *able to read and write, having education*. These formulations suggest continua: being able to read/write or having education is not a simple 'yes/no' affair. At the more advanced end of the continuum is, for example Marx, able to 'read' Hegel and to write *Das Kapital*, while nearer the initiate end is the 'literate' person so labelled in some countries for the purposes of literacy census on the grounds of merely being able to recognise her/his name in some script. One might protest that a person just able to recognise her name is neither literate nor educated. But in making this protest, one is implicitly recommending a specific point on the continuum as the 'true' referent of the terms, identifying 'the' norm for being judged literate and educated. It is reasonable to ask: who ratifies the validity of this norm? Where do such ratifiers of norms derive their legitimacy from?

Quite obviously preference for any standard of literacy is ultimately evaluative: it is a covert demand to accept a certain view point; and this inevitably raises questions about the basis of its own validity. On the other hand, this act of evaluation is more or less thrust on us: where the referential space is as elastic as with literacy, a preference for some point or other on the continuum is unavoidable. So it seems apposite to ask whether the literacy of Marx and that of the initiate are the same kind of social and cognitive facts, whether a preference for the kind of literacy demonstrated by Marx is just a matter of social prejudice, simply pandering to dominant interests of the elite. If not, what makes the two different?

An important step toward answering these questions may be taken by treating the referential indeterminacy of the term *literacy* as a positive starting point: literacy is not the name of some fixed state; it refers to a developmental process. This implies, in turn, that its nature can be known effectively through the practices its development enables. If literacy is an ongoing process whose present transforms into its future stages, then each of its stages should be identifiable by reference to some distinction in practices that the process of literacy at that stage enables. Let us ask, then, what practice is specific to the initial stage – to the very onset of literacy?

## 2.1   Defining the onset of literacy

Dictionaries are agreed on reading/writing as the *sine qua non* of literacy, but reading/writing are specific and complex practices; they cannot be taken as the onset of literacy itself. Underlying these more complex activities there must be a simpler less specific ability. I suggest that this less specific ability is *the grasp of the principle of representation*. This ability consists of relating two qualitatively different types of phenomenon – an expression and a content – to each other so that the significance of one is understood in terms of the other. So becoming literate in the sense of being able to read/write presupposes the ability to 'see' a phenomenon as 'standing for' something other than itself. In fact, the ability to relate expression and content in this way is a necessary condition for using any semiotic system whatever. From this point of view, the fundamental attribute for the onset of literacy is the ability to engage in acts of meaning: to be an initiate in literacy is to be able to make sense.

Defining the onset of literacy as the *ability to make sense* construes it as a variety of semiotic praxis: literate acts are acts of semiosis. This conceptualisation of the basic nature of literacy is significant on several counts. First, it emphasises the commonalities between different classes of sign, for example, a gesture, a symptom, a picture, a painting, a sonnet, and so on. One thing these have in common is their nature as signs: as signs, their coming into being is a licence to their being interpreted, while the fact that they are capable of being interpreted makes them signs. Secondly, interpretation is at once both formally and socially grounded. It is formally grounded in that a sign comes to be that sign, having that interpretation, by virtue of its relation to other signs in the system; it is socially grounded because the meaning of a sign becomes tangible for the user in the context of his/her life-situations; in other words, the relations of one sign to other signs have to be perceived as such and so by interpreters who are by definition socially positioned. Thirdly, and related to the last point, if the interpretation of a sign relies on the user's experience of how it functions in her/his life-situations, and if even in the same community different persons' life-situations differ, it follows that their variant experience of the sign's function in the living of life will contribute to the development of a disposition for variant interpretations of what might be called *the same sign* from some point of view. Finally, for most of us the experience of signing involves co-interpreting signs from a number of distinct sign systems: for instance, the picture of the skull and cross-bones with the legend *Danger! High Voltage!* combines conventionalised pictorial and linguistic signs to create a single semiotic whole.[2] The computer screen often presents a configuration of the pictorial and the verbal. Sign interpretation is thus entirely context sensitive – it is sensitive to the context of its own system; to the users' context of social situations; and it is sensitive to other simultaneously operating sign systems.

If these characteristics apply to all sign systems alike, then clearly the onset of literacy bears no special relation to reading/writing which are specifically language-based practices. There are other semiotic systems than just language; and they are just as amenable to interpretation. This might tempt one to conclude that the term *literacy* should be decoupled from the specific semiotic system of language, that it should be construed simply as the ability to make sense. In fact, this view of literacy already exists in pedagogic discourse where many scholars prefer to talk about *literacies*. The use of the plural underlines the assumption that literacy, at least in one of its senses,[3] consists in making sense of *anything* that can be/is taken as expression. There is more than a hint in the literature that it is conservative to define literacy as simply making sense of linguistic signs, as most dictionaries do; that the practice unjustifiably 'privileges' language; and that it is desirable – progressive? egalitarian? – to give literacy a definition that is neutral as to the semiotic character of what is being interpreted. How justified are these positions?

Before we begin to answer this question, it is best to be clear that the views recounted above involve two related but somewhat different positions: (i) that the term *literacy* should be decoupled from any specific sign system whatever; and (ii) that *literacy* should be decoupled specifically from language. We will examine both these positions in turn.

## 2.2 Literacy as simply making sense

Typically, definitions of literacy have been formulated in the context of pedagogic goals. From this point of view literacy, as simply the ability to make sense, raises some serious problems. For example, if this definition is accepted, then what pedagogic practices would be deemed relevant to the achievement of its goals? Indeed, what precisely are these goals, and what would count as evidence for their successful achievement? What attributes would be implied as necessary to engage as teachers or pupils in the processes of developing such literacy? Attempts to answer these questions highlight the problems in conceptualising literacy as simply concerned with sense-making without relating the process of sense-making to some specific signing modality: it appears impossible to devise any pedagogic program around the notion. Literacy so defined is unteachable in any known or imaginable schooling context.

Part of the problem is of course that while for purposes of analysis one might dissociate the act of interpretation from that which is being interpreted, in actual practice this is about as impossible as 'languaging' without using grammar! Note also that there exists the term *semiosis* to refer to this analytically isolated process of interpretation, but the idea that there can actually occur any process of semiosis dissociated from any semiotic system(s) whatever is simply nonsense. The semantic structure underlying terms such as *interpretation, making sense, semiosis*, etc., is inherently relational, implying a duality; the terms refer to processes which relate two phenomena – the meaning and the form – to each other. One cannot just make sense; one must make sense of some type of sign. And since signs are sensitive to the context of their own system, a specific sign cannot be interpreted independently of the system to which it pertains. Literacy, as the ability to make sense in dissociation from specific sign systems, is thus an incoherent concept; interpretation has to be anchored in some signing modality or other. Hence the need for a modifier, for example, in expressions such as *media literacy, map literacy*, and so on.

This does not mean that we have to abandon our claim about the nature of the onset of literacy; we have already seen that to think of literacy as founded on the grasp of the principle of interpretation reveals the sign-based nature of this process, allowing us to deduce certain important characteristics of the process (cf. section 2.1. above). But to say that the onset of literacy consists in the grasp of the principle of representation is simply to claim that the process of literacy, whatever its specific evolving character, cannot proceed without this ability which is thus its necessary condition. By contrast, conceptualising the entire gamut of the process of literacy as simply the ability to interpret, is to be highly reductive, elevating the necessary condition to the status of a sufficient one! This is problematic not least because the nature of literacy is not static. And if literacy is an ongoing process, then its onset must be differentiated in some critical way from its more evolved stages. The conclusion seems inevitable that literacy cannot be taken to refer to just the ability to interpret; the term cannot be meaningfully decoupled from specific semiotic system(s). But does this necessarily mean the term should be coupled, as it has traditionally been, with language?

## 2.3    Literacy as language-based semiosis

My brief response to this question is to say that in the last resort the issue is purely terminological since the character and role of language in human life is such that irrespective of what name is given to its development, it will always have an important position in both pedagogic and everyday contexts: reference to it will need to be made. It is certainly true that language is only one among many semiotic systems and that in many important ways the various sign systems are alike (see section 2.1. above). This, however, does not mean that they are identical in all respects. For example, they differ considerably in their potentiality. The potentiality of a sign system can be estimated by reference to how far the system impinges on the significant life-situations of a community; the more it does so, the higher its potentiality.

A sign system's having a higher potential is not a MORAL GOOD of any kind; however, borrowing the jargon of economics *à la* Bourdieu, one might claim that a sign system with a higher potential will have *higher investment returns* for those who can appropriate it; by the same token, those who cannot, face a liability. So it seems reasonable to argue that control over a sign system with a higher potential is relatively more important, and there is no virtue in treating all sign systems on an equal footing. Besides, no matter how successfully one mouths the jargon of revolutionary discourse, the issue is not that the various sign systems – or even the various disciplines – must be treated impartially; the issue worthy of revolution, if one is really keen on bringing one about, is rather that the users of the sign systems must enjoy an equal opportunity for appropriating higher potential sign systems! The term *privileged* is often used in educational discourse almost as an emotion-laden war cry. But to say that some semiotic system, for example, language, is being privileged at the cost of others simply because it receives greater attention, reveals a lack of analytic acuity; there is no attempt in such declarations to engage with the variability in the efficacy of the various sign systems in the life of the community. One can hardly deny that, compared to most sign systems, language has an exceedingly high potential; its investment value is bound to be a good deal higher as by its very nature it will always impinge more on the production and maintenance of social life whether in its *esoteric* or its *mundane* manifestation. We need no deep theoretical insight to establish that neither of these manifestations of human social life can come about in the absence of language. Moreover, contrary to popular belief, the rise of multi-media has further strengthened the position of language as a hidden accomplice in many crucial social processes. The more reluctant we are to recognise overtly the importance of language, the more dangerous it can be as a tool of domination, both inside and outside pedagogic contexts.

These considerations suggest that if the term *literacy* is decoupled from language, then a language-based interpretive praxis will still resurface under some other name[4] still holding an important position in the pedagogic context: language is just too powerful a means of control to be ignored or set aside in the prime controlling environment of pedagogic action. It is true that none of the above arguments necessarily force us actually to retain the traditional coupling of literacy with language, but it is also obvious that such a coupling will have to be recognised under some name or other; there seems to be no advantage whatever in re-semanticising literacy and coining another to take its place! In my view what would be helpful is to recognise the conventional reference of the term, without accepting conventional views about language. So this debate might be concluded by saying that literacy develops into a *specific kind of semiosis*; its specificity resides in the fact that *this kind of semiosis uses language as its resource*. While the onset of literacy is an undifferentiated stage, entry into literacy processes has a relatively more specific character: it is this which differentiates the unqualified term *literacy* from such coined phrases as *computer literacy, map literacy*, and so on.[5] This perspective returns us to the traditional dictionary definition of literacy but with some significant differences: unlike the dictionary, we conceptualise literacy as an inherently variable semiotic process without restricting it to reading and writing.

## 3   Learning literacy – teaching literacy

Literacy in the sense of using language to mean has two simultaneous lines of development. In the first place, literacy in the sense of linguistic semiosis develops in the context of *mundane* or *quotidian* activities. The child's learning of language is taken for granted. Or to be more precise, it is a completely unremarkable fact that by a certain maturational stage every normal child will have begun to speak to those around it; what draws attention to itself is rather the absence of this semiotic development. Moving from the physiologically mediated, pre-semiotic behaviour (Trevarthen 1974; Trevarthen and Hubley 1977) to the individual-based protolinguistic stage, the child finally enters the language of its immediate community – its mother tongue (Halliday 1975; Painter 1984). And although technically this completes what is known as 'language acquisition', the process of learning how to mean is in actual fact a life-long one. Ways of interacting with differentiated others, of engaging in varied processes, continue to be learned in the course of the daily living of life. Obviously, this quotidian development of literacy in the sense of growing prowess in semiosis by language is shaped to a very large extent by the learners' life-situations – by their social positioning – and the mode of literate engagement in this line of development tends to be the spoken word. The learners' daily living of life might or might not also introduce them to the mysteries of the world of print. Increasingly, in the Western world at least, all segments of the society are 'exposed' to print, and it seems reasonable to believe that in the natural line of literacy development most members of the society come to have at least a passive acquaintance with writing. However, not all members of the community will naturally develop 'command' of all forms of written and/or spoken discourse, and there will be definitely some segment which will not engage in meaning by writing along their natural line of literacy development.

Alongside this 'natural' quotidian line of literacy development is a second, *exotic* or specialised one: this is THE literacy development as it is conceptualised in the official pedagogic contexts. And while in all societies known to us this line of literacy development both chronologically postdates and logically relies on the gains from the quotidian one, it is this second line of literacy development that is the more socially salient, the more politically effective, in the sense that those whose literacy development successfully follows this route are, all else being equal, also very likely to be socially saliently located. This line of literacy development also happens to be the one that is much closer to the dictionary's view of literacy. It is here that the spoken mode must be less valued and writing must be elevated to a higher status,[6] the everyday modes of interaction are underrated; the specialised ones are given prestige.

There are some important points of contrast between these two lines of literacy development. Building on Vygotsky's notion of 'intellectualisation' (Vygotsky 1978; Hasan 1992b; 1995b), I would claim that typically there are two levels of intellectualisation of language: one, a speaking subject's self-conscious view of what language is like, and the other, an unself-conscious 'feel' for language. It is the latter that is in fact more important in giving shape and character to the speaking subject's actual semiotic practices, whereas the former is typically produced in lay discourses about language. In the quotidian line of development, the unself-conscious feel for language is dialectically engaged with the speaking subject's social life, shaping and being shaped by it. In the exotic – specialised or pedagogic – line of development, it is the self-conscious view of language that has supremacy, which is to say the view of language here is not that by which we live as socio-semiotically active creatures, but rather one which is in many respects a counterfeit. Typically, underlying this line of literacy development is a conception of language far removed from language as social semiotic practice, and typically, the goals of exotic literacy development are consciously set, while in the quotidian line of development there is hardly any awareness of goals – there is simply social action, successful or otherwise. Further, both the view of language and the consciously designed goals for pedagogic literacy development derive from needs that are not necessarily felt to be needs by all the learning subjects, whereas logically in the quotidian line of development this disjunction just cannot occur. Finally, the goals set for the pedagogic literacy development are objectively better suited for, and familiar to, some section(s) of the community, thus perpetuating the inequalities of social positioning through the workings of the pedagogic system.

It is in the uneasy co-existence of these two lines of literacy development that the secret of the complexity of the notion of literacy lies: this is where we must look to trace the origin of our problems. Literacy in the sense of untutored quotidian language development without the intervention of official pedagogy is already complex enough – simply because speaking is a social act of immense consequence; literacy in the sense of language development, following the image of language which is self-consciously conceptualised by largely linguistically unsophisticated pedagogues, compounds the complexity even further. In the following sections, for lack of space, I shall directly approach the various conceptions of literacy in the pedagogic context, referring to the mundane line of literacy development only occasionally.

### 3.1   Teaching literacy[7]

The dictionaries firmly define literacy as the ability to read and write. This formulation gives pride of place in the activities of literacy to the grasp of what is known in linguistics as the orthographic system – the correspondence between the marks on the paper and the sounds 'of' the words of a language. This particular cycle of expression-content – what written marks signify what sounds – is, however, a later development both in the history of individuals and in that of the human race (Goody 1968; Goody and Watt 1972; Halliday 1985). So whoever begins learning to read and/or write must already have been using some language as a resource for making meanings by speaking, and there are some languages of the world which, as the popular phrase puts it, have still not been 'reduced' to writing. With literacy defined as the use of the linguistic system for making meanings, control over the ortho-graphy-phonology correspondence is not a necessary part of being literate, since meanings can be made without the use of orthography.[8] Indeed, some scholars (e.g., Basso 1980) have argued that the invention of orthography adds nothing to the acts of meaning-making; that all it does is to shift the making of mean-ing from one channel, the phonic-acoustic, to another, the graphic-visual. Others (e.g., Goody 1977; Olson 1977) have sug-gested, explicitly or implicitly, that the invention of orthography has been a significant step in the evolution of humanity. I shall say no more on this important controversy (for a discussion of the rel-evant issues see Halliday (1985) and also this volume).

## 3.2 Recognition literacy

It is no secret that the correspondence between orthography and phonology forms the major thrust of literacy teaching in many schools. Most of us have gone through the *bat, pat, hat, mat* stage in our schooling; most of us remember the wise words 'dot your i's and cross your t's'. Such injunctions are designed to teach us how orthography and phonology in calibration act as the expression of the lexical items *bat, pat, hat, mat*, and how to form letters the right way so the appearance of, say, *tame* is not confused with that of *lame*, etc. Though much has been written against the limiting nature of this conception of literacy development which focuses on teaching sound-shape correspondence, and which is known in the trade as the *coding approach*, it remains alive and well in many schools even today. A remarkable thing about this entire process is that in the intensity of the focus on expression – what the shape looks like, what sound it represents – the issue of meaning can and often does get ignored (Kress 1982; Wells 1987). In coding literacy the more complex forms of meaning-making by language remain alien to the developmental program. This unwarranted focus on expression leads to a fragmentation of linguistic facts. Thus words are grouped and brought to the pupils' attention not on the basis of the words' meaning potential but because of their sound-shape correspondences, either because this correspondence is regular (cf. *bat, pat*) or because it is irregular (cf. *shun, ocean, nation, commission*). Language as a mode of social action is ignored; language as inventory of forms has precedence. So pupils may be asked to 'turn' active sentences into passive; to cite tense conjugation of verbs, for example, *catch, latch, shoot, loot*; to find a substitute for some word. I will refer to this entire spectrum as **recognition literacy**.

Underlying this kind of pedagogic literacy development program is a conception of language far removed from language as social semiotic practice. This is not to claim that the kinds of relation which form the centre of attention in recognition literacy are unnecessary for the development of the ability to make linguistic meanings; on the contrary, these relations constitute important means for meaning. The problem is not that recognition literacy is concerned with script, or grammatical features, or lexical paraphrases which are expendable elements of language; they are not. The problem is that, in the absence of an approach to language which sees it as a mode of social action, the nature and function of these aspects of language is badly conceived, and worse still, these unfounded conceptions have often become the very end of literacy teaching in the pedagogic context. Most textbooks are witness to the focus on the isolated sentence, the recognition of paradigm memberships, and so on. It is not surprising then that the pupil's progress is usually measured precisely in terms of these 'skills' – how good the pupil is at giving the definition of the parts of speech, of spelling trick words, conjugating verbs with exceptional patterns, the list goes on and on. Note, however, that the popular idea of what literacy is all about is very close to this letter-sound-word correspondence: when politicians, ministers of education, and newspapers talk about the forever declining standards of literacy, they very often have in mind the spelling and punctuation conventions, the fairly obvious features of linguistic form, for example, for English, such features as the concord between subject and finite verb, tense sequence in hypotactic clause complexes, the contrast between *that* and *which* in the defining relative clause, etc. They have hardly any idea of grammar as a resource for meaning (Halliday 1975, 1994).

What expertise would a teacher need in order to be able to teach the elements of recognition literacy? It is easy to underestimate the degree of expertise required for the purpose, *provided* the teaching is to be done with understanding. The relations between the patterns of language are not transparent: for example, the principles underlying the calibration of orthography and phonology in English are very complex (Albrow 1972); and the same is true of the lexicogrammar and semantics (Halliday 1994; Matthiessen 1995). Teachers need this expertise to understand the nature of that which they are teaching, but they seldom possess such understanding. The irony lies in the fact that if they did possess this expertise, then it is highly likely that they would also recognise the futility of attempting to develop literacy this way. Since this understanding is more often lacking than not, the so-called rules of spelling, punctuation, and grammar that the teachers teach are rules *by fiat*: someone has set up those standards, and the teachers are supposed to inculcate them in their pupils. This implies they have to be willing to accept certain 'facts' without seeking explanations. Obviously, when these features of recognition literacy are stated overtly, very few would admit to supporting it. Yet the surprising fact remains that it is the most persistent form of teaching literacy.[9]

The learning done by the pupils in recognition literacy can be discussed at least on two levels. Assuming that the teaching is successful, the pupils will learn to recognise the correspondences that form the centre of such pedagogic action. This is the manifest level of learning. At a deeper level, the pupils also learn the value of conformity. Recognition literacy has limited ways of answering a *why* question. So if you ask: why does the letter *b* represent the sound /b/? why is the subject typically in concord with the finite verb in the English language? why and where can *why* substitute *what is the reason that?*, these questions can only be answered either by appealing to tradition – this is just how we do it – or by appealing to the internal properties of language – this is what language is like. Aspects of language thus appear either blind tradition or entirely unmotivated form – a view that is accepted even by some linguists. We know that the norms of language children are taught in school are precisely those which conform to the practices of a certain segment of the society. But since, according to recognition literacy, linguistic choice is arbitrary, the social motivations for the choice of a particular variety as the favoured one in the pedagogic environment cannot be effectively highlighted. Standards of correctness are simply given, to be accepted not to be questioned. At a deeper level of learning, then, the underlying message of this approach is to go on doing what others have been doing, to regard language as not socially motivated, and perhaps to conclude that at least some systems of knowledge are not open to questioning. By presenting language as pure form, recognition literacy creates an ideology of language as plastic and powerless. As pure form, language only has the power to reflect pre-existing meanings passively, just as a mirror might reflect passively without playing any active part in the creation and maintenance of that which it reflects. This is very far from the role language actually plays in the mundane sphere of our lives where much of our social universe is created and maintained with the complicity of language. A good amount of disquiet about the teaching of literacy can be attributed precisely to what the pupils are learning in learning recognition literacy. But just as the lay perception of literacy is very close to recognition literacy, so also popular ideas about the nature of language itself are in agreement with the ideas about language that underlie this view of literacy. And it is not simply the proverbial layman who shares this emasculated picture of language which underlies recognition literacy. Talk to academics, and you will find that irrespective of their intellectual prowess in some field of learning or other, they too are very likely to echo precisely the same view. This is not surprising since most of us have been schooled in recognition literacy, which remains the most popular pedagogic perspective even today.[10]

The persistence of recognition literacy might make one think that it must be enabling in some significant way, or else why invest so many resources, so much energy and time to it? But the fact of the matter is that recognition literacy persists thanks to ill-informed politicians in search of power and equally mis-informed but opinionated educators who believe that simply because being tutored by life they can use language to mean, therefore they know all about the nature of language. For the hours of schooling we put into this futile mode of developing literacy, the return is pathetic. Certainly, many of us who have been taught a second language largely by methods akin to recognition literacy have been dismayed to find that after years of such learning, we are not able to use that language for exchanging meanings: it is one thing to turn an active sentence into a passive as a formal exercise, it is quite another to know where to use the one or the other. When this same pedagogic method is applied – as it is very often – to the development of the pupils' mother tongue, this creates a peculiar situation. On the one hand, it contributes very little, if anything, to the actual development of the pupils' ability to use language effectively to mean; on the other, thanks to the quotidian line of literacy development, this fact remains largely invisible because at least some pupils' abilities to use language develop in the 'right' direction anyway. There are, of course, those whose natural literacy development does not converge with the direction required by the pedagogic context. For example, they are not able to answer comprehension questions or to write reports or essays satisfactorily. In these cases the responsibility for the failure can be laid at the pupils' door: after all, the other pupils are doing well with the same 'teaching', aren't they? It is no secret that the pupils whose natural development diverges from the pedagogic standards typically belong to the disadvantaged classes of the community. The construction of a specific section of the community as willing failures despite 'good teaching' is a strong reason for disquiet with the teaching of recognition literacy in schools.

Logically, the ideals of recognition literacy demand pupils who are not likely to ask questions, who are willing to follow wherever authority in the guise of the teacher leads them; they have to be pupils who do not expect their educational knowledge of language to have any direct relevance to what they do with language in the living of their life. To use Bernstein's descriptions these pupils have to be 'flexible and conformist'. So recognition literacy would flourish best in societies that are authoritarian, with a routinisation of conduct, or at least where the nature of educational knowledge is non-negotiable. How is it then that recognition literacy can be still found in practice in the so-called progressive societies? There are at least three reasons for this. First, progressive societies, despite their proclamations, are authoritarian, and possess hidden mechanisms for the preservation of the power of authority. Secondly, the cost of implementing recognition literacy is substantially low: it is low both in terms of what it costs to appear to be teaching literacy and also in terms of who it is that suffers from such teaching. Those who suffer most, particularly when recognition literacy is applied to mother-tongue teaching-learning contexts, come from the disadvantaged groups in a community; their voice is not the voice of authority, and it is not represented in the schooling systems. Finally, an equally important reason for the perpetuation of recognition literacy is the ideology of language it perpetuates. When it comes to ideas about language, we are caught in something of a catch-22 situation. Generally, thanks to being schooled in recognition literacy, we tend to mis-recognise the nature of language, failing to appreciate its character as a social semiotic; so when it comes to designing language curricula, then given our mistaken views of language, it is not surprising that our creations leave much to be desired. We give recognition literacy in schools to get back recognition literacy in the curriculum, to perpetuate the mis-recognition of language by being schooled in recognition literacy! This cycle recycles itself. It should, however, be obvious that if literacy counts as the ability to use language for making meanings, then recognition literacy does not really meet that ideal. The disquiet against literacy teaching practices in schools should not be attributed to the privileging of language, as some scholars put it. It would be nearer the mark to attribute it to common ignorance about language.

## 3.3   Literacy and language use

This discussion of recognition literacy has emphasised that if literacy is seen as linguistic semiosis, then the *ability to read and write*, which dictionaries cite as the quality of being literate, cannot be equated simply with the pairing of certain visual shapes with certain sounds, and being educated cannot be synonymous with knowing the conjugations of weak and strong verbs. What more is needed, then, to make reading and writing semiotic acts, and how does it – whatever that 'it' is – contribute to being educated? To answer these questions, let us focus on that aspect of language which is largely ignored by recognition literacy.

What is missing from recognition literacy is any concern with those processes that lie at the centre of the actual use of language. When these processes are taken into account, the focus is shifted from fragmentary language to contextualised language. I am using the term *contextualised language* to draw attention to two types of context that are central to any language use: one is the *verbal context* of the ongoing talk, and the other is the *situational context.* I have already suggested (in section 2.1.) that a sign can take on meaning only in the context of other signs, and that signing always occurs in some context of social situation. Language in use is no exception. It does not come in a fragmented form as words, phrases, sentences arranged in lists according to some formal or semantic feature; it comes as *texts*. This means it has both the property of texture and of structure. The sayings that the speakers produce typically bear some relevance to what else has been or is about to be said; at the same time, the way that a talk progresses as a whole displays the speakers' awareness of the relevance of the occasion of talk to that talk (Halliday and Hasan 1976, 1985). This quality of *double relevance* is such a typical feature of linguistic acts of meaning that where this feature is absent, the absence is taken as an indication of some kind of pathology. So, if literacy is a variety of semiosis that consists in linguisitc acts of meaning, and linguistic acts of meaning entail the production of contextualised language, then an important part of literacy development should be the development of *discursive ability*, that is, the ability to engage in discourses which display this *double relevance*.

Scholars are agreed that in the very early stages of the development of their language, children's language use does not display this double relevance. Speakers are not born with discursive ability; its emergence is a developmental phenomenon, which begins sometime after the *protolinguistic* stage (Halliday 1973; 1975; Bruner 1975; Dore 1977; McTear 1985; Painter 1984). As the child approaches the end of the *transition* which heralds entry into the mother tongue, the contribution of the social experience of talk comes to play a more decisive part (Halliday 1976; Andersen 1986; Painter 1989). Through their interactions with others in their environment, children naturally develop double relevance. They learn that signs relate to signs, and the act of signing as a whole relates to what one uses signing for. This is not to say that children know consciously about either kind of relevance – what it consists in – it is simply to say that they know how to 'act relevant' using their language.

But doesn't this way of looking at literacy development dismiss the need for the pedagogy of literacy in the sense of development of discursive ability? Since discursive ability develops 'naturally' through the use of language for meaning-making in social contexts, it follows that, pedagogy or no pedagogy, as speaking social beings we will have this ability. In fact, even the kindergarten learners come to school already with considerable discursive ability. Why do we need literacy development programs to teach them this same thing? The answer to these questions is implied in my discussion of the natural, quotidian line of literacy development. The naturally developed literacy of social subjects will be socioculturally specific: different segments of a society will be literate in different ways, depending on what variety of language they use, for what, and with whom. As a modality of meaning-making, language is riven by diversity precisely because it is so deeply implicated in creating social boundaries: men do not speak as women do; old people do not speak as young do; city-dwellers do not speak as people in the villages do; and certainly, members from different socio-economic strata speak differently. This being the case, children from different segments of the society come to school speaking differently: their literacy development will take different forms. Because this literacy is the product of the natural line of development, their voice will be the voice of their own immediate group, their own speech fellowship (Firth 1957).

### 3.3.1   Language as social action and linguistic variation

In formal linguistics, speaking differently has been treated as simply some difference in expression (Labov 1972; Trudgill 1978); so members of a community are said to speak different *social dialects* with *different accents*. This is a limited view of what it means to speak differently as other forms of variation exist which implicate meanings, not simply expression. Consider first the notion of *register variation* (Halliday, McIntosh and Strevens 1964), or *speech variety* (Hymes 1972). This difference has to do with the fact that people talk differently about the same thing depending on who they are talking to, apropos of performing what social activity, and how their interaction with the other is organised. Take, as an example, talk about the *water cycle*. A teacher engaged in the social activity of presenting information about the water cycle to a class of nine year olds will talk differently from one who is addressing a high school class in performing the same activity, and, compared to both these, another teacher doing the same thing with a class of university students will talk differently yet again. Then again, the same teachers will talk differently to the same learners depending on whether they are presenting information or revising already presented information. For example, a presentation lesson is likely to be more monologic, even though spoken, while, by comparison, the revision one would tend to be dialogic. Consider yet another vector of differentiation. Suppose that we have a chapter in a textbook, which presents information about the water cycle. We might think of this as the written analogue to the spoken presentation lesson. Here again we will find that the written presentation lesson – the textbook chapter – will differ according to which group of learners it is aimed at, as Cross (1991) has demonstrated. So given the same subject matter, teachers will talk differently depending on what activity is going on, presentation or revision; who they are addressing, young school children or university students; and whether the same activity is being carried out by speaking or writing, lesson to present information or chapter to do the same. So variation in register is motivated by variation in social activity, in speaker-addressee relations, and by variation in the controls on the progression of this interaction. These contextual factors are relevant to both what overall structure the interaction will have, and what meanings and wordings will appear in the texts. The structure of a presentation lesson will be different from that of a revision one; the strucutre of a presentation lesson addressed to university students will be different from that addressed to the high school pupils; and a spoken presentation lesson will have a different structure from that which it would have when presented as a chapter. The forms of discourse, that is, the meanings we mean and the wordings with which we make these meanings, thus differ from one social process to another, and the double relevance that I spoke of as the defining characteristic of discursive ability has its genesis in this relation between the social contexts and the linguistic meanings typically associated with them (Halliday and Hasan 1976, 1985; Hasan 1995a).

One very important fact to recognise about register variation is that not every member of a society enjoys the possibility of engaging in every kind of social activity: the limits placed on these possibilities are entirely social, even though sometimes they are presented as 'natural'. For example, take cooking: in Pakistan, only women engage in this activity, unless it is performed as a professional activity, carrying cash in return for labour, when it is typically performed by men; bathing children, feeding and dressing them, domestic cleaning, chores around the house are typically women's activities, whether as paid labour or as mistress of the house; the pursuit of professions such as driving taxis, trains, other vehicles or acting as mechanics, gas-pump attendants etc., are men's activities; playing chess, bridge, etc., is typically a male (upper) middle-class activity; only women of the highest social class may engage in these activities. Similarly, certain sorts of relationship are enjoyed by some but not by others. On the

Indo-Pakistani sub-continent, relations between males and females are typically conceptualised in terms of kinship. A woman is someone's wife, mother, daughter, daughter-in-law, sister, etc. Up until quite recently, being just 'good colleagues' was not recognised as a legitimate relation between a man and a woman. What all this means is that the registers prevalent in a society as a whole are not 'available' in the normal course of living to every speaker in that society because people engage in different social processes depending on their 'place' in society; in fact, this is partially how their place in society is recognised. (Try presenting a budget speech without 'being' the federal treasurer; try being a federal treasurer without being able to make a budget speech!) Register variation needs to be seen from two perspectives in the present context: first, the use of language varies depending on variation in social processes; and secondly, not all speakers enjoy the possibility of engaging in all social processes. It follows that pupils will come to the school with differing discursive abilities, with differing experience of participation in registers – simply because of the differences in their social position. Speaking in the 'voice of one's speech fellowship' will refer not simply to accent and social dialect but also to *register repertoire* – what people use their language for, what social processes they engage in.

### 3.3.2    Semantic variation and natural literacy development

This brings us to the next kind of linguistic variation involving meaning. It is true that the possibility of engaging in social processes is not the same for every group in a society, but of course the groups do not differ **absolutely** in this respect. There will certainly be some social processes in every society that would be in common to its larger segments. For example, most people will have the experience of talking to neighbours, swapping jokes or telling stories to friends or kin, and most mothers will attempt to control their children's behaviour, or give them information about the world, and so on. But while most people might do the same thing, their ways of meaning by way of carrying out these activities could be critically different. Speakers are oriented towards different ways of saying and meaning depending on the material conditions of their social existence. It is this meaning orientation that Bernstein (1986, 1987, 1990) talks about as *coding orientation.* According to him, the coding orientations of the dominating classes in a society are critically different from those of the dominated ones. My sociolinguistic research has shown that both in controlling their children and in giving them information, mothers of the dominating classes differed significantly from those of the subordinate classes. There is, thus, a good deal of *semantic variation* across social strata; different social segments of a community develop different predispositions for meaning-making, different ideological stances, so that given the same social process, they will tend to say and mean different sorts of things (Hasan 1989, 1991, 1992a, 1992b; Hasan and Cloran 1990).

It is important to recognise this form of linguistic variation, as it allows us to appreciate the complexities of speaking within what might be called the same speech community: on the one hand, social groups are distinguished by having distinct register reper-toires by virtue of engaging in different social processes; and, on the other, where they do engage in 'the same' social processes, there the difference in their ideological stances is still sufficient to maintain the distinction between their discursive practices. The voice of the speech fellowship the pupils bring to the classroom will, thus, represent the pupils' experience of accents, dialects, registers, seen with the eyes of an ideology that is specific to their social positioning. What this means is that the conditions of being, of doing, and of saying in a community are represented in the classroom through the make-up of the learning subjects. I suggest that all these aspects of sociolinguistic variation are relevant, in different ways, to debates on literacy. It ought to be a matter of primary interest to teachers of language, that within one and the same text, within a single exchange of meaning, there may be combined different strands of socially engendered variation: that of dialect and accent, that of register, and that of the ideological perspective resulting in semantic variation.

## 3.4   *Action literacy*

If what I am saying about pupils' linguistic experiences is correct, then discursive ability is a complex concept. People don't just either have it or not; they can 'have' different degrees and differ-ent varieties of discursive abilities. True, thanks to the natural line of literacy development, pupils will come to school with some dis-cursive abilities, and true that even if they are not schooled in literacy, they will develop some discursive ability. These things are not in question; what is in question is whether they will all come to school with the sort of discursive ability which will permit them to engage in the educational process with equal facility. It seems to me that here three considerations are relevant. First, the exotic, specialised contexts of education are somewhat remote from the contexts of everyday living so that it is rather doubtful that the ability to engage in educational discourses could develop naturally without experience of the educational processes. Secondly, while it is true that the educational context is a specialised context for most members of a community, different social classes in the community are placed differently in this respect. Members of the dominating classes do engage more often, than do those of the dominated ones, in practices of saying and meaning which are closer in their discursive properties to educational discourses. The best way to express the nature of this closeness might be to say that there is an ideological congruence between the two. To report again from my sociolinguistic research, it appears that irrespective of who their pupils are, teachers' classroom discourses tend to be, ideologically, significantly closer to those of the middle-class mothers' (Hasan 1987, 1988): they display a similar perspective on what it means to learn, what counts as knowledge, and how knowledge should be 'produced'. And finally, turning to the schooling context, so long as we do not opt out of the educational system altogether, and so long as we hold the ideal of egalitarian education, there will be a need to teach literacy in the sense of developing pupils' discursive abilities in relation to educational registers, since this is a necessary condition for 'having education', for getting to know knowledge! In fact, it would be difficult to draw a distinction between the pupils' knowledge of an academic discipline and their discursive ability to listen/read, speak/write the discourses of that discipline. Academic disciplines are, after all, largely a constellation of certain types of discourse, and, in the end, what counts as knowing a discipline is the ability to participate successfully in the discourses of that discipline. Turning briefly to the question of writing and reading, to the extent that educational discourses make use of reading and writing, to that extent an essential characteristic of being educated would be the ability to use reading and writing to participate in discourses of knowledge. And to the extent that certain aspects of the creation and maintenance of knowledge depend on the invention of writing, to that extent being educated implies being able to read and write. So, we can begin to perceive a deeper truth in the dictionaries' juxtaposition of *being literate* and *having education,* and in its paraphrase of *the state of being literate* as *being able to read and write, having education.*

Now, like dictionaries, educational systems too have always recognised the close link between the development of discursive ability, and the state of being educated. This can be seen from the fact that, following on recognition literacy in schools, the very next step tends to be that of teaching pupils 'connected writing', comprehension and composition, the art of self-expression, creative writing, and the like. Whatever reservations we may have about these approaches, the fact that such pedagogies exist and have always existed is a way of acknowledging that the goal of literacy has to extend beyond the mastery of lists and paradigms; it has to go past the stage of recognition literacy to the development of an ability to use language for the exchange of meanings. Inspired by linguisitcs, several new approaches to the teaching of literacy as discursive ability have arisen over the past few decades. Let me mention here one such pedagogic approach, developed under the leadership of my colleague, J.R. Martin (1985, 1986, 1989, 1992), which has gained a great deal of momentum in educational linguistics in Australia. Known as *genre-based pedagogy,* this approach is deeply concerned with issues in literacy teaching, as many of its representative writings show (Painter and Martin 1986; Martin, Christie and Rothery 1987; Christie 1988, 1991; and Rothery 1989, etc.). Of the various existing programs for the teaching of discursive literacy, genre-based pedagogy is, perhaps, the one that makes its assumptions and arguments most explicit. According to this approach, the goal of education should be to provide equal opportunities for all pupils to develop their discursive abilities precisely in those respects which are essential to their education. Pupils must be schooled to participate successfully in educational genres because of the consequences education has for life chances in a society. Compared with the traditional approach to, say, creative writing or self-expression, genre-based pedagogy differs significantly in its arguments and in its methodology, not least because of its commitment to language as a social semiotic. But if I speak generally of pedagogies concerned with the development of discursive abilities, then these pedagogies fall within the same group. Each has the aim of enabling the pupils to do something with their language, and in this sense they are all action oriented. I will use the term *action literacy* to refer to this entire spectrum of literacy pedagogy. Action literacy ranges from the more traditional practices of getting the pupils to produce some form of connected writing to the more linguistically informed text-based approaches, of which genre-based pedagogy is the best example. Let us ask then what sorts of pedagogic practice are associated with the achievement of this goal.

Naturally, the answer depends on how discursive ability is conceptualised. If it is thought of simply as the ability to comprehend and convey one's thoughts and feelings, to read and produce 'connected writing', then with this rather simplistic view, teachers might draw attention to awkward expressions, comment on some part of a pupil's writing as good or bad, whether the writing was effective, and so on. Turning to actual language patterns they may teach how sentences should be put together, which expression goes better with which expression, and which part of a passage was 'saying' what, etc. The students could be set such tasks as to write a story, summarise some given text (fragment), answer questions which require understanding some part of some prescribed written material, express their views on some situation or other. As to teacher expertise, most of this teaching could be carried out on an *ad hoc* basis, without any awareness of what social factors are criterial to the production of discourse, and what part the patterns of language play in making these socially activated meanings.

At the other end of this spectrum of literacy pedagogies – that is to say, with genre-based pedagogy – discursive ability is conceptualised as the mastery of educational genres. So in this pedagogy teachers would try to get pupils to produce the sorts of texts which would belong to the various educational genres. And to achieve this goal, ideally they will themselves need to be aware of the specific properties of these genres. They will need to know the ways in which talking science (Lemke 1990) is different from writing science (Halliday and Martin 1993), which is different from writing history (Eggins, Wignell and Martin 1993), which is again different from writing about literature. Participation in a discipline calls for discursive abilities which differ to some extent from one discipline to another. Since a crucial distinction across genres is in their schematic structure (Martin 1985, 1989), pupils will need to know how texts in the target genres are structured. One important aim of teaching would be to develop precisely this ability in the pupils to produce well-formed texts in the genres. It follows that pupils will need to know what stages characterise the various target genres, how these stages are sequenced, and so on. A second closely related aspect of controlling the production of well-formed texts is to know those lexicogrammatical patterns which typically occur in these various stages. According to genre-based pedagogy, the teachers' task is to make these aspects of educational genres accessible to the pupils. Through these and similar teaching foci, the teachers would be able to increase pupils' awareness of what counts as a report, and what as a description; how an instruction for carrying out an experiment differs from an essay on the evils of racism, and so on.

What can the pupils be expected to learn through the pedagogies of action literacy? Clearly, the more aware teachers are of the theoretical underpinnings of textual production, the more effective would be their intervention in developing the pupils' discursive ability. So for example, given genre-based pedagogy, ideally the pupils will learn to produce language of the type that is required of them to succeed in the educational system. This makes it likely that at least a higher proportion of pupils will succeed in getting their educational credentials, and it would not be unreasonable to expect that the experience of participation in this kind of literacy pedagogy would also enable pupils to act more confidently with their language in other social activities than just those specific to the educational context. It is obvious, then, that the pedagogy of action literacy at its best has considerable edge over recognition literacy. Pupils' learning and their doing will be not isolated from each other, something that makes recognition literacy so ineffectual in real-life situations. It is important to note, though, that in order to achieve the goals of action literacy, pupils will need to have internalised the sorts of information that form the content of recognition literacy: they will need to be able to recognise the relations between the written shape and the spoken words, and they will need to know about the lexicogrammar. But there is a crucial difference. In action literacy, all this learning will be harnessed to some act of meaning.

What do pupils learn at the deeper level of learning from the teaching practices associated with action literacy? Before answering this question, let me repeat that there is a world of difference between the teaching practices of the more recent linguistically informed approaches such as genre-based pedagogy and those of the traditional ones, which are devoted to teaching the reading and writing of connected prose, focusing on comprehension and composition, or on the development of creative aesthetic sensibilities. This difference is evident in how the pedagogic steps are visualised in the two types of approaches. In genre-based pedagogy these steps are explicitly identified on the basis of a conscious understanding of the target genres and of language as meaning potential (see, for example, Veel and Coffin and also Macken-Horarik, this volume). This understanding is itself based on the linguistic analyses of genres valued in the educational system. In the traditional teaching of reading and writing connected prose, etc., the reliance is on 'intuitive' understanding. It is assumed without debate that because teachers can themselves read and write, therefore they are competent to teach reading and writing. But this silent assumption is false. After all, not all competent native speakers of a language are competent teachers of that language. So there are some very important differences between the two ends of the spectrum, which are classed together here purely on the grounds that both are concerned with textual production, not with fragments of language.

Since the primary aim of action literacy is to teach pupils how to do certain things with their language in the ways that those things are done linguistically in the pupils' culture, this necessarily implies using existing models of discourse. Pupils are provided with standards for some selected aspects of language use – how to structure discourse, how to use the lexicogrammatical resources – and their task is to produce texts, the criterial features of which match those of the approved models. In effect, then, pupils are being schooled to reproduce the selected discursive models, and on this basis, certain varieties of action literacy have been criticised for subscribing to *social reproduction* (cf. Luke, this volume). Their critics claim that action literacy ends up teaching pupils to go on doing precisely what (some) others have been doing in their society, thus reproducing social relations. Again, the issues in this debate are complex, and the scope of this chapter does not allow discussion of all aspects of this critique. Let me first say that I agree with the observation: there certainly is a strong reproductive element in action-based literacy of all varieties. However, I disagree with the conclusion drawn from this, namely that this necessarily renders action literacy unfit as a pedagogic program. Let me elaborate on this comment.

In the first place, I will emphasise once again the wide range of rather disparate literacy pedagogies which are included under the label *action literacy*. For example, the traditional comprehension-composition approaches or the self-expression, creative writing movements differ significantly from genre-based literacy which is founded on a deeper understanding of language as social semiotic; it is explicit in its methodology, and in my view it has produced some of the best language teaching resources for teachers to date. Now it is significant that sociologists of education and proponents of critical literacy have appeared more worried by the reproductive nature of genre-based literacy; in fact hardly anyone has raised this as an issue with regard to the other forms of literacy pedagogies. Why? I believe one reason for this lies in the strengths of genre-based literacy: since its intellectual program is made explicit, it permits discussion about itself in a way that the fuzz around the traditional approaches cannot. But these traditional approaches too are reproductive. Take, for example, the seemingly less likely candidate – the self-expression, creative writing movement: what is 'self'? How is it constituted? What steps do these teachers take to ensure that the 'self' is not a reproductive projection? In fact, criteria for creativity, excellence, accuracy, and other such 'nice' attributes cannot be defined without reference to standards set up within the society where the criteria makers live. Operating independently of socially given standards is the prerogative of the mystic or the mentally deranged (Douglas 1975). Genre-based pedagogy, which makes its assumptions visible, and so easier to criticise, operates on the assumption that pupils' chances of success in education will be considerably enhanced if they are enabled to produce the sorts of discourse which are valued within the educational context. In this sense, this kind of literacy pedagogy could be said to be consciously *aiming* to be reproductive. And they seem to be right in making these assumptions: educational systems are inherently evaluative, which implies the acceptance of some standard by reference to which evaluation can be made. As teachers, most of us have some time or other refused to 'pass' an essay because it did not conform to certain discursive criteria. In other words, teachers have to, and do, operate with some ideas about what pupils' essays should be like, how reports should be produced, what counts as a précis, and so on. Teaching and the idea of successful teaching are inalienably related; so long as we are willing to operate with teaching systems of any kind whatever, we will also operate with models and standards.

Typically, these models and standards will come from (some section of[11]) the society to which the educational systems belong. In short, the brutal fact about the human condition is that to live in a society is to collude to maintain at least some of the ways of being, doing and saying that are prevalent in that society; no one has yet shown us that to live in society can mean anything else, and the natural line of literacy development is largely a process of reproduction (see, for example, the results of my sociolinguisitc research). Critical literacy may be right in saying that to teach educational genres is to reproduce existing knowledge structures, but as against this there remains the much more disturbing fact that to fail to master educational genres is to almost certainly collude in the reproduction of the inequalities of the social system at the cost of precisely those whose voice is absent from the educational curricula! It may be true that educational capital is not automatically converted into economic gain: to succeed educationally may not necessarily mean moving to positions of power. But there does remain the fact that without educational success the chances for the majority of us to attain any power over the course of our lives are almost non-existent. Moreover, there is no convincing evidence for assuming that in order to change a society, its members have to be INNOCENT of the prevalent ways of being, doing, and saying; that to show the young how their society lives by language would entirely prevent them from moving towards social change, though I believe that there is no ground for supposing that the production of the ability to act linguistically as some others act in our culture will necessarily equip pupils to contribute to change (Hasan 1995a). It seems to me that the issue of reproduction has been exaggerated and it is very likely that it stands in need of much deeper reflection.

My critique of genre-based literacy, which incidentally is the only literacy pedagogy worthy of serious attention in the entire range of action literacy, is rather different: I believe that the introduction of planned, consciously designed change requires the ability to analyse, reflect, and judge the underlying motivations for those actions. I believe also that while much of education consists in reproduction/recontextualisation of knowledge (see note 11) the endpoint of education has to be production of knowledge. So an important question is whether in learning discursive ability through genre-based pedagogy, one is also learning the ability to analyse and to challenge the desirability of the prevalent ways of being, doing and saying. To my knowledge, in the range of pedagogic practices that are associated with genre-based literacy, there is no explicit element designed to encourage such reflection.[12] The implied underlying message of this pedagogy is conformism, a respect for convention which is not required to be tempered by analytical reflection. In this respect, recognition literacy and action literacy are alike: both encourage conformism; the difference is that recognition literacy does not enable discursive action, whereas action literacy equips pupils to act with their language.

## 3.5   Literacy and knowledge

Following discursive conventions – talking the way that others in our society talk – is the norm of social life; it is what we mean, in large part, by the expression *socially adapted* or *well adjusted*. The great strength of action literacy, and particularly of genre-based literacy is that it introduces pupils to certain norms of discourse and of knowledge. But paradoxically, this is also the source of the weakness of action literacy. Since the norms of language and knowledge are both filtered through the educational system itself, if the learning of these norms was treated as the ultimate goal of literacy, we would naturally inherit whatever shortcomings there may be in the educational norms. This applies inevitably to all pedagogies of the type I have referred to as action literacy. For example, if we take the self-expression variety of action literacy, a pupil may be asked to write his reactions to a poem, but to be approved by the teacher, his reactions have to be written in the ways in which one is supposed to write one's reactions about poems in the school system; and, interestingly, even the reactions have to be reactions of a certain category; so it won't do at all to just write *I didn't like that poem because it was a load of rubbish*, even if this represents the pupil's conscious apprehension of his reaction. As a second example, take genre-based pedagogy as a notable example of a linguistically inspired case of action literacy. Unlike the self-expression variety of pedagogy, it recognises its aims. Its acknowledged aim is to teach pupils the norms for reading, writing, and speaking about some sort of educational knowledge, but these norms are naturally norms recognised and upheld as norms for doing those same things within the schooling context. There is, then, a certain circularity about the enterprise. Discourse norms that, for example, genre-based literacy teaches are the

norms of what is considered good discourse in the educational
environment; the norms of knowledge it teaches are norms of
what counts as knowledge within the educational context. If this
reasoning is correct, then we end up teaching literacy *for* schooling, creating the literate subject in the image of the existing
standards of education. It could be argued then that it is an instrument for the perpetuation of the standards of the existing
educational system, and one might go on to argue that if the ideal
goal of teaching is to enable pupils to PRODUCE knowledge, not just
replicate it, then genre-based literacy falls short of this ideal.

How is it that using the norms of the educational system puts us
into this quandary? After all, education is popularly thought to be
a means for the *transmission of knowledge and cultural values.* If that
is so, then why criticise genre-based literacy for perpetuating the
norms of education? And how is it that following these norms fails
to enable pupils to produce knowledge? Sociologists of educational knowledge have argued that school knowledge is typically
knowledge that is produced elsewhere; it is relocated into the curricula; and the standards of the educational system simply
demand a degree of the mastery of this already produced knowledge as a sign of educational success. So school knowledge comes
to have norms largely by treating knowledge as a finished product
– something that has been created in the past by some other producers. But when it comes to the process of producing knowledge,
the situation is qualitatively different. Here the existing knowledge is simply the point of departure for the creation of
something significantly different from it; the very idea of *right
knowledge* has to be viewed with caution, if not with suspicion, for
the essential nature of knowledge in this context is to change
within a framework of seeming stability. Its changing nature
becomes evident only when viewed from a time-distance. At one
time in our knowledge, the earth was flat, not round; there was no
evolution of species: the human species grew as a result of the first
female's foibles; sickness had no physical basis: it was the work of
the devil; and so on. That in these respects our knowledge is different now shows that we were able to reflect, to analyse, and to
challenge that which was taken to be *true in nature* though it was
*true only by convention.* In making this reflection, this analysis, and
this challenge, the discursive conventions, too, must have had to
change from those which had appeared *natural* for talking about
the earth, about creation, or the creator. And in as much as acts of

reflection, of analysis, and of challenge call into question systems of belief that are *naturally* accepted, they also call on speakers to speak *un-naturally*, to use un-natural locutions, un-natural collocations. I am arguing, then, that both the norms of knowledge and of discourse change, and they change together; that like knowledge, the essential nature of language is to change within a framework of seeming stability. This similarity is not accidental: the possibilities of knowledge and the potentiality of human language cannot be understood in isolation from each other. Discourse and knowledge go hand in hand. It so happens then that while in the schooling system the norms of knowledge and of discourse are treated as stable and fixed; outside this system, both the ways of using language and of construing knowledge continue to evolve with the result that the norms for both are subject to change.

But should we as teachers be concerned about the evolution of knowledge? If so, why? There are good reasons for this. Scholars have argued for some time now that the evolution of knowledge is a highly significant process in human history, because it serves a function very much like the function of the bodily evolution in animals. In both cases, the function is to enable the species to survive (Vygotsky 1978; Popper 1979). To quote the philosopher, Popper,

> Animal evolution proceeds largely ... by the modification of organs ... or the emergence of new organs. ... Human evolution proceeds largely by developing new organs outside our bodies or persons: 'exo-somatically' as biologists call it ... man, instead of growing better eyes and ears, grows spectacles, microscopes, telescopes, telephones, and hearing aids...              (Popper 1979: 238)

The close link between the exo-somatic evolution of human beings and the growth of knowledge is quite obvious. It is the evolution of knowledge that allows us to produce the technical aids that Popper talks about as exo-somatic organs. With this argument, the production of knowledge becomes a condition of human survival. Popper goes on to suggest that as human beings we experience three orders of phenomena. First, we know *the world of physical states*; secondly, there is *the world of mental states*; and thirdly, there is *the world of objective contents of thought*. The last of these, known as Popper's WORLD 3, is what some might describe as communal heritage of knowledge. Popper believes that this

WORLD 3 exists independently of specific individuals; it is autonomous. For example, the theory of relativity remains an element of this world, irrespective of whether or not Einstein is still alive. The elements of this world, described in general terms, are *theoretical systems, problem situations, the state of critical arguments and of discussion*. This WORLD 3 develops as a result of individuals interacting with the elements of WORLD 3, or, to put it another way, knowledge evolves through reflection and analysis of the elements of communal knowledge. The elements of WORLD 3 are thus resources for the creation of further knowledge because they carry a certain set of implications. Whether we know about these implications or not, they exist; they are *objectively* there. From this point of view, it is immaterial that it was Einstein who produced the theory of relativity; what matters is that the germs of the theory were already there in the implications of the existing theoretical systems, the problems they gave rise to, and their close analysis. For knowledge to evolve, what we need is someone – anyone – to perceive the problem(s), to develop the implications; this implies a search for explanations, raising *how-questions and why-questions*, using existing knowledge only as a point of departure, not as the end of an intellectual journey.

## 3.6   Reflection literacy

It follows from these views, that if we are actively interested in the evolution of knowledge, then we cannot take for granted the certainty of facts simply on the ground that those facts have generally been treated as facts; nor can we treat the prevalent ways of saying and meaning as utterly binding on us simply because these happen to be the accepted ways of doing things with our language. Neither the norms of knowledge nor those of discourse can be treated as stable, arrested at some point in time; change is the only abiding condition for human existence. This puts the emphasis on a qualitatively different aspect of discursive ability than that which underlies pedagogies of action literacy. Participation in the production of knowledge will call for an ability to use language to reflect, to enquire and to analyse, which is the necessary basis for challenging what are seen as facts. So, if our aim is to enable pupils to produce knowledge, then we would need a view of literacy designed to develop these faculties. This literacy will necessarily prioritise reflection, enquiry and analysis. For this reason I refer to it as *reflection literacy*. Reflection literacy should not be confused with critical literacy. The notion nearest to reflection literacy is Wells' idea of *epistemic literacy*.[13]

At this point two important questions arise: is reflection literacy teachable? and even if it is, is it necessary? Taking the first question first, I do believe that reflection literacy is teachable. After all, we have somehow succeeded in keeping the evolution of knowledge going. So unless we believe in born theoreticians, born scientists, sociologists, and so on, we would have to grant that some variety of reflection literacy is not only teachable but must be being taught at some level of education to permit the production of knowledge rather than just replication. And while it is true that normally the students' contribution to knowledge production occurs at a fairly late stage in the educational system, it must also be true that the orientations that assist them in this task must begin to develop long before the event. Actually, I believe that the sorts of perspectives typically needed for knowledge production are taught throughout schooling but they are taught *invisibly*. In analysing the language of the classroom in a picture-reading session in the first year of schooling in some suburban schools in Australia, I found (Hasan 1987) that as early as the very first year of schooling, teachers already insisted on *objective* evidence; they rejected answers that were not explicitly supported by some evidence in the picture. They also rejected conclusions that were not *logical*; to be received with approval, conclusions had to be *implicational* in their reasoning; and the responses which the teachers favoured highly were those presented as *universal* generalisations. Of course, it is these discursive features which are primarily relevant to the sort of knowledge production that Popper values so highly. But it must be pointed out that this invisible pedagogy would have meaning only for *some* pupils, not for all; the pupils for whom it would have meaning are those who are familiar with this voice as the voice of their own speech fellowship. They would be able to *log in*, as it were, because the code is their code. My research has shown also that these ways of meaning are typical of the mothers of the dominating classes in the Australian society; they do not represent the voice of the dominated classes (Hasan 1988, 1989, 1991, 1992b, 1992c). To say that the pedagogy is invisible is to say that the teachers themselves are not aware of what they are doing; this being the case, they would find it difficult to employ such a pedagogy systematically in such a way as to develop reflection literacy in all pupils, irrespective of their *natur-ally developed* voice. So far as the teaching of reflection literacy is concerned, we really do not have many alternatives: either we have to teach reflection literacy so as to develop the potential of all pupils to participate in the production of knowledge, or we should abandon claims that our educational system is egalitarian. These arguments are pretty much the same as those employed by Martin in support of his genre-based pedagogy.

The answer to the second question is already implicit in this discussion. It is often thought that the ability to reflect and to enquire is a divine gift; some have it, others don't. But the very concept of *native intelligence* is problematic. We have no clear idea of the range of intelligence levels enjoyed by infants at birth, and whatever that range may be it is not sufficient for the living of life without further development. The development of higher mental functions that we think of as guided by intelligence is essentially fashioned by the living of life in society, and this means that it is guided by semiotic inter-acts of one kind or another, but largely of linguistic semiosis (Vygotsky 1962, 1978; Halliday 1975, 1979; Donaldson 1978; Bernstein 1972, 1987; Hasan 1988, 1992b; Painter, this volume). What is specifically relevant to reflection literacy is *semantic orientation* (see section 3.3.2) since it is speakers' orientation to meaning, their ideological stance, that underlies their disposition to make enquiries, analyses, challenges of one kind or another. An important feature of language is that as a meaning-making resource it is not dedicated to any specific purpose. In theory, it can be used by any one of us to conform or to question. But, in practice, because all members of a community do not occupy identical social positions, their naturally developed meaning-making dispositions are not identical, and it cannot be assumed that along the natural line of literacy development, everyone in a community will naturally come to possess the disposition to enquire, to analyse and to challenge in ways that are considered necessary for the production of knowledge (Hasan 1992c; 1995b). If literacy is what education is about, and education is supposed to be truly egalitarian, and if the aim of education is to enable participation in the production of knowledge – and not just reproduction – then it follows that we would need to develop in all pupils the ability to reflect, to enquire, to analyse and to challenge.

But what sorts of teaching-learning practices are implied by this view of literacy? To put a question to a text – to ask why the said is being said, what it implies, and on what grounds – calls for a much deeper understanding of language as a resource for meaning. So teachers will need to sensitise pupils to not simply the overall schematic structure of the text, which is just one aspect of discursive ability; they would also be concerned to show what alternative ways there are of saying the 'same thing'. The point is that one can never say exactly the same thing using a different wording; so in fact, the teachers will need to make pupils aware of the sorts of difference in meaning that may arise from putting it one way as opposed to another. If it is true, as I claimed earlier, that within the same text is interwoven evidence of the various sorts of linguistic variation, then there are many ways in which a text can be read. This does not mean that *meaning is in the reader*, as the postmodernist sentiment has it (Rosenau 1991: 25ff); rather, it means that our perceptions of meaning are coloured by our point of view, and our point of view – in as much as it is capable of being studied and taken into account – is related to who we are, socially speaking. To say that a community has many voices is to say that there are experiences of saying and meaning which differ from one social group to the next; this includes the possibility that the way a locution is evaluated in one segment of the community might be critically different from that in another. So it becomes important to ask whose point of view does the writing represent? whose point of view is implied in which reading? It is from this kind of deeper understanding of what 'the' text means that we can move to explanation questions. For example, pupils would not simply note the way a text is structured, but they would also ask why it is structured in the way it is; what would change, for whom and at what price, if the structure were to be changed? They would not simply observe whose voice(s) underly messages of what category, they would also ask why these voices and these messages go together, what voices are absent and why. This is indeed to question the very norms of discourse. Just as teachers will need a good deal of expertise and understanding of language as a meaning potential in order to be able to help develop this kind of discursive perspective in their pupils, so also they will need to be deeply familiar with the nature of the disciplines they are to discuss with their classes. What issues does it problematise? What methods for the resolution of such problems were employed in the past? What today? What counts as a fact and why? What sort of evidence upholds the status of a fact as fact?

Schooling in reflection literacy is, then, literacy for educating to produce knowledge. If the pedagogy is successful, it should ideally produce in the pupils a disposition to distrust *doxic knowledge*, that is, knowledge whose sole authority is the authority of someone in authority. Since the history of a discipline is also the history of how it has changed, this pedagogy should create a perspective which refuses to consider the accepted ways of doing things in a culture as beyond questioning. So, apart from questioning the norms of discourse and of knowledge, a literacy of this kind would seek to examine the norms of education itself. For example, why do systems of education always insist on using the standard dialect? Why is educational success distributed in a society the way it is? Why does the production of knowledge get appropriated by a particular segment of the society? Why is knowledge conceptualised as it is? In what sense do the accepted Western notions of the evolution of knowledge represent progress? How should we understand the term *progress* when it comes to the survival of humanity? Indeed, how should we understand the term *survival?* In what sense can we talk about the evolution of knowledge contributing to the *progress* and *survival* of humanity in an environment where both are linked to the idea of competing successfully against some other? We might justifiably expect that such literate pupils might be able to question the wisdom of the short-sighted goals that we have embraced the world over. They might indeed be able to ask what we have lost by gaining control over the environment, while ignoring all notions of self-control, by construing knowledge as a competitive enterprise, while failing to acknowledge the centrality of the other in our very survival as human beings. A literacy that can turn back upon the very systems that perpetuate the literacy teaching practices in a society is indeed worth striving for. If and when literacy and education stand in this relation, then we shall indeed be justified in paraphrasing *literate* as *educated,* and *educated* as *displaying qualities of culture or learning.*

## 4    Literacy, talk, and society

We have travelled a good distance in this chapter from *bat, pat, hat, mat,* from weak and strong verbs, from paraphrases, and the like.

Perhaps the chapter has given some indication of how the uneasy co-existence of the two lines of literacy development in essentially non-egalitarian societies contribute to the complexities of literacy pedagogy. This perspective draws attention to the close links between literacy, everyday talk, and society. The voice of the speech fellowship that the child brings to the school is the voice developed in everyday talk. So far as the exotic pedagogic line of literacy development is concerned, the one thing that can always be taken for granted is that all children will have had experience of ordinary everyday talk. There will be many, of course, who will also have had the additional experience of having been read to or of acquaintance with print. But how parents read with their children tends to vary from one social segment to another (Williams 1990, 1994); and secondly, this experience, unlike that of everyday talk, cannot be taken for granted as a universal feature. For example, do we know what goes on in these respects in some small remote villages of Uzbekistan, or of the interior of Australia, or in the remote north of Pakistan? The answer to this is not always available, but what we do know is that there, too, parents and the immediate meaning group – those who form the core of the child's speech fellowship – talk to the child, and it is this experience that gives the child his/her voice. Just because it is certain that every child will come to school with the voice of his/her speech fellowship, it is also certain that the educational system will encounter linguistic variation in the many ways in which voices can vary. It is equally important that the ordinary, everyday talk occurs in the course of some social action, that it is really the semiotic aspect of those social processes. The implications of the varying experience of social processes that pupils bring to the pedagogic context need urgent attention not only in the teaching of literacy, but in all pedagogic activity. A serious source of disquiet with literacy teaching practices is precisely that the educational systems deal with this variability by simply ignoring it – by raising one voice as the only legitimate voice, and that voice happens to be the voice of the dominating segments of the society. If education represents a social resource, then this resource is appropriated with the greatest ease by those same social classes which also control the society's material resources, thus making the strength of their control that much more formidable.

It should not surprise us that literacy poses so many issues. Literacy in the sense of making meaning by language, imports the most socially sensitive signing system, namely language, into the educational arena. Language is not a mirror that just reflects the social inequalities and hierarchies which exist in our society, mocking our claims of egalitarianism. Language is, in fact, actively involved in the creation and maintenance of social inequalities, because human social systems are *unmakeable* without language. Here is cause enough for problems, especially when we know whose linguistic norms are the silently endorsed norms in the educational system. But this problem is made worse by a mis-recognition of the nature of language. People typically think of language as passive, a clothing for meanings and ideas which are external to it. This popular but false ideology prevents us from raising questions about language. The inability of teachers to understand the nature of language as a powerful social instrument does not, indeed cannot, help them in any way to recognise, much less to respect, the many voices in their classroom or reflect on the genesis of those voices; teachers that are so ill-equipped to reflect on language cannot be expected to scrutinise the 'rationality' of the choice of norms and standards which they inculcate. Keeping teachers of literacy uninformed about the close relation between the development of language, everyday talk, learning, and society, in fact, plays into the hands of the dominating segments of society, whose ideologies remain the ideologies of education. Thus the cry against privileging language raised by some proponents of critical literacy is ironically an aid to the domination they profess to abhor rather than a release from it!

## 5   Concluding remarks: the many faces of literacy

In opening this chapter I suggested that literacy is a many-faceted process. Identifying the onset of literacy as *semiosis*, I located it topologically in the same domain as any other semiotic practice with which it shares many critical attributes. I went on to claim that its specific and decisive character consists in being *language-based semiosis*. If it is desirable to extend the use of the term *literacy* (cf. 'media literacy', etc.), this does not appear to be a serious problem worthy of much deliberation. The fact worth emphasising is that *language-based semiosis* under whatever name will occupy a central position in any discussion of education. We can, if we choose, turn language classes into sites for the discussion of wider social issues, for raising pupils' consciousness about any pressing social problems. The choice is not between bringing such issues to the students' attention *or* developing understanding of language as a powerful social semiotic. Both need to be done, and a more relevant question is: what is the best way to do both? Those who argue against focusing on language, on the explication of its internal character, on the power of lexicogrammar to construe reality, or on the efficacy of discursive knowledge speak from a less than adequate understanding of the role of language in the living and shaping of social life. Whatever else literacy pedagogy needs to be, one thing it cannot avoid is to help pupils to 'intellectualise' in the Vygotskian sense of the term[14] the nature of language. Learning about the nature and structure of language is not an expendable educational activity.

I have talked about the three facets of literacy, each being presented in a rather idealised form, as if each existed or was able to exist on its own. This is of course not true. What is true is that different educational systems, different institutions attach different degrees of importance to these facets. Each facet has its own focus. Recognition literacy is concerned primarily with language as expression; action literacy focuses on language as expression and content in relation to social processes, while reflection literacy is concerned with the reflexive capacities of language when it functions as meta-discourse, analysing both the nature of expression and of content by relating both to the exchange of meanings by socially positioned speakers for the living of life in society. Different as these three perspectives on literacy are, they are none the less logically related to each other. To see this we need to separate analytically what the various facets focus on as the material for teaching and how they actually do it. It is the former that is important for my claim of the interrelatedness of the three facets of literacy developed here. Let me elaborate this point.

I have suggested earlier that the pedagogy of action literacy presupposes the sorts of understanding about language that form the content of recognition literacy. I will ignore once again the comprehension-composition and self-expressive, creative pedagogies on the grounds that from the point of view of understanding language as a social semiotic system such pedagogies are deplorably inadequate. Consider, however, genre-based literacy: to talk about the structure of a text is to talk about what meanings construe its various elements/stages, and to talk about the meanings is to talk about the lexicogrammar that will construe those meanings, with the implication that an awareness of lexicogrammar as functionally focused on the construal of meanings is important. But lexicogrammar is the most abstract part of language (Hasan 1995a); what impinges on the human senses is the manifestation of these categories in phonic and/or orthographic form. Thus the phonology-orthography correspondence to lexis and grammar is an essential part of the understanding of language. The success of genre-based literacy – and there is no doubt that it is successful at teaching language – resides in the fact that it has appropriated these aspects of recognition literacy, harnessing them to language in use in social contexts. A similar relation can be shown to exist between reflection literacy and genre-based literacy. If, for example, we wish to understand why politicians toss language education around like a football in the field of political gains, if we wish to ask why sociology only pays lip-service to language, if we want to ask why literary scholars sidetrack issues of language when the universe of literary art is anchored to our intelligence purely by the mediation of linguistic meaning, if we wish to understand how critical literacy can be a program for literacy development without a viable basis in an understanding of the workings of language, if we wonder how and why women have colluded in the processes of their own oppression, then we will need to be able to read, and read with understanding the many discourses that reveal the principles underlying these positions. We will need to become familiar with how 'they do it' – how they put these perspectives across, what justifications they offer, from whose perspective. It means being sensitive to discursive strategies, and being able to deconstruct the already constructed discourses in one's society. Reflection presupposes understanding; and understanding a point of view is synonymous with understanding discourse.

Let me make it quite clear, though, that I am not talking about a temporal ordering here: I am not saying that genre-based literacy must be taught *before* reflection literacy, or that recognition literacy has to be taught *before* genre-based literacy. It is possible to pursue all three perspectives within one and the same teaching stage. So the issue is not of temporal sequence but of logical implication. In the natural line of literacy development, patterns of language are learned in discourse: genre-based literacy must logically presuppose the development of patterns of language. Its program, from this point of view, is successful to the extent that learning about discourse is also learning about 'how language does it'. Similarly, the pedagogy of reflection literacy depends on being able to analyse the existing discourses of knowledge from the point of view of what they present as the norms of discourse and of knowledge. It is in understanding discourse as discourse that the critical faculty will develop. Logically, it is impossible to achieve this goal without bringing in the sorts of understanding that are essential to the creation of texts. So these three facets of literacy are related by logical inclusion: reflection literacy includes a well informed variety of action literacy such as genre-based literacy, and the latter includes recognition literacy; the reverse is, however, not true.

This has a practical implication: in theory there exists a possible choice of perspective in the teaching of literacy, but because of this inclusion relation, the choice can only proceed in one direction. One may be limited to recognition literacy without action literacy, or to action literacy without reflection literacy, but if reflection literacy is to be developed, this will necessarily involve insights that form a linguistically well-informed variety of action literacy such as Martin's framework, and that in turn will entail the pedagogy of the structural working of language. The cry of *back to basics* does a good deal of harm, because those who utter this war-cry often do not really know what they want and why. But perhaps my account of the logical relations between the three facets of literacy clarifies why knowing about language is important. It is important *only if and in as much as* it contributes to a conscious understanding of the resources of one's language for acting with it. The ability to act with language is important because it contributes to our ability to analyse those same acts. So all three facets of literacy are equally important. What we need to avoid is the danger of ending up by focusing only on formal structures of language without relating them to their social functions – that is, getting locked into recognition literacy – taking it as the resting point without moving to action; similarly, I would not wish to end up with focus on action literacy without moving to include reflection. I have tried to point out how each of these resting points will have different consequences in terms of the kind of social world it will help to produce. Literacy is not simply a semantically saturated term; what it refers to is a socially powerful process, which can be used in different ways – some perhaps more beneficial to a society, some to only some persons in it!

# Notes

1 This is a revised and abridged version of a plenary paper presented at the 5th Anniversary Symposium of the Society of Pakistani English Language Teachers (SPELT), held in Karachi, 4 July 1989. My thanks are due to the organisers of the SPELT Symposium for release of the manuscript for publication here.

2 See van Leeuwen and Humphrey, this volume, for a discussion of how graphic signs such as maps, pictures, co-operate with the linguistic materials in a geography text.

3 There are at least two other senses in which the term *literacies* is used. The plural is used to show that being literate in any one educational discipline (or discipline cluster) differs from being literate in some other(s). In this sense, one might talk about, say, *science literacy, social science literacy,* and so on. Secondly, the plural is used to show that different segments of the society are literate in different ways, depending upon the point of view they bring to the *reading*. In this sense, one might talk about *feminist literacy, dominant literacy,* and so on.

4 For a discussion of this point see also Halliday, this volume.

5 Note the close analogy with *language*. The unqualified use of this word means natural human language; its use can be extended as in *sign language, body language, computer language,* and so on.

6 From this point of view Derrida's diatribe against the 'privileging' of speech by linguists is a curious twist that calls for a re-assessment.

7 My thanks are due to Jennifer Hammond (University of Technology, Sydney) with whose help I developed many of the ideas presented in this and subsequent subsections, specifically those concerning the pedagogies specific to each of the three perspectives on literacy development.

8 We note once again the tension between the mundane line of literacy development and the exotic, pedagogic one.

9 Often it is argued that we neither have the time nor the resources (cf. Terry Threadgold, personal communication) for familiarising teachers with the relevant aspects of language such as its nature, its form, its function, all of which are, of course, interdependent. It is worthy of reflection though that neither time nor resources are allocated to the pedagogic system by an act of nature; they are the expression of our commitment to the so-called 'egalitarian education' and need to be scrutinised, even though such scrutiny is very much less dramatic in its impact on audience than certain forms of rhetoric.

10 A couple of years ago, a national Australian newspaper proudly announced the emergence of yet another 'innovative' literacy program, 'developed at Baltimore's John Hopkins University' which

some Australian researchers in the Education Department of a prestigious university were hoping to use so as to 'help poor or deprived children' in this country. The accompanying photograph showed a blackboard with the following 'meaningful utterances': *I am Pam. See the map, Pam. Sam is on the mat. Pat Sam.* (*Sydney Morning Herald*, September 11, 1993). And no doubt more advanced and innovative literacy programs have been introduced since, which are, in effect, not very different from the *bat, pat, hat, mat* variety of recognition literacy. This type of 'language-based' literacy development is a cause for worry, not because it privileges language but because it privileges ignorance of language, hiding its true nature and power.

11  One may of course question, as sociologists of education have done, the inequity of choosing the point of view of a particular section of society. Criticising the educational system for being monopolised by the 'ruling classes' is, however, a somewhat different issue from criticising it for 'reproducing' knowledge and/or social relations, for it could be argued that education IS largely nothing but reproduction under a different name. In this sense to oppose reproduction in education *altogether* is to imply the need for the replacement of education by some other institution, whatever that may be. If this is the position taken by critical literacy, then there is as yet very scant indication of any viable alternative or of any strategy by which the alternative could be achieved.

12  Attention should be drawn to the fact that genre-based literacy is not a static package. It has shown a good deal of responsiveness to its critique by colleagues and, more recently, elements are being introduced in this form of pedagogy to overcome the shortcomings. See, for example, Macken-Horarik, this volume.

13  Although Hammond and I developed our system of literacy classification on which my account here is based (with some revision) independently of Wells (1987), it is interesting to note that Wells recognises four levels of literacy which cover approximately the same space as the three perspectives presented in this paper. He refers to his first level of literacy as *performative literacy*. I prefer the term *recognition literacy* because it is a clear reminder of what this literacy pedagogy is about: it helps us recognise a language pattern as a pattern of a specific kind. Besides, all literacy involves performance of some kind, but not all literacy requires focus on recognition of isolated patterns. My term *action literacy* covers approximately the same area as Wells' *functional* and *informational literacy*. Wells distinguishes between these two as *literacy in interpersonal communication* and in *communication of knowledge*, respectively. The basis for this distinction is not very obvious to me: from my point of view all discursive language is both interpersonal and informational, though the distinction between everyday genres and educational knowledge genres does

appear valid. If this is the distinction, then in the spectrum covered by my *action literacy*, genre-based pedagogy is nearest to *informational literacy*. Finally, my term *reflection literacy* is quite close to Wells' notion of *epistemic literacy*, which according to him provides *ways of acting upon and transforming knowledge.*

14  By 'intellectualisation' Vygotsky (1962, 1978) meant the process of making a concept one's own in such a way that a person becomes able to recall it at will, use it in conjunction with other concepts, see it as part of some system(s) of ideas – make it pliable.

# References:

Albrow, K.H. 1972. *The English writing system: notes towards a description.* London: Longman.

Andersen, Elaine S. 1986. The acquisition of register variation in Anglo-American children. In *Language socialisation across cultures*, edited by Bambi B. Schieffelin and Elinor Ochs. London: Cambridge University Press.

Basso, Keith. 1980. Review of Jack Goody (ed.), *The domestication of the savage mind. Language in Society*, **9**: 72–80.

Bernstein, Basil. 1972. A sociolinguistic approach to socialization: with some reference to educability. In *Directions in sociolinguistics: the ethnography of communication*, edited by John J. Gumperz and Dell Hymes. London: Blackwell.

Bernstein, Basil. 1975. On the classification and framing of educational knowledge. In *Knowledge, education and cultural change*, edited by R. Brown. London: Tavistock.

Bernstein, Basil. 1986. On pedagogic discourse. In *Handbook of theory and research in the sociology of education*, edited by J.G. Richardson. London: Greenwood.

Bernstein, Basil. 1987. Elaborated and restricted codes: an overview 1958–85. In *Sociolinguisitcs/Soziolinguistik: an international handbook Vol. 1*, edited by Ulrich Ammon, Norbert Dittmar and Klaus J. Mattheier. Berlin: W de Gruyter.

Bernstein, Basil. 1990. *The structuring of pedagogic discourse: class, codes and control Vol. IV.* London: Routledge.

Bourdieu, Pierre and Jean-Claude Passeron. 1977. *Reproduction in education, society and culture.* (2nd edn) London: Sage.

Bruner, Jerome K. 1975. The ontogenesis of speech acts. *Journal of Child Language* **2(1)**: 1–19.

Christie, F. 1988. The construction of knowledge in the primary school. In *Language and socialisation: home and school, Proceedings from the Working Conference on Language in Education, Macquarie University November 17–21,*

*1986*, edited by L. Gerot, J. Oldenburg, and T. van Leeuwen. Sydney: Macquarie University.

Christie, F. 1991. (ed.) *Literacy in social processes: papers from the Inaugural Conference of the Australian Systemic Functional Association.* Darwin: Centre for the Studies of Language in Education, Northern Territory University.

Cross, Marilyn. 1991. *Choice in text: a systemic approach to computer modelling of variant text production.* PhD thesis, Macquarie University.

Donaldson, Margaret. 1978. *Children's minds.* London: Fontana.

Dore, J. 1977. Children's illocutionary acts. In *Discourse: comprehension and production*, edited by R. Freedle. Hillsdale, NJ: Lawrence Erlbaum.

Douglas, Mary. 1975. *Implicit meanings: essays in anthropology.* London: Routledge & Kegan Paul.

Eggins, S., P. Wignell and J.R. Martin. 1993. The discourse of history: distancing the recoverable past. In *Register analysis: theory into practice*, edited by Mohsen Ghadessy. London: Pinter.

Firth, J.R. 1957. Personality and language in society. In *Papers in general linguistics 1934–1951.* London: Oxford University Press.

Goody, Jack. 1968. *Literacy in traditional societies.* Cambridge: Cambridge University Press.

Goody, Jack. 1977. *The domestication of the savage mind.* Cambridge: Cambridge University Press.

Goody, Jack and I. Watt. 1972. The consequences of literacy. In *Language and social context*, edited by Pier Paolo Giglioli. Harmondsworth: Penguin.

Halliday, M.A.K. 1973. Relevant models of language. In *Explorations in the functions of language.* London: Edward Arnold.

Halliday, M.A.K. 1975. *Learning how to mean: explorations in the development of language.* London: Edward Arnold.

Halliday, M.A.K. 1976. Early language learning: a sociolinguistic approach. In *Language and man: anthropological issues*, edited by S.A. Wurm and W.C. McCormack. The Hague: Mouton.

Halliday, M.A.K. 1979. Three aspects of children's language development: learning language, learning through language, learning about language. In *Oral and written language development: impact on schools*, edited by Yetta M. Goodman, Myna M. Haussler and Dorothy M. Strickland. International Reading Association and National Council of Teachers of English: Proceedings from the 1979–1980 IMPACT conferences [no date given].

Halliday, M.A.K. 1985. *Spoken and written language.* Geelong, Vic.: Deakin University Press.

Halliday, M.A.K. 1992. How do you mean? In *Advances in systemic linguistics: recent theory and practice*, edited by Martin Davies and Louise Ravelli. London: Pinter.

Halliday, M.A.K. 1994. *Introduction to functional grammar.* (2nd edn). London: Arnold.

Halliday, M.A.K. and Ruqaiya Hasan. 1976. *Cohesion in English.* London: Longman.

Halliday, M.A.K. and Ruqaiya Hasan. 1985. *Language, context and text: aspects of language in a social-semiotic perspective.* Oxford: Oxford University Press.

Halliday, M.A.K. and J.R. Martin. 1993. *Writing science: literacy and discursive power.* London: Falmer.

Halliday, M.A.K., Angus McIntosh and P. Strevens. 1964. Users and uses of language. In *Linguistic sciences and language teaching.* London: Longman.

Hasan, Ruqaiya. 1987. Reading picture reading: invisible instruction at home and in school. *Proceedings from the 13th Conference of the Australian Reading Association, Sydney* [no date; no editor].

Hasan, Ruqaiya. 1988. Language and socialisation: home and school. In *Language in the processes of socialisation,* edited by L. Gerot, J. Oldenburg and T. van Leeuwen. Sydney: Macquarie University.

Hasan, Ruqaiya. 1989. Semantic variation and sociolinguistics. *Australian Journal of Linguistics* **9(2)**: 221–76.

Hasan, Ruqaiya. 1991. Questions as a mode of learning in everyday talk. In *Language education: interaction and development,* edited by Thao Lê and Mike McCausland. Launceston: University of Tasmania (pp. 70–119).

Hasan, Ruqaiya. 1992a. Rationality in everyday talk: from process to system. In *Directions in corpus linguistics: proceedings of Nobel Symposium 82, Stockholm, 4–8 August 1991,* edited by Jan Svartvik. Berlin: Mouton de Gruyter.

Hasan, Ruqaiya. 1992b. Meaning in sociolinguistic theory. In *Sociolinguistics today: international perspectives,* edited by Kingsley Bolton and Helen Kwok. London: Routledge.

Hasan, Ruqaiya. 1992c. Speech genre, semiotic mediation and the development of higher mental functions. *Language Sciences* **14(4)**: 489–528.

Hasan, Ruqaiya. 1995a. The conception of context in text. In *Discourse in society: systemic functional perspectives,* edited by Peter H. Fries and Michael Gregory. Norwood NJ: Ablex.

Hasan, Ruqaiya. 1995b. On social conditions for semiotic mediation: the genesis of mind in society. In *Knowledge and pedagogy: the sociology of Basil Bernstein,* edited by Alan R. Sadovnik. Norwood, NJ: Ablex.

Hasan, Ruqaiya and Carmel Cloran. 1990. A sociolinguistic interpretation of everyday talk between mothers and children. In *Learning, keeping and using language Vol. 1: selected papers from the 8th World Congress of Applied Linguistics, Sydney 16–21 August 1987,* edited by M.A.K. Halliday, John Gibbon and Howard Nicholas. Amsterdam: Benjamins (pp. 67–100).

Hymes, Dell. 1972. On communicative competence. In *Sociolinguistics,* edited by J.B. Pride and J. Holmes. Harmondsworth: Penguin.

Kress, Gunther. 1982. *Learning to write*. London: Routledge.

Labov, William. 1972. *Sociolinguistic patterns*. Philadelphia, PA: University of Pennsylvania Press.

Lemke, Jay L. 1990. *Talking science: language, learning and values*. Norwood NJ: Ablex.

Luke, Allan. 1988. *Literacy, textbooks and ideology*. London: Falmer.

Martin, J.R. 1985. Process and text: two modes of human semiosis. In *Systemic perspectives on discourse, Vol. 1: selected theoretical papers from the 9th International Systemic Workshop*, edited by J.D. Benson and W.S. Greaves. Norwood NJ: Ablex.

Martin, J.R. 1986. Intervening in the process of writing development. In *Writing to mean: teaching genres across the curriculum*, edited by Clare Painter and J.R. Martin. Occasional Paper No. 9. Budoora, Vic.: Applied Linguistics Association of Australia.

Martin, J.R. 1989. *Factual writing: exploring and challenging social reality*. Geelong, Vic: Deakin University Press.

Martin, J.R. 1992. *English text: system and structure*. Amsterdam: John Benjamins.

Martin, J.R., F. Christie and J. Rothery. 1987. Social processes in education. In *The place of genre in learning*, edited by Ian Reid. Geelong, Vic.: Deakin University Press.

Matthiessen, Christian. 1995. *Lexicogrammatical cartography: English Systems*. Tokyo: International Language Sciences Publisher.

McTear, Michael. 1985. *Children's conversations*. London: Blackwell.

Olson, David R. 1977. From utterance to text: the bias of language in speech and writing. *Harvard Educational Review* **47(3)**: 257–81.

Painter, Clare. 1984. *Into the mother tongue*. London: Pinter.

Painter, Clare. 1989. Learning language: a functional view of language development. In *Language development: learning language, learning culture: studies for Michael Halliday*, edited by Ruqaiya Hasan and J.R. Martin. Norwood NJ: Ablex.

Painter, Clare and J.R. Martin. 1986. (eds) *Writing to mean: teaching genres across the curriculum*. Applied linguistics Association of Australia, Occasional Paper No. 9.

Popper, Karl R. 1979. *Objective knowledge: an evolutionary approach*. (Revised edn.) Oxford: Oxford University Press.

Rosenau, Pauline Marie. 1991. *Post-modernism and the social sciences: insights, inroads and intrusions*. Princeton, NJ: Princeton University Press.

Rothery, J. 1989. Learning about language. In *Language development: learning language, learning culture: studies for Michael Halliday*, edited by Ruqaiya Hasan and J.R. Martin. Norwood NJ: Ablex.

Trevarthen, C. 1974. The psychobiology of speech development. In

*Language and brain: developmental aspects, neuroscience research progress bulletin* (Boston) **12**, edited by E.H. Lenneberg (pp. 570–85).

Trevarthen, C. and P. Hubley. 1977. Secondary intersubjectivity: confidence, confiding and acts of meaning in the first year. In *Action, gesture and symbol: the emergence of language,* edited by A. Lock. New York: Academic.

Trudgill, Peter. 1978. *Sociolinguisitc patterns in British English.* London: Edward Arnold.

Vygotsky, L.S. 1962. *Thought and language,* edited and translated by Eugenia Hanfmann and Gertrude Vakar. Cambridge, MA: MIT Press.

Vygotsky, L.S. 1978. *Mind in society: the development of higher psychological processes,* edited by Michael Cole, Vera John-Steiner, Sylvia Scribner and Ellen Souberman. Cambridge, MA: Harvard University Press.

Wells, Gordon. 1987. Apprenticeship in literacy. *Interchange* **18(1/2)**: 109–23.

Williams, Geoffrey. 1990. Variation in home reading contexts. *Proceedings from the 16th Conference of Australian Reading Association,* held at Canberra [no date, no editor].

William, Geoffrey. 1994. Joint book-reading and literacy pedagogy: a socio-semantic examination. Unpublished PhD dissertation, School of English, Linguisitcs and Media, Macquarie University.

# Index